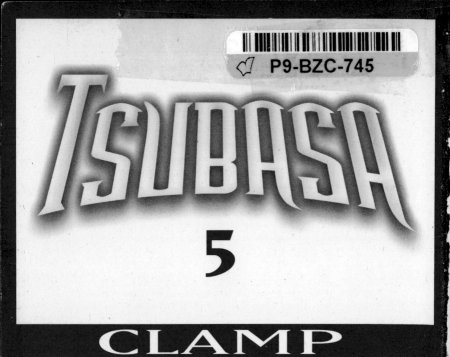

# TSUBASA

## 5

## CLAMP

TRANSLATED AND ADAPTED BY
William Flanagan

LETTERED BY
Dana Hayward

BALLANTINE BOOKS • NEW YORK

P9-BZC-745

*Tsubasa* crosses over with *xxxHOLiC*. Although it isn't necessary to read *xxxHOLiC* to understand the events in *Tsubasa*, you'll get to see the same events from different perspectives if you read both!

*Tsubasa*, Volume 5 is a work of fiction. Names, characters, places, and incidents are the products of the author's imagination or are used fictitiously. Any resemblance to actual events, locales, or persons, living or dead, is entirely coincidental.

A Del Rey Books Trade Paperback Original

Copyright © 2005 CLAMP.

All rights reserved.

Published in the United States by Del Rey Books, an imprint of The Random House Publishing Group, a division of Random House, Inc., New York.

Del Rey is a registered trademark and the Del Rey colophon is a trademark of Random House, Inc.

First published in serialization and subsequently published in book form by Kodansha Ltd. Tokyo in 2004.

ISBN 0-345-47792-8

Printed in the United States of America

Del Rey Books website address: www.delreymanga.com

9  8  7

Lettered by Dana Hayward

# Contents

# Honorifics

Throughout the Del Rey Manga books, you will find Japanese honorifics left intact in the translations. For those not familiar with how the Japanese use honorifics and, more important, how they differ from American honorifics, we present this brief overview.

Politeness has always been a critical facet of Japanese culture. Ever since the feudal era, when Japan was a highly stratified society, use of honorifics — which can be defined as polite speech that indicates relationship or status — has played an essential role in the Japanese language. When addressing someone in Japanese, an honorific usually takes the form of a suffix attached to one's name (example: "Asuna-san"), or as a title at the end of one's name or in place of the name itself (example: "Negi-sensei," or simply "Sensei!").

Honorifics can be expressions of respect or endearment. In the context of manga and anime, honorifics give insight into the nature of the relationship between characters. Many translations into English leave out these important honorifics, and therefore distort the "feel" of the original Japanese. Because Japanese honorifics contain nuances that English honorifics lack, it is our policy at Del Rey not to translate them. Here, instead, is a guide to some of the honorifics you may encounter in Del Rey Manga.

-san:   This is the most common honorific, and is equivalent to Mr., Miss, Ms., Mrs., etc. It is the all-purpose honorific and can be used in any situation where politeness is required.

-sama:  This is one level higher than "-san." It is used to confer great respect.

-dono:  This comes from the word "tono," which means "lord." It is an even higher level than "-sama" and confers utmost respect.

-kun:   This suffix is used at the end of boys' names to express familiarity or endearment. It is also sometimes used by men among friends, or when addressing someone younger or of a lower station.

-chan: This is used to express endearment, mostly toward girls. It is also used for little boys, pets, and even among lovers. It gives a sense of childish cuteness.

Bozu: This is an informal way to refer to a boy, similar to the English term "kid" or "squirt."

Sempai: This title suggests that the addressee is one's senior in a group or organization. It is most often used in a school setting, where underclassmen refer to their upperclassmen as "sempai." It can also be used in the workplace, such as when a newer employee addresses an employee who has seniority in the company.

Kohai: This is the opposite of "sempai," and is used toward underclassmen in school or newcomers in the workplace. It connotes that the addressee is of lower station.

Sensei: Literally meaning "one who has come before," this title is used for teachers, doctors, or masters of any profession or art.

-[blank]: Usually forgotten in these lists, but perhaps the most significant difference between Japanese and English. The lack of honorific means that the speaker has permission to address the person in a very intimate way. Usually, only family, spouses, or very close friends have this kind of permission. Known as *yobisute*, it can be gratifying when someone who has earned the intimacy starts to call one by one's name without an honorific. But when that intimacy hasn't been earned, it can also be very insulting.

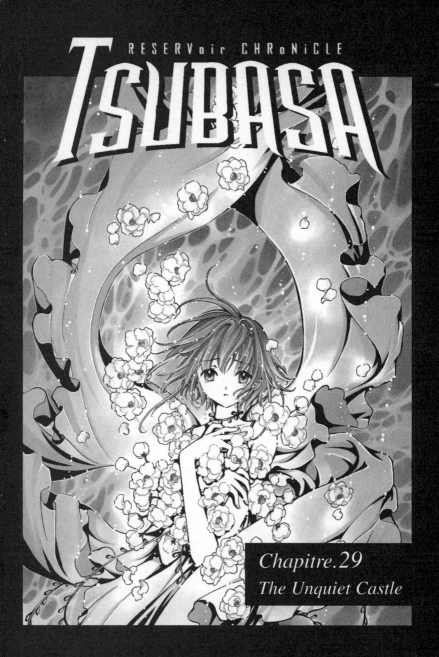

RESERVoir CHRoNiCLE

# TSUBASA

Chapitre.29

*The Unquiet Castle*

ツバサ

RESERVoir CHRoNiCLE

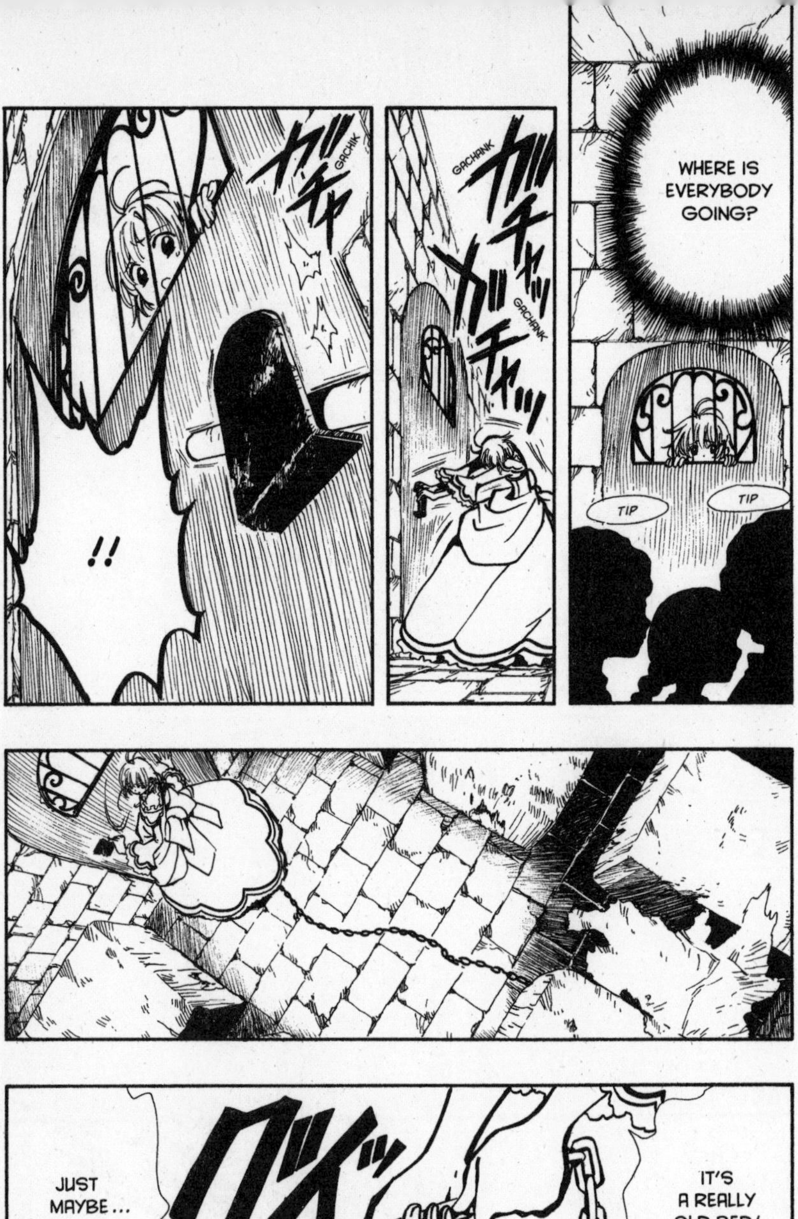
WHERE IS EVERYBODY GOING?
TIP
TIP
ガチャッ
GACHANK
ガチャッ
GACHANK
ガチャ
GACHIK
!!
IT'S A REALLY OLD BED!
CHINK
グイッ
GRMP
JUST MAYBE ...

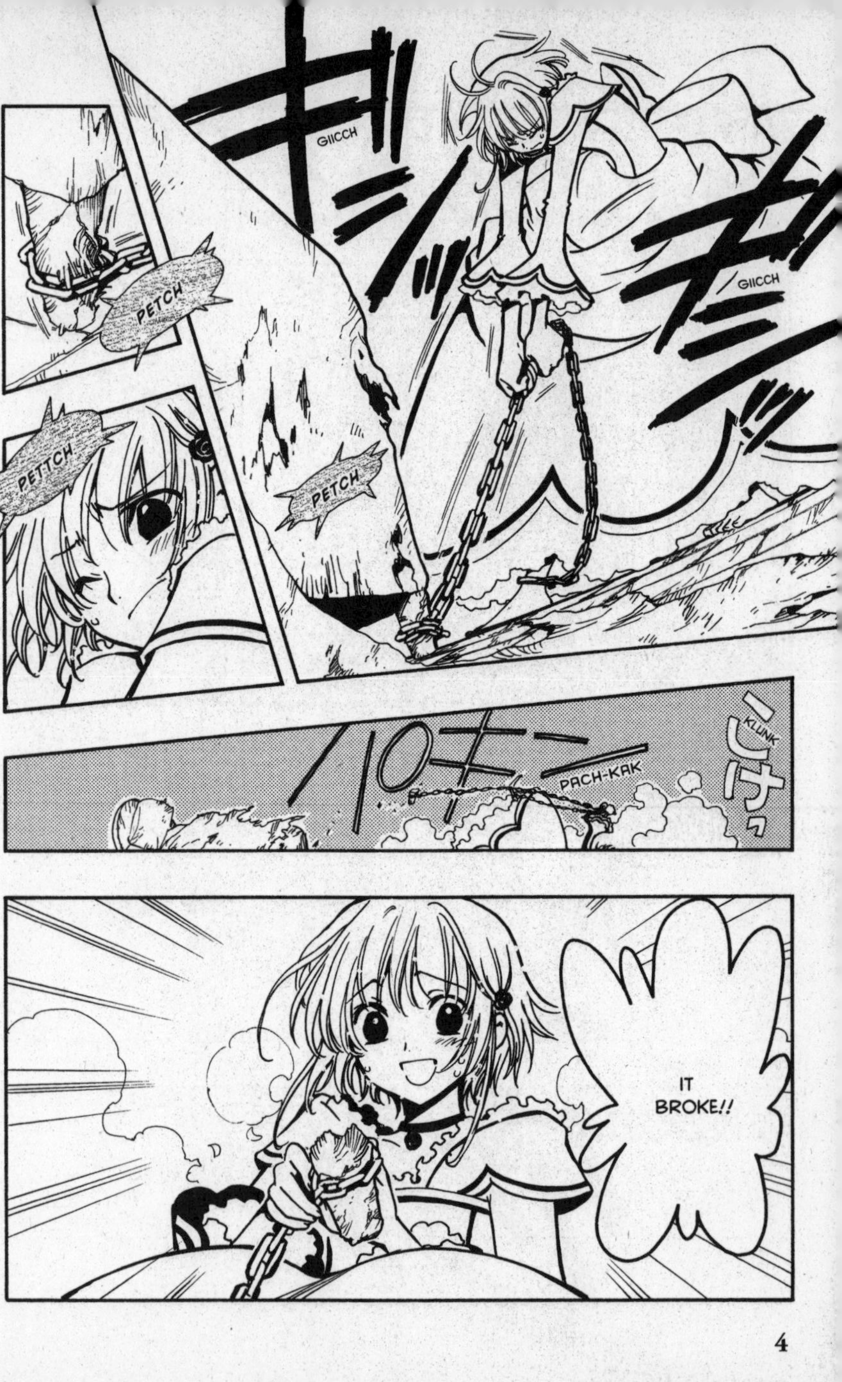
GIICCH
GIICCH
PETCH
PETCH
PETTCH
KLUNK
PACH-KAK
IT BROKE!!

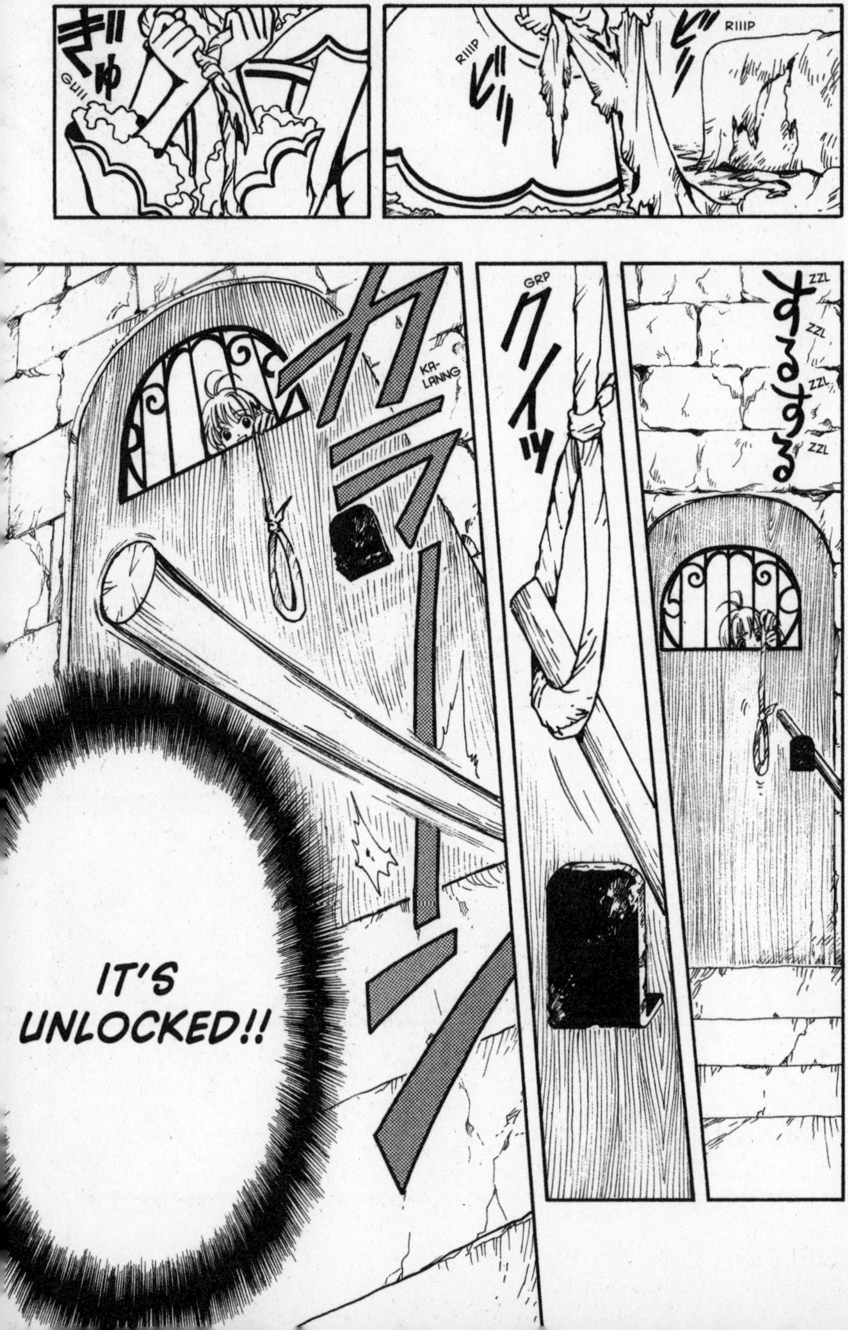
ビリ
RIIIP
ビリ
RIIIP
ぎゅ
GUIII
するする
ZZL
ZZL
ZZL
ZZL
クイッ
GRP
カラーン
KA-LANNG
IT'S UNLOCKED!!

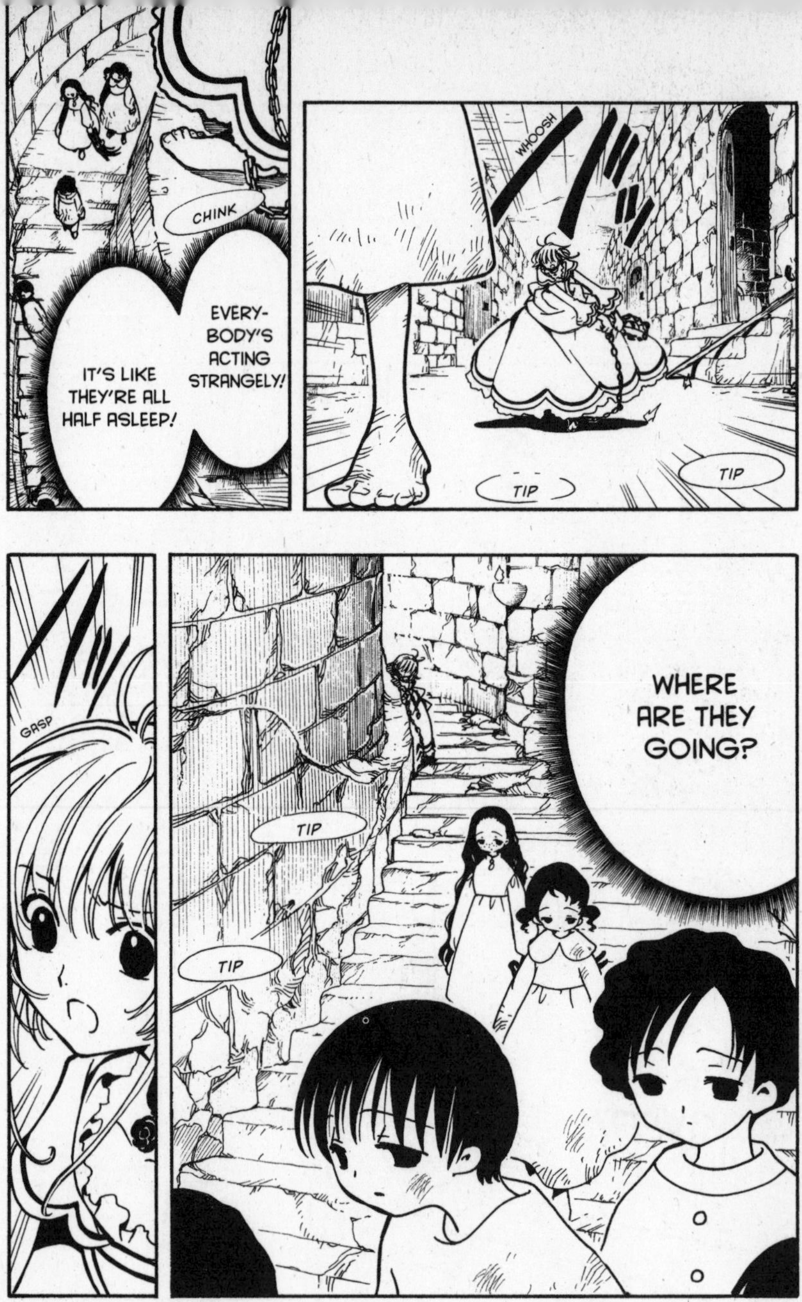
WHOOSH
TIP
TIP
CHINK
EVERY-BODY'S ACTING STRANGELY!
IT'S LIKE THEY'RE ALL HALF ASLEEP!
WHERE ARE THEY GOING?
TIP
TIP
GASP

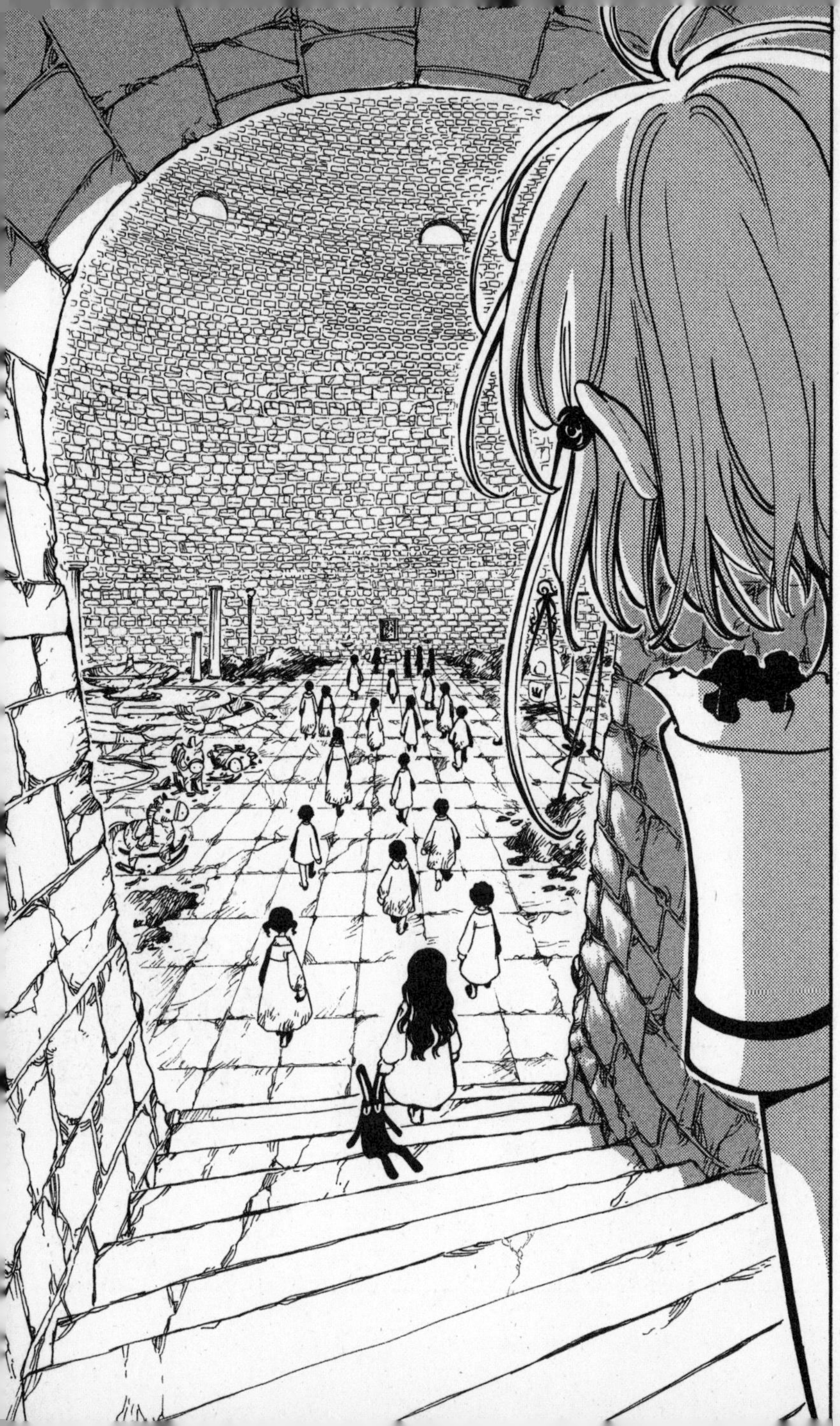

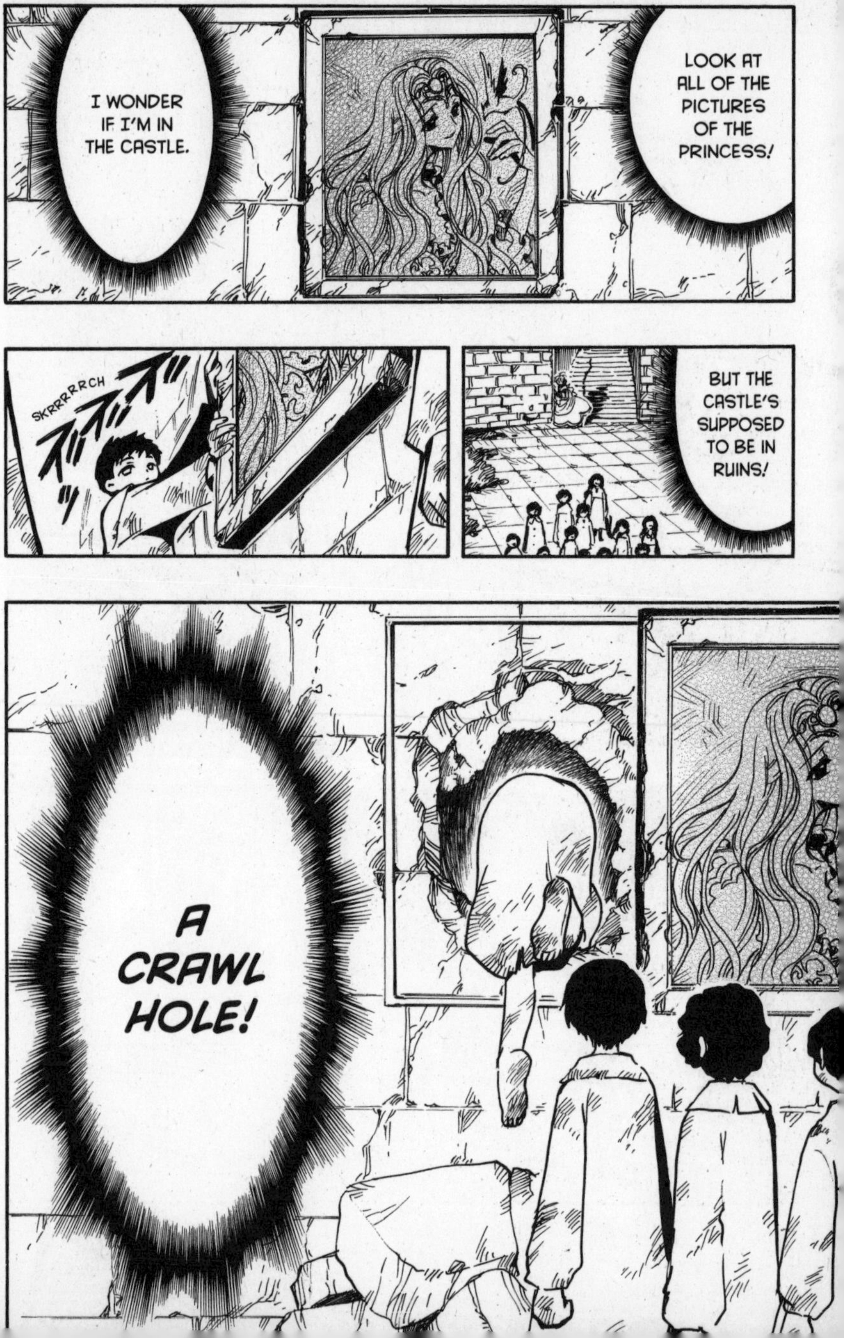
LOOK AT ALL OF THE PICTURES OF THE PRINCESS!
I WONDER IF I'M IN THE CASTLE.
BUT THE CASTLE'S SUPPOSED TO BE IN RUINS!
SKRRRRRCH
A CRAWL HOLE!

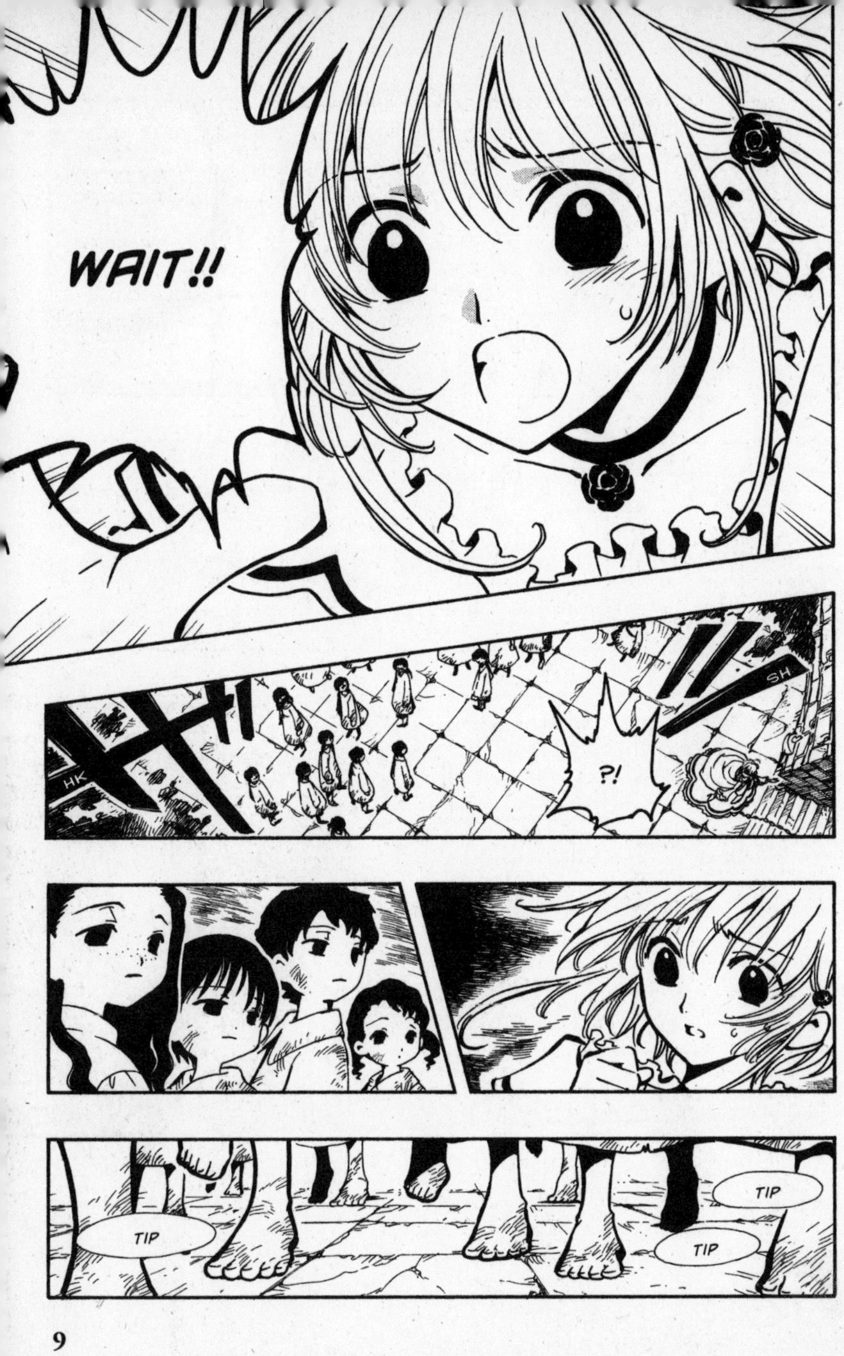
WAIT!!
SH
?!
HK
TIP
TIP
TIP

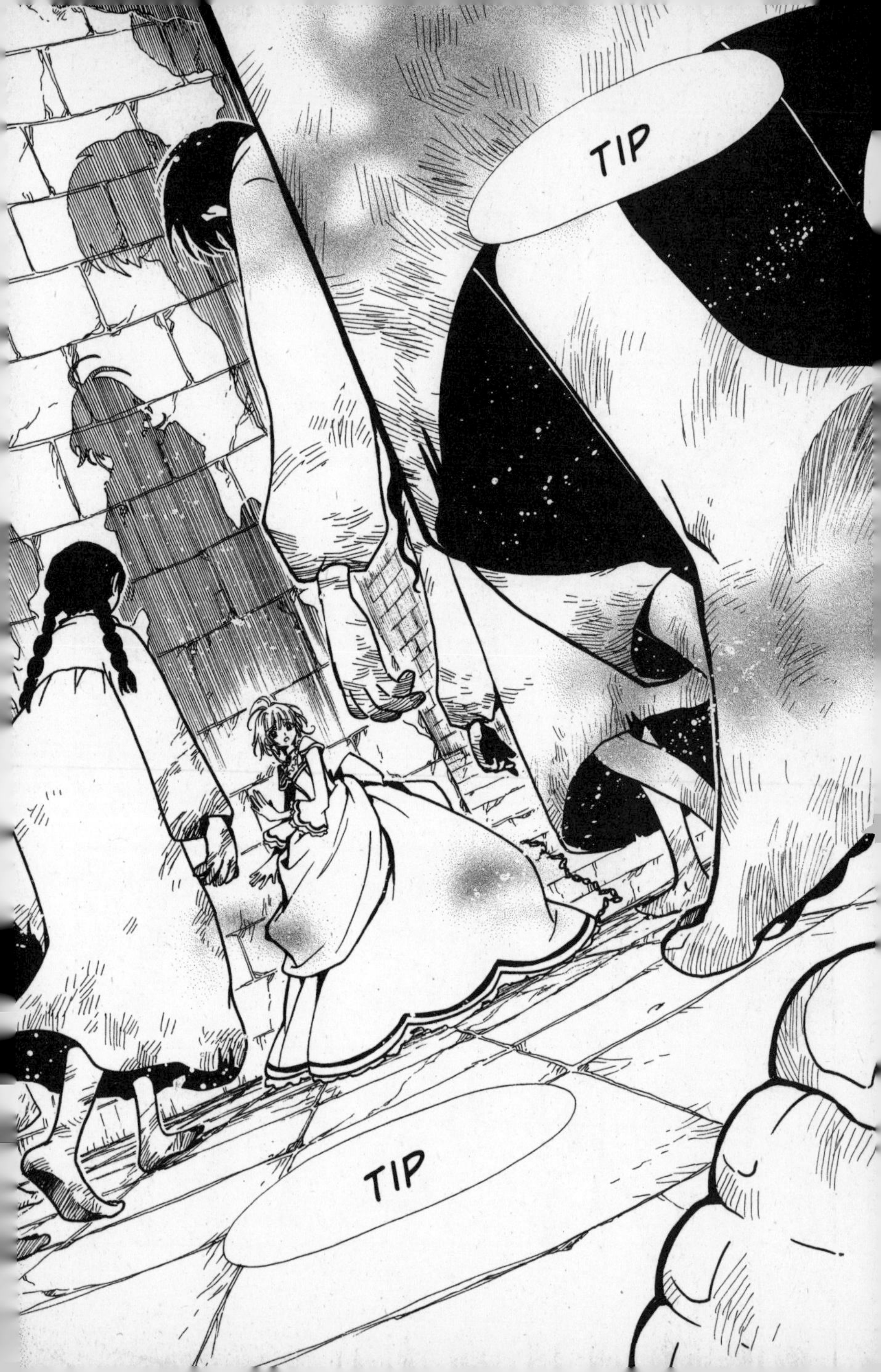
TIP
TIP

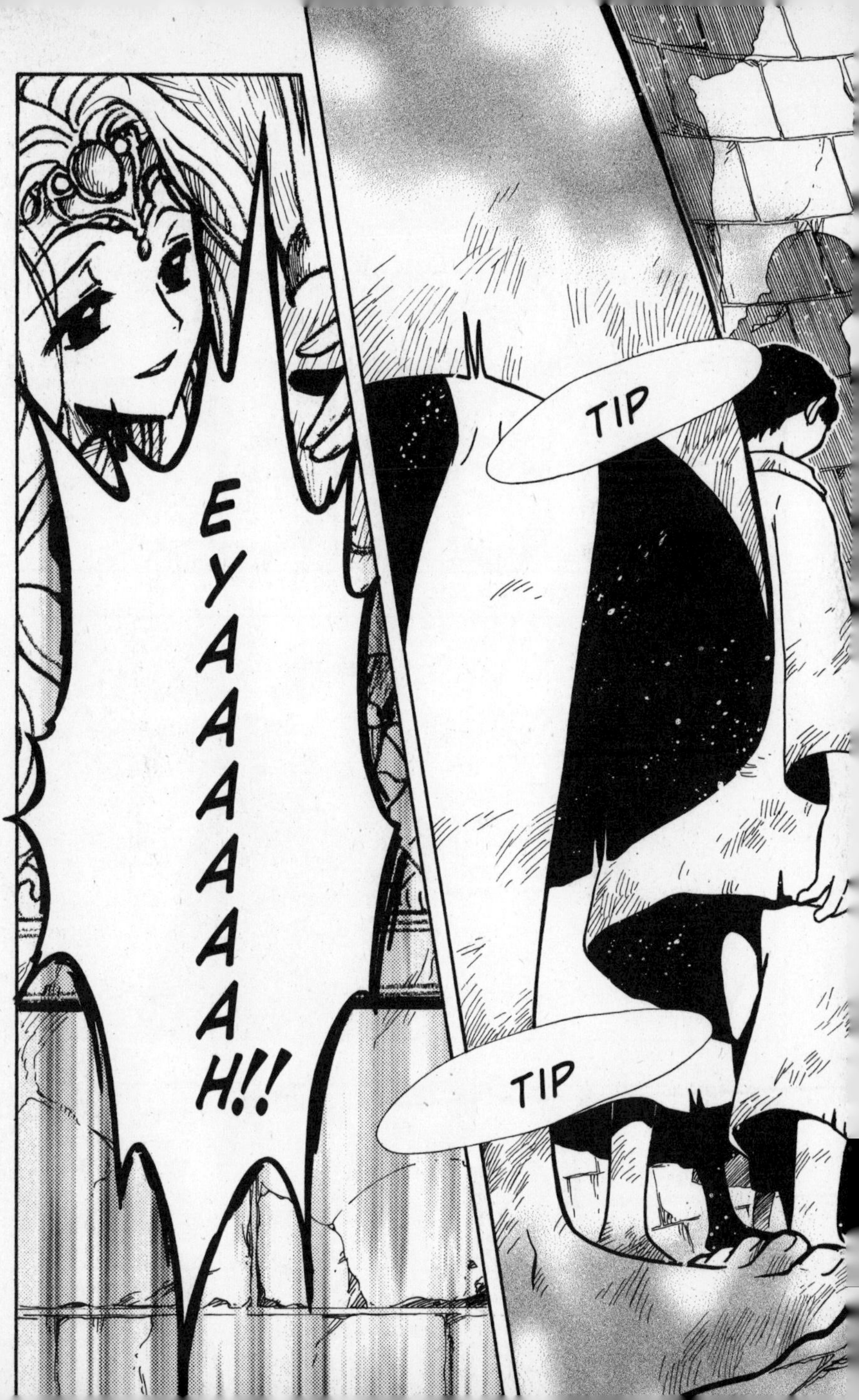
TIP
TIP
EYAAAAAAH!!

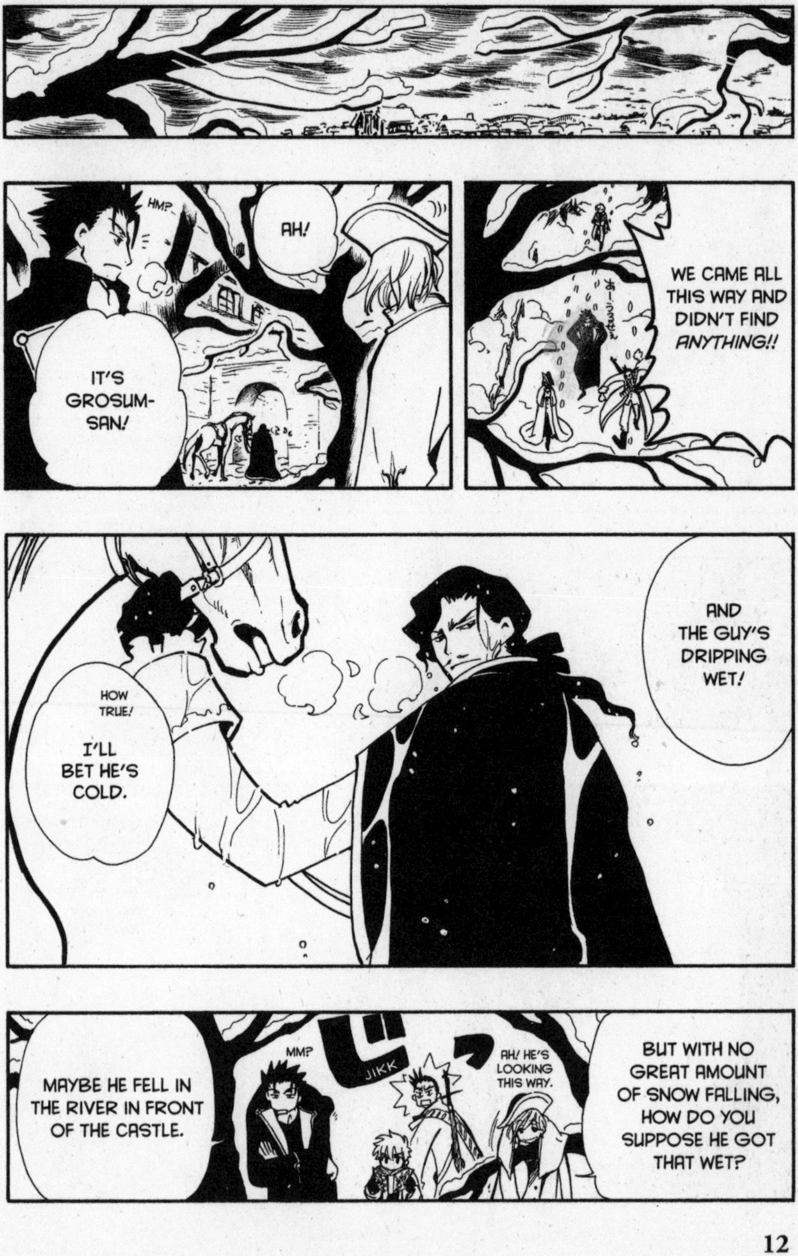
WE CAME ALL THIS WAY AND DIDN'T FIND *ANYTHING!!*
AH!
HM?
IT'S GROSUM-SAN!
AND THE GUY'S DRIPPING WET!
HOW TRUE!
I'LL BET HE'S COLD.
BUT WITH NO GREAT AMOUNT OF SNOW FALLING, HOW DO YOU SUPPOSE HE GOT THAT WET?
AH! HE'S LOOKING THIS WAY.
JIKK
MM?
MAYBE HE FELL IN THE RIVER IN FRONT OF THE CASTLE.

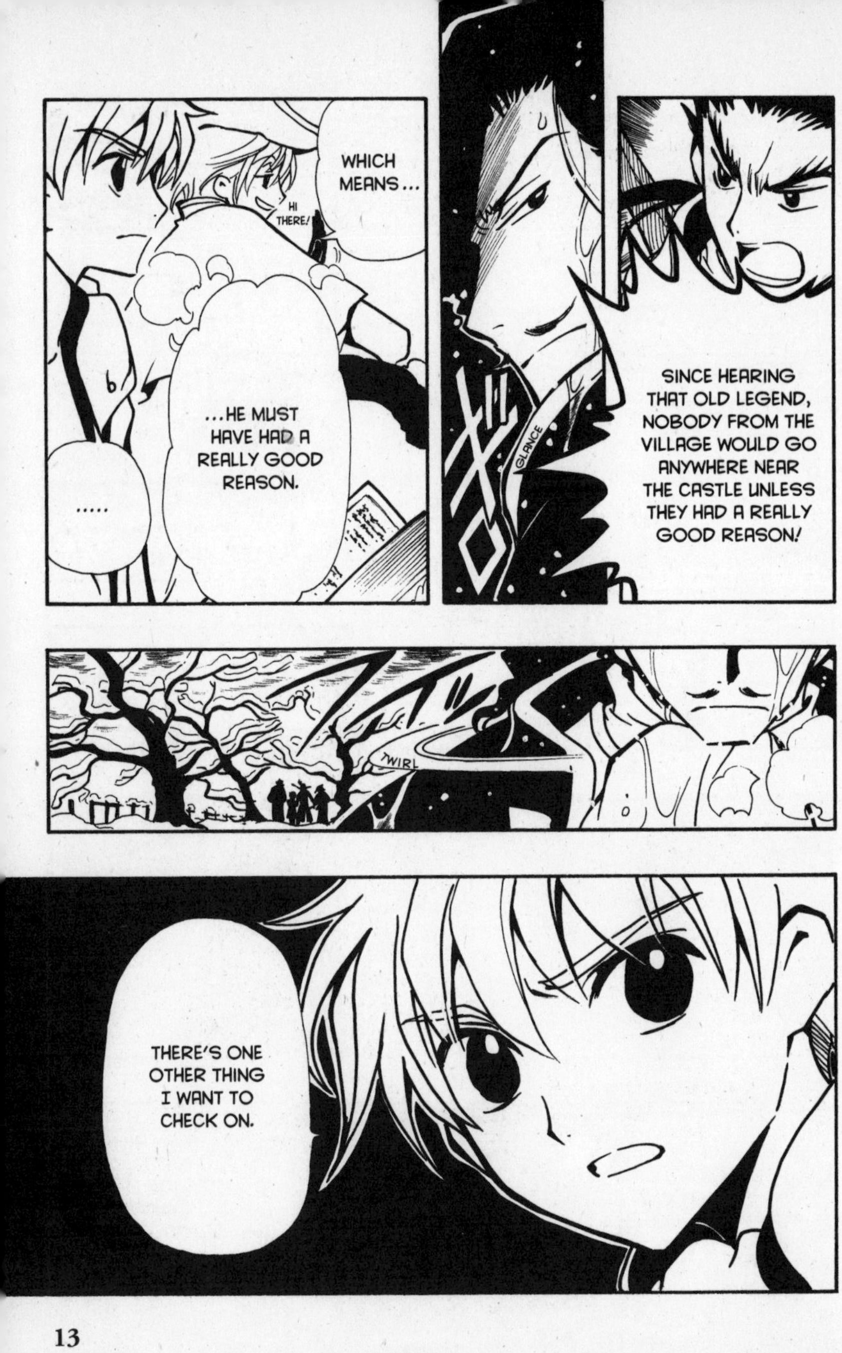
SINCE HEARING THAT OLD LEGEND, NOBODY FROM THE VILLAGE WOULD GO ANYWHERE NEAR THE CASTLE UNLESS THEY HAD A REALLY GOOD REASON!
GLANCE
WHICH MEANS...
HI THERE!
...HE MUST HAVE HAD A REALLY GOOD REASON.
.....
TWIRL
THERE'S ONE OTHER THING I WANT TO CHECK ON.

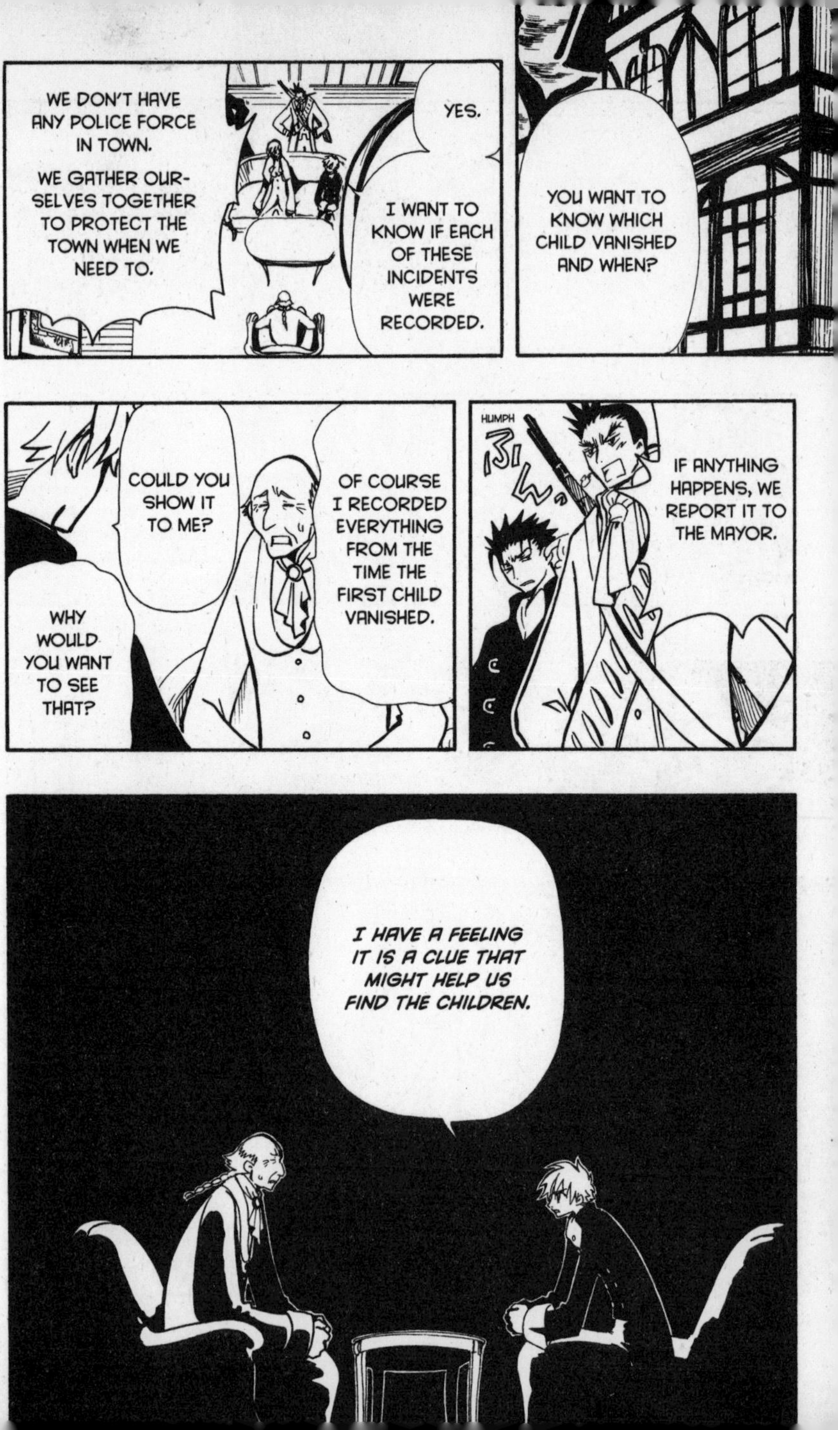
YOU WANT TO KNOW WHICH CHILD VANISHED AND WHEN?
YES.
I WANT TO KNOW IF EACH OF THESE INCIDENTS WERE RECORDED.
WE DON'T HAVE ANY POLICE FORCE IN TOWN.
WE GATHER OUR-SELVES TOGETHER TO PROTECT THE TOWN WHEN WE NEED TO.
HUMPH
IF ANYTHING HAPPENS, WE REPORT IT TO THE MAYOR.
OF COURSE I RECORDED EVERYTHING FROM THE TIME THE FIRST CHILD VANISHED.
COULD YOU SHOW IT TO ME?
WHY WOULD YOU WANT TO SEE THAT?
I HAVE A FEELING IT IS A CLUE THAT MIGHT HELP US FIND THE CHILDREN.

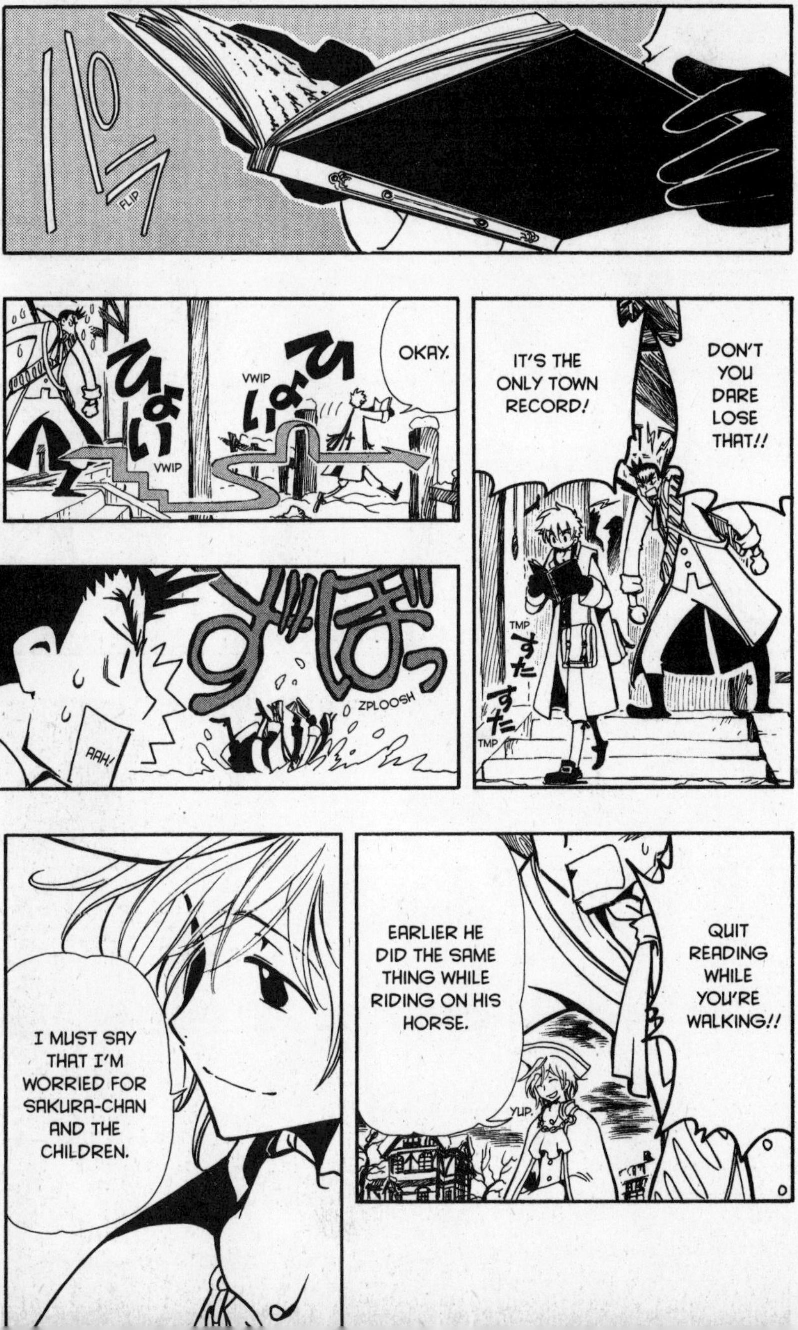
パラ
FLIP
DON'T YOU DARE LOSE THAT!!
IT'S THE ONLY TOWN RECORD!
すた
TMP
すた
TMP
OKAY.
ひょい
VWIP
ひょい
VWIP
ずぼっ
ZPLOOSH
AAH!
QUIT READING WHILE YOU'RE WALKING!!
EARLIER HE DID THE SAME THING WHILE RIDING ON HIS HORSE.
YUP.
I MUST SAY THAT I'M WORRIED FOR SAKURA-CHAN AND THE CHILDREN.

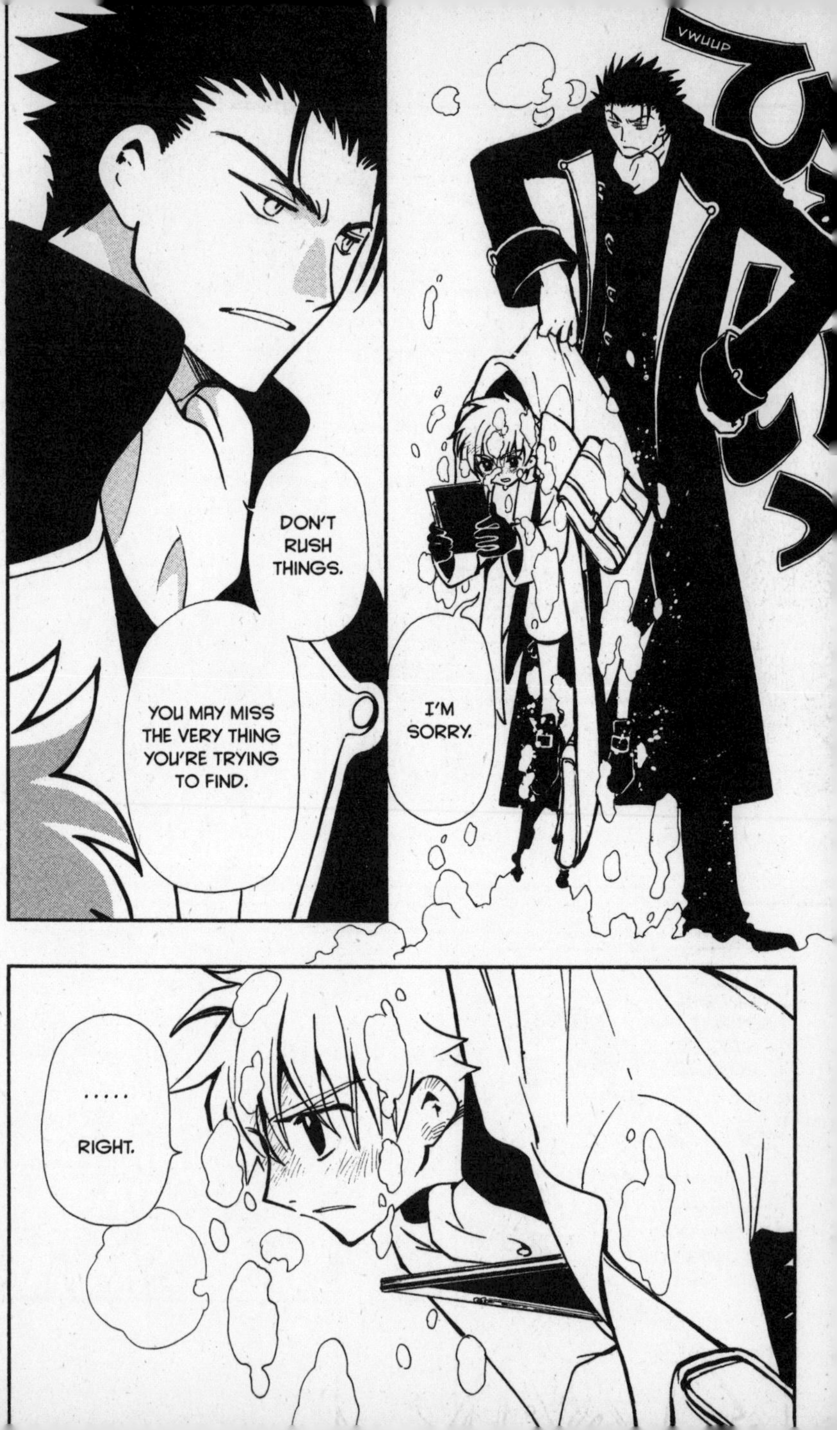
VWUUP
I'M SORRY.
DON'T RUSH THINGS.
YOU MAY MISS THE VERY THING YOU'RE TRYING TO FIND.
..... RIGHT.

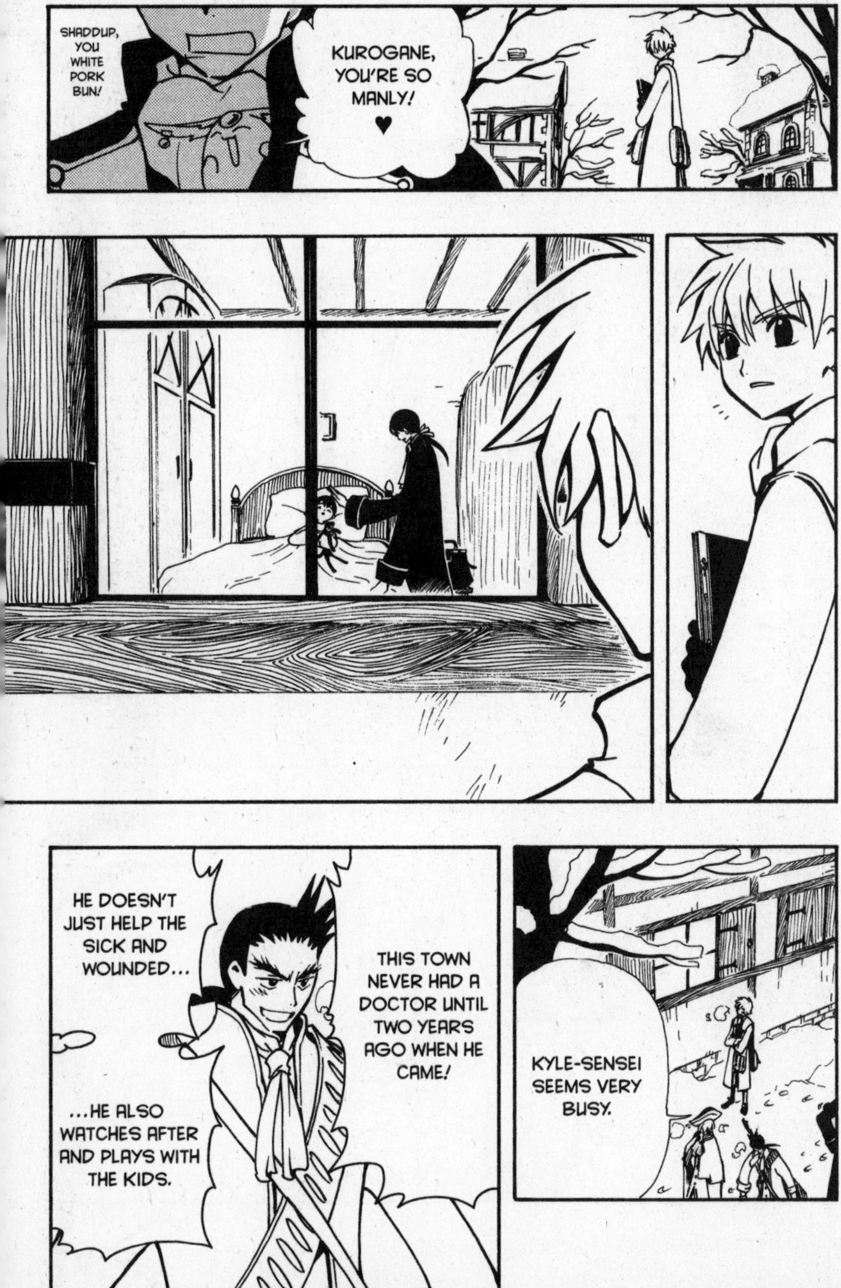
KUROGANE, YOU'RE SO MANLY! ♥
SHADDUP, YOU WHITE PORK BUN!
KYLE-SENSEI SEEMS VERY BUSY.
THIS TOWN NEVER HAD A DOCTOR UNTIL TWO YEARS AGO WHEN HE CAME!
HE DOESN'T JUST HELP THE SICK AND WOUNDED...
...HE ALSO WATCHES AFTER AND PLAYS WITH THE KIDS.

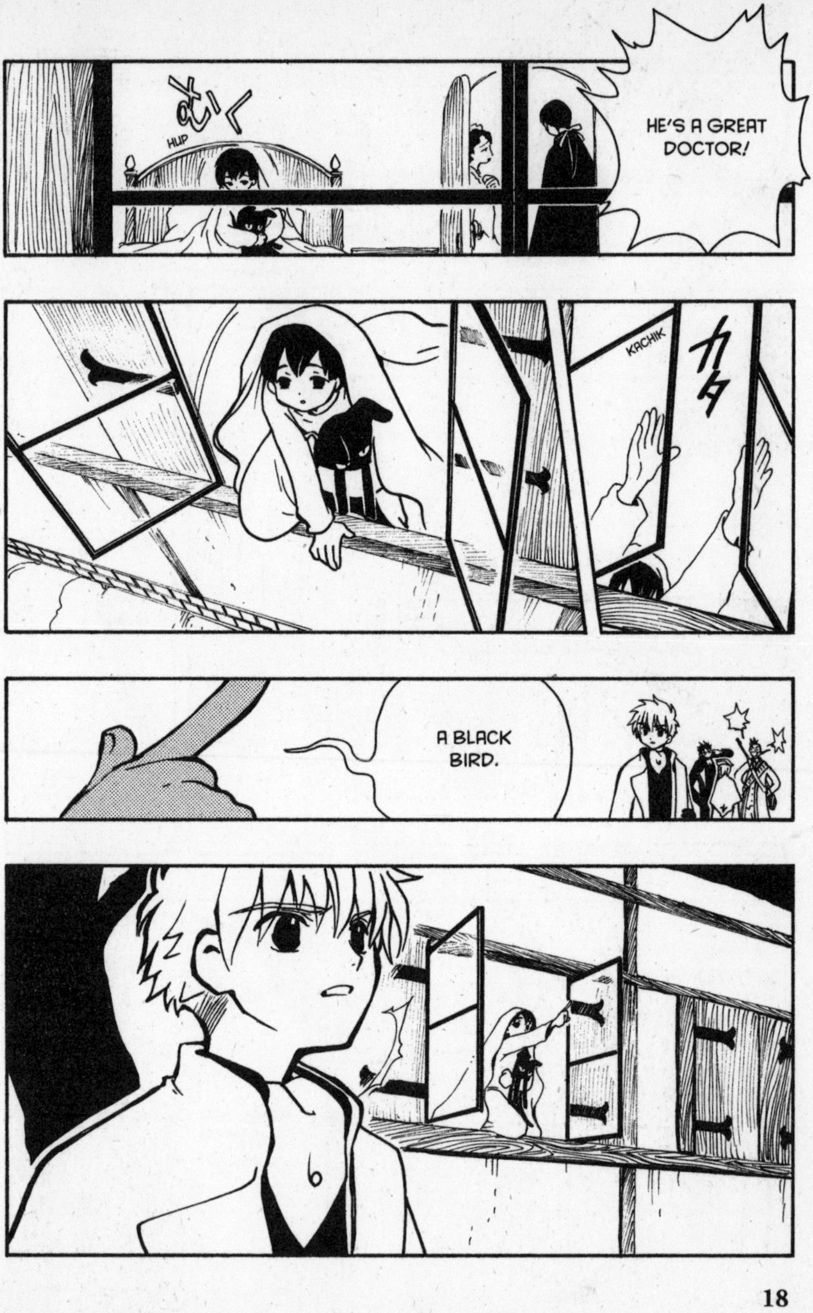
HE'S A GREAT DOCTOR!
むく
HUP
カタ
KACHIK
A BLACK BIRD.

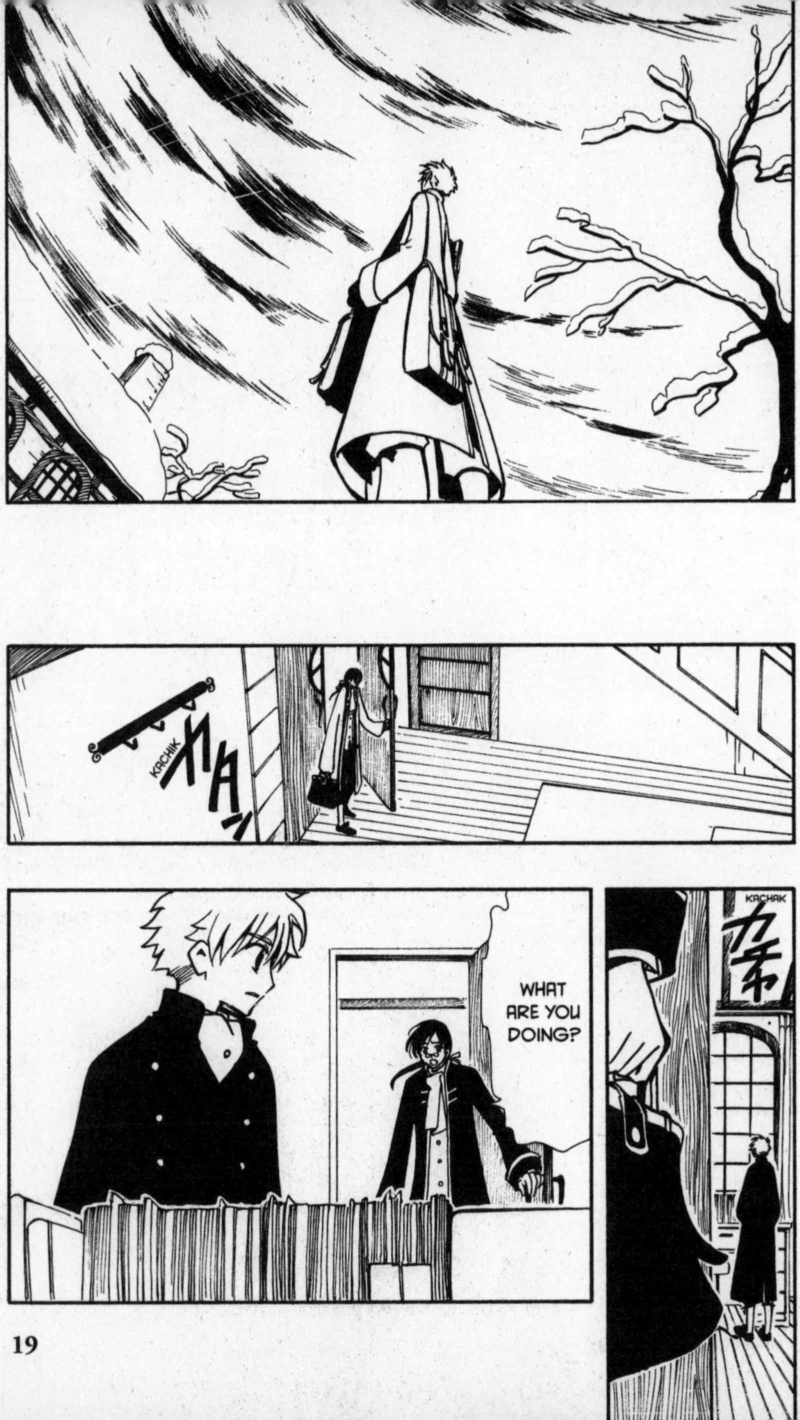
KACHIK
KACHAK
WHAT ARE YOU DOING?

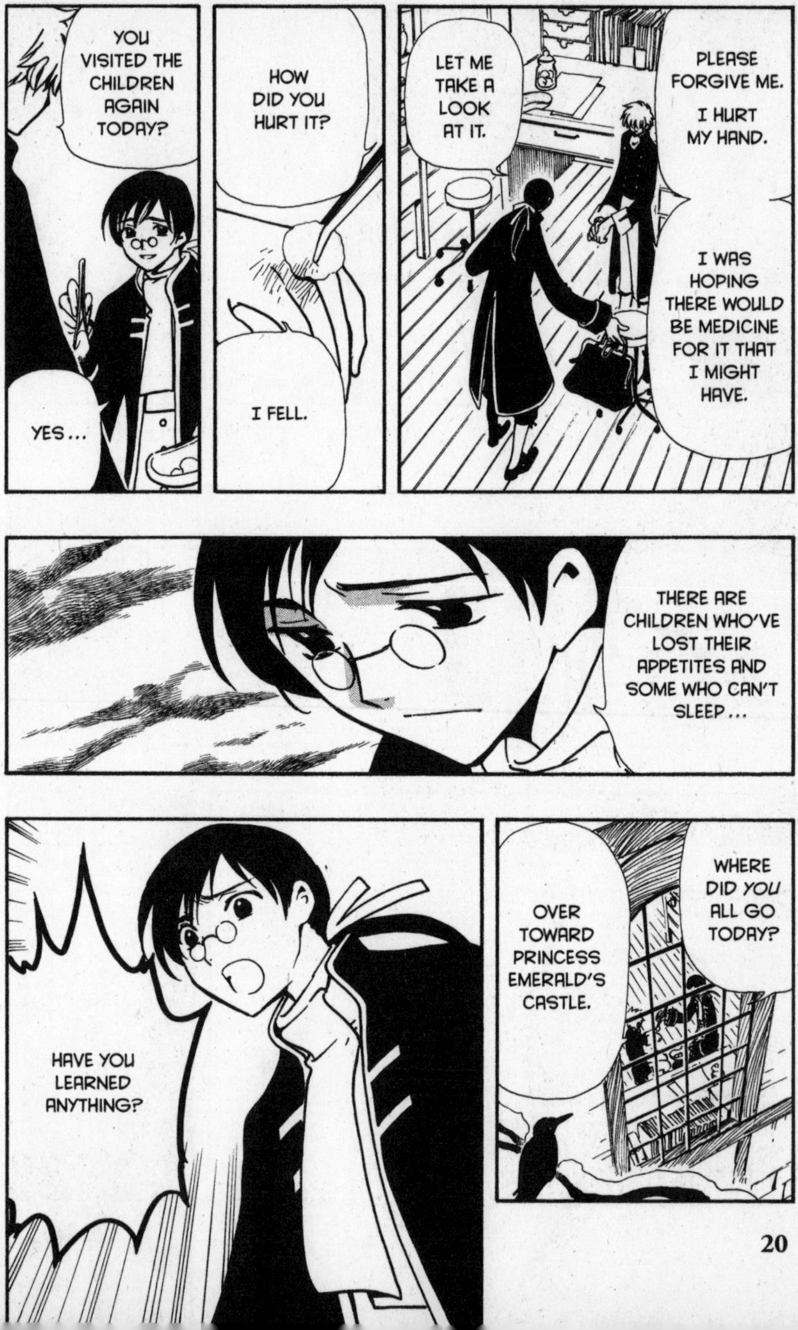
PLEASE FORGIVE ME.
I HURT MY HAND.
I WAS HOPING THERE WOULD BE MEDICINE FOR IT THAT I MIGHT HAVE.
LET ME TAKE A LOOK AT IT.
HOW DID YOU HURT IT?
I FELL.
YOU VISITED THE CHILDREN AGAIN TODAY?
YES...
THERE ARE CHILDREN WHO'VE LOST THEIR APPETITES AND SOME WHO CAN'T SLEEP...
WHERE DID *YOU* ALL GO TODAY?
OVER TOWARD PRINCESS EMERALD'S CASTLE.
HAVE YOU LEARNED ANYTHING?

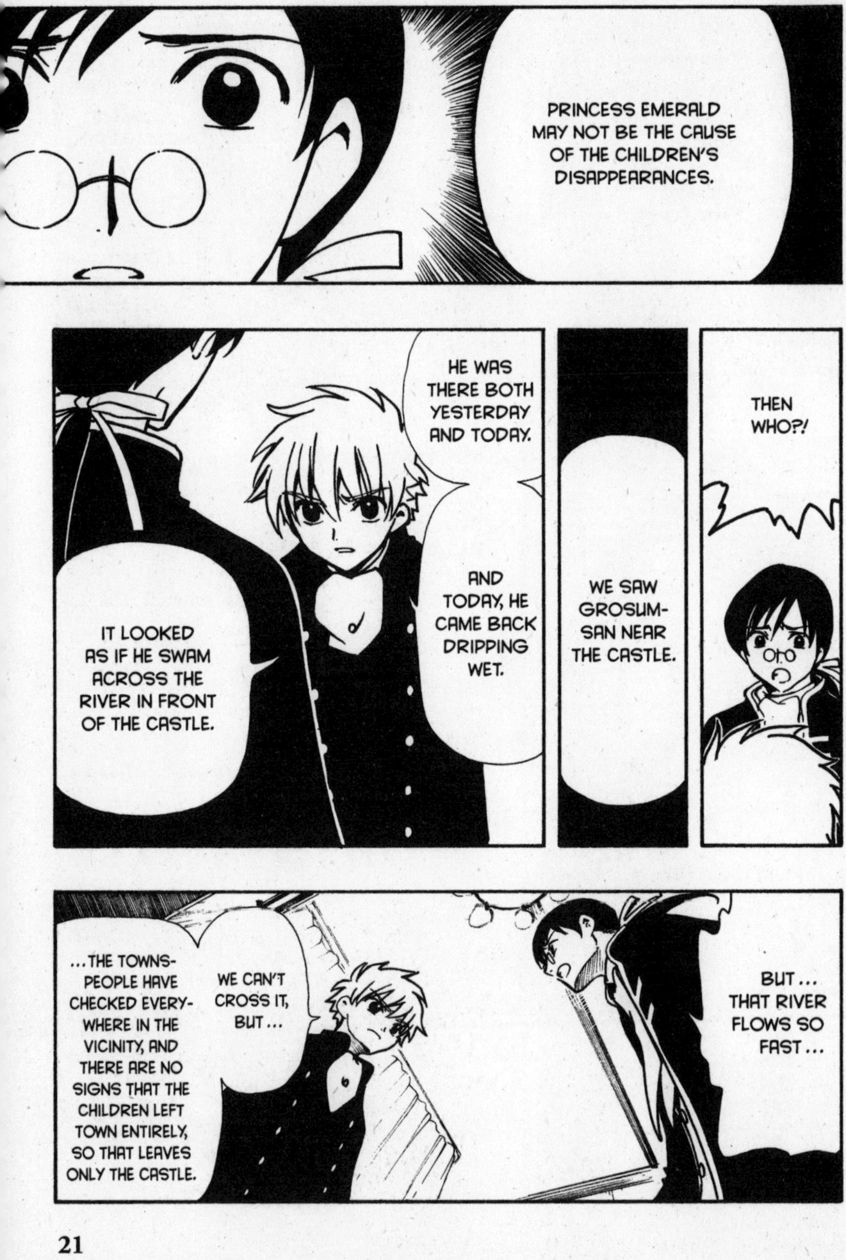
PRINCESS EMERALD MAY NOT BE THE CAUSE OF THE CHILDREN'S DISAPPEARANCES.
THEN WHO?!
WE SAW GROSUM-SAN NEAR THE CASTLE.
HE WAS THERE BOTH YESTERDAY AND TODAY.
AND TODAY, HE CAME BACK DRIPPING WET.
IT LOOKED AS IF HE SWAM ACROSS THE RIVER IN FRONT OF THE CASTLE.
BUT... THAT RIVER FLOWS SO FAST...
WE CAN'T CROSS IT, BUT...
...THE TOWNS-PEOPLE HAVE CHECKED EVERY-WHERE IN THE VICINITY, AND THERE ARE NO SIGNS THAT THE CHILDREN LEFT TOWN ENTIRELY, SO THAT LEAVES ONLY THE CASTLE.

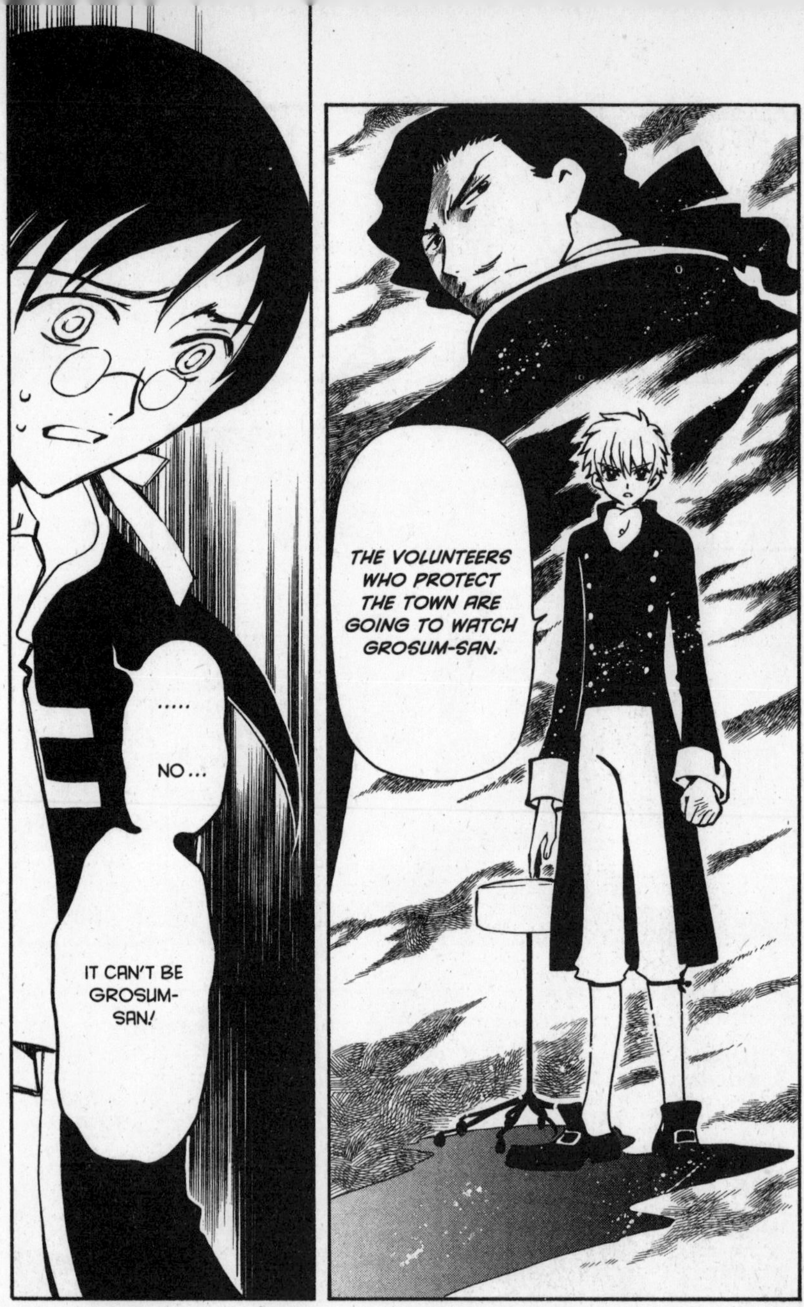
THE VOLUNTEERS WHO PROTECT THE TOWN ARE GOING TO WATCH GROSUM-SAN.
.....
NO...
IT CAN'T BE GROSUM-SAN!

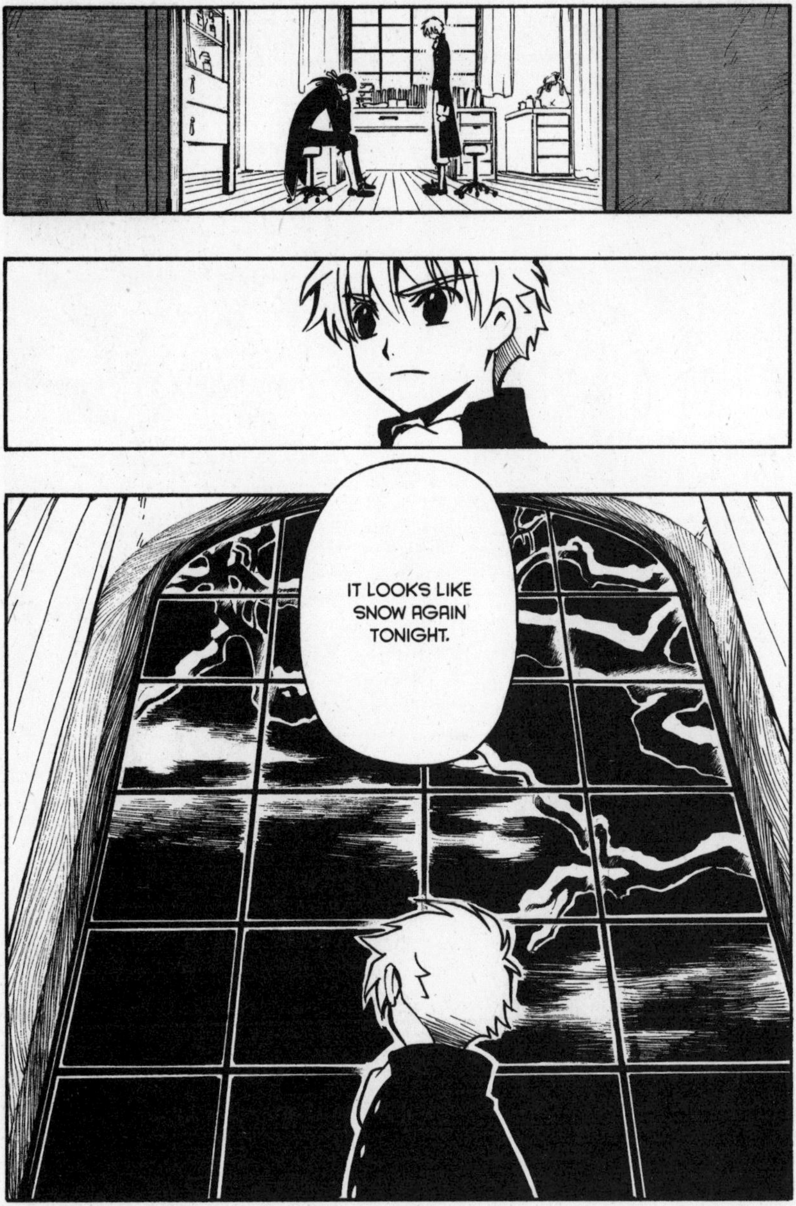
IT LOOKS LIKE SNOW AGAIN TONIGHT.

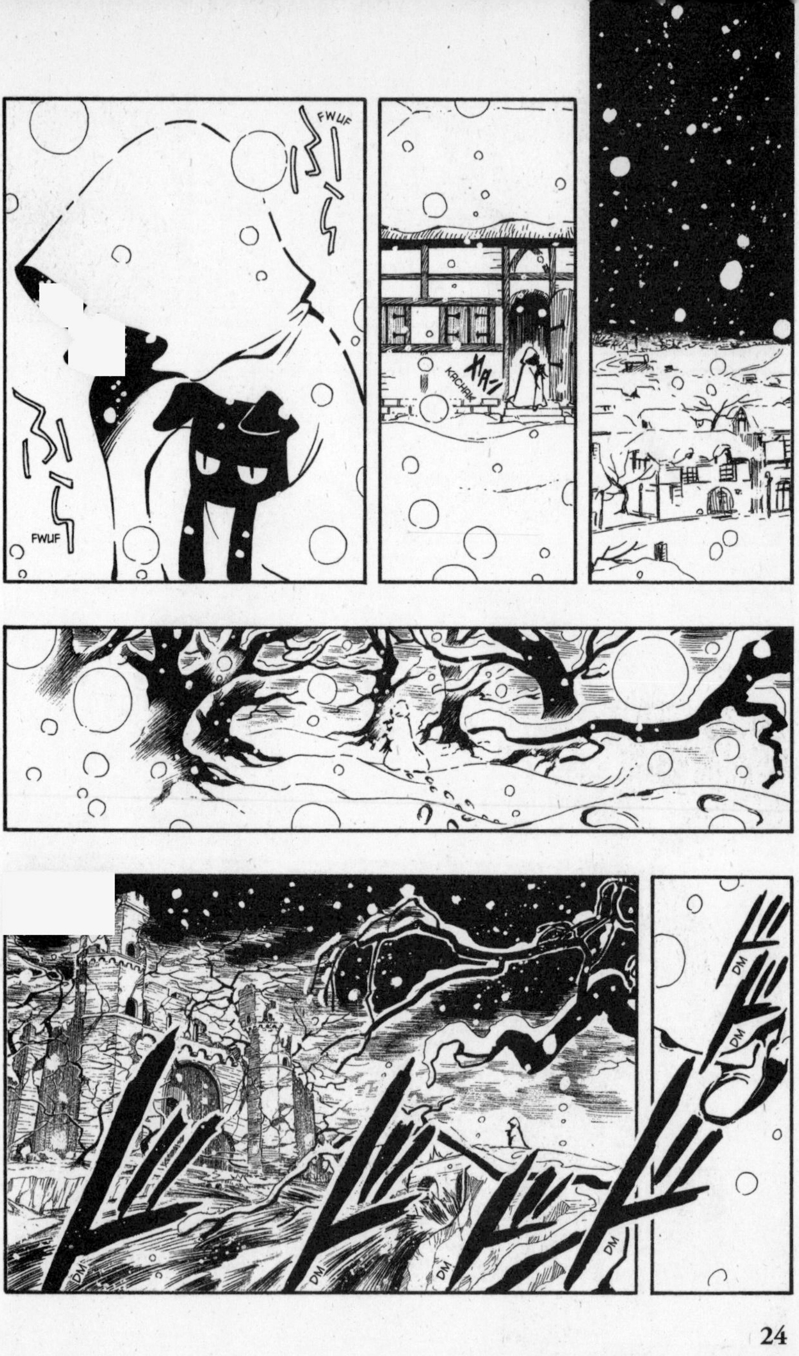
KACHAK
FWUF
FWUF
DM
DM
DM
DM
DM
DM

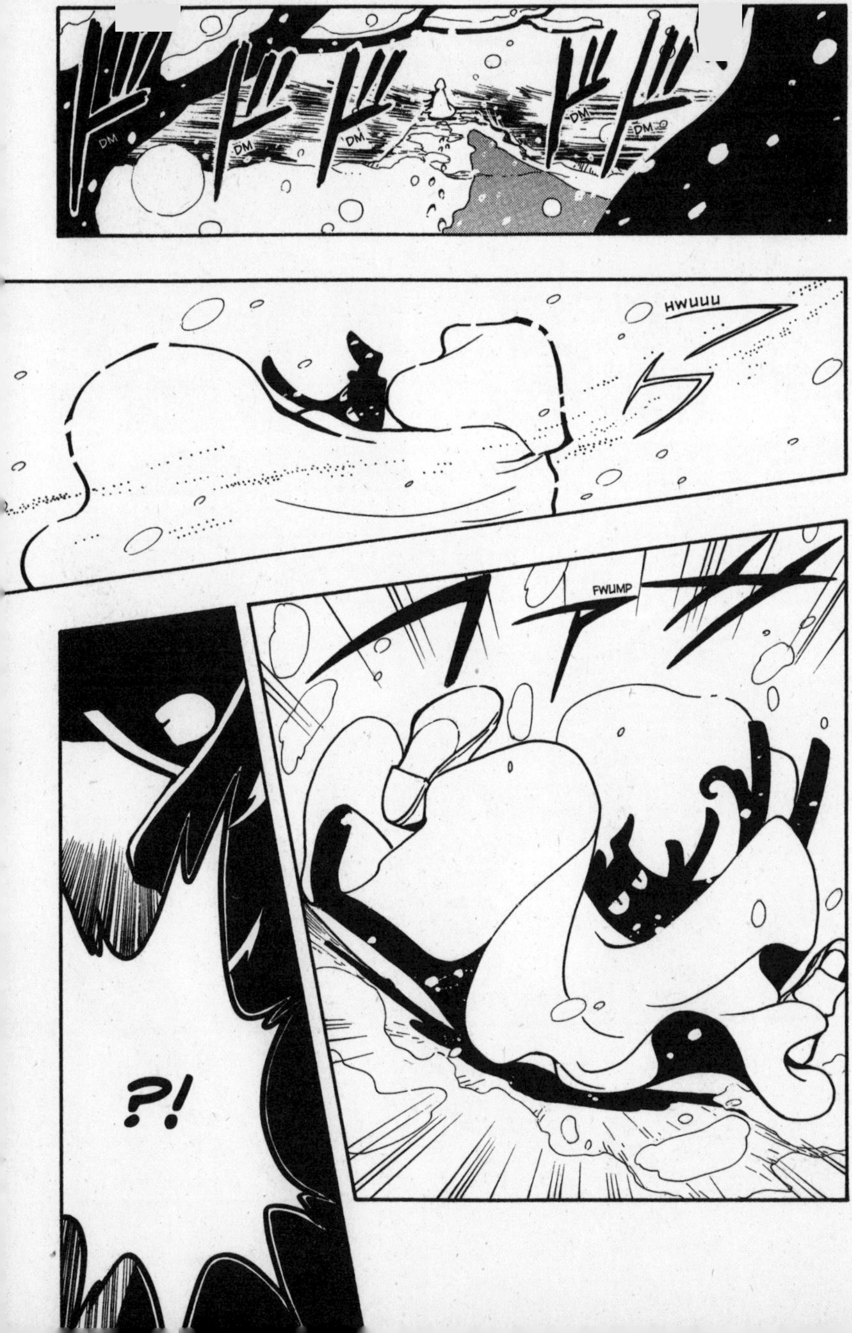
DM
DM
DM
DM
DM
HWUUU
FWUMP
?!

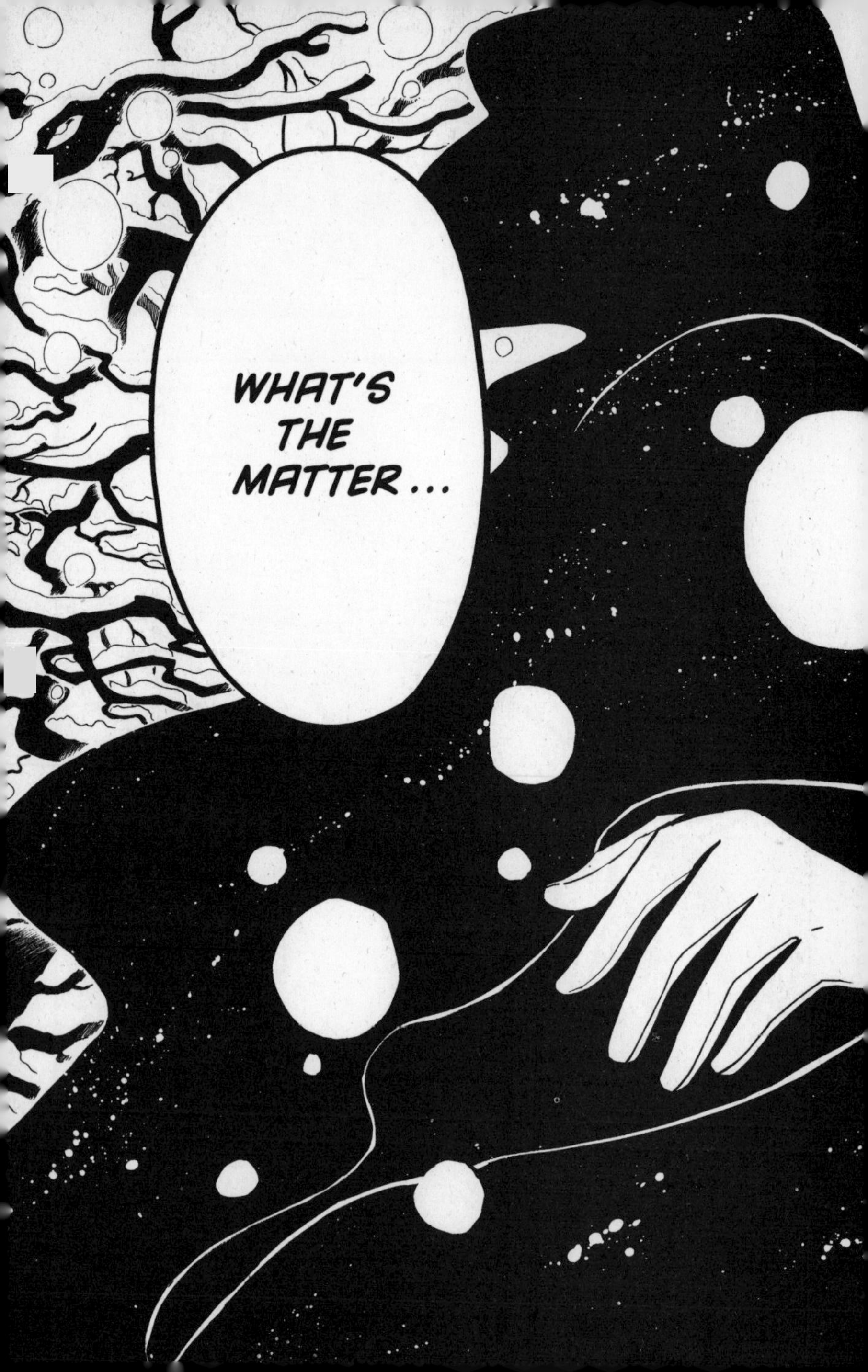
WHAT'S THE MATTER...

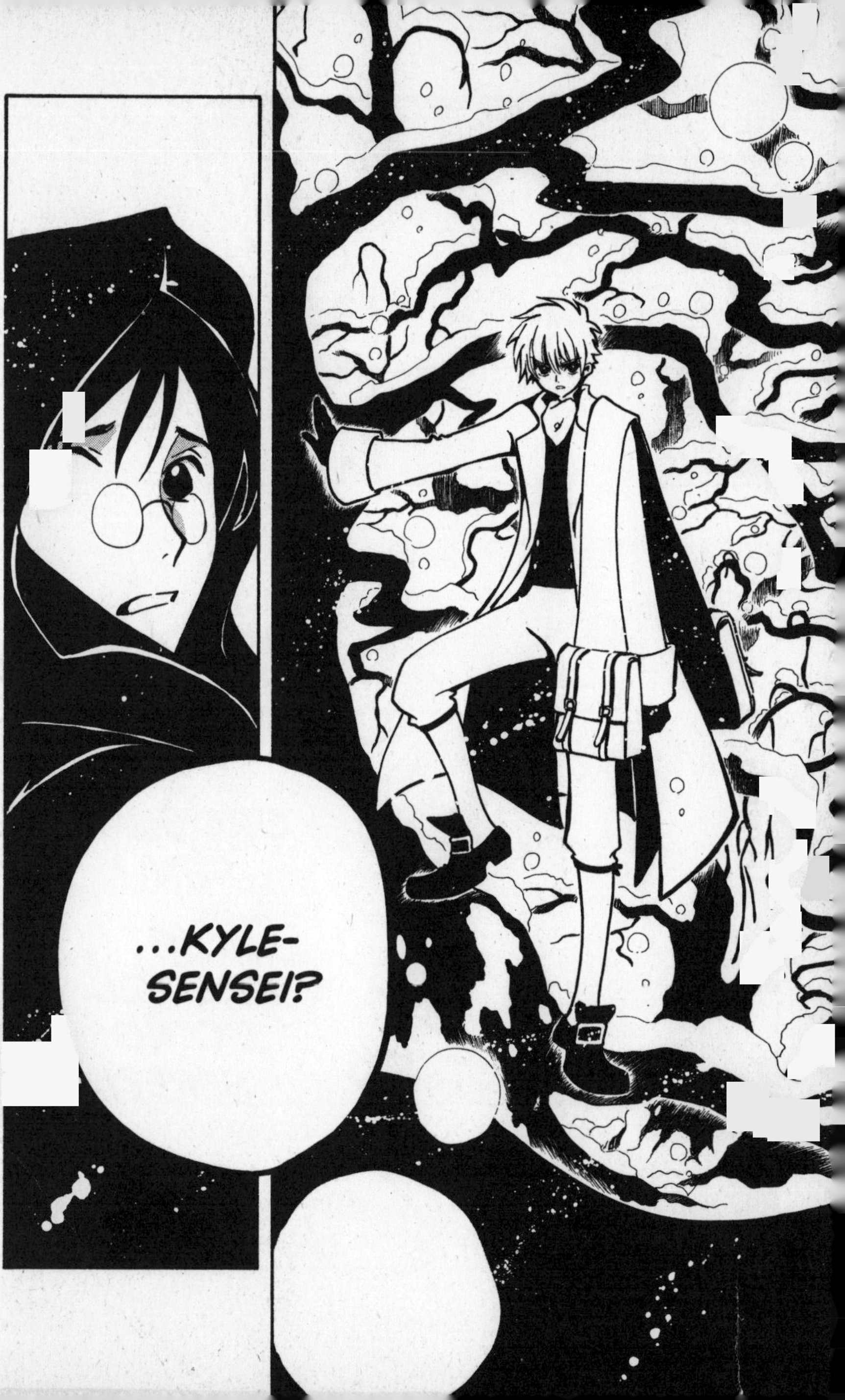
...KYLE-
SENSEI?

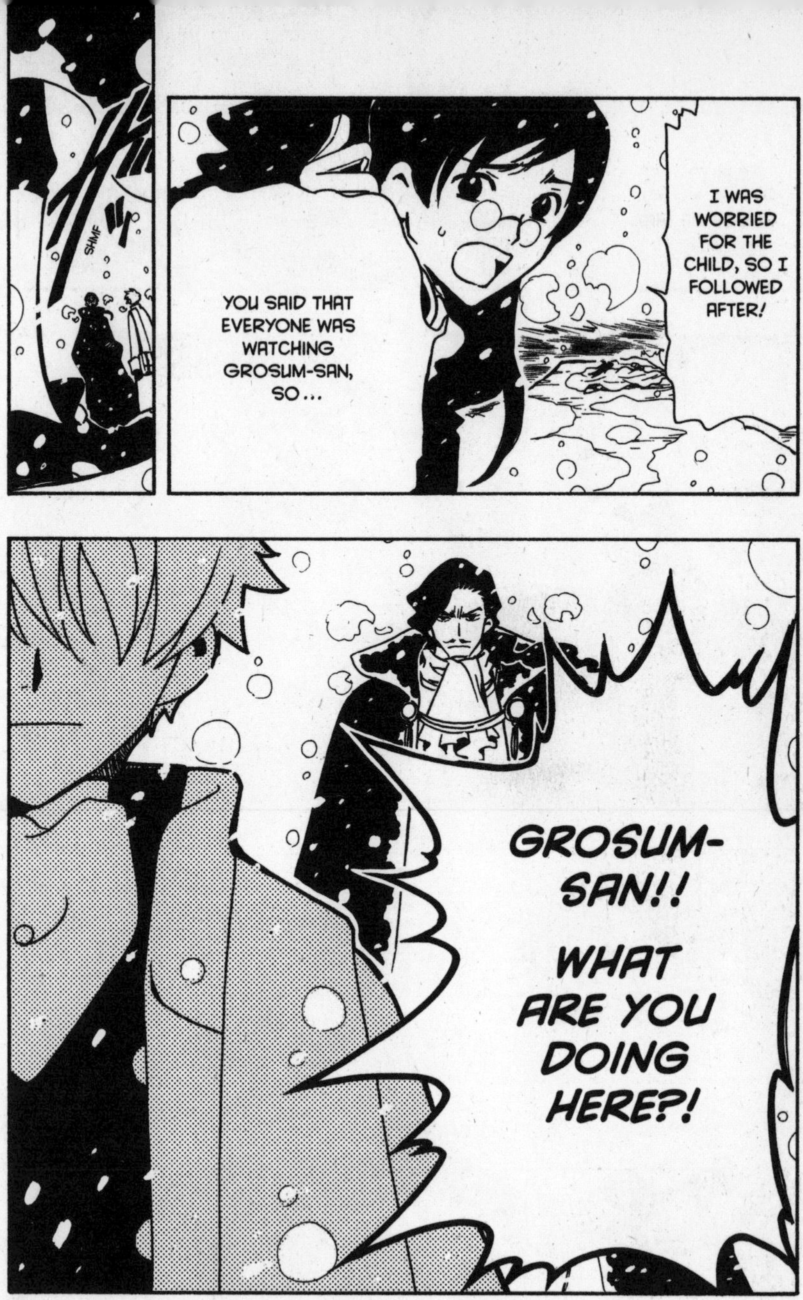
I WAS WORRIED FOR THE CHILD, SO I FOLLOWED AFTER!
YOU SAID THAT EVERYONE WAS WATCHING GROSUM-SAN, SO...
SHMF
GROSUM-SAN!!
WHAT ARE YOU DOING HERE?!

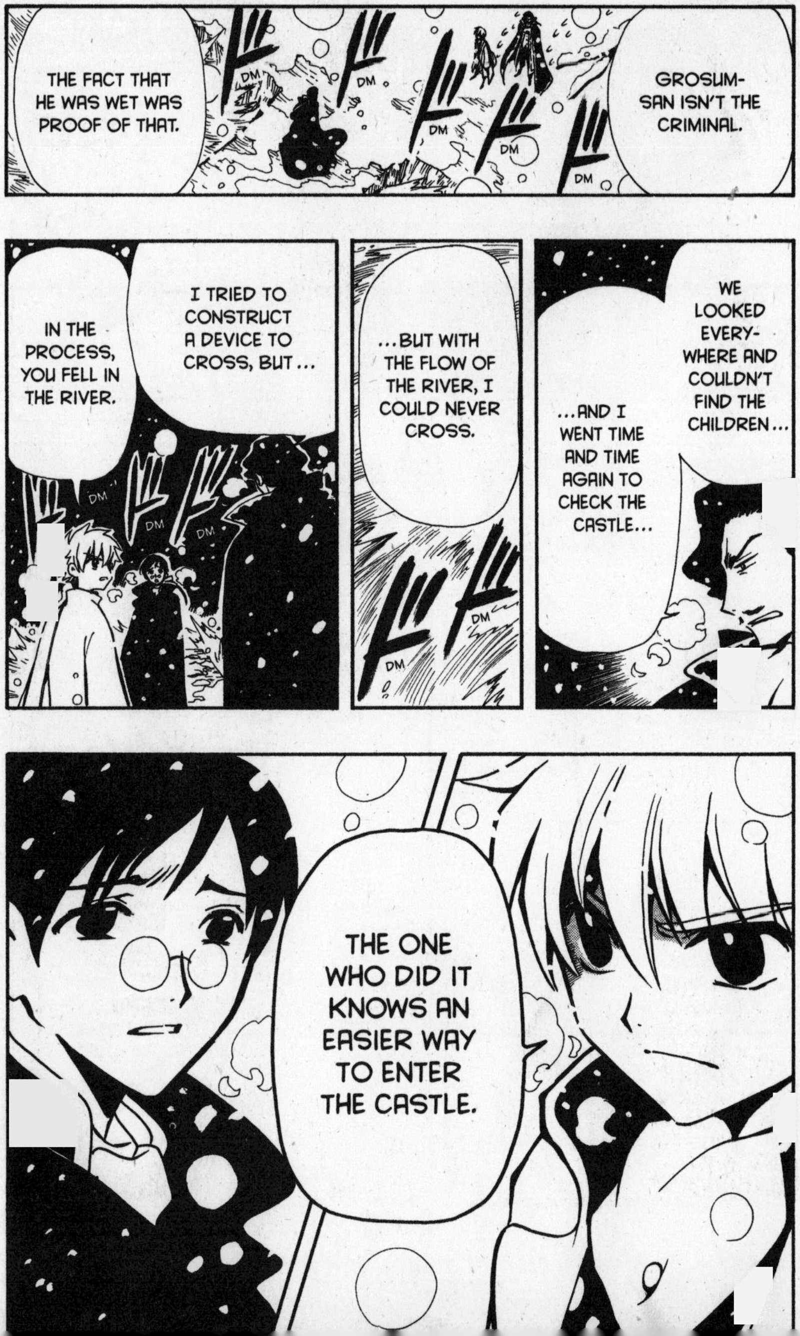
GROSUM-SAN ISN'T THE CRIMINAL.
DM
DM
DM
DM
DM
THE FACT THAT HE WAS WET WAS PROOF OF THAT.
WE LOOKED EVERY-WHERE AND COULDN'T FIND THE CHILDREN...
...AND I WENT TIME AND TIME AGAIN TO CHECK THE CASTLE...
...BUT WITH THE FLOW OF THE RIVER, I COULD NEVER CROSS.
DM
DM
I TRIED TO CONSTRUCT A DEVICE TO CROSS, BUT...
IN THE PROCESS, YOU FELL IN THE RIVER.
DM
DM
DM
THE ONE WHO DID IT KNOWS AN EASIER WAY TO ENTER THE CASTLE.

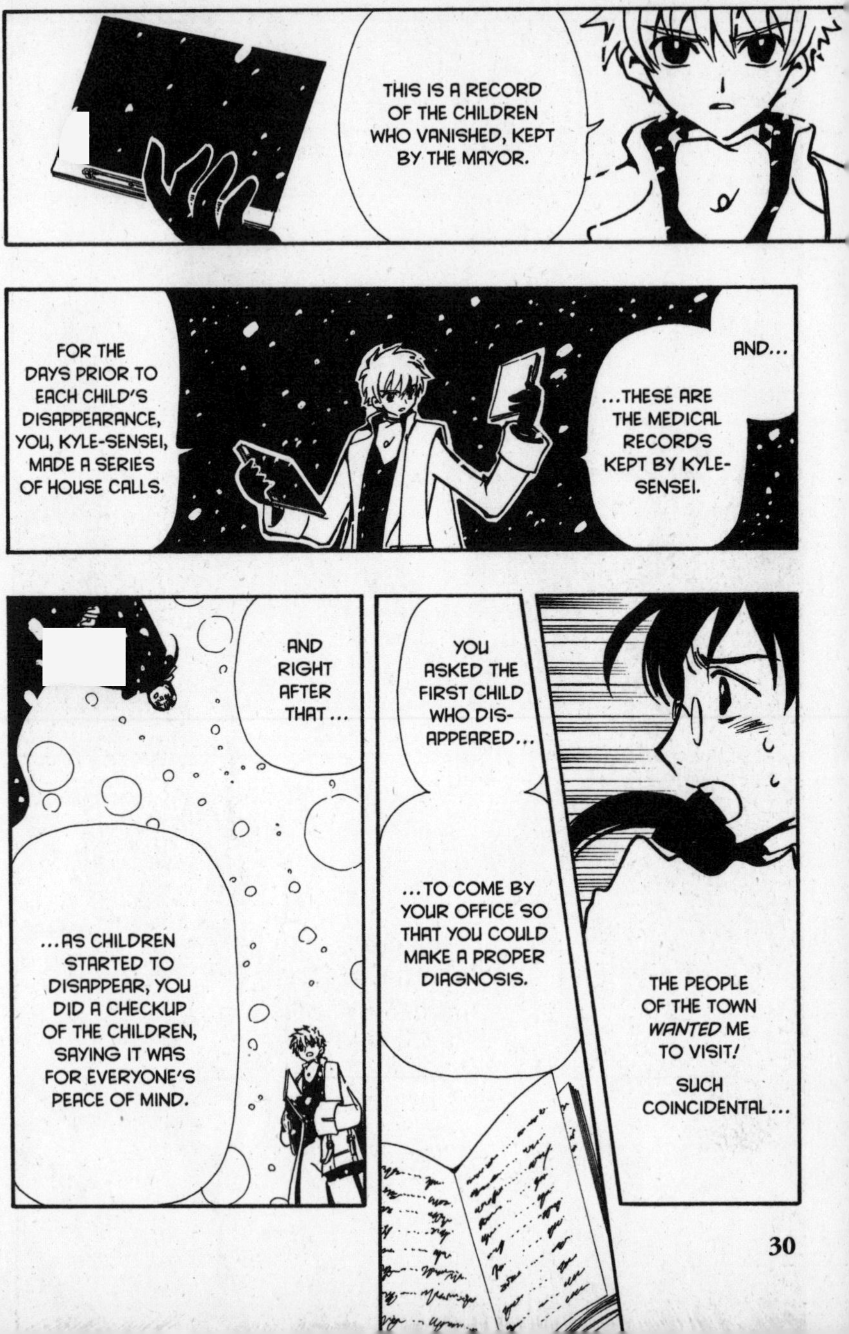
THIS IS A RECORD OF THE CHILDREN WHO VANISHED, KEPT BY THE MAYOR.
AND...
...THESE ARE THE MEDICAL RECORDS KEPT BY KYLE-SENSEI.
FOR THE DAYS PRIOR TO EACH CHILD'S DISAPPEARANCE, YOU, KYLE-SENSEI, MADE A SERIES OF HOUSE CALLS.
THE PEOPLE OF THE TOWN *WANTED* ME TO VISIT!
SUCH COINCIDENTAL...
YOU ASKED THE FIRST CHILD WHO DIS-APPEARED...
...TO COME BY YOUR OFFICE SO THAT YOU COULD MAKE A PROPER DIAGNOSIS.
AND RIGHT AFTER THAT...
...AS CHILDREN STARTED TO DISAPPEAR, YOU DID A CHECKUP OF THE CHILDREN, SAYING IT WAS FOR EVERYONE'S PEACE OF MIND.

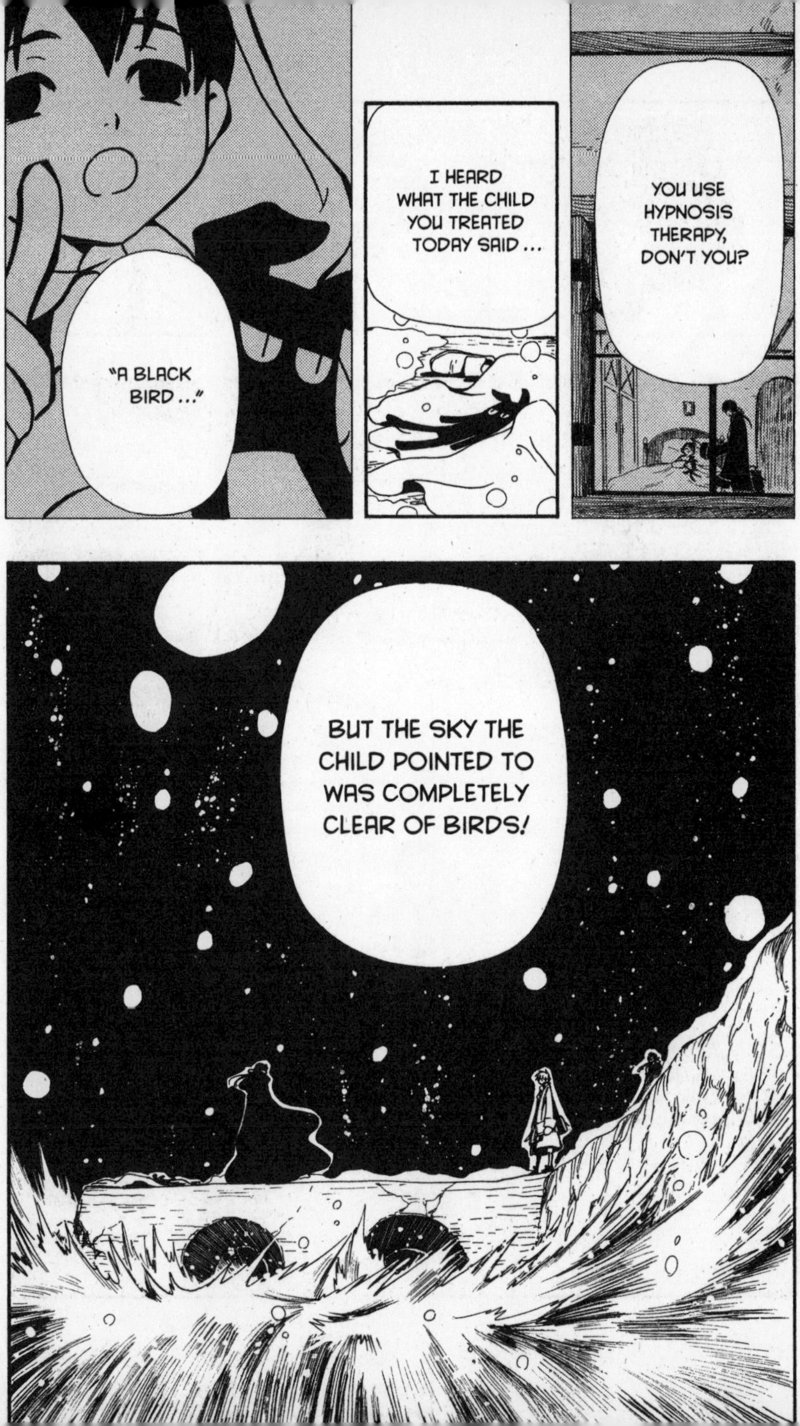
YOU USE HYPNOSIS THERAPY, DON'T YOU?
I HEARD WHAT THE CHILD YOU TREATED TODAY SAID...
"A BLACK BIRD..."
BUT THE SKY THE CHILD POINTED TO WAS COMPLETELY CLEAR OF BIRDS!

YOU IMPLANTED A HYPNOTIC SUGGESTION IN THE CHILD.

ON SNOWY NIGHTS WHEN THEIR TRACKS WILL BE COVERED OVER, THE CHILDREN CHASE IMAGINARY BLACK BIRDS... AND VANISH ON THEIR OWN.

THEN WHERE HAVE THE CHILDREN GONE?

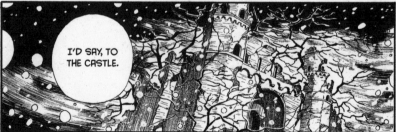

I'D SAY, TO THE CASTLE.

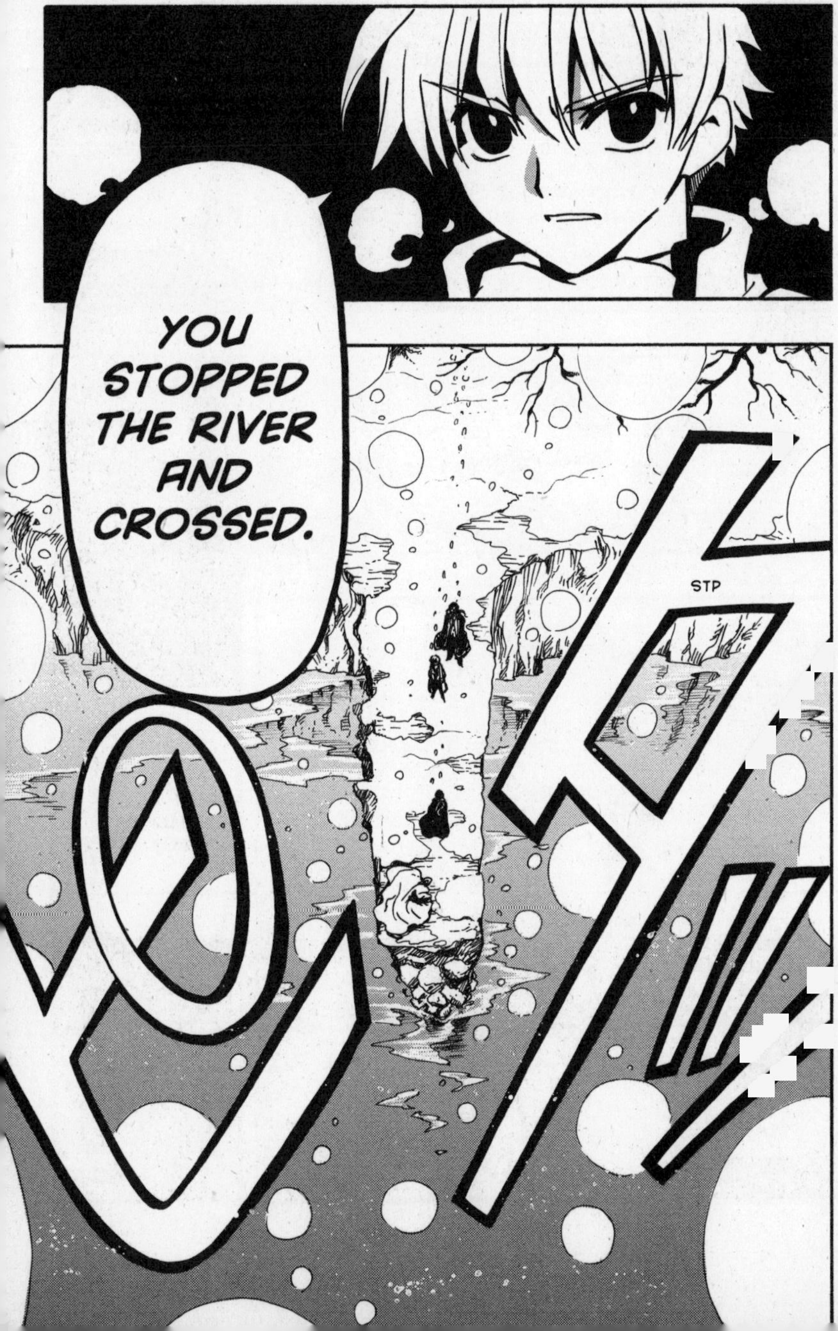
YOU STOPPED THE RIVER AND CROSSED.
STP

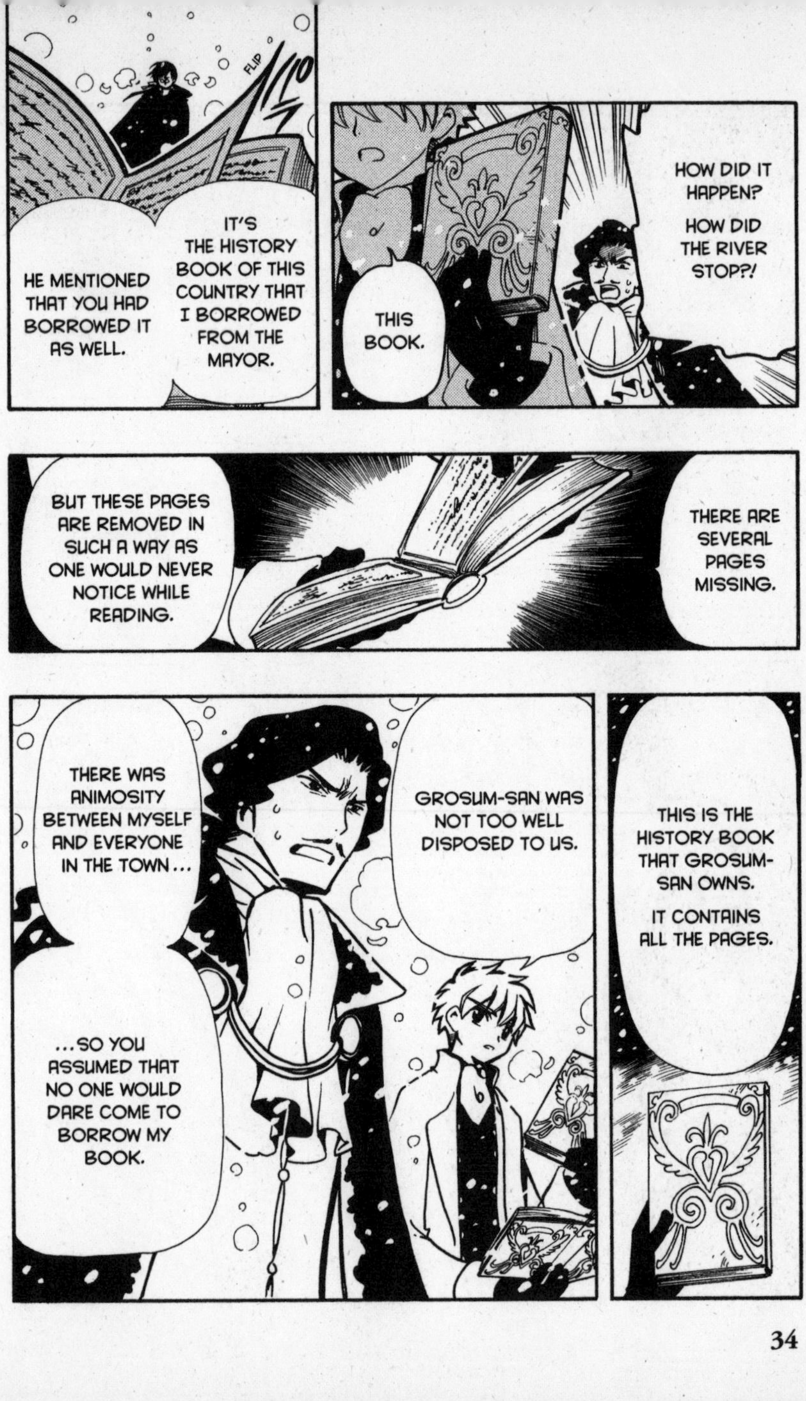
HOW DID IT HAPPEN?
HOW DID THE RIVER STOP?!
THIS BOOK.
FLIP
IT'S THE HISTORY BOOK OF THIS COUNTRY THAT I BORROWED FROM THE MAYOR.
HE MENTIONED THAT YOU HAD BORROWED IT AS WELL.
THERE ARE SEVERAL PAGES MISSING.
BUT THESE PAGES ARE REMOVED IN SUCH A WAY AS ONE WOULD NEVER NOTICE WHILE READING.
THIS IS THE HISTORY BOOK THAT GROSUM-SAN OWNS.
IT CONTAINS ALL THE PAGES.
GROSUM-SAN WAS NOT TOO WELL DISPOSED TO US.
THERE WAS ANIMOSITY BETWEEN MYSELF AND EVERYONE IN THE TOWN...
...SO YOU ASSUMED THAT NO ONE WOULD DARE COME TO BORROW MY BOOK.

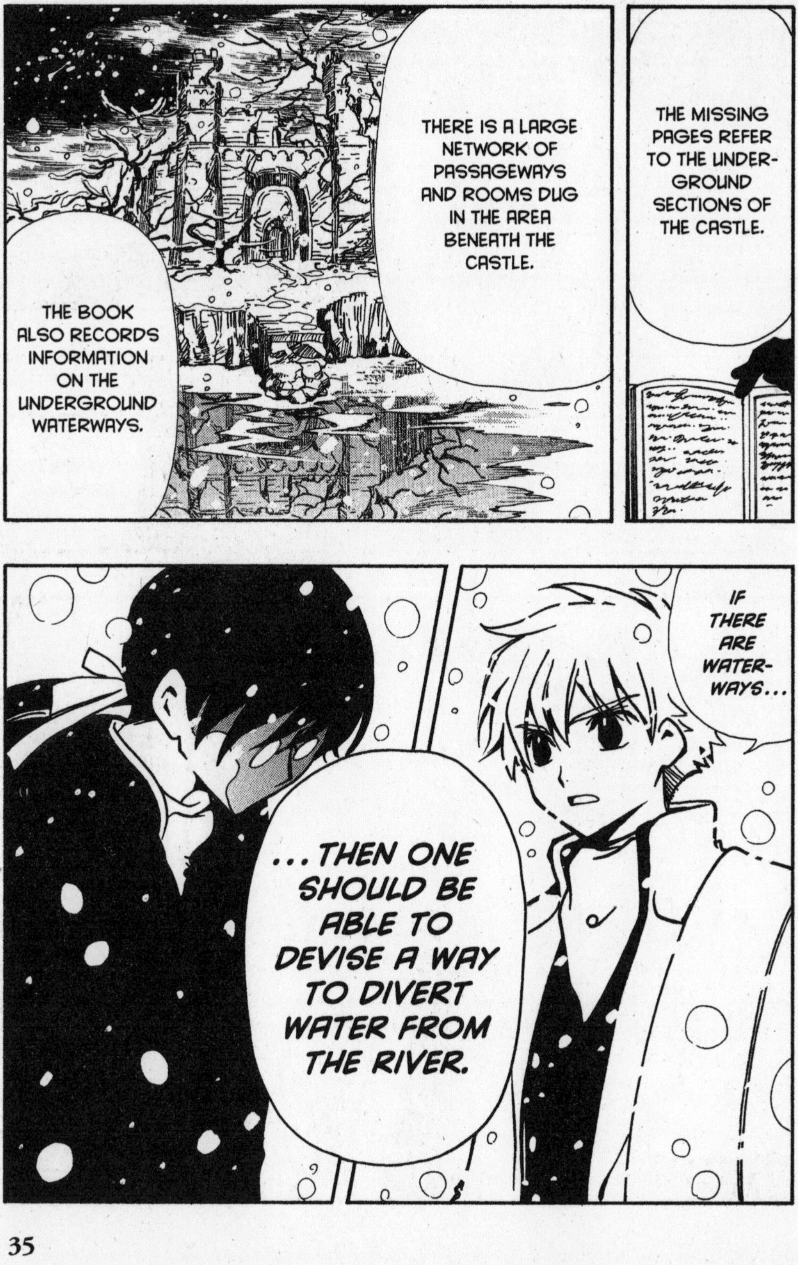
THE MISSING PAGES REFER TO THE UNDER-GROUND SECTIONS OF THE CASTLE.
THERE IS A LARGE NETWORK OF PASSAGEWAYS AND ROOMS DUG IN THE AREA BENEATH THE CASTLE.
THE BOOK ALSO RECORDS INFORMATION ON THE UNDERGROUND WATERWAYS.
IF THERE ARE WATER-WAYS...
...THEN ONE SHOULD BE ABLE TO DEVISE A WAY TO DIVERT WATER FROM THE RIVER.

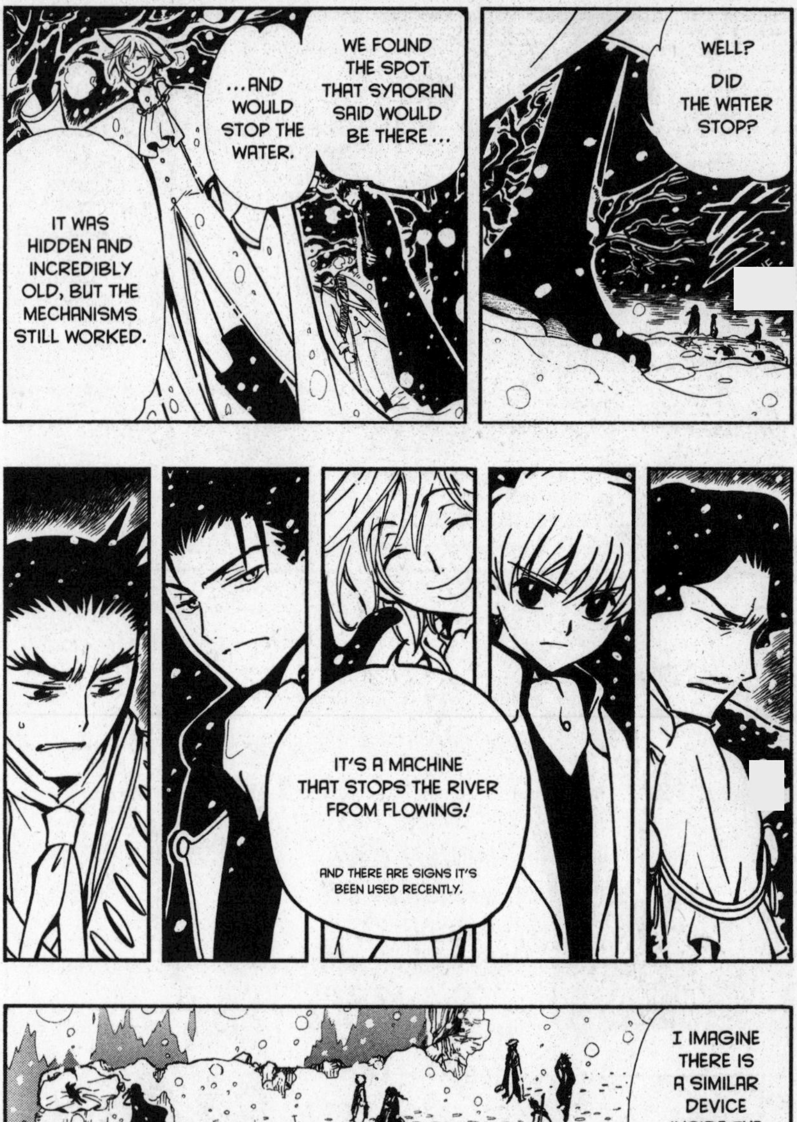
WELL? DID THE WATER STOP?
WE FOUND THE SPOT THAT SYAORAN SAID WOULD BE THERE...
...AND WOULD STOP THE WATER.
IT WAS HIDDEN AND INCREDIBLY OLD, BUT THE MECHANISMS STILL WORKED.
IT'S A MACHINE THAT STOPS THE RIVER FROM FLOWING!
AND THERE ARE SIGNS IT'S BEEN USED RECENTLY.
I IMAGINE THERE IS A SIMILAR DEVICE INSIDE THE CASTLE AS WELL.

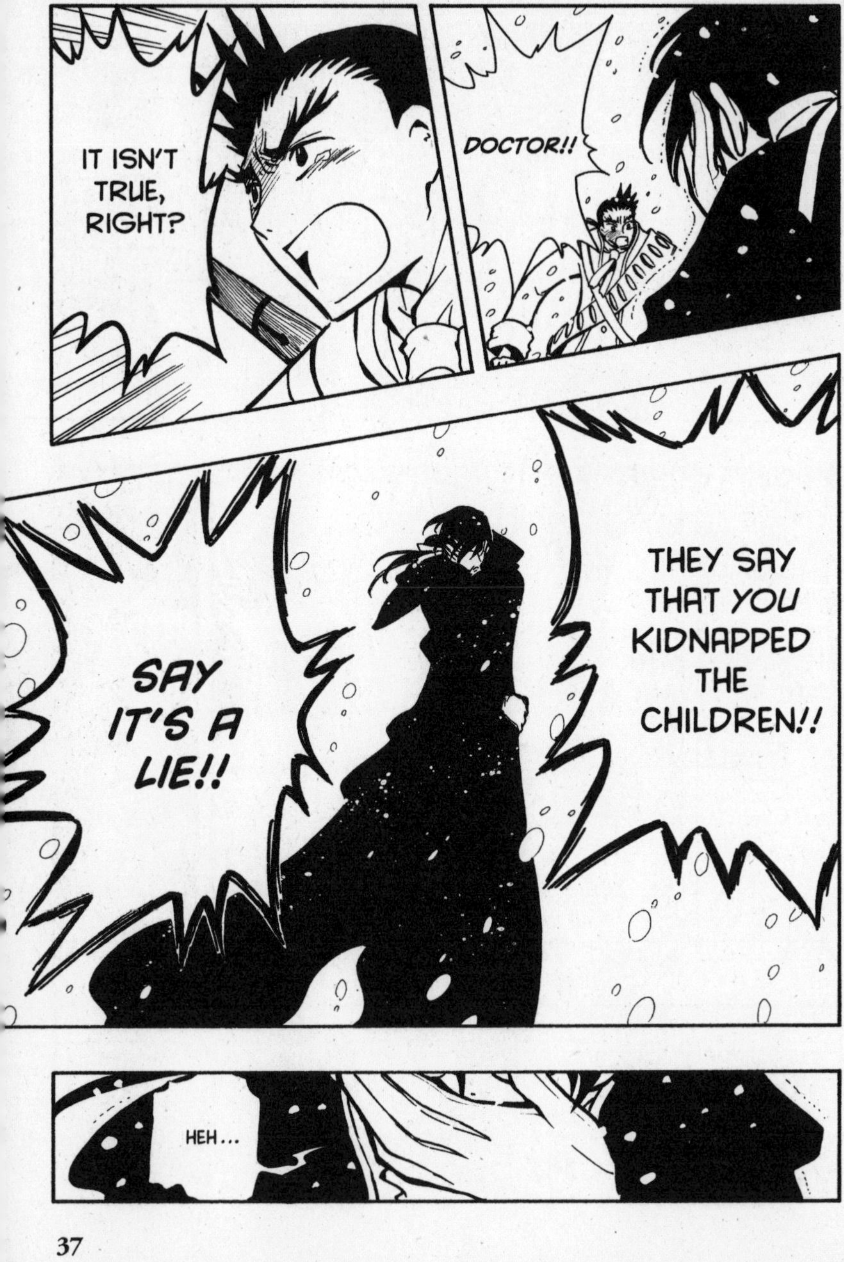
DOCTOR!!
IT ISN'T TRUE, RIGHT?
THEY SAY THAT *YOU* KIDNAPPED THE CHILDREN!!
SAY IT'S A LIE!!
HEH...

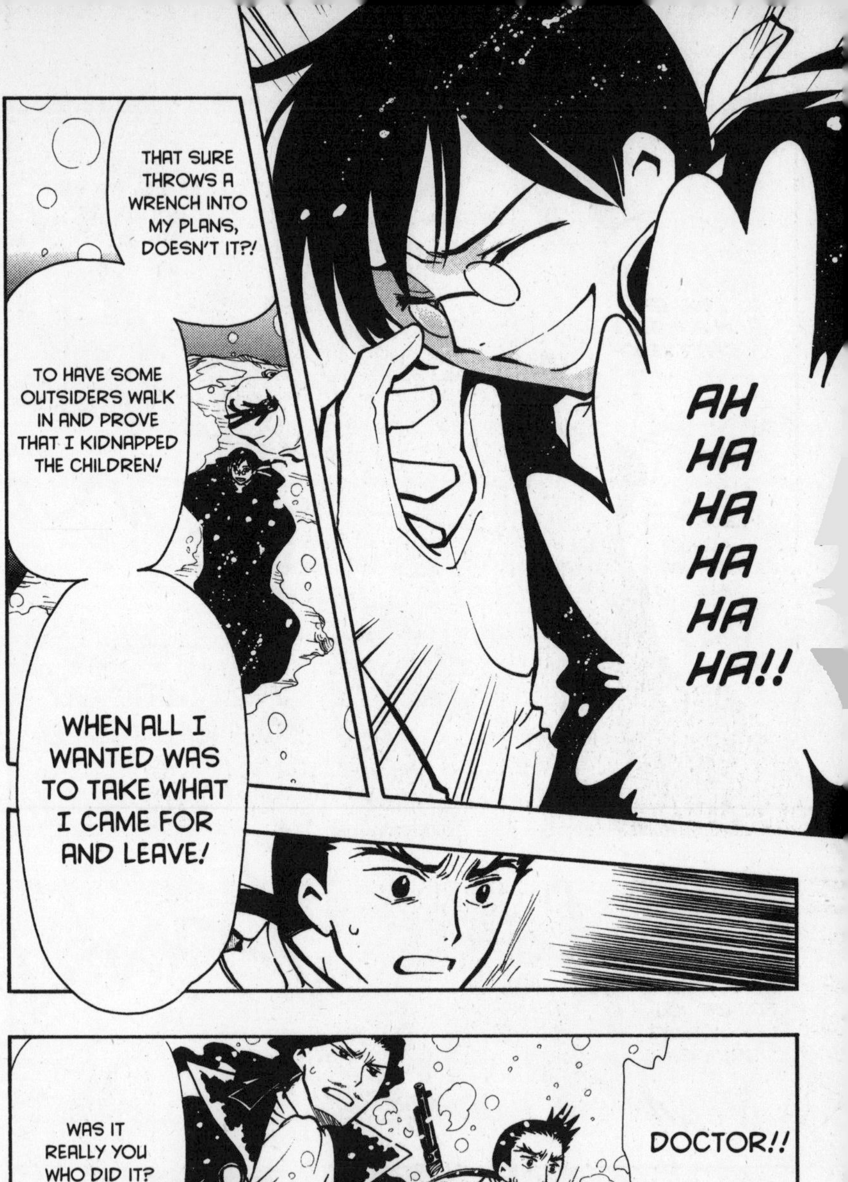
AH HA HA HA HA HA!!
THAT SURE THROWS A WRENCH INTO MY PLANS, DOESN'T IT?!
TO HAVE SOME OUTSIDERS WALK IN AND PROVE THAT I KIDNAPPED THE CHILDREN!
WHEN ALL I WANTED WAS TO TAKE WHAT I CAME FOR AND LEAVE!
DOCTOR!!
SHF
WAS IT REALLY YOU WHO DID IT?

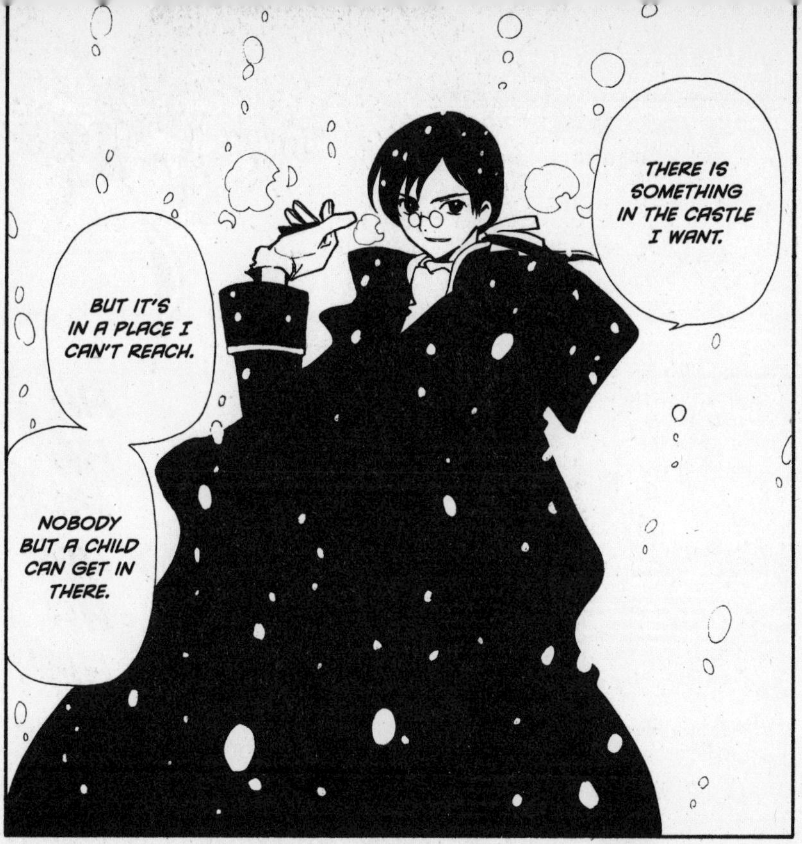
THERE IS SOMETHING IN THE CASTLE I WANT.
BUT IT'S IN A PLACE I CAN'T REACH.
NOBODY BUT A CHILD CAN GET IN THERE.

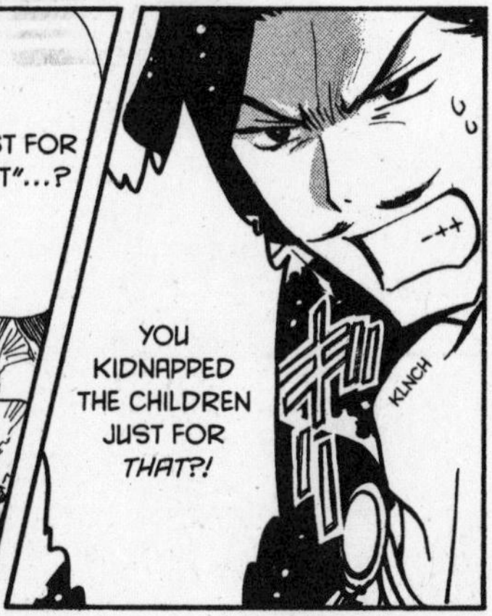
YOU KIDNAPPED THE CHILDREN JUST FOR *THAT*?!
KLNCH

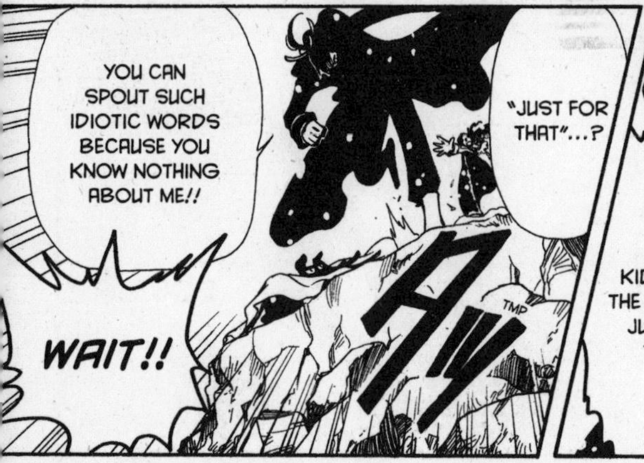
"JUST FOR THAT"...?
YOU CAN SPOUT SUCH IDIOTIC WORDS BECAUSE YOU KNOW NOTHING ABOUT ME!!
TMP
WAIT!!

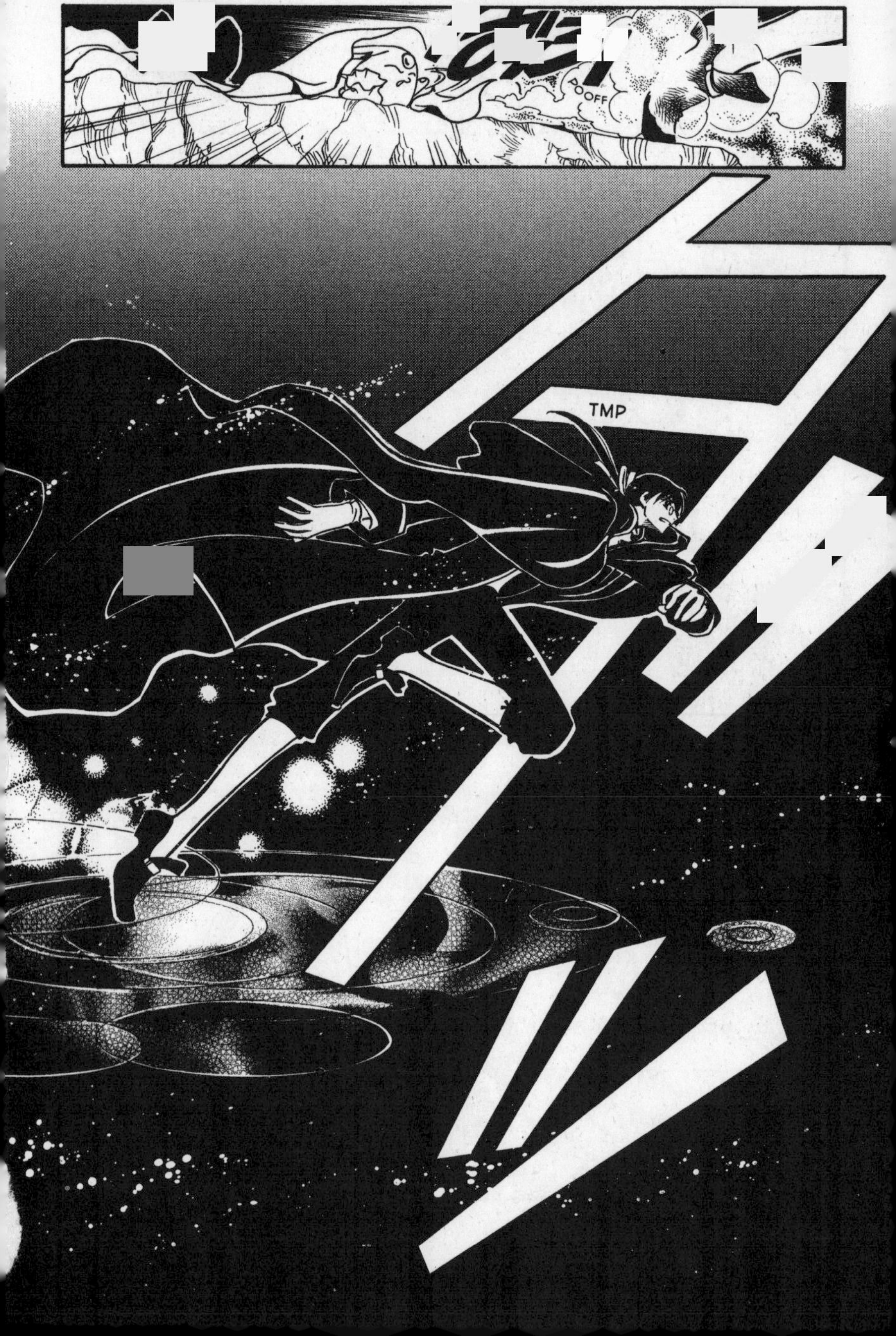
POOFF
TMP

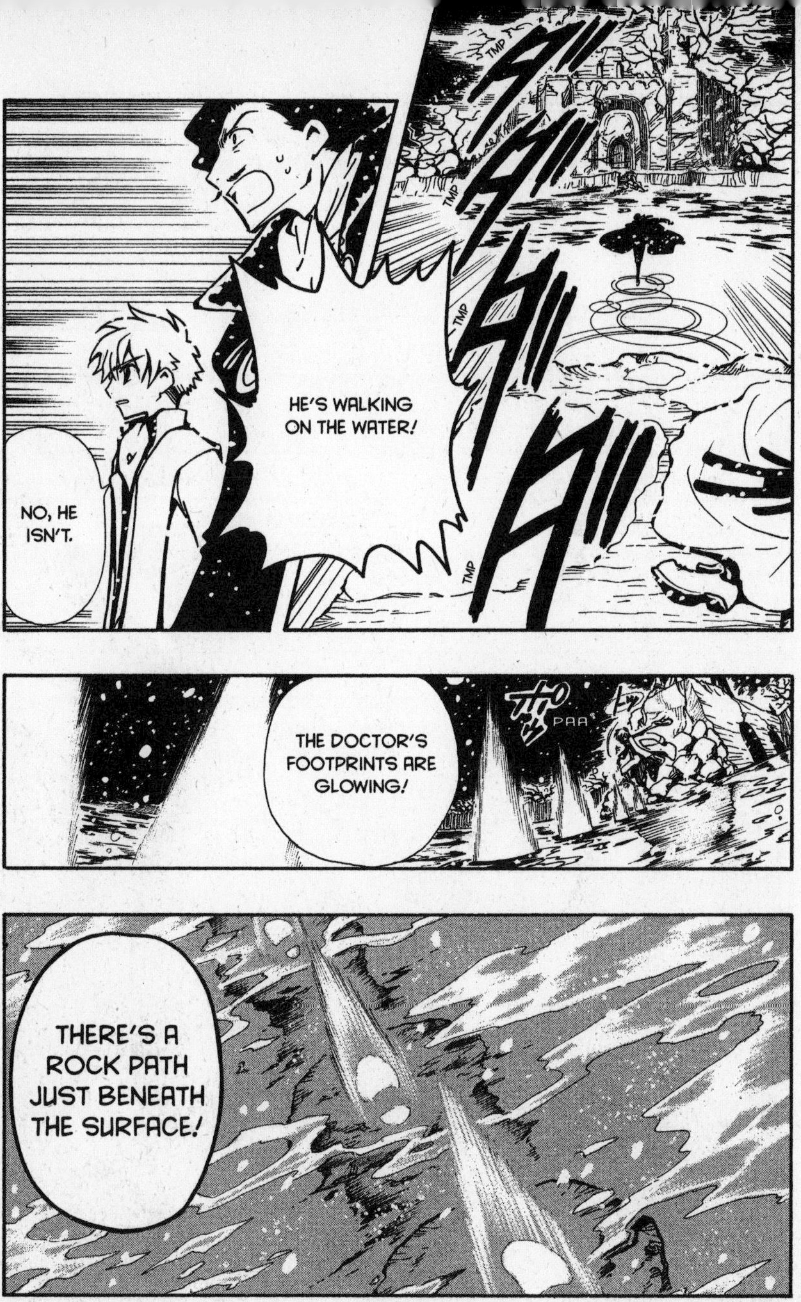
TMP
TMP
TMP
TMP
HE'S WALKING ON THE WATER!
NO, HE ISN'T.
PAA
THE DOCTOR'S FOOTPRINTS ARE GLOWING!
THERE'S A ROCK PATH JUST BENEATH THE SURFACE!

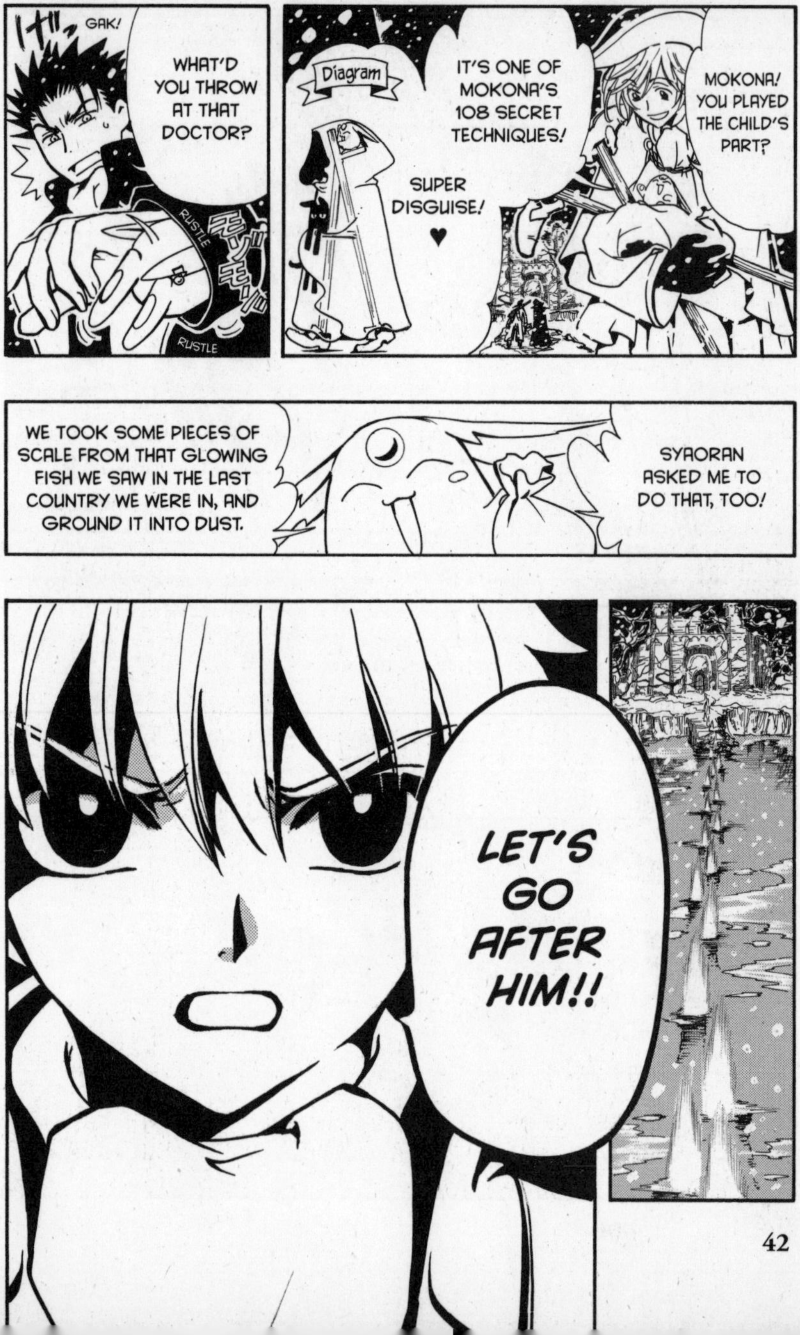
MOKONA! YOU PLAYED THE CHILD'S PART?
IT'S ONE OF MOKONA'S 108 SECRET TECHNIQUES!
Diagram
SUPER DISGUISE! ♥
WHAT'D YOU THROW AT THAT DOCTOR?
GAK!
RUSTLE
RUSTLE
SYAORAN ASKED ME TO DO THAT, TOO!
WE TOOK SOME PIECES OF SCALE FROM THAT GLOWING FISH WE SAW IN THE LAST COUNTRY WE WERE IN, AND GROUND IT INTO DUST.
LET'S GO AFTER HIM!!

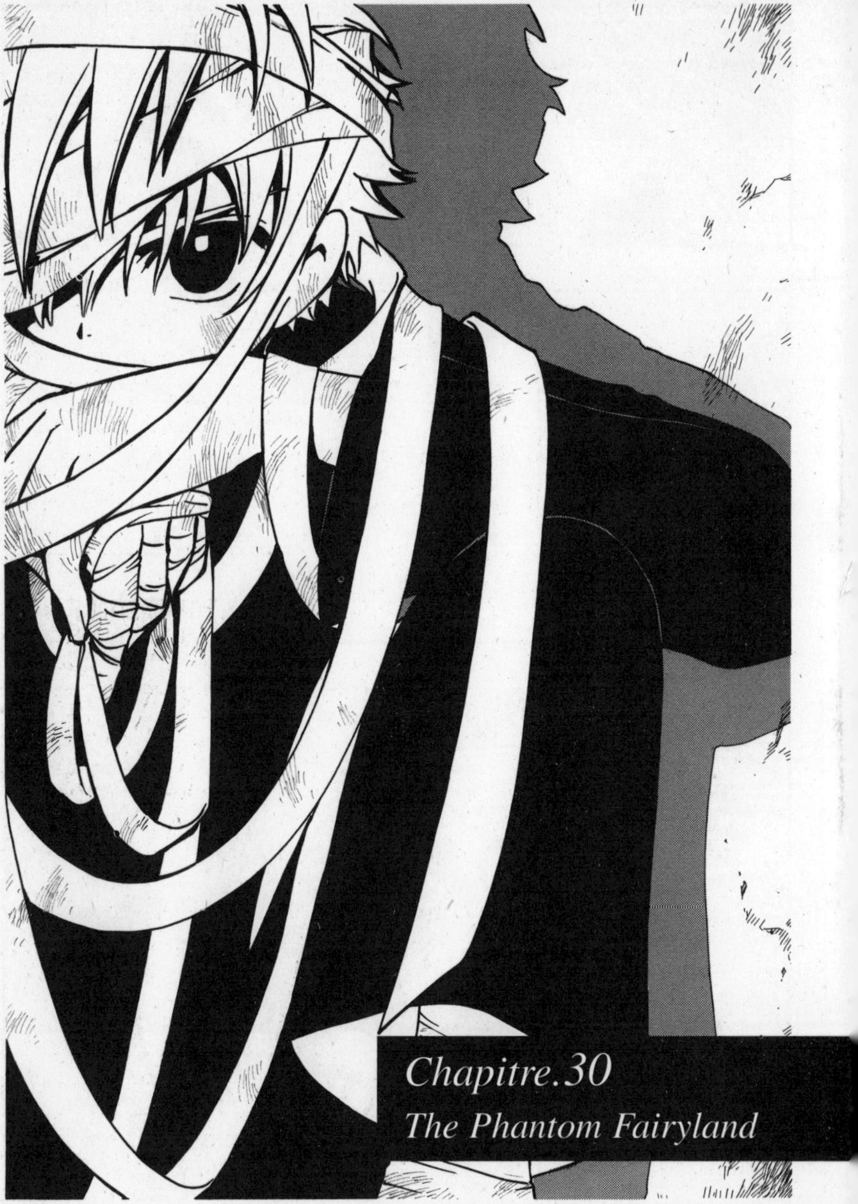

# Chapitre.30
## The Phantom Fairyland

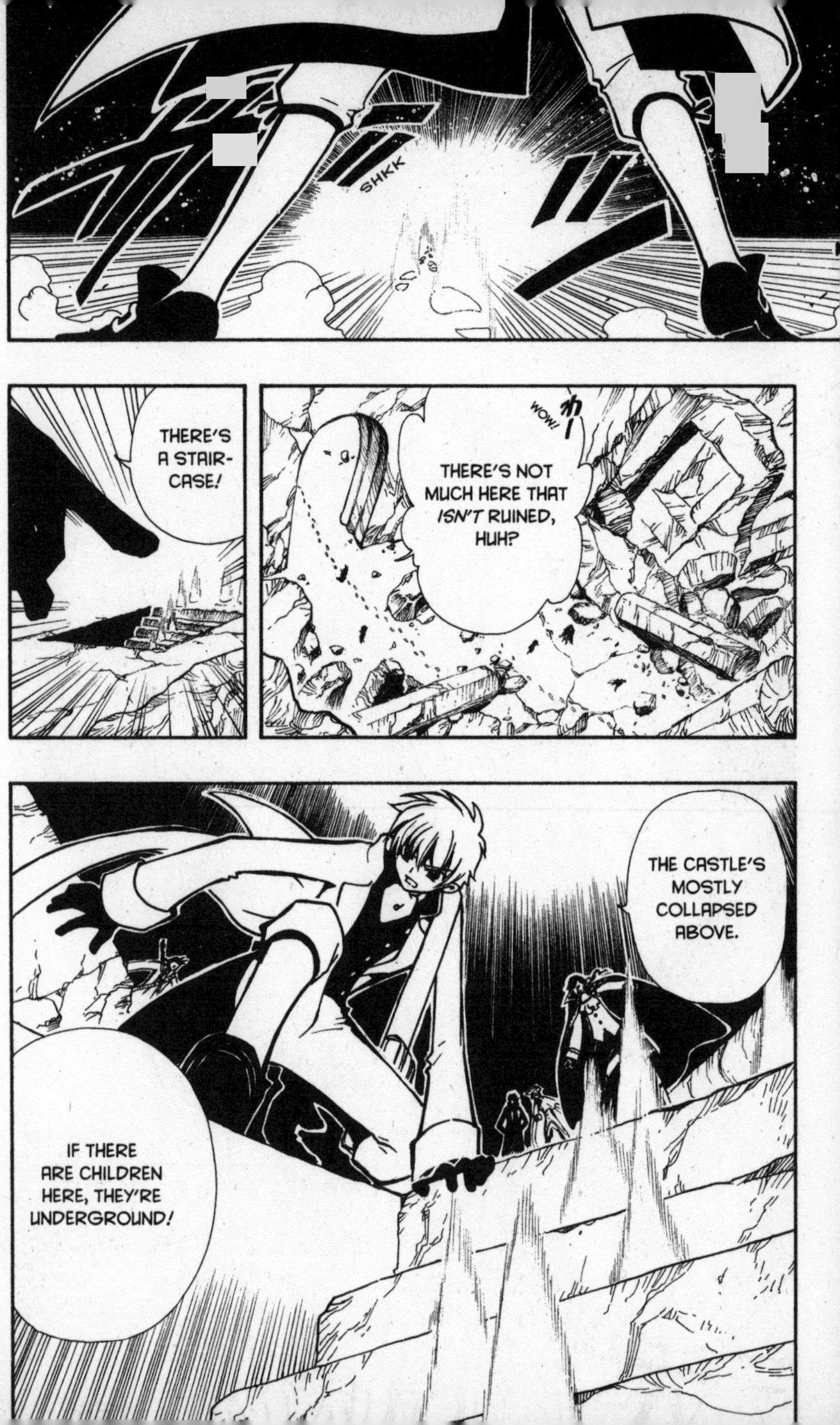
SHKK
WOW!
THERE'S NOT MUCH HERE THAT *ISN'T* RUINED, HUH?
THERE'S A STAIR-CASE!
THE CASTLE'S MOSTLY COLLAPSED ABOVE.
IF THERE ARE CHILDREN HERE, THEY'RE UNDERGROUND!

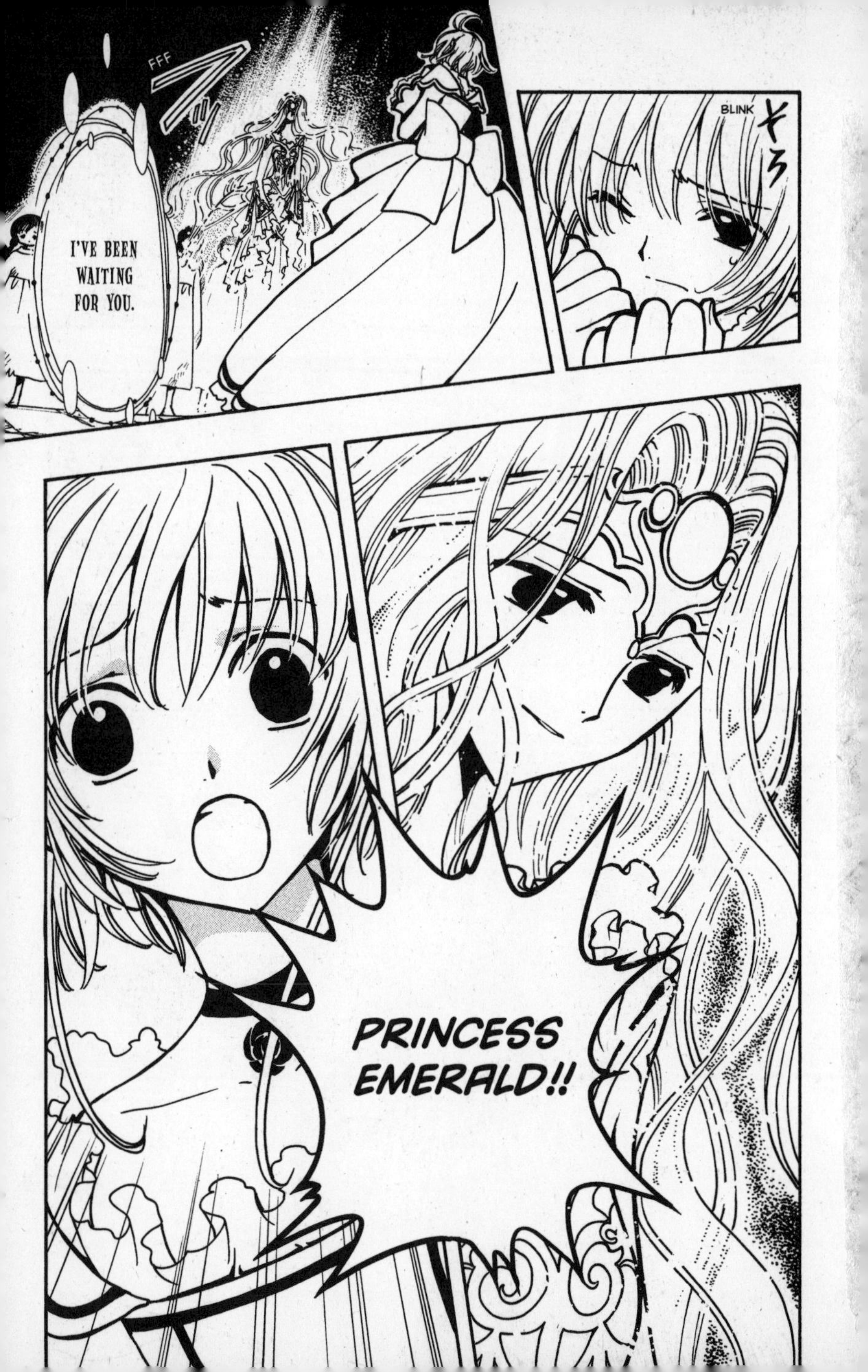
BLINK
FFF
I'VE BEEN WAITING FOR YOU.
PRINCESS EMERALD!!

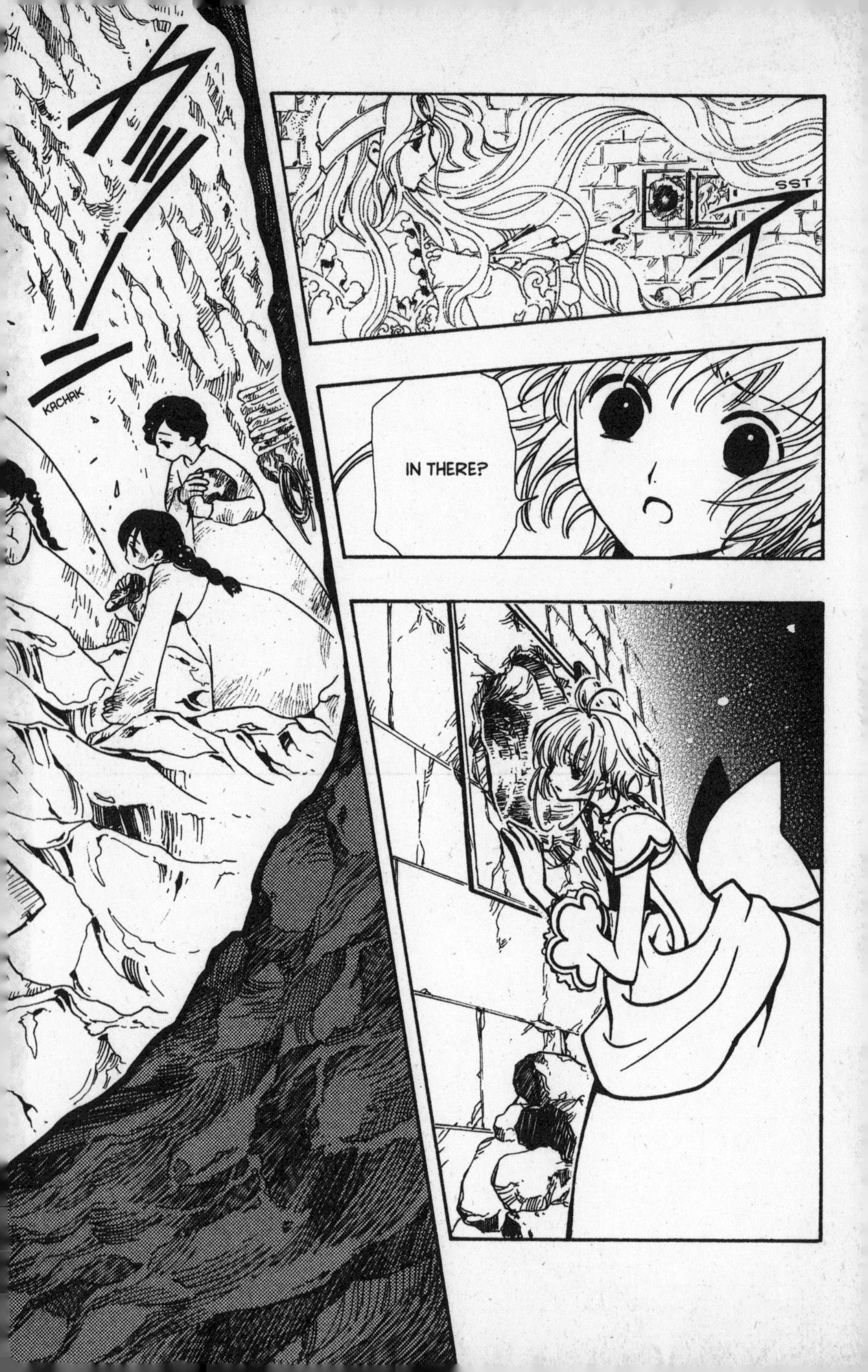
SST
IN THERE?
KACHAK

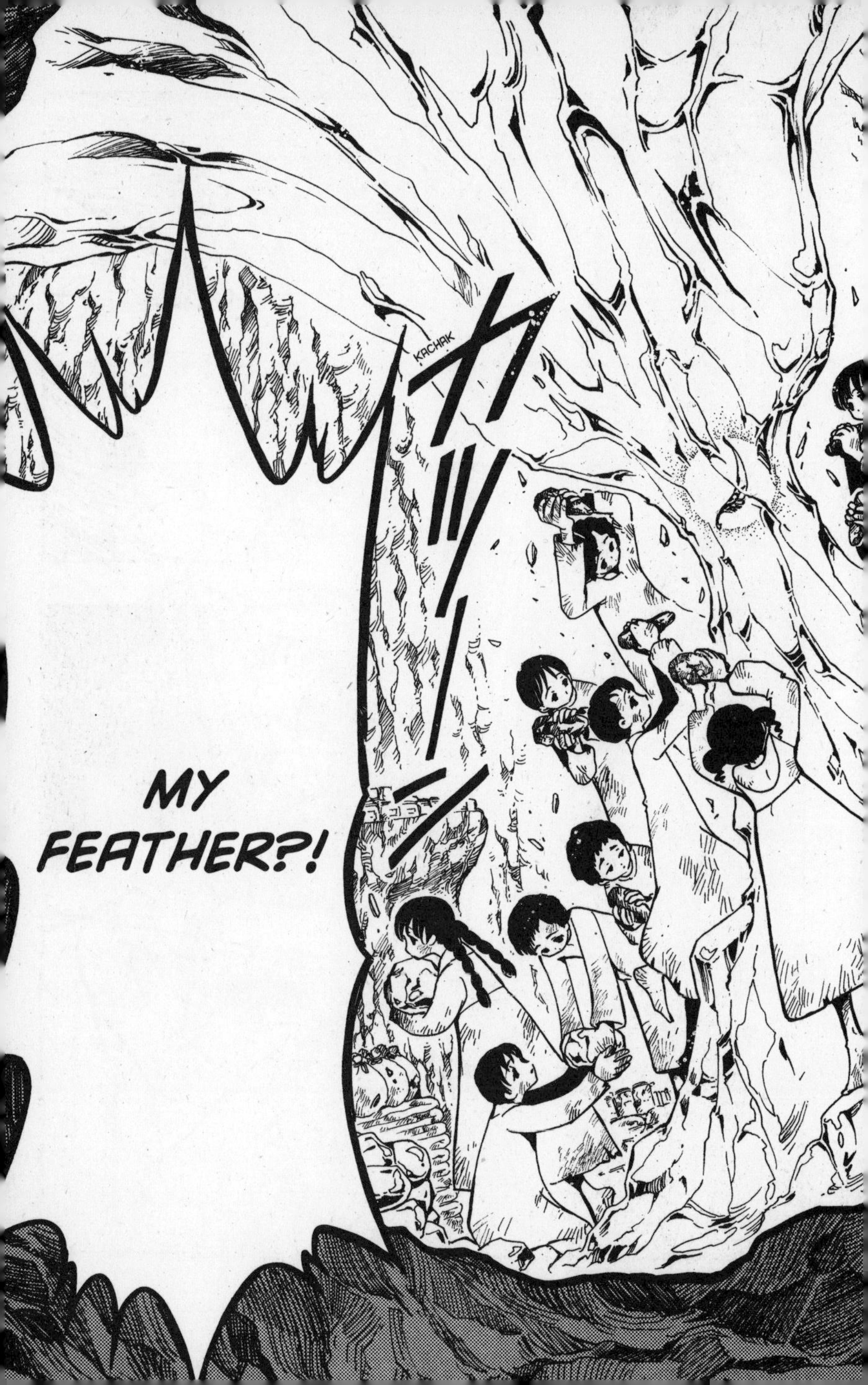
MY FEATHER?!
KACHAK

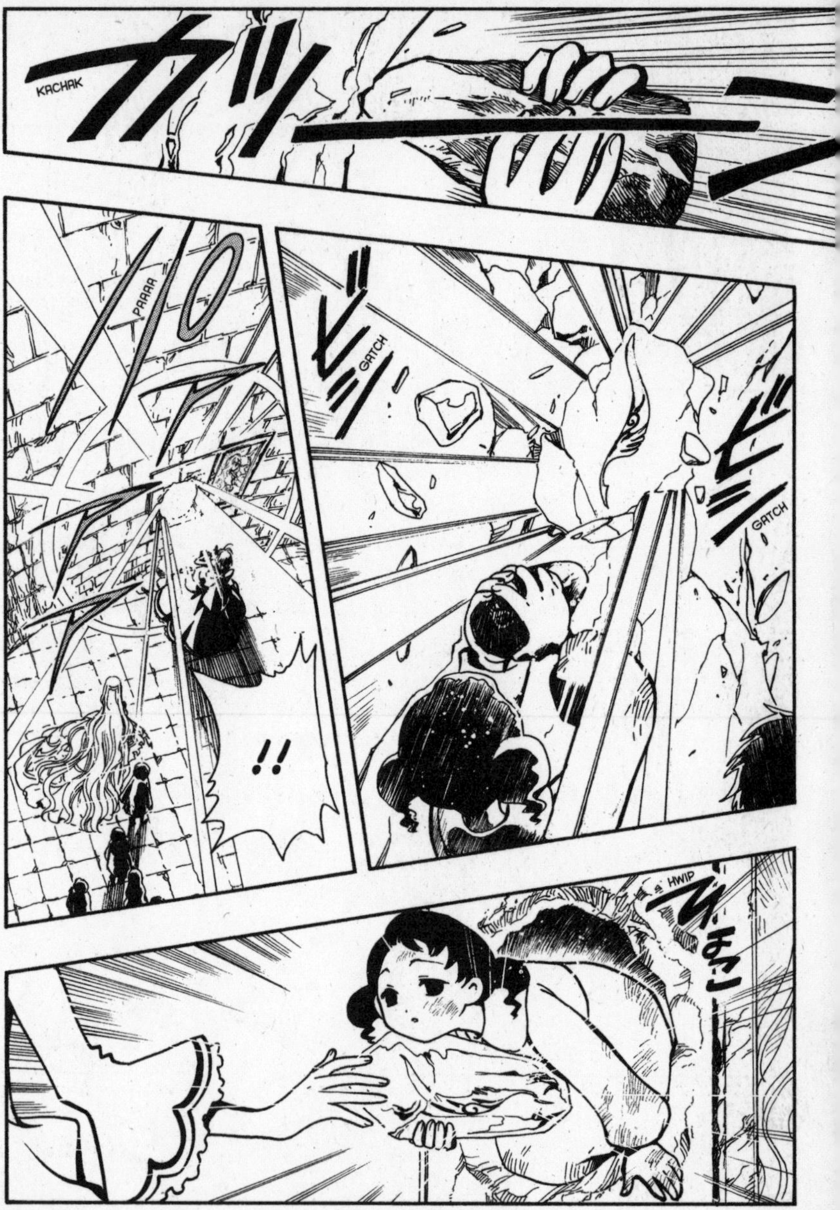
カッ
KACHAK
ビッ
GATCH
ビッ
GATCH
PAAAA
!!
HWIP
ぴょこ

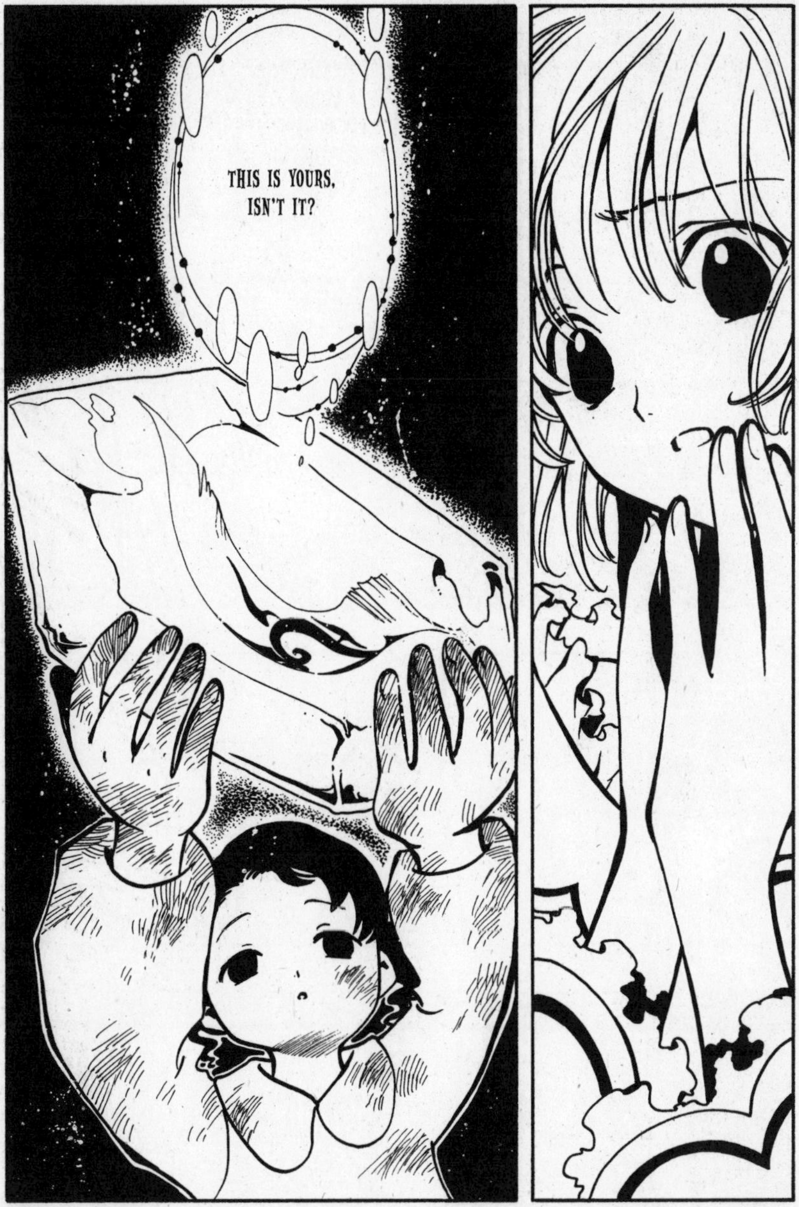
THIS IS YOURS,
ISN'T IT?

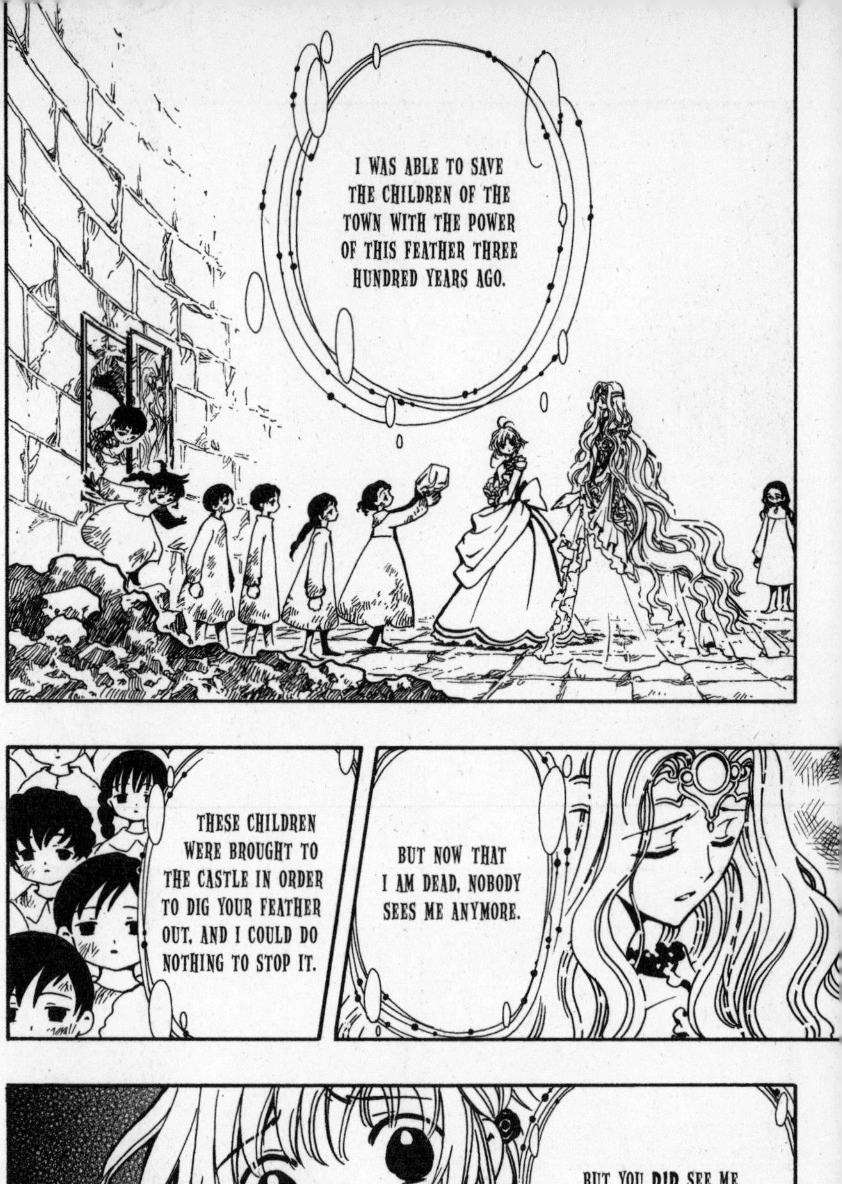
I WAS ABLE TO SAVE THE CHILDREN OF THE TOWN WITH THE POWER OF THIS FEATHER THREE HUNDRED YEARS AGO.
BUT NOW THAT I AM DEAD, NOBODY SEES ME ANYMORE.
THESE CHILDREN WERE BROUGHT TO THE CASTLE IN ORDER TO DIG YOUR FEATHER OUT, AND I COULD DO NOTHING TO STOP IT.
BUT YOU **DID** SEE ME, AND CAME HERE.

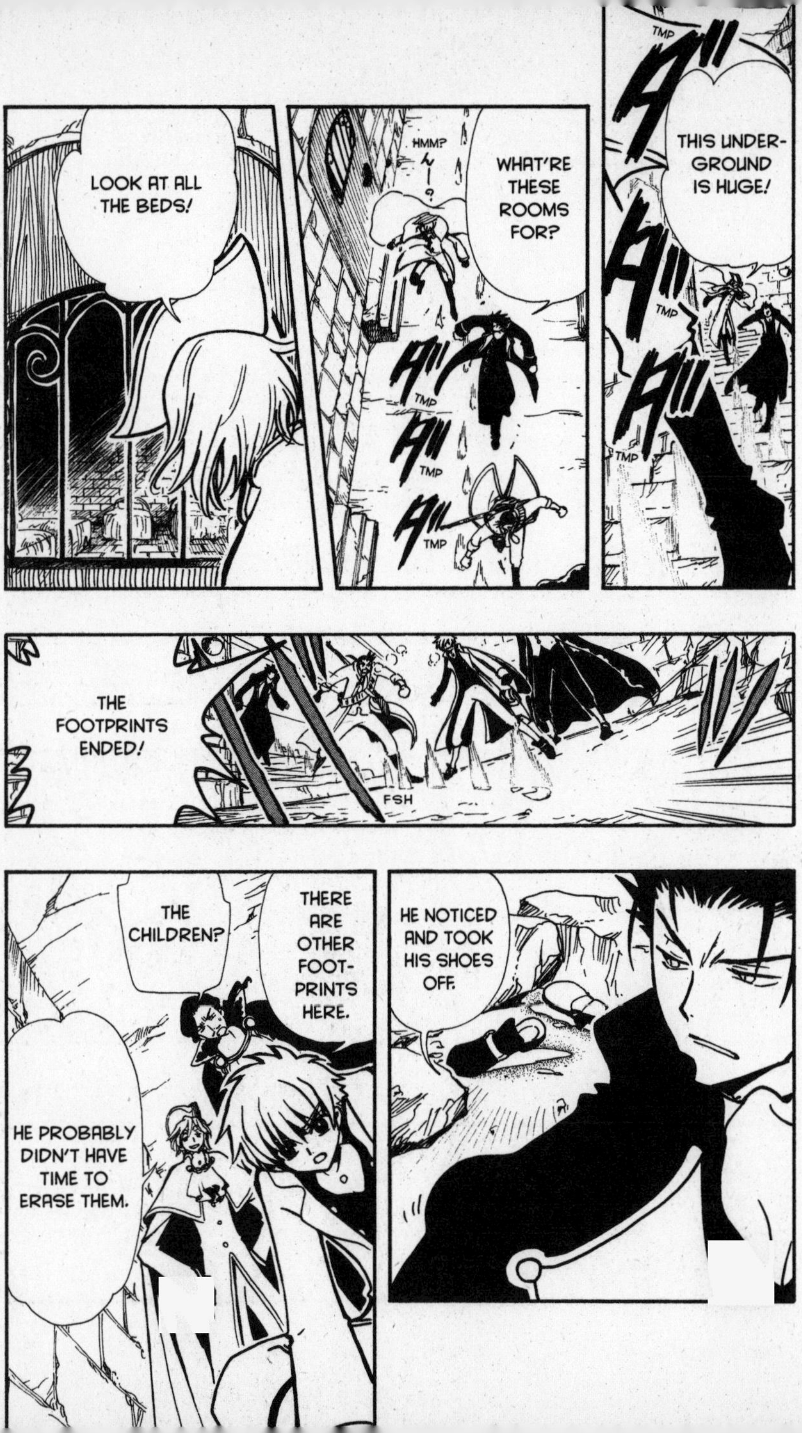
TMP
THIS UNDER-GROUND IS HUGE!
TMP
TMP
HMM?
WHAT'RE THESE ROOMS FOR?
TMP
TMP
TMP
LOOK AT ALL THE BEDS!
THE FOOTPRINTS ENDED!
FSH
HE NOTICED AND TOOK HIS SHOES OFF.
THERE ARE OTHER FOOT-PRINTS HERE.
THE CHILDREN?
HE PROBABLY DIDN'T HAVE TIME TO ERASE THEM.

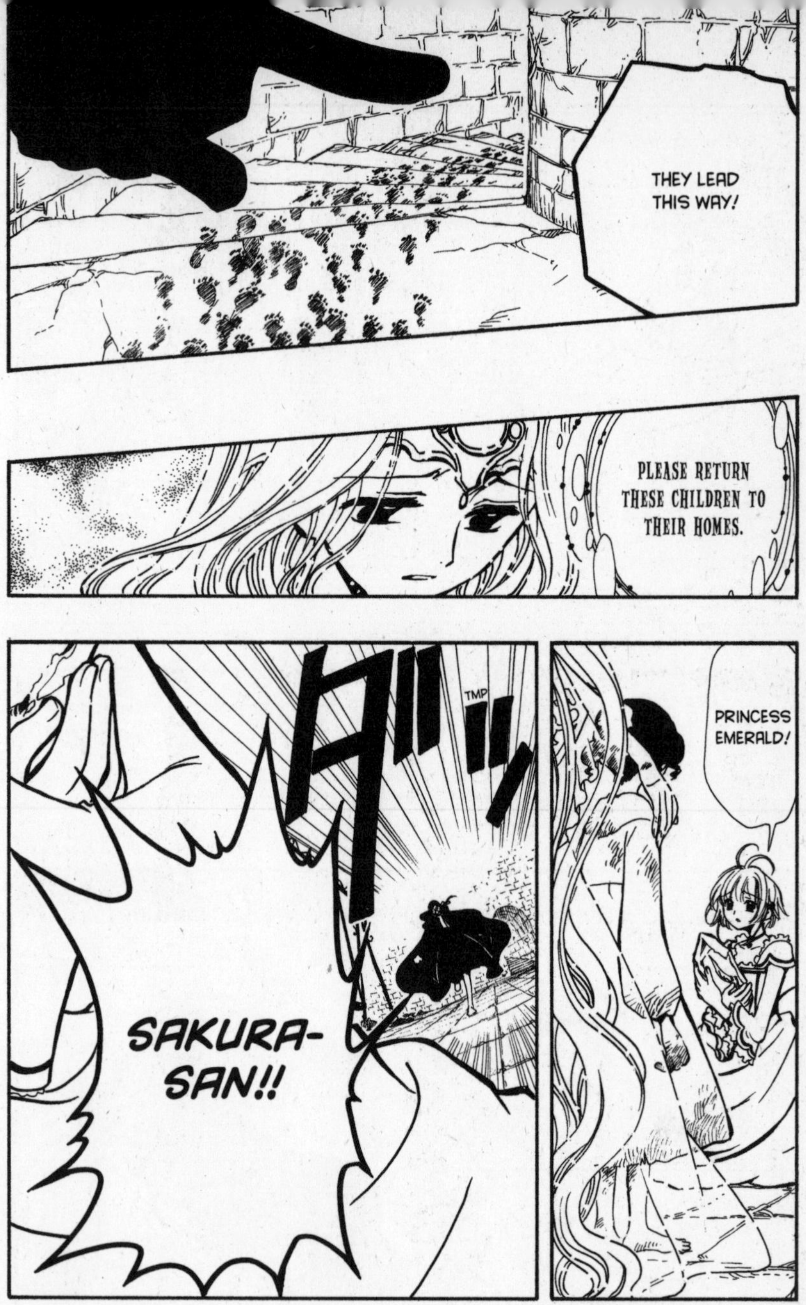
THEY LEAD THIS WAY!
PLEASE RETURN THESE CHILDREN TO THEIR HOMES.
PRINCESS EMERALD!
TMP
SAKURA-SAN!!

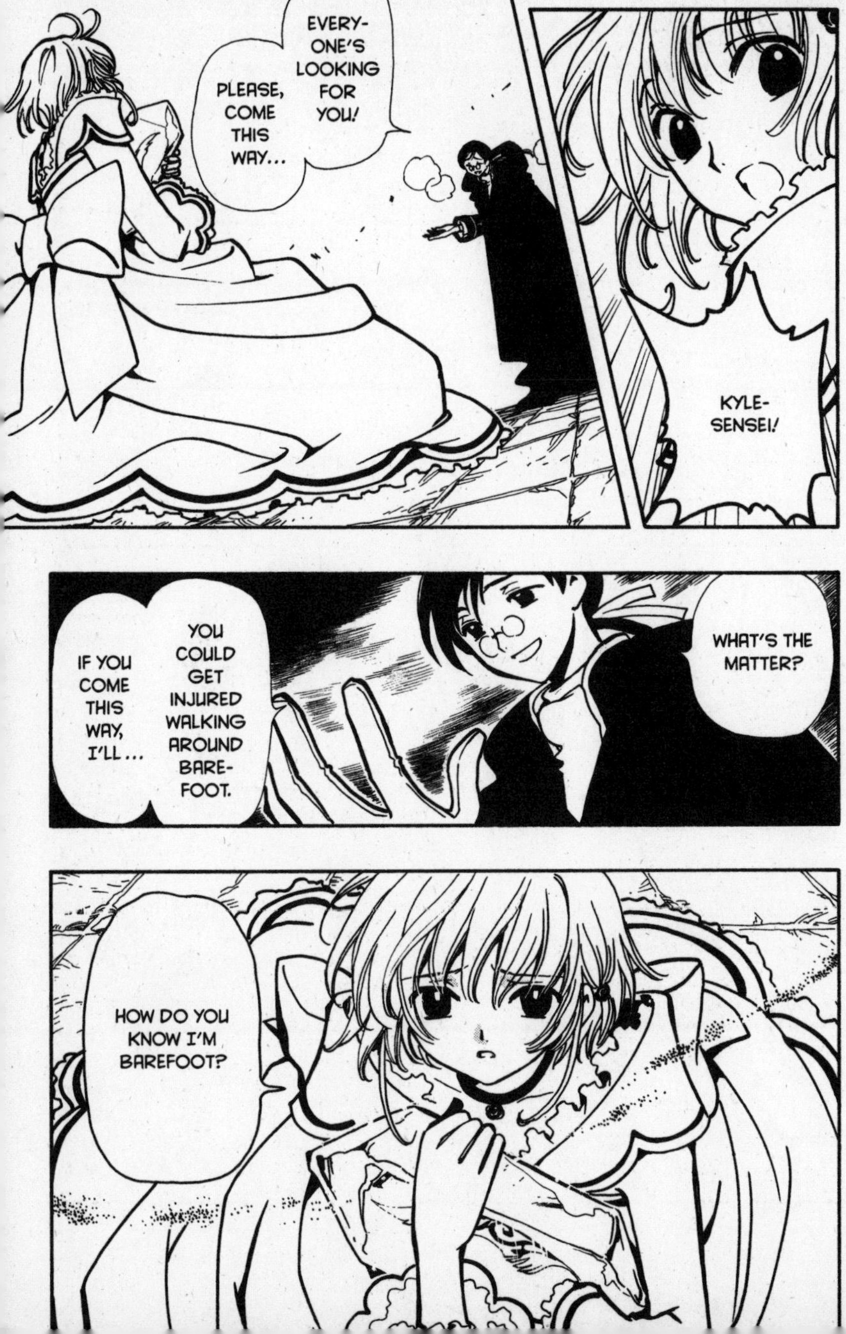
KYLE-SENSEI!
EVERY-ONE'S LOOKING FOR YOU!
PLEASE, COME THIS WAY...
WHAT'S THE MATTER?
YOU COULD GET INJURED WALKING AROUND BARE-FOOT.
IF YOU COME THIS WAY, I'LL...
HOW DO YOU KNOW I'M BAREFOOT?

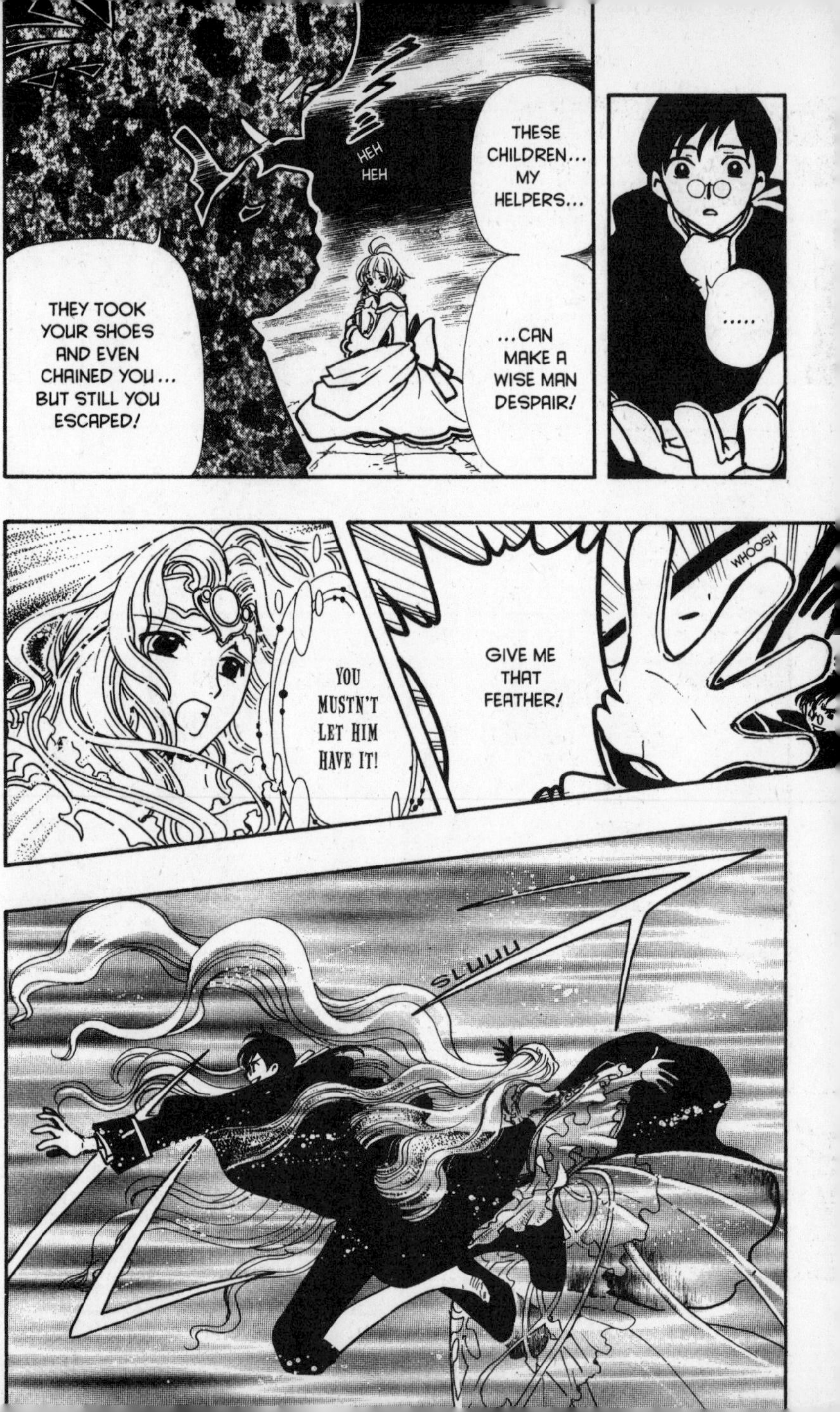
.....
THESE CHILDREN... MY HELPERS...
HEH HEH
...CAN MAKE A WISE MAN DESPAIR!
THEY TOOK YOUR SHOES AND EVEN CHAINED YOU... BUT STILL YOU ESCAPED!
WHOOSH
GIVE ME THAT FEATHER!
YOU MUSTN'T LET HIM HAVE IT!
SLUUU

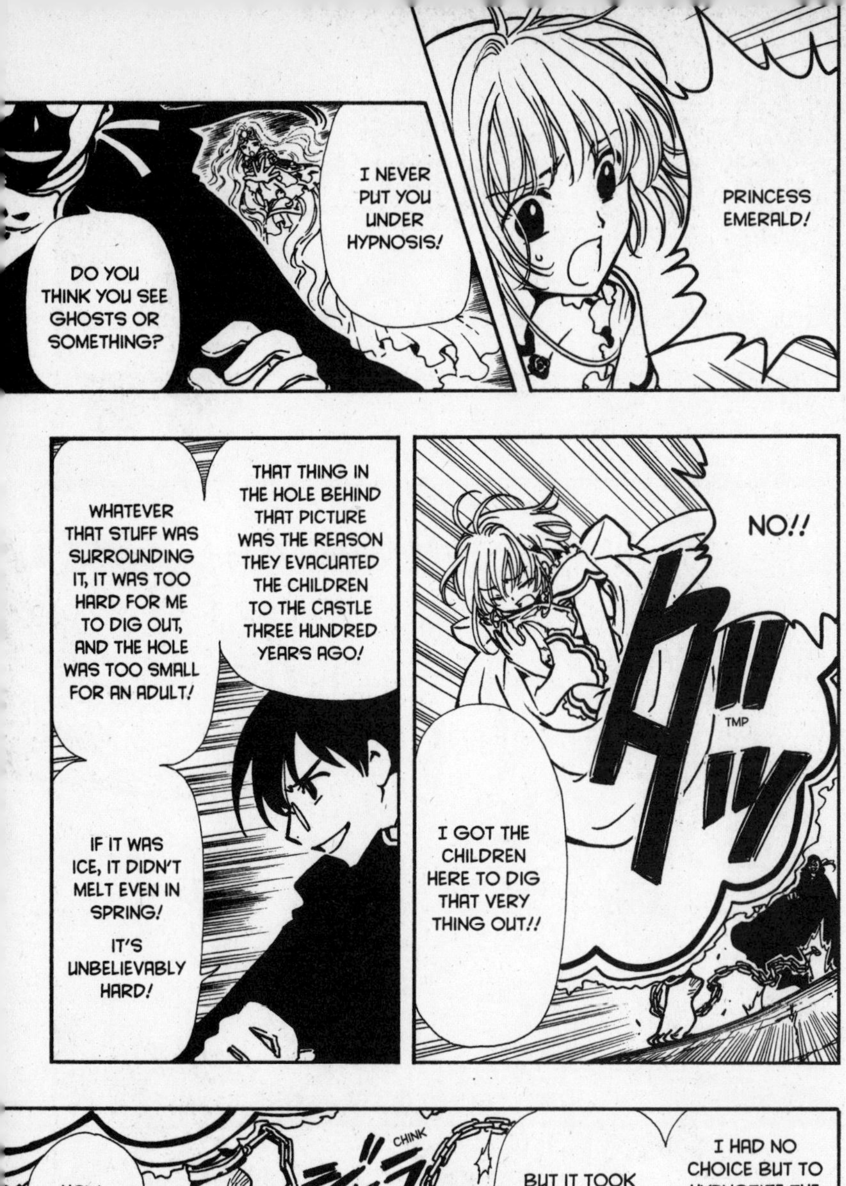
PRINCESS EMERALD!
I NEVER PUT YOU UNDER HYPNOSIS!
DO YOU THINK YOU SEE GHOSTS OR SOMETHING?
NO!!
TMP
I GOT THE CHILDREN HERE TO DIG THAT VERY THING OUT!!
THAT THING IN THE HOLE BEHIND THAT PICTURE WAS THE REASON THEY EVACUATED THE CHILDREN TO THE CASTLE THREE HUNDRED YEARS AGO!
WHATEVER THAT STUFF WAS SURROUNDING IT, IT WAS TOO HARD FOR ME TO DIG OUT, AND THE HOLE WAS TOO SMALL FOR AN ADULT!
IF IT WAS ICE, IT DIDN'T MELT EVEN IN SPRING!
IT'S UNBELIEVABLY HARD!
I HAD NO CHOICE BUT TO HYPNOTIZE THE CHILDREN AND HAVE THEM DIG IT OUT!
BUT IT TOOK MORE TIME THAN I THOUGHT!
CHINK
CHANG
HOW-EVER...

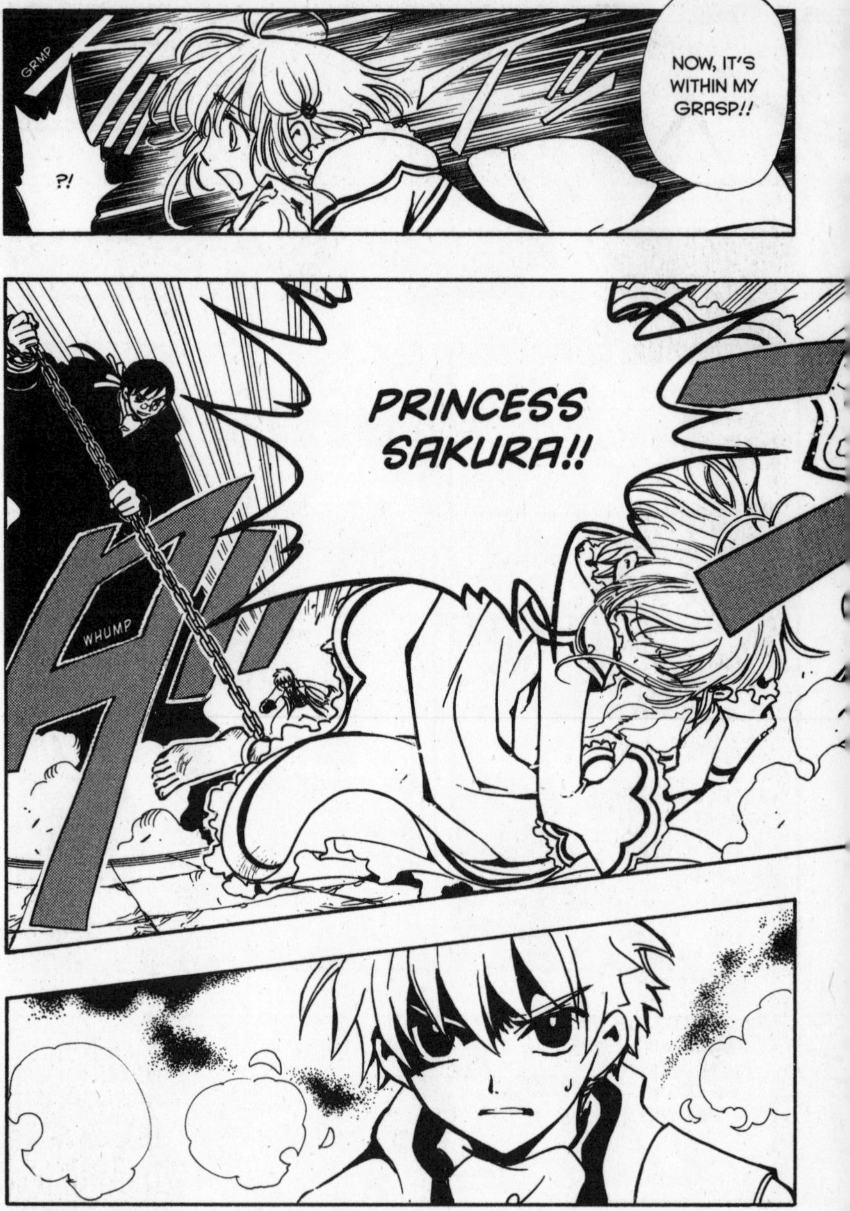
NOW, IT'S WITHIN MY GRASP!!
GRMP
?!
PRINCESS SAKURA!!
WHUMP

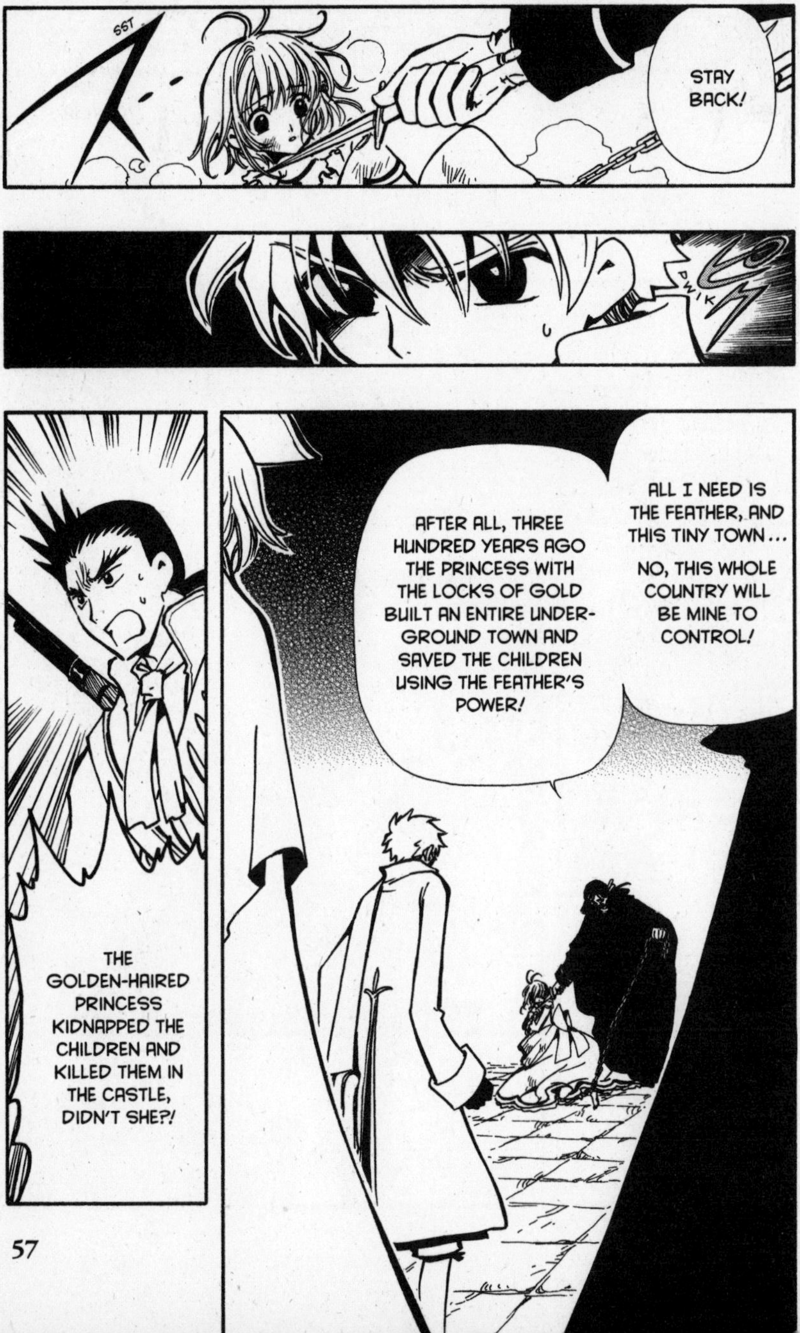
SST
STAY BACK!
PWIK
ALL I NEED IS THE FEATHER, AND THIS TINY TOWN... NO, THIS WHOLE COUNTRY WILL BE MINE TO CONTROL!
AFTER ALL, THREE HUNDRED YEARS AGO THE PRINCESS WITH THE LOCKS OF GOLD BUILT AN ENTIRE UNDER-GROUND TOWN AND SAVED THE CHILDREN USING THE FEATHER'S POWER!
THE GOLDEN-HAIRED PRINCESS KIDNAPPED THE CHILDREN AND KILLED THEM IN THE CASTLE, DIDN'T SHE?!

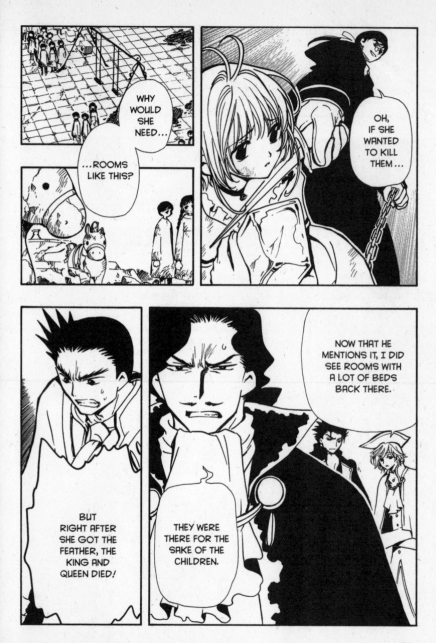

OH, IF SHE WANTED TO KILL THEM...
WHY WOULD SHE NEED...
...ROOMS LIKE THIS?
NOW THAT HE MENTIONS IT, I DID SEE ROOMS WITH A LOT OF BEDS BACK THERE.
THEY WERE THERE FOR THE SAKE OF THE CHILDREN.
BUT RIGHT AFTER SHE GOT THE FEATHER, THE KING AND QUEEN DIED!

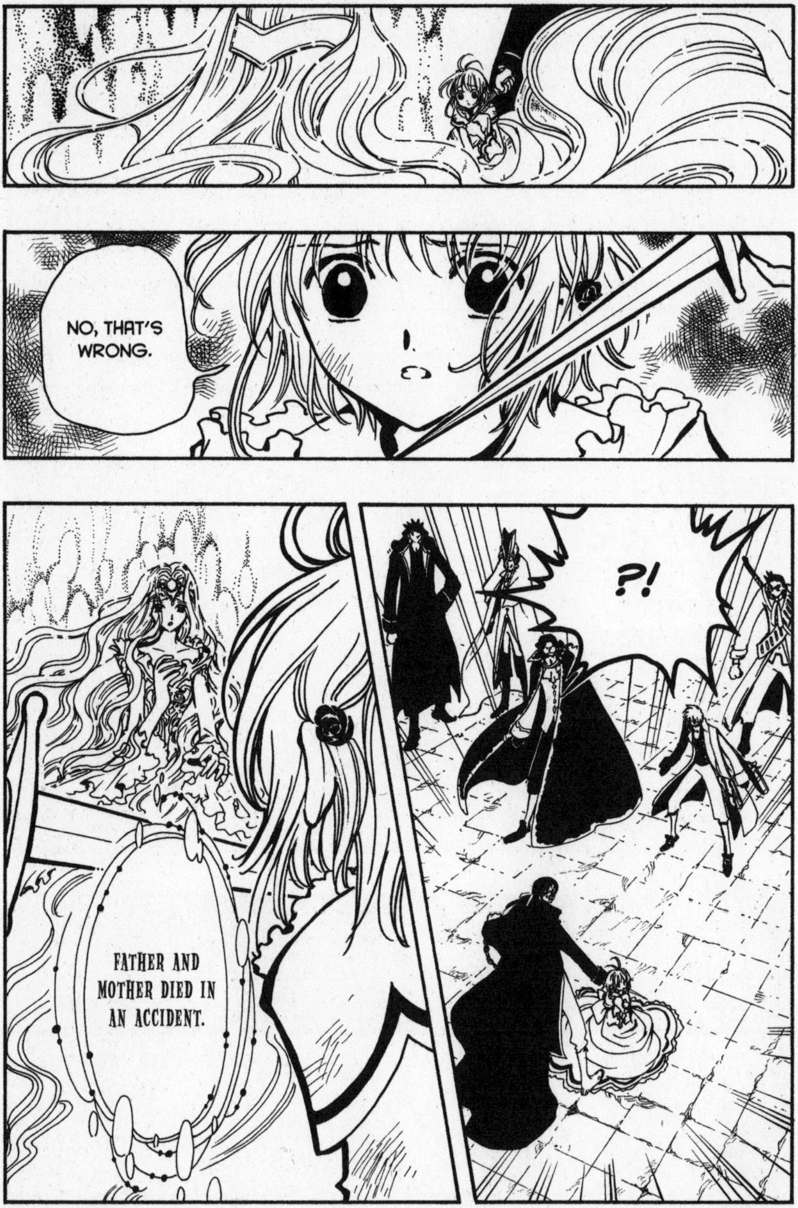
NO, THAT'S WRONG.
?!
FATHER AND MOTHER DIED IN AN ACCIDENT.

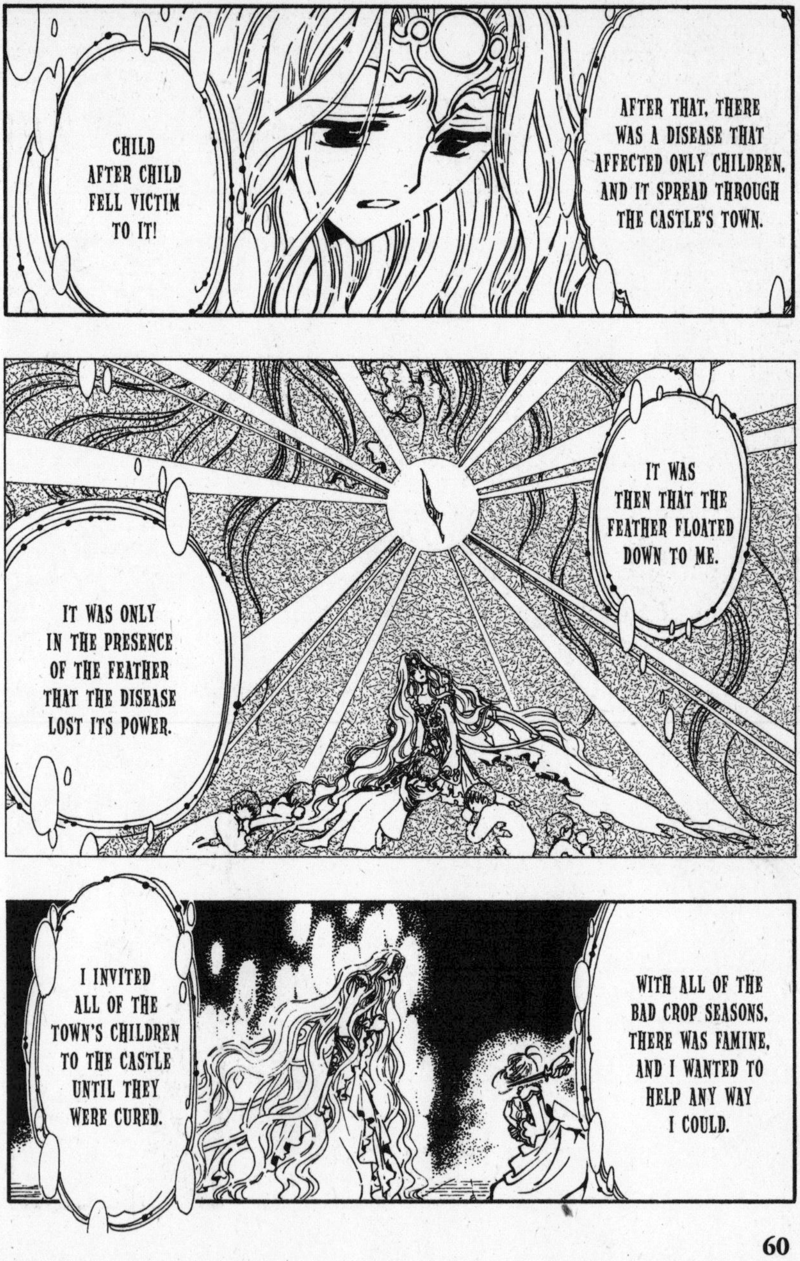
AFTER THAT, THERE WAS A DISEASE THAT AFFECTED ONLY CHILDREN, AND IT SPREAD THROUGH THE CASTLE'S TOWN.
CHILD AFTER CHILD FELL VICTIM TO IT!
IT WAS THEN THAT THE FEATHER FLOATED DOWN TO ME.
IT WAS ONLY IN THE PRESENCE OF THE FEATHER THAT THE DISEASE LOST ITS POWER.
WITH ALL OF THE BAD CROP SEASONS, THERE WAS FAMINE, AND I WANTED TO HELP ANY WAY I COULD.
I INVITED ALL OF THE TOWN'S CHILDREN TO THE CASTLE UNTIL THEY WERE CURED.

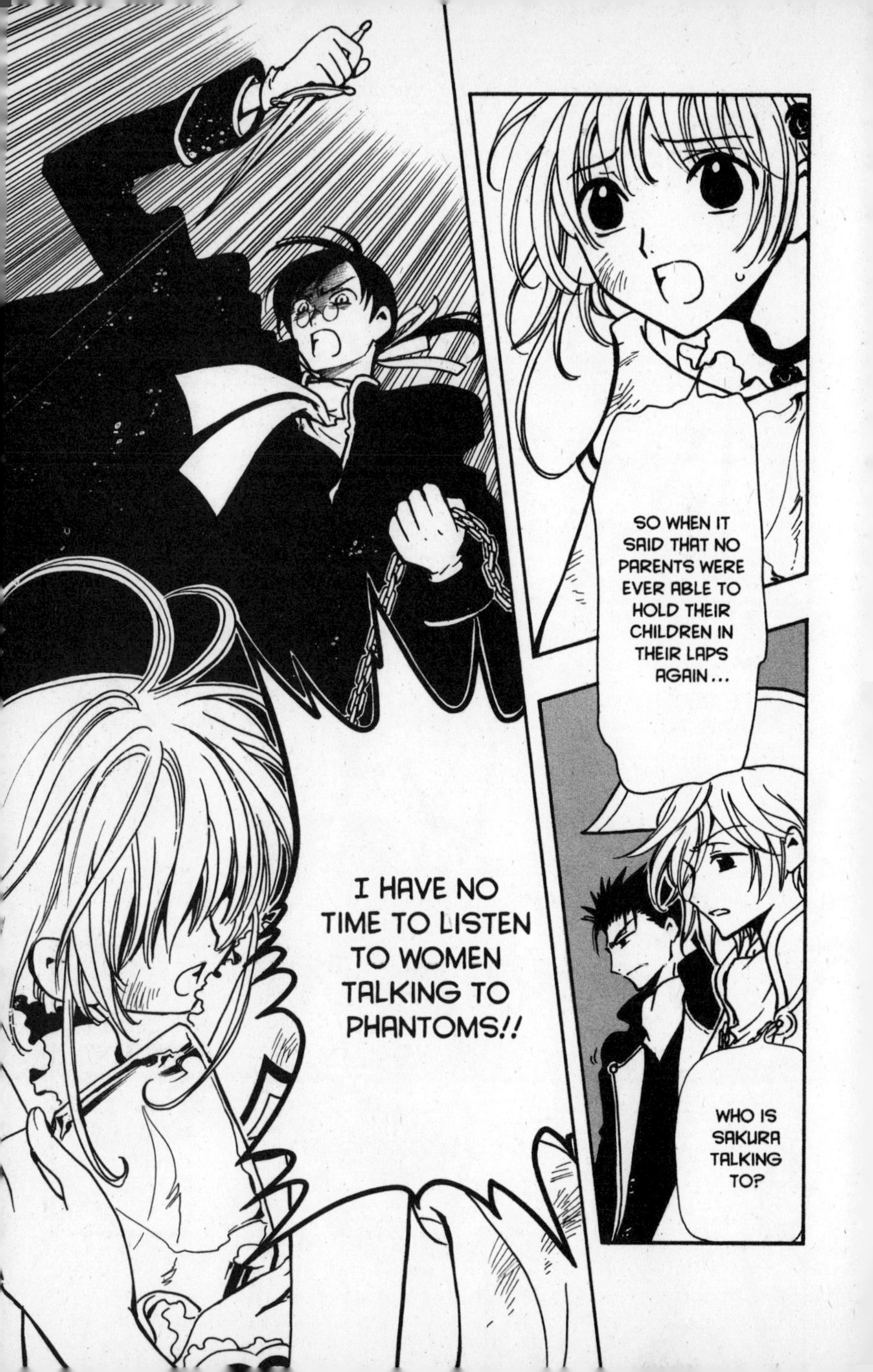
SO WHEN IT SAID THAT NO PARENTS WERE EVER ABLE TO HOLD THEIR CHILDREN IN THEIR LAPS AGAIN...
WHO IS SAKURA TALKING TO?
I HAVE NO TIME TO LISTEN TO WOMEN TALKING TO PHANTOMS!!

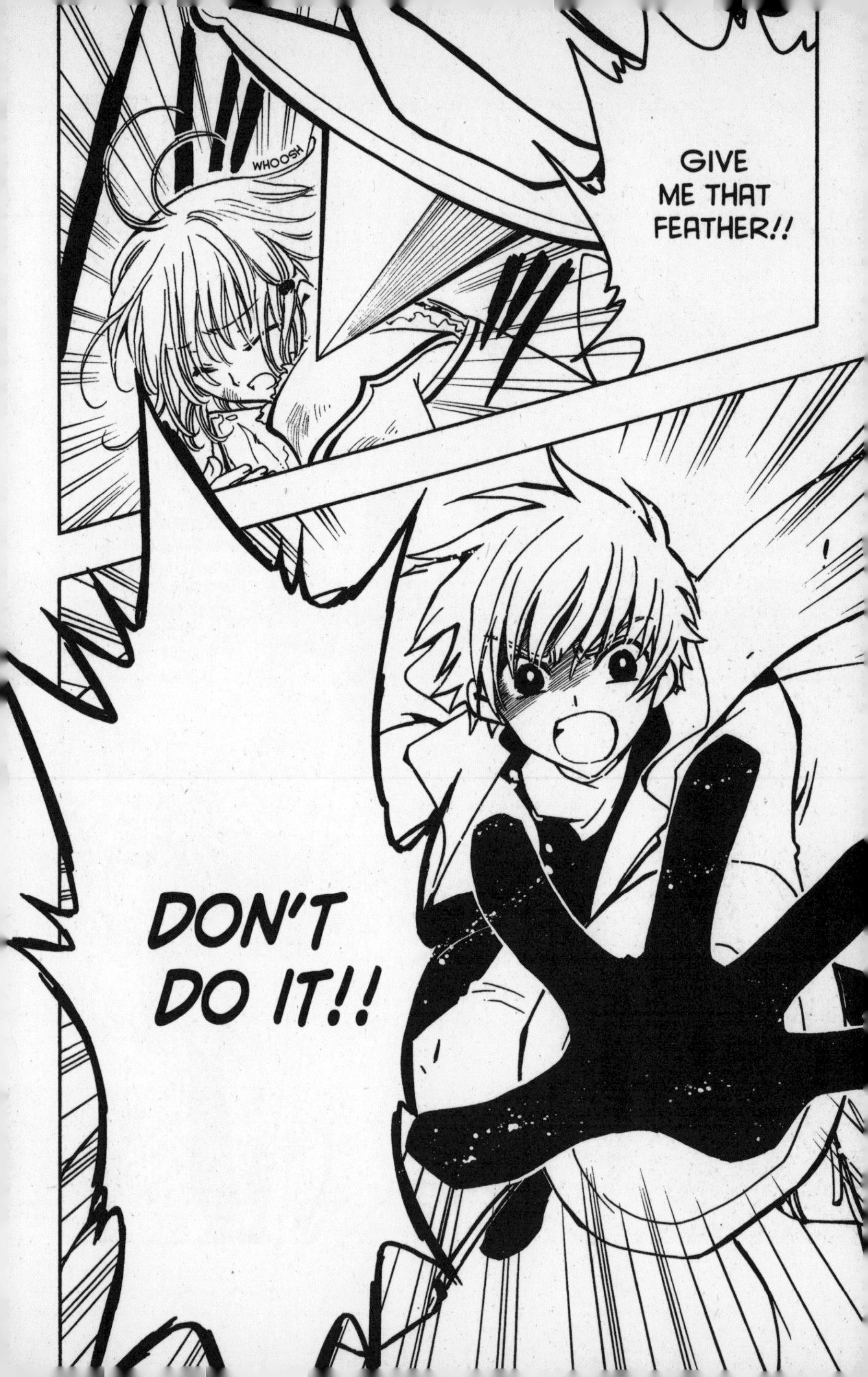
GIVE ME THAT FEATHER!!
WHOOSH
DON'T DO IT!!

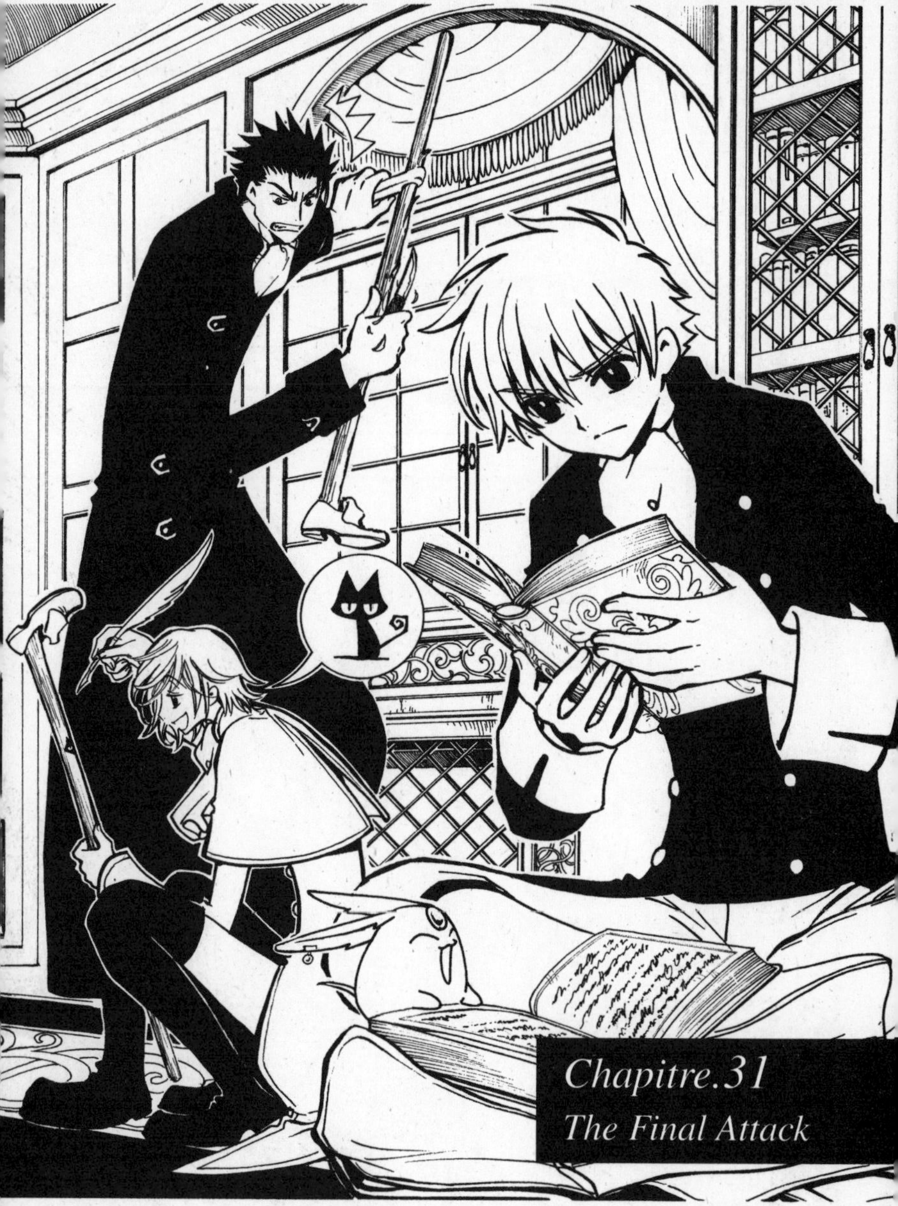
Chapitre.31
The Final Attack

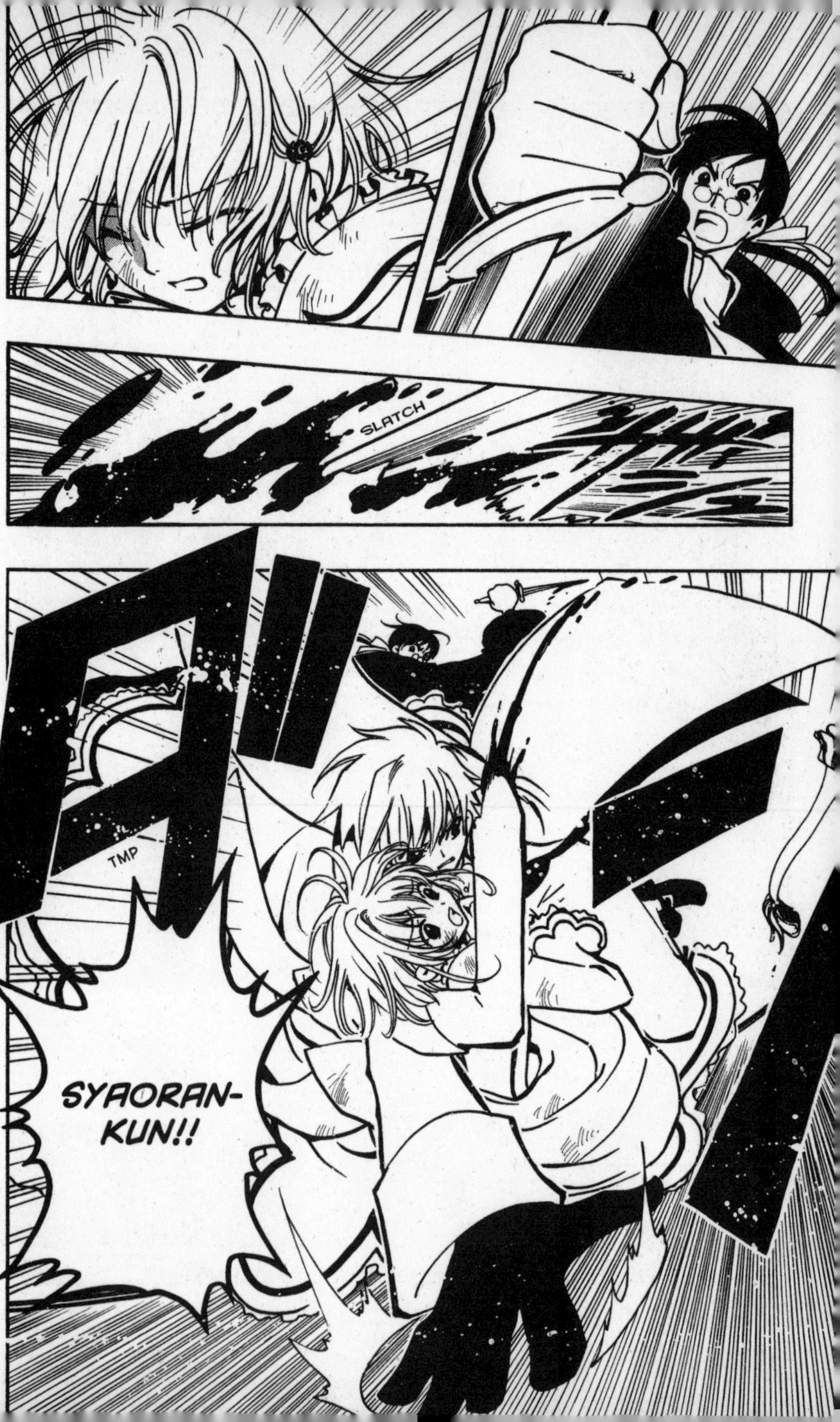
SLATCH
TMP
SYAORAN-KUN!!

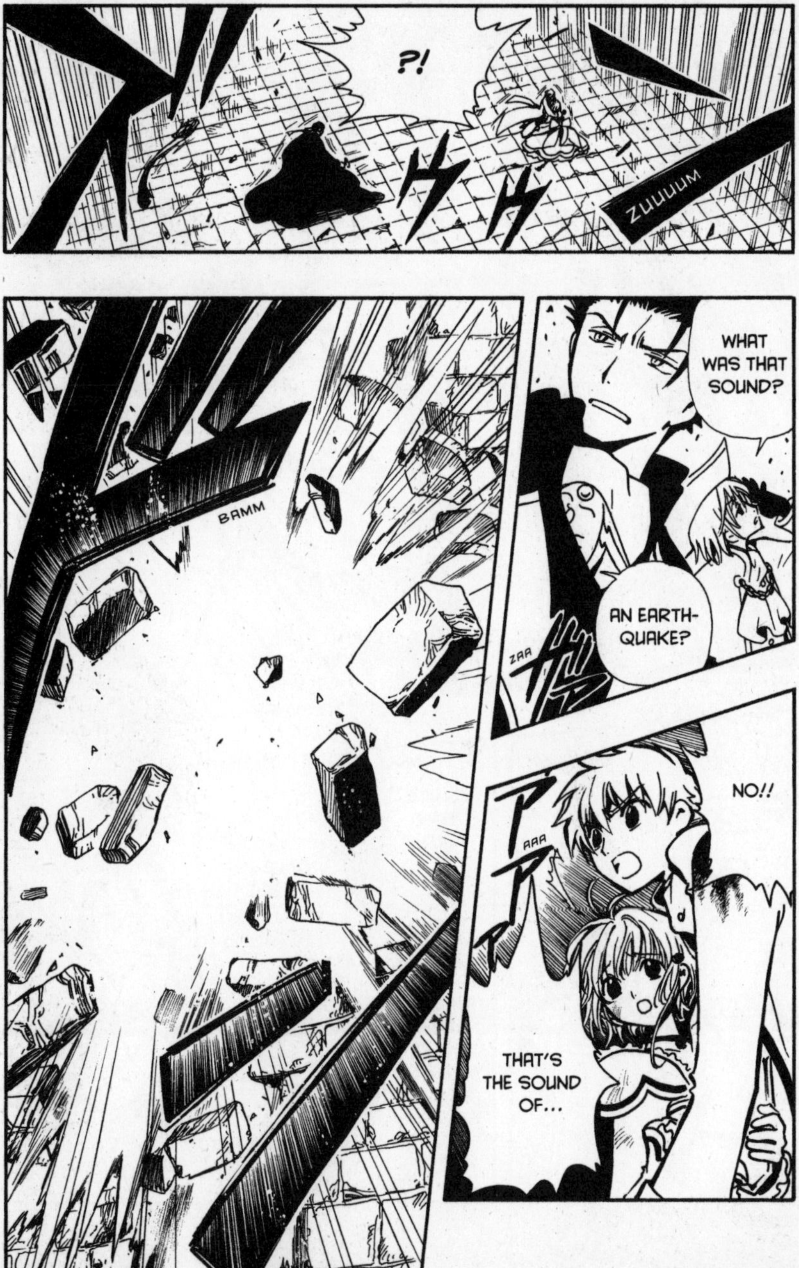
?!
ZUUUUM
WHAT WAS THAT SOUND?
ZAA
AN EARTH-QUAKE?
NO!!
AAA
THAT'S THE SOUND OF...
BAMM

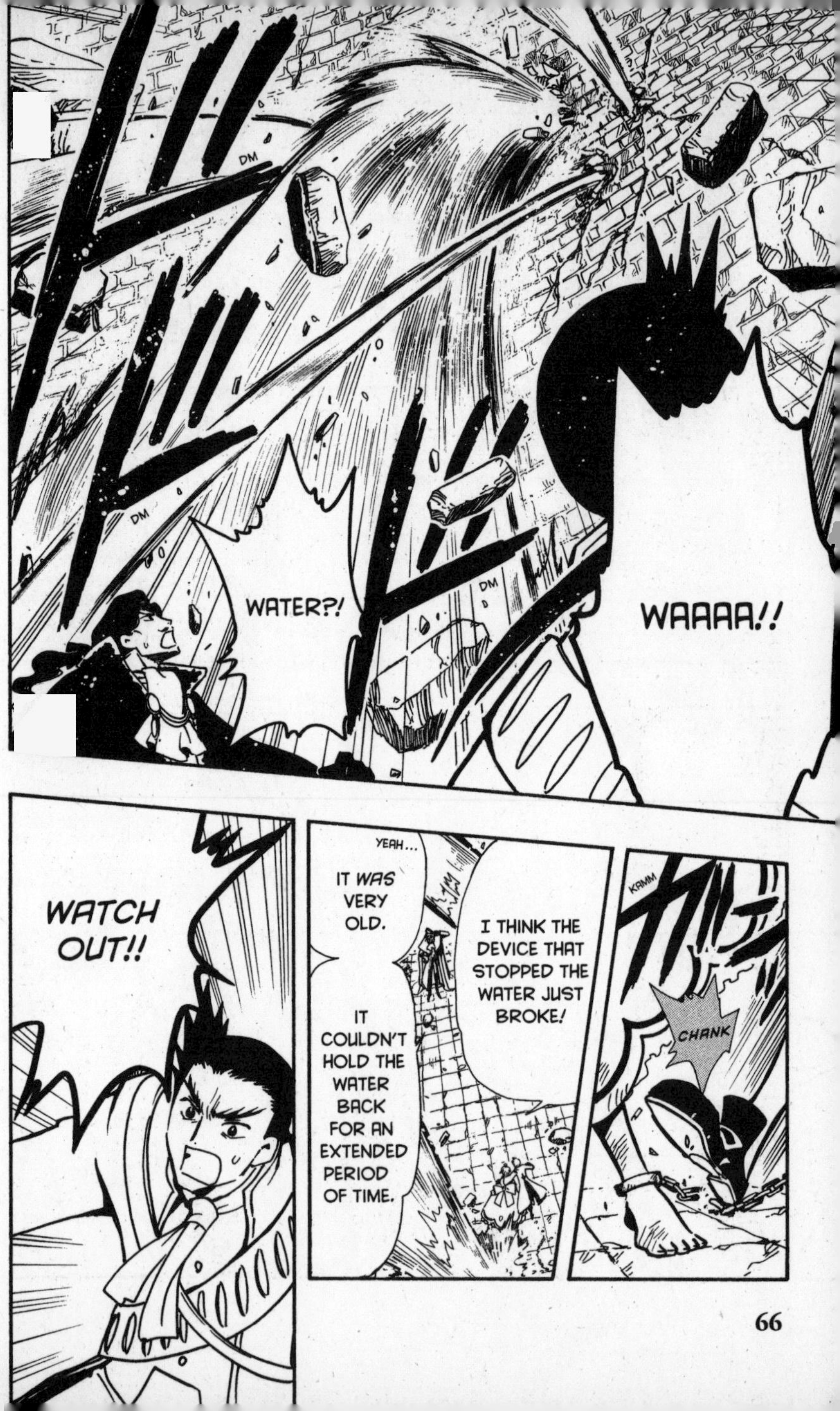
DM
DM
DM
WAAAA!!
WATER?!
KAMM
CHANK
I THINK THE DEVICE THAT STOPPED THE WATER JUST BROKE!
YEAH...
IT WAS VERY OLD.
IT COULDN'T HOLD THE WATER BACK FOR AN EXTENDED PERIOD OF TIME.
WATCH OUT!!

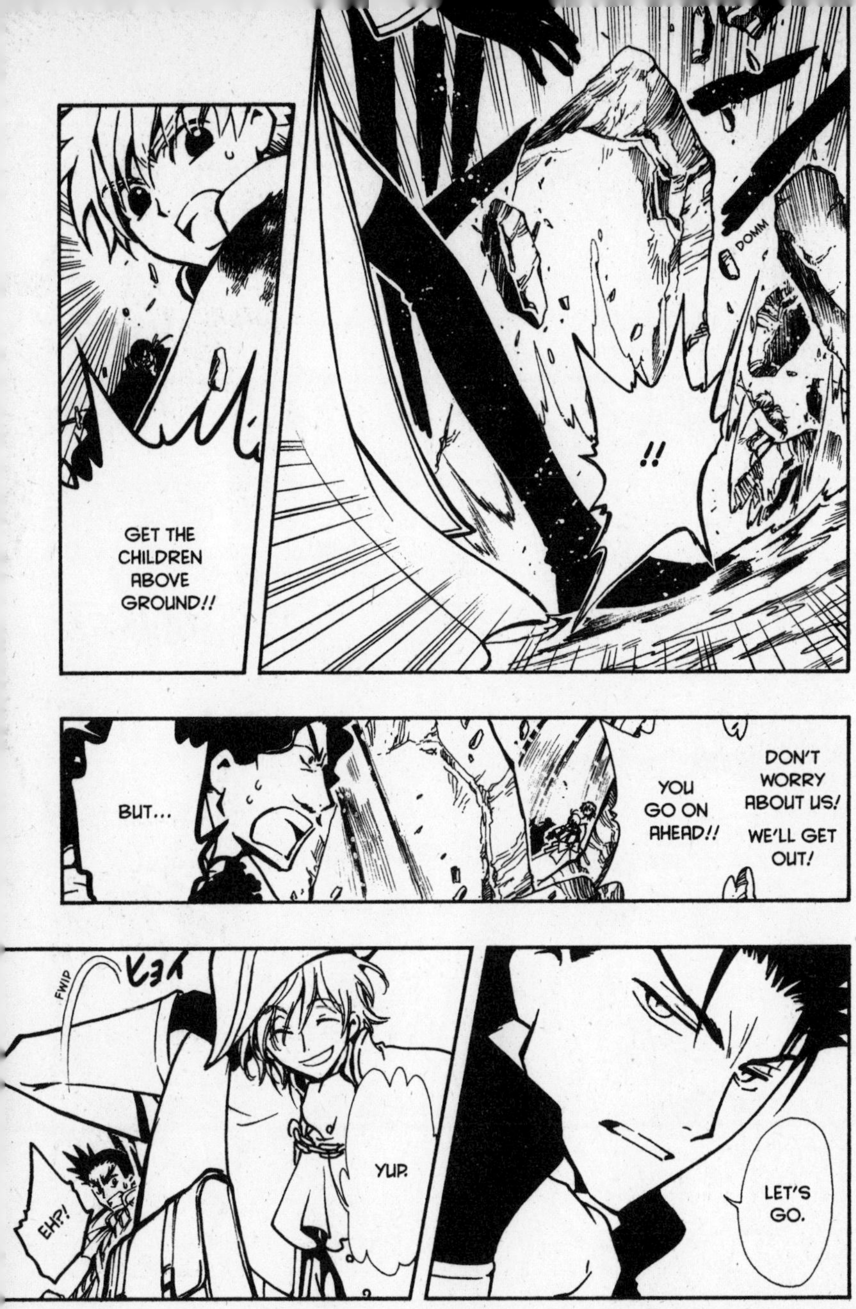
DOMM
!!
GET THE CHILDREN ABOVE GROUND!!
DON'T WORRY ABOUT US!
WE'LL GET OUT!
YOU GO ON AHEAD!!
BUT...
LET'S GO.
ヒョイ
FWIP
YUP.
EH?!

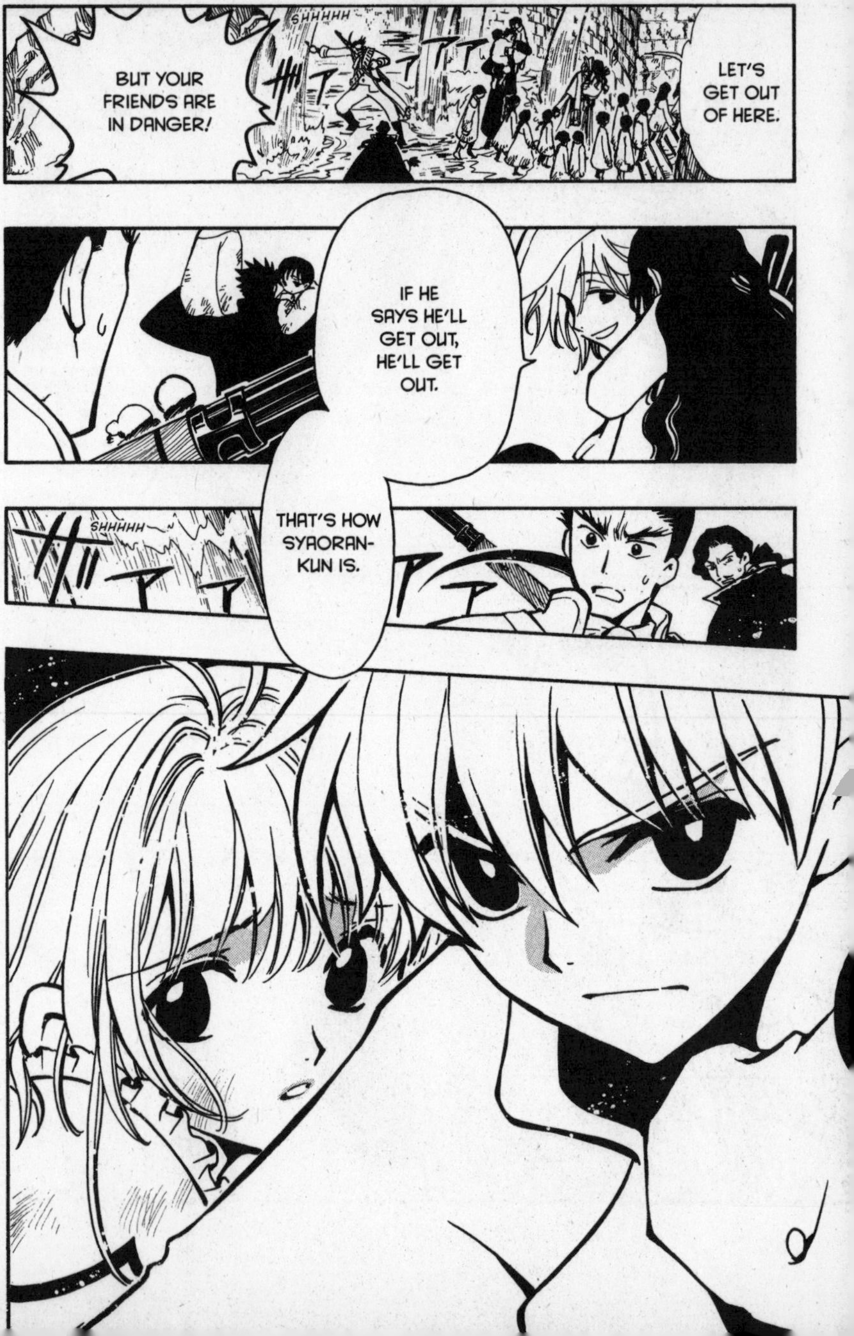
LET'S GET OUT OF HERE.
SHHHHH
BUT YOUR FRIENDS ARE IN DANGER!
IF HE SAYS HE'LL GET OUT, HE'LL GET OUT.
THAT'S HOW SYAORAN-KUN IS.
SHHHHH

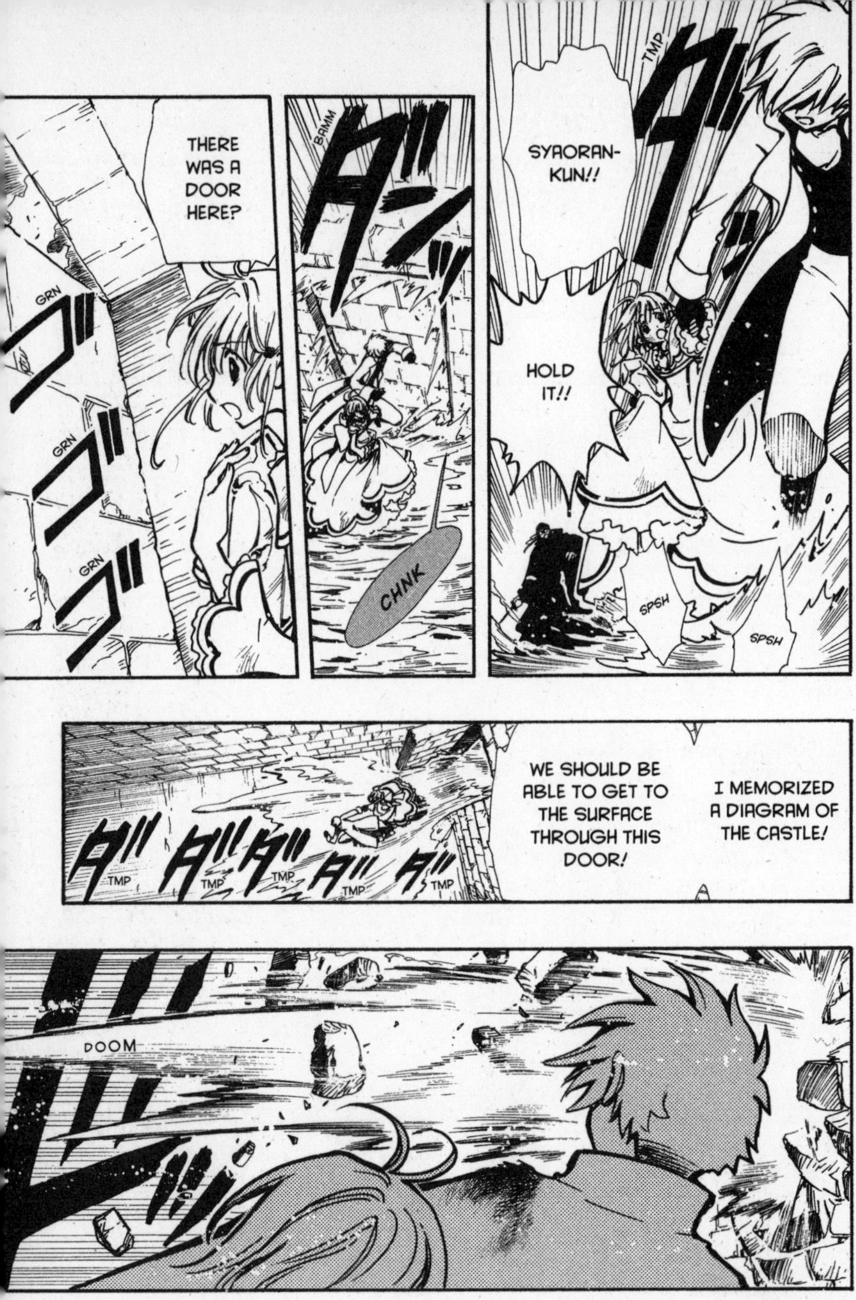
TMP
SYAORAN-KUN!!
HOLD IT!!
SPSH
SPSH
BAMM
CHNK
THERE WAS A DOOR HERE?
GRN
GRN
GRN
I MEMORIZED A DIAGRAM OF THE CASTLE!
WE SHOULD BE ABLE TO GET TO THE SURFACE THROUGH THIS DOOR!
TMP
TMP
TMP
TMP
TMP
DOOM

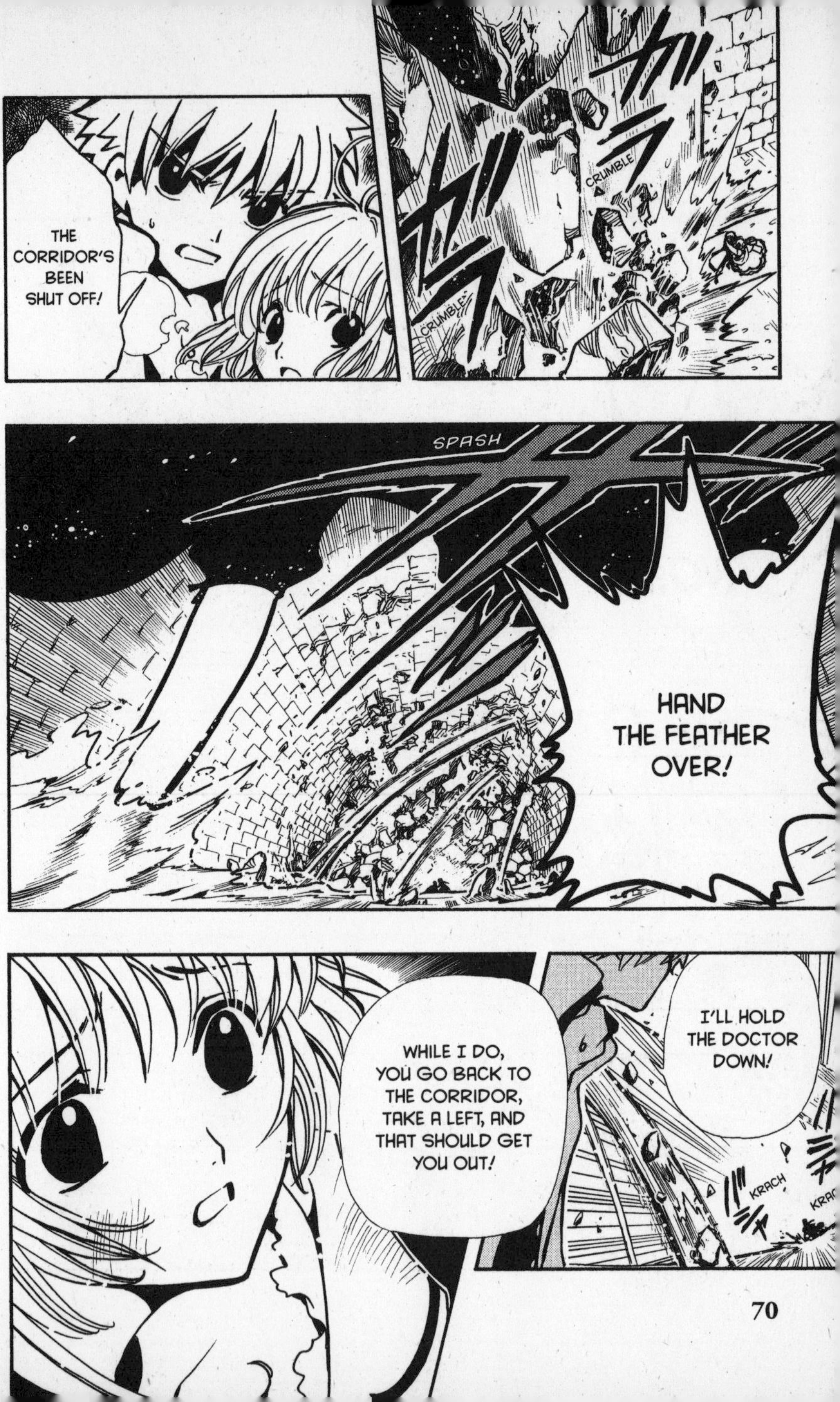
CRUMBLE
CRUMBLE
THE CORRIDOR'S BEEN SHUT OFF!
SPASH
HAND THE FEATHER OVER!
I'LL HOLD THE DOCTOR DOWN!
KRACH
WHILE I DO, YOU GO BACK TO THE CORRIDOR, TAKE A LEFT, AND THAT SHOULD GET YOU OUT!

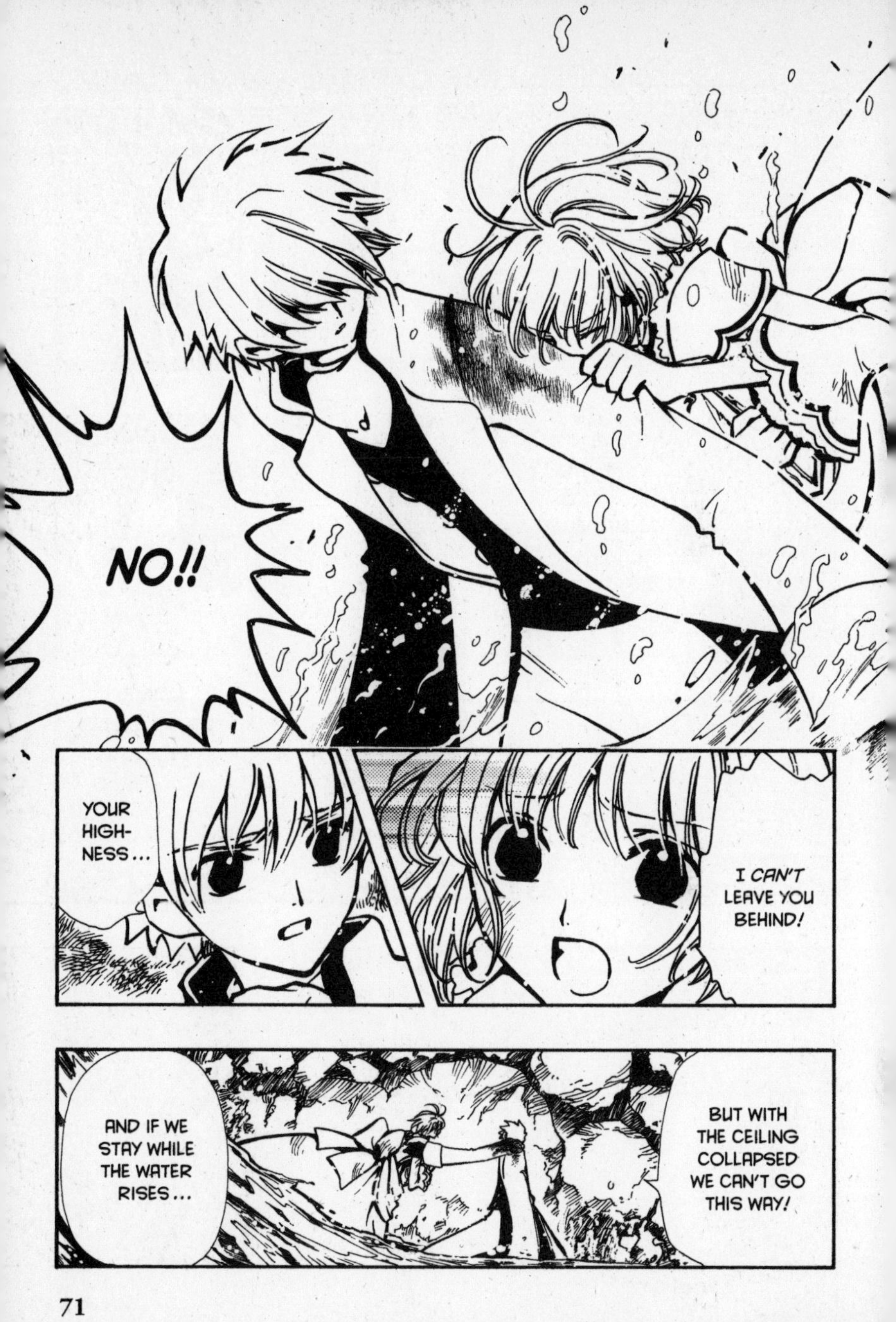
NO!!
I CAN'T LEAVE YOU BEHIND!
YOUR HIGH-NESS...
BUT WITH THE CEILING COLLAPSED WE CAN'T GO THIS WAY!
AND IF WE STAY WHILE THE WATER RISES...

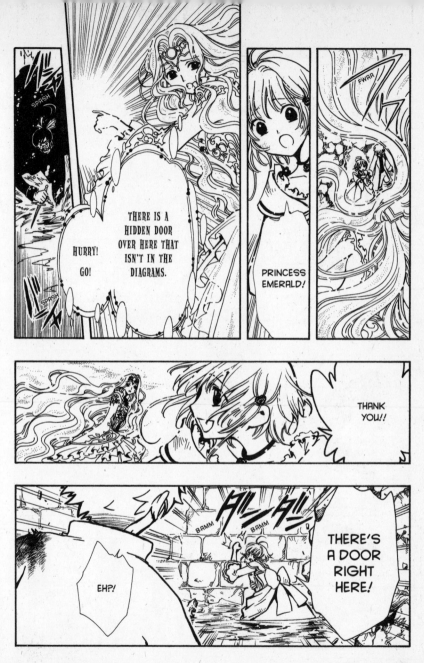

FWAA
PRINCESS EMERALD!
THERE IS A HIDDEN DOOR OVER HERE THAT ISN'T IN THE DIAGRAMS.
HURRY! GO!
SPASH
SPASH
THANK YOU!!
THERE'S A DOOR RIGHT HERE!
BAMM
BAMM
EH?!

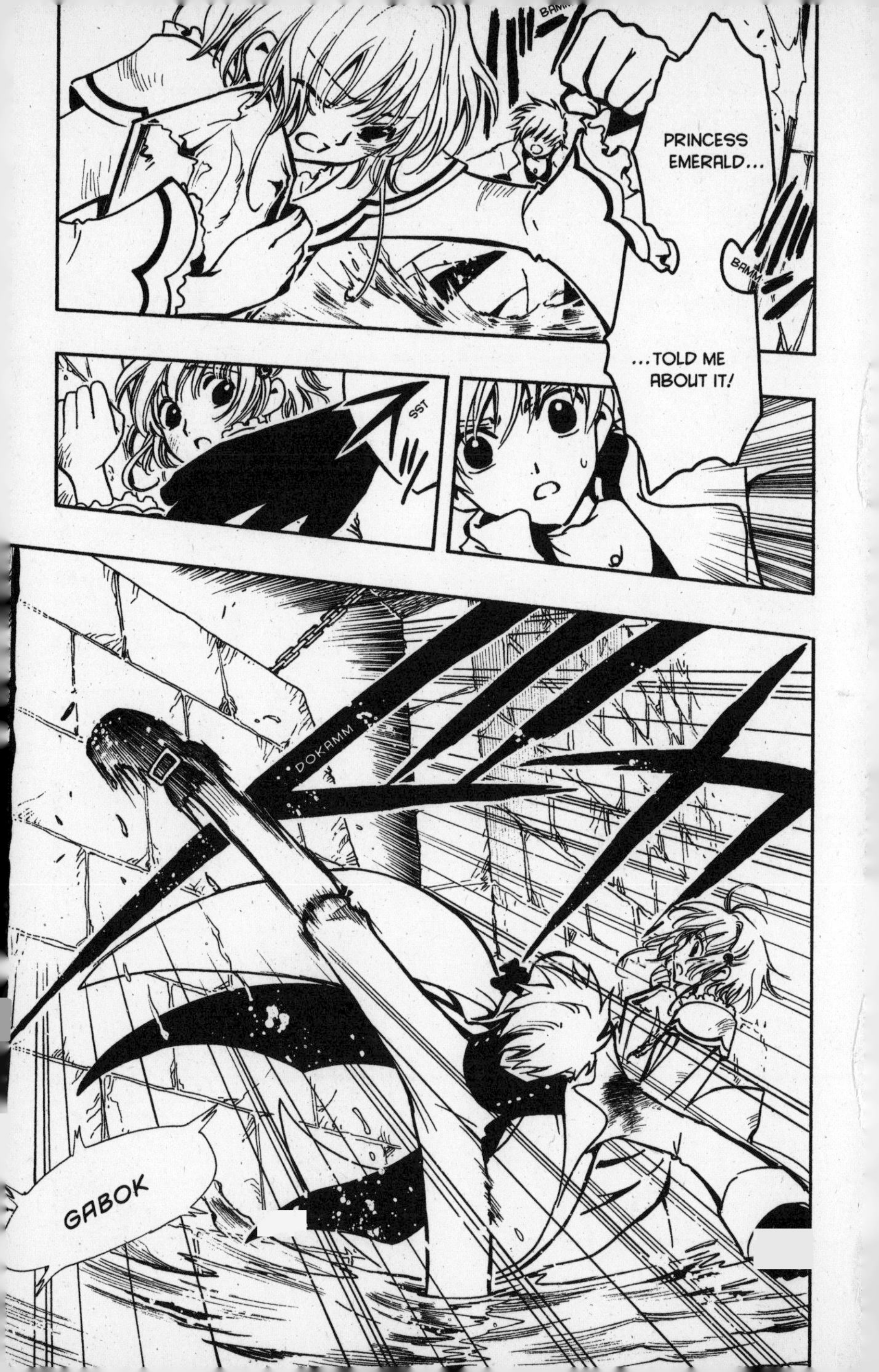
BAMM
PRINCESS EMERALD...
BAMM
...TOLD ME ABOUT IT!
SST
DOKAMM
GABOK

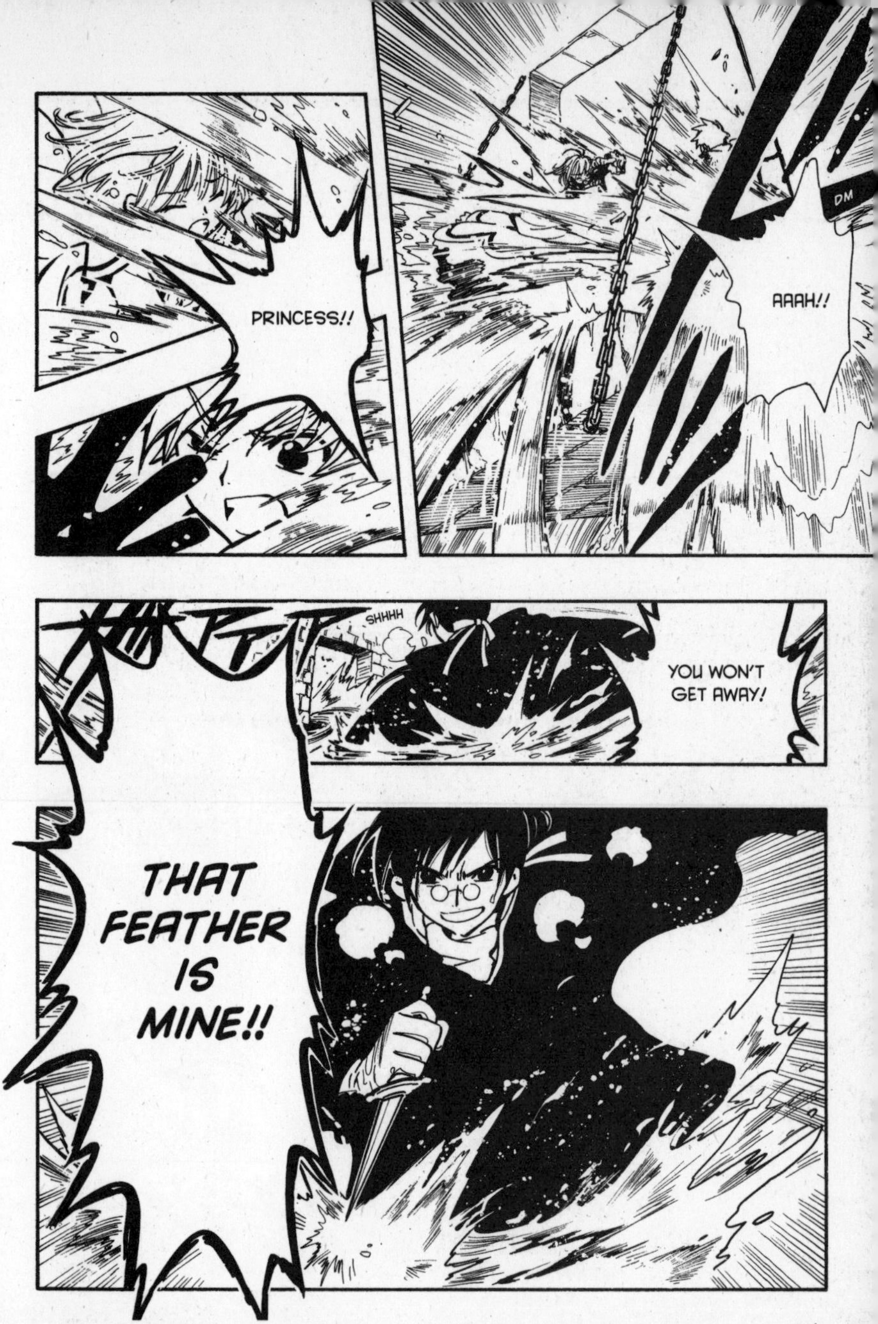
DM
AAAH!!
PRINCESS!!
YOU WON'T GET AWAY!
SHHHH
THAT FEATHER IS MINE!!

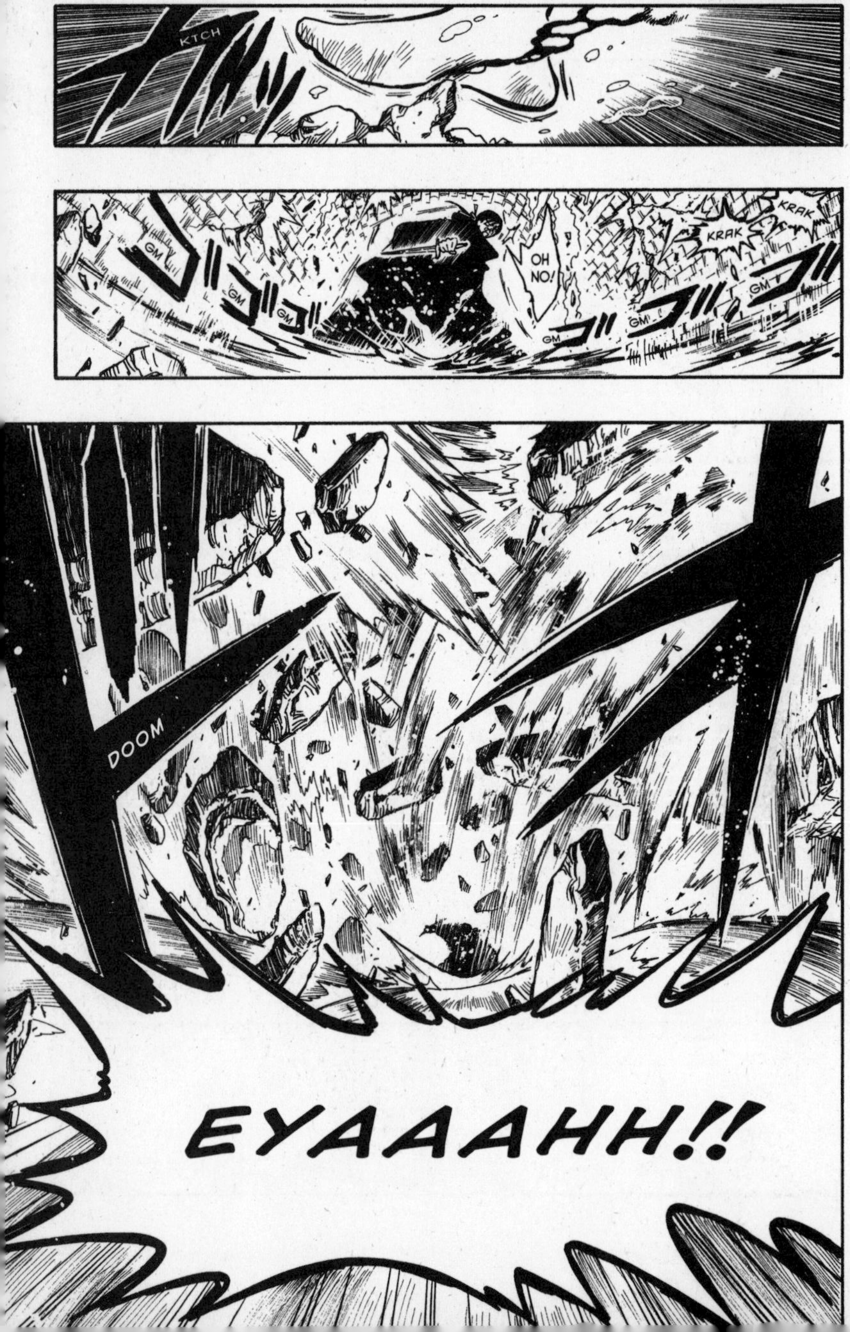
KTCH
KRAK
KRAK
GM
OH NO!
GM
GM
GM
GM
GM
DOOM
EYAAAHH!!

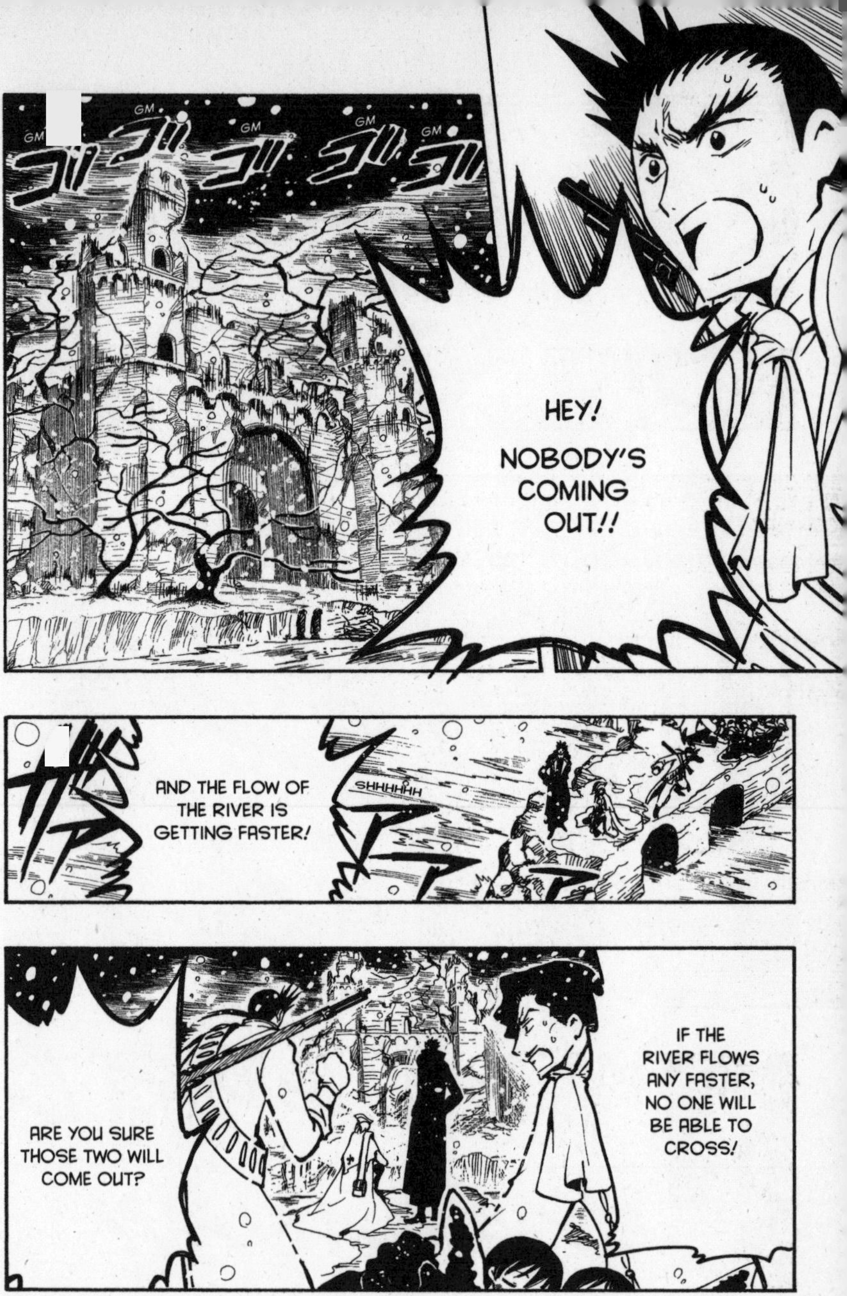
HEY!
NOBODY'S COMING OUT!!
GM GM GM GM GM
AND THE FLOW OF THE RIVER IS GETTING FASTER!
SHHHHHH
IF THE RIVER FLOWS ANY FASTER, NO ONE WILL BE ABLE TO CROSS!
ARE YOU SURE THOSE TWO WILL COME OUT?

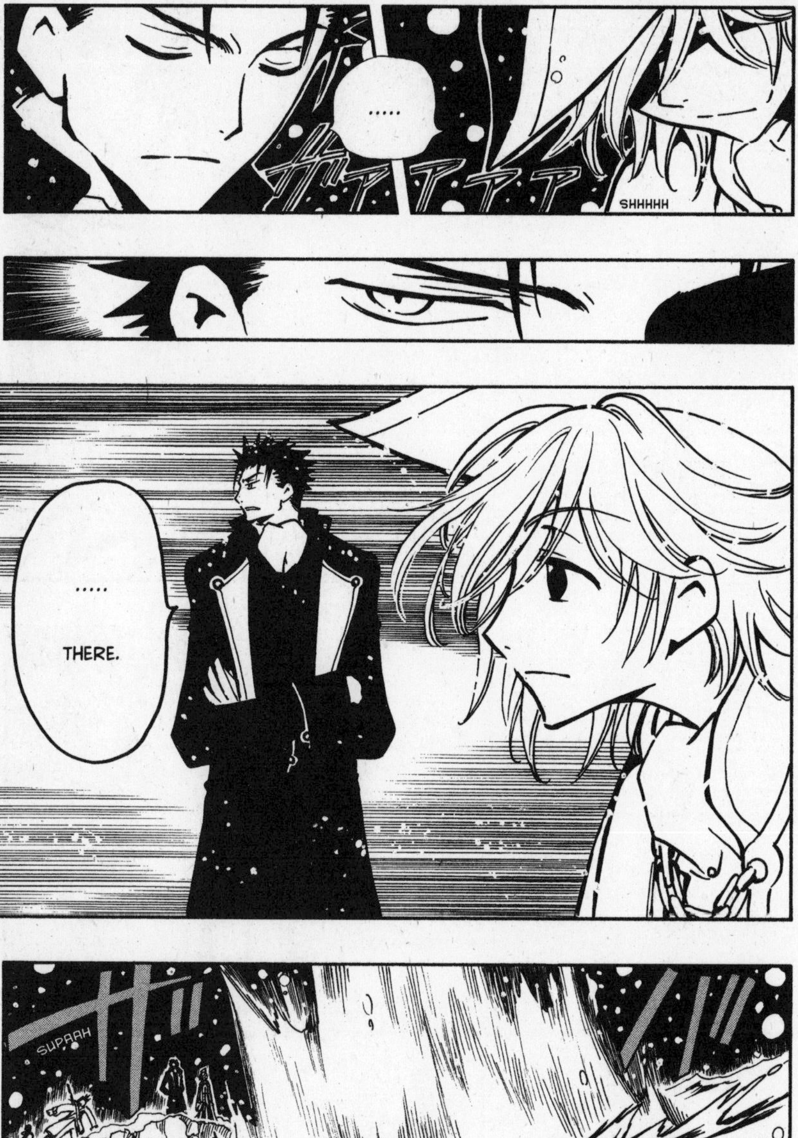
SHHHHH
......
......
THERE.
SUPAAH

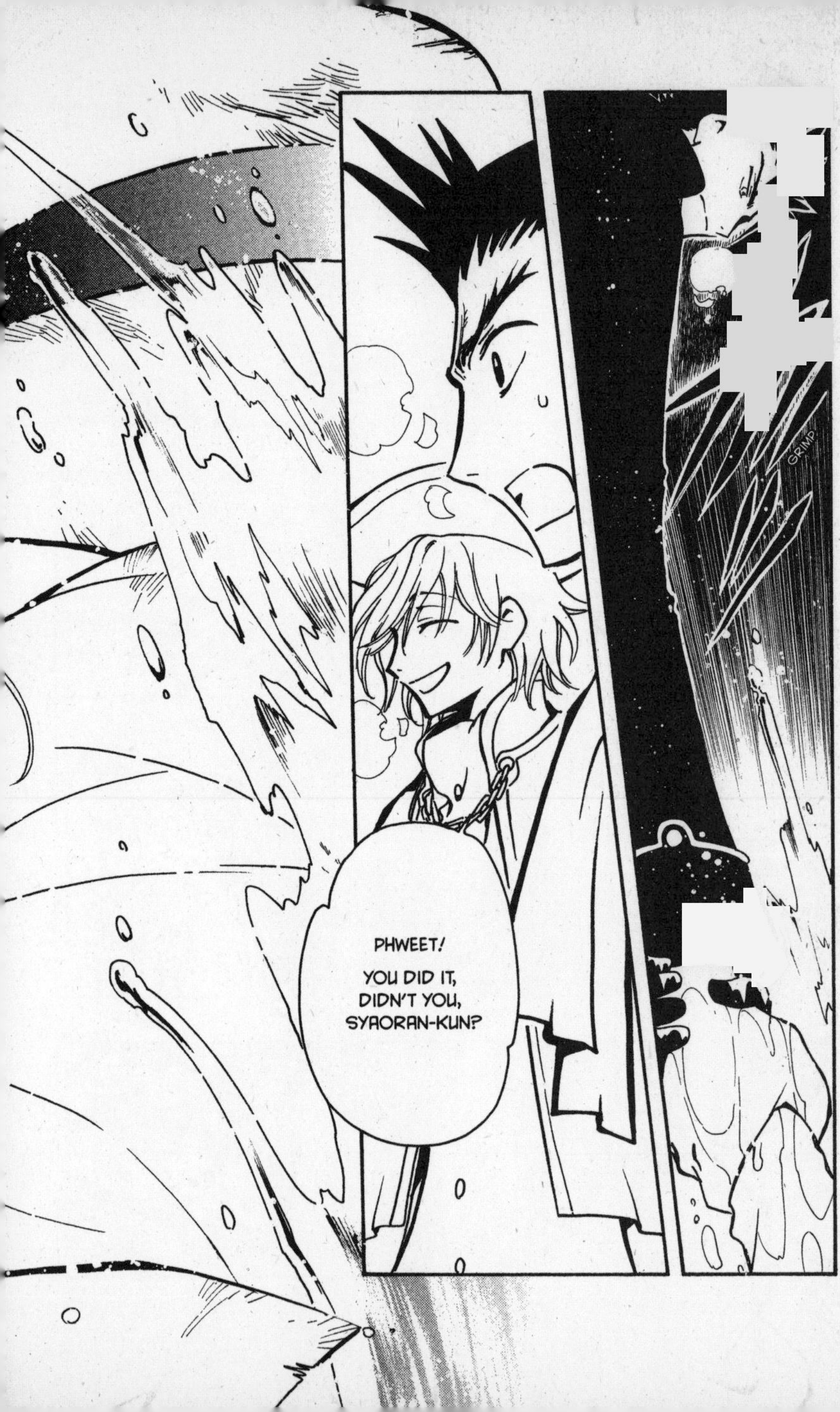
GRIMP
PHWEET!
YOU DID IT, DIDN'T YOU, SYAORAN-KUN?

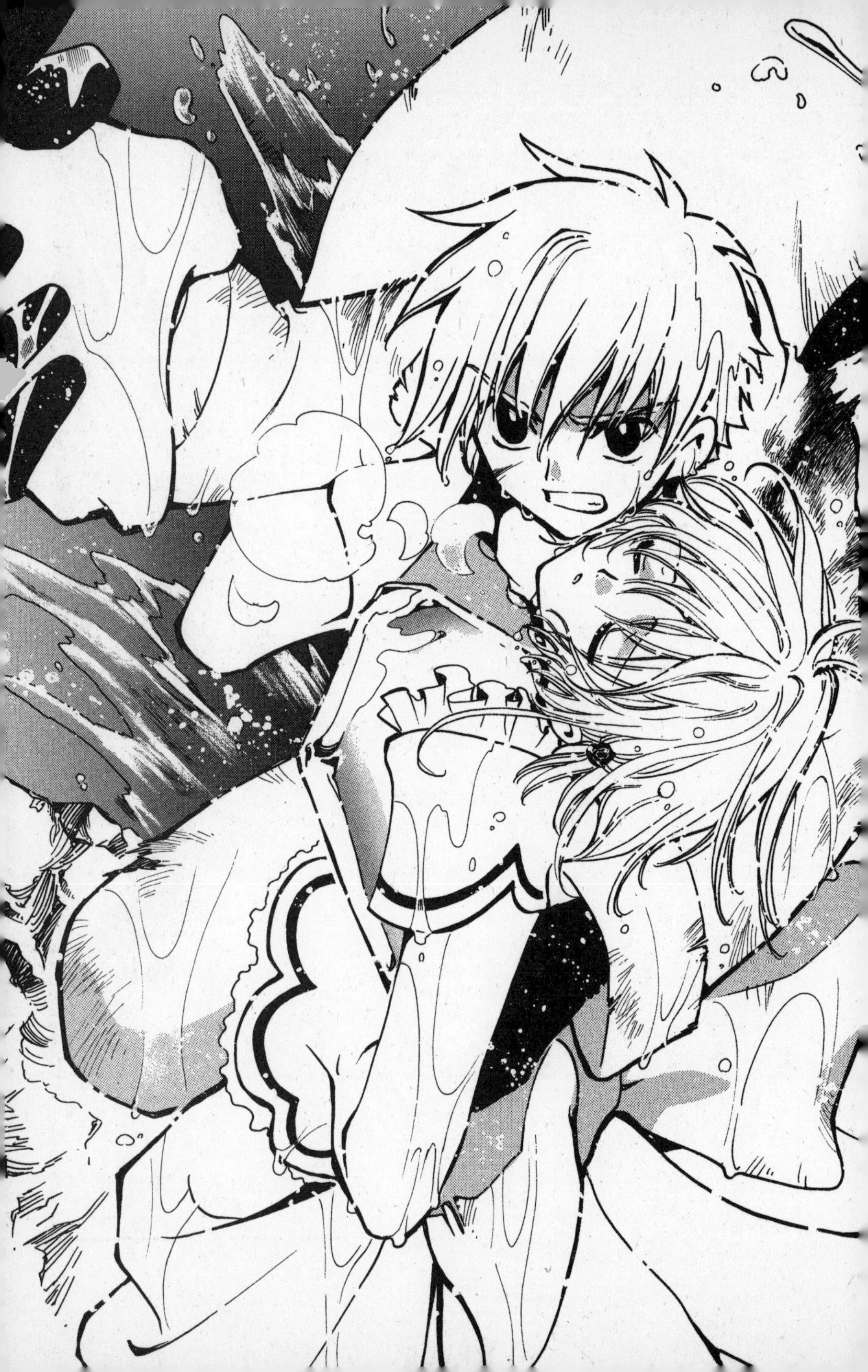

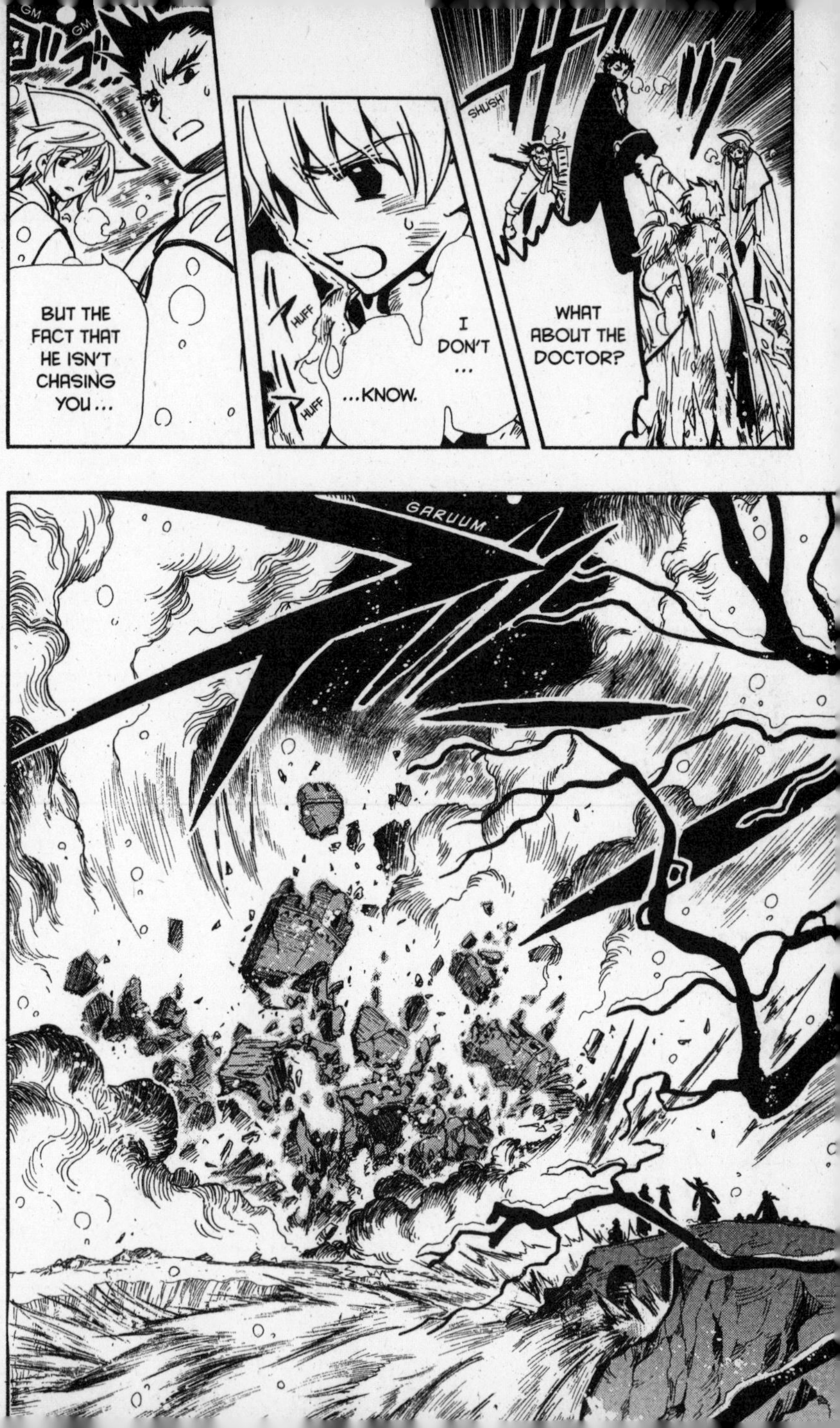
SHUSH
WHAT ABOUT THE DOCTOR?
I DON'T ...
HUFF
HUFF
...KNOW.
GM
GM
BUT THE FACT THAT HE ISN'T CHASING YOU...
GARUUM

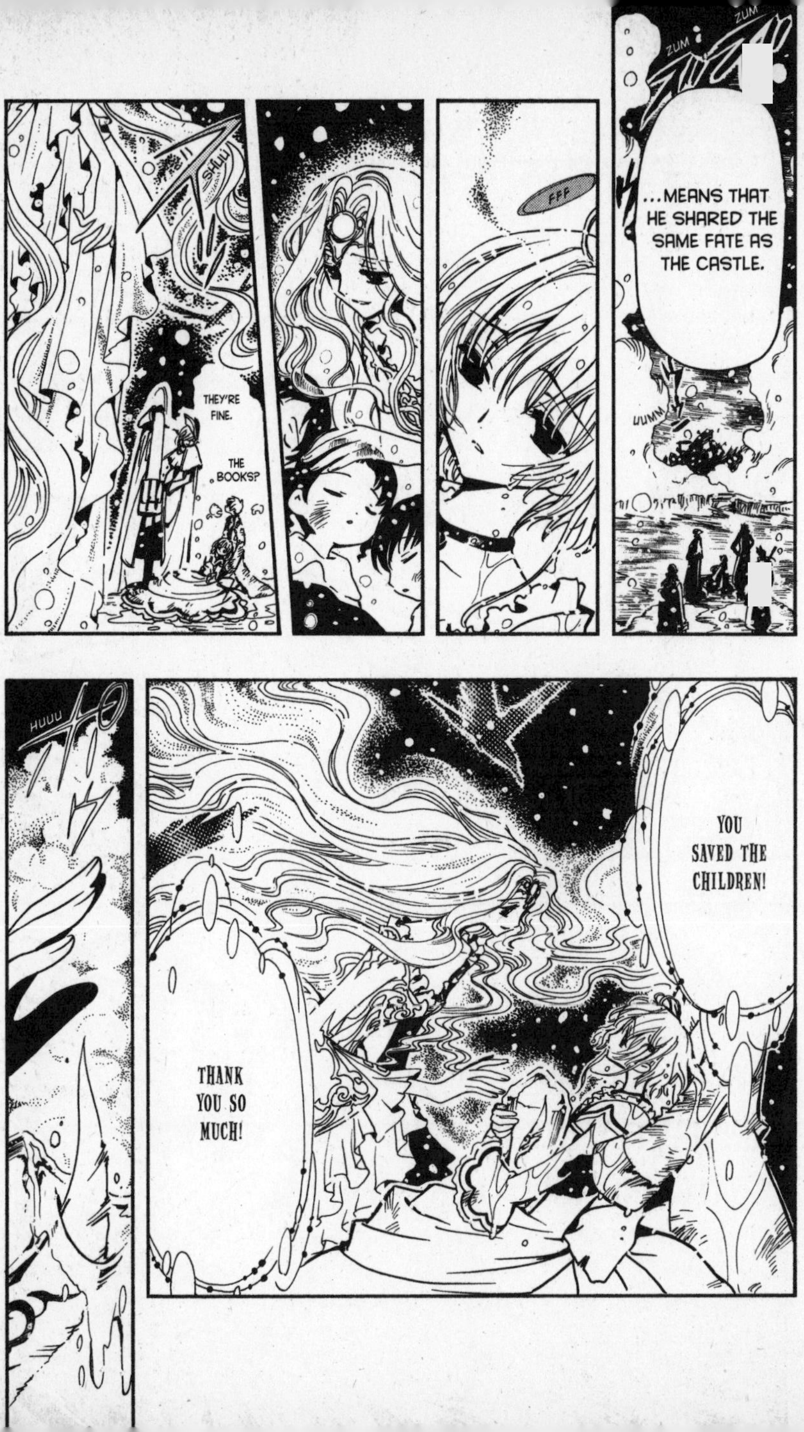
ZUM
ZUM
...MEANS THAT HE SHARED THE SAME FATE AS THE CASTLE.
UUMM
FFF
SHUU
THE BOOKS?
THEY'RE FINE.
YOU SAVED THE CHILDREN!
THANK YOU SO MUCH!
HUUU

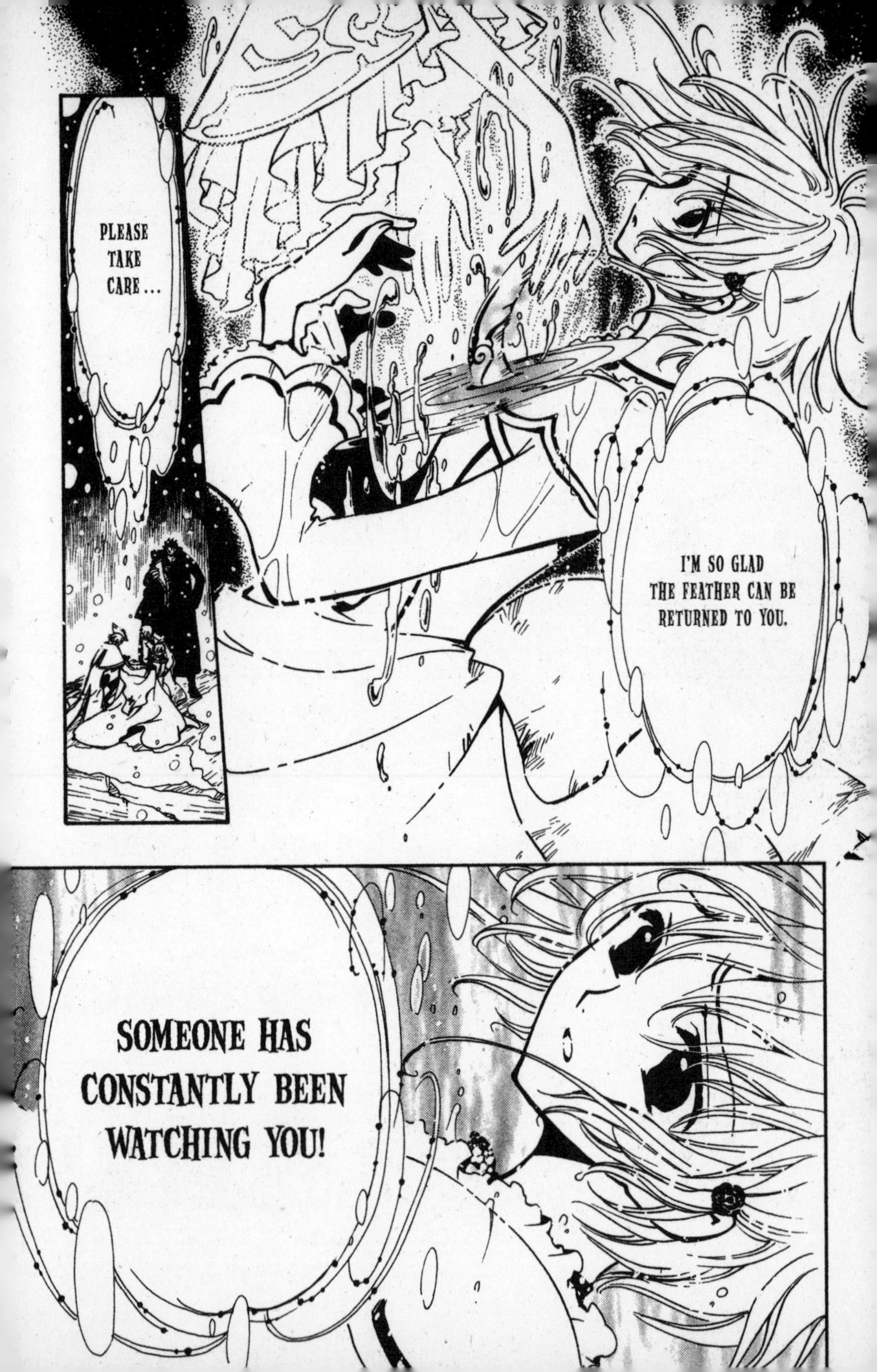
I'M SO GLAD THE FEATHER CAN BE RETURNED TO YOU.
PLEASE TAKE CARE...
SOMEONE HAS CONSTANTLY BEEN WATCHING YOU!

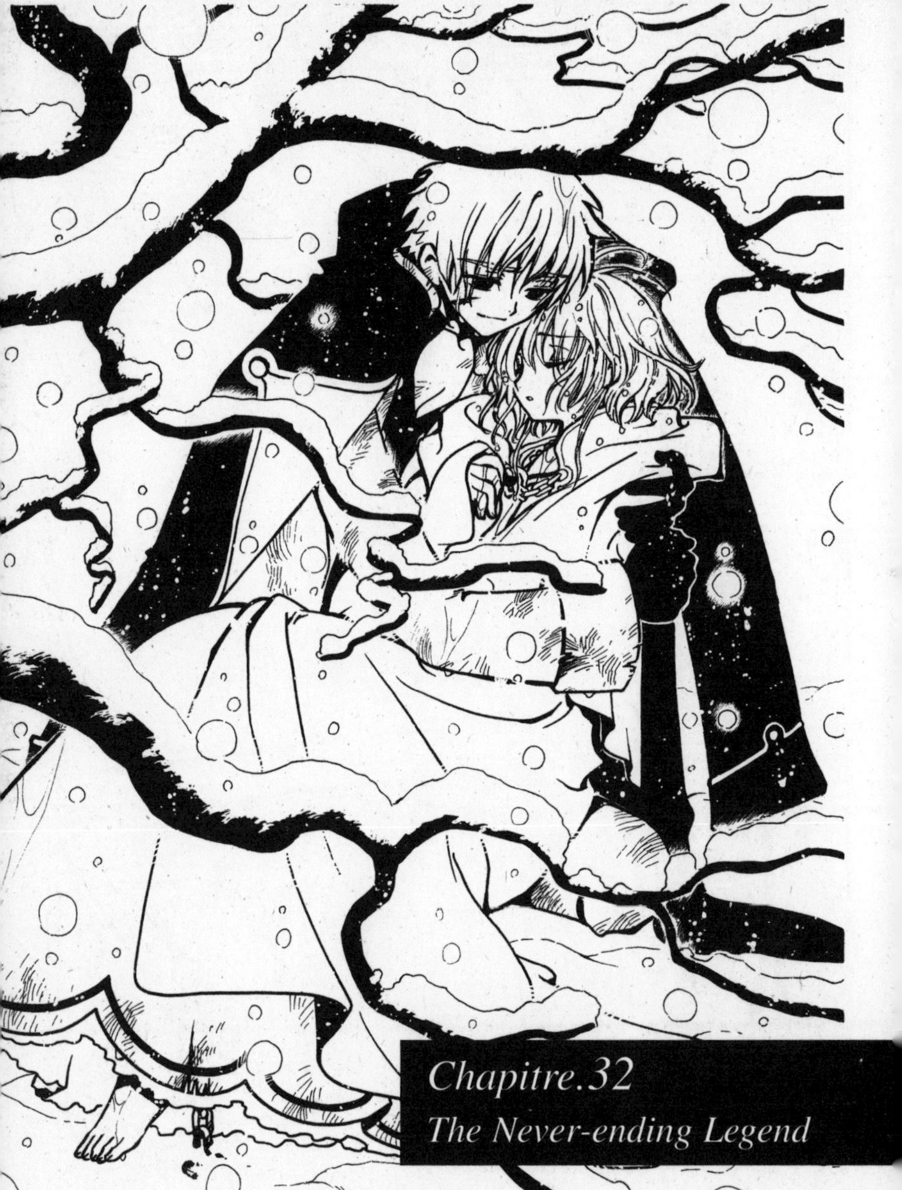

# Chapitre.32
## The Never-ending Legend

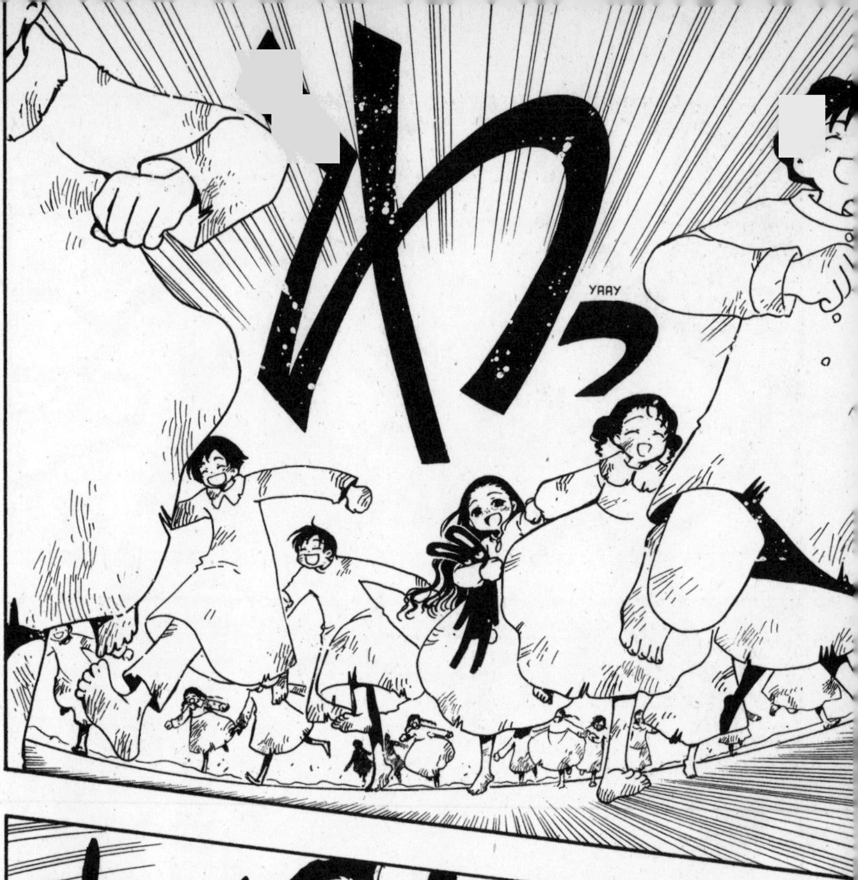
わっ
YAAY

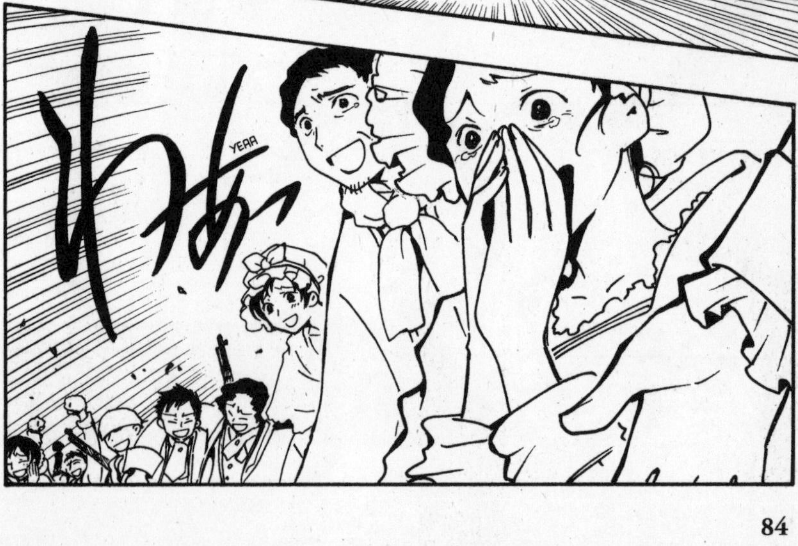
わあっ
YEAA

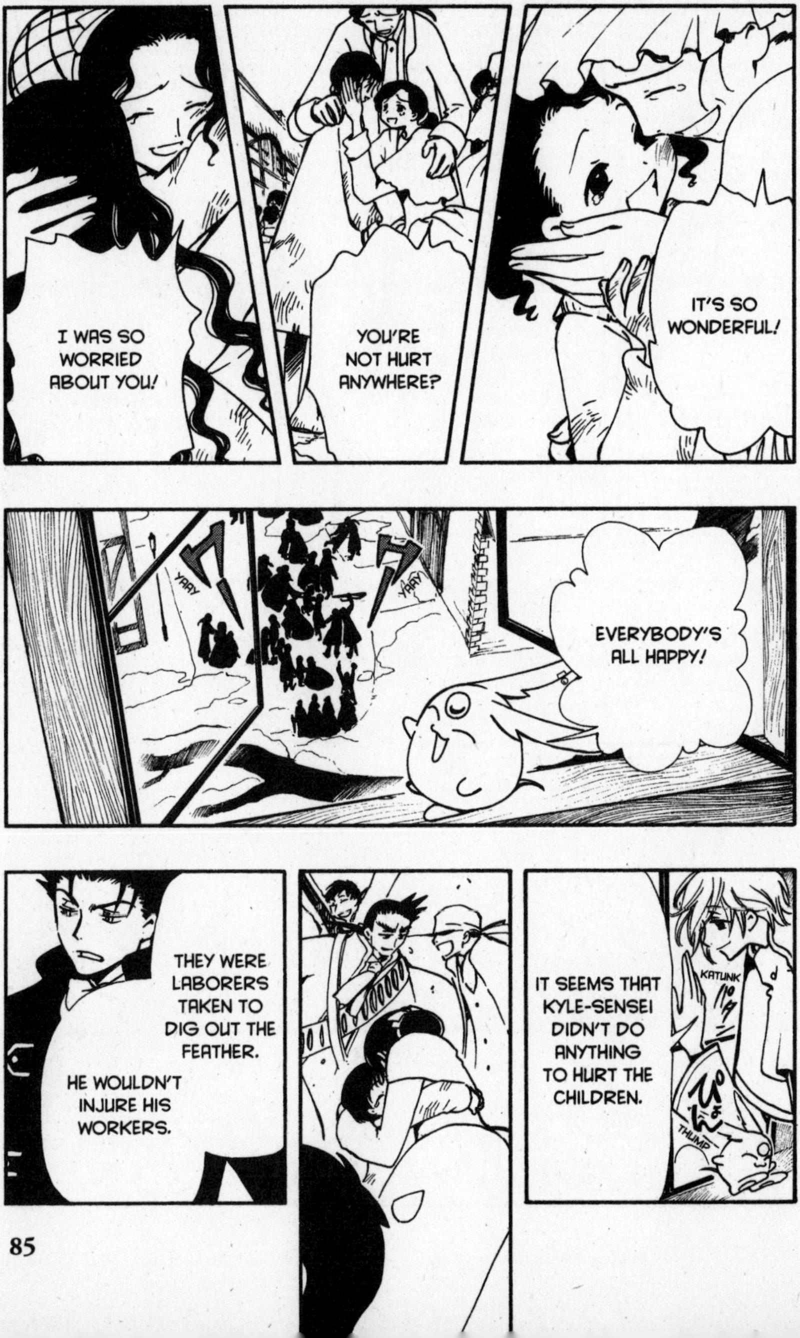
IT'S SO WONDERFUL!
YOU'RE NOT HURT ANYWHERE?
I WAS SO WORRIED ABOUT YOU!
EVERYBODY'S ALL HAPPY!
YAAY
YAAY
IT SEEMS THAT KYLE-SENSEI DIDN'T DO ANYTHING TO HURT THE CHILDREN.
KATUNK
ぴょん
THUMP
THEY WERE LABORERS TAKEN TO DIG OUT THE FEATHER.
HE WOULDN'T INJURE HIS WORKERS.

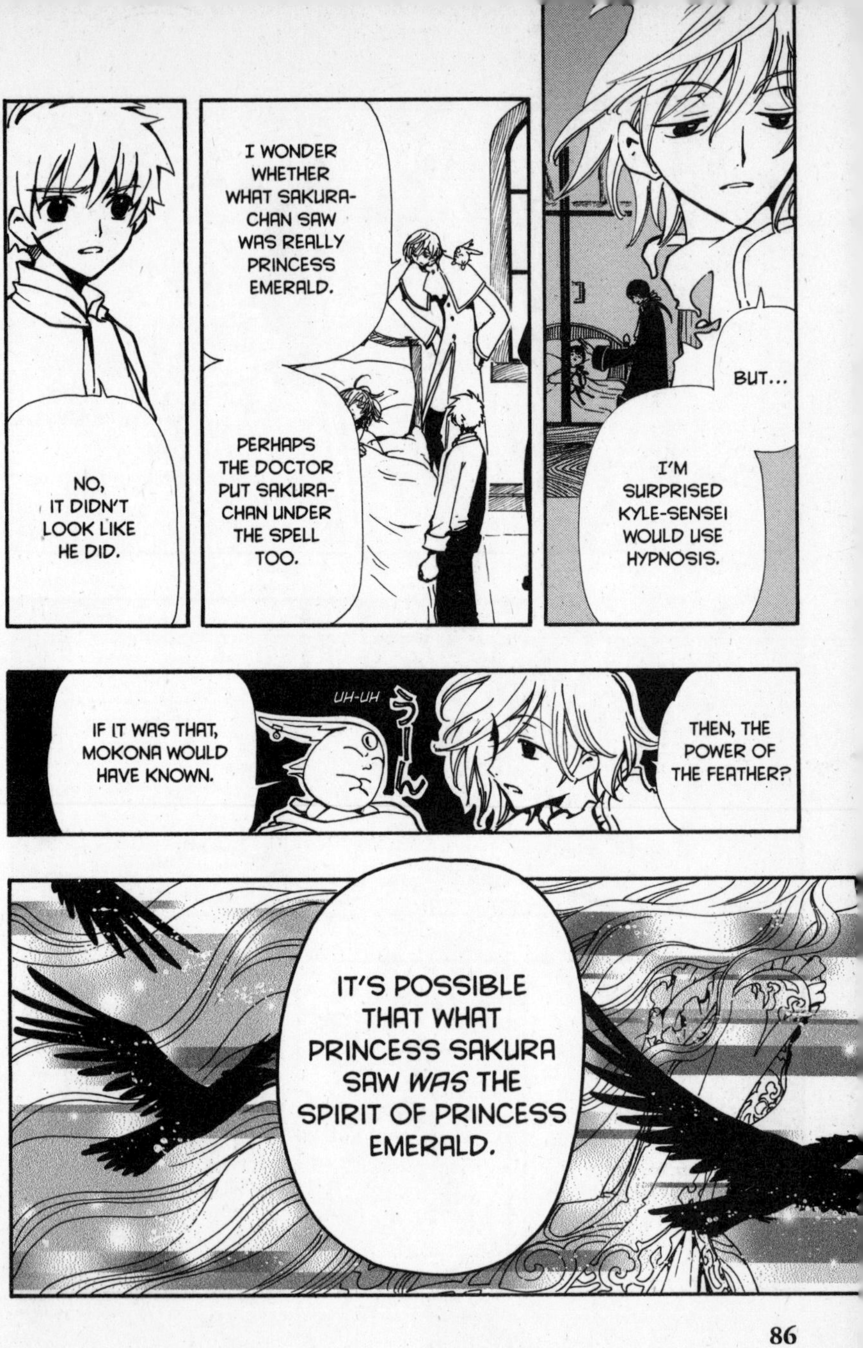
BUT...
I'M SURPRISED KYLE-SENSEI WOULD USE HYPNOSIS.
I WONDER WHETHER WHAT SAKURA-CHAN SAW WAS REALLY PRINCESS EMERALD.
PERHAPS THE DOCTOR PUT SAKURA-CHAN UNDER THE SPELL TOO.
NO, IT DIDN'T LOOK LIKE HE DID.
THEN, THE POWER OF THE FEATHER?
UH-UH
うーん
IF IT WAS THAT, MOKONA WOULD HAVE KNOWN.
IT'S POSSIBLE THAT WHAT PRINCESS SAKURA SAW *WAS* THE SPIRIT OF PRINCESS EMERALD.

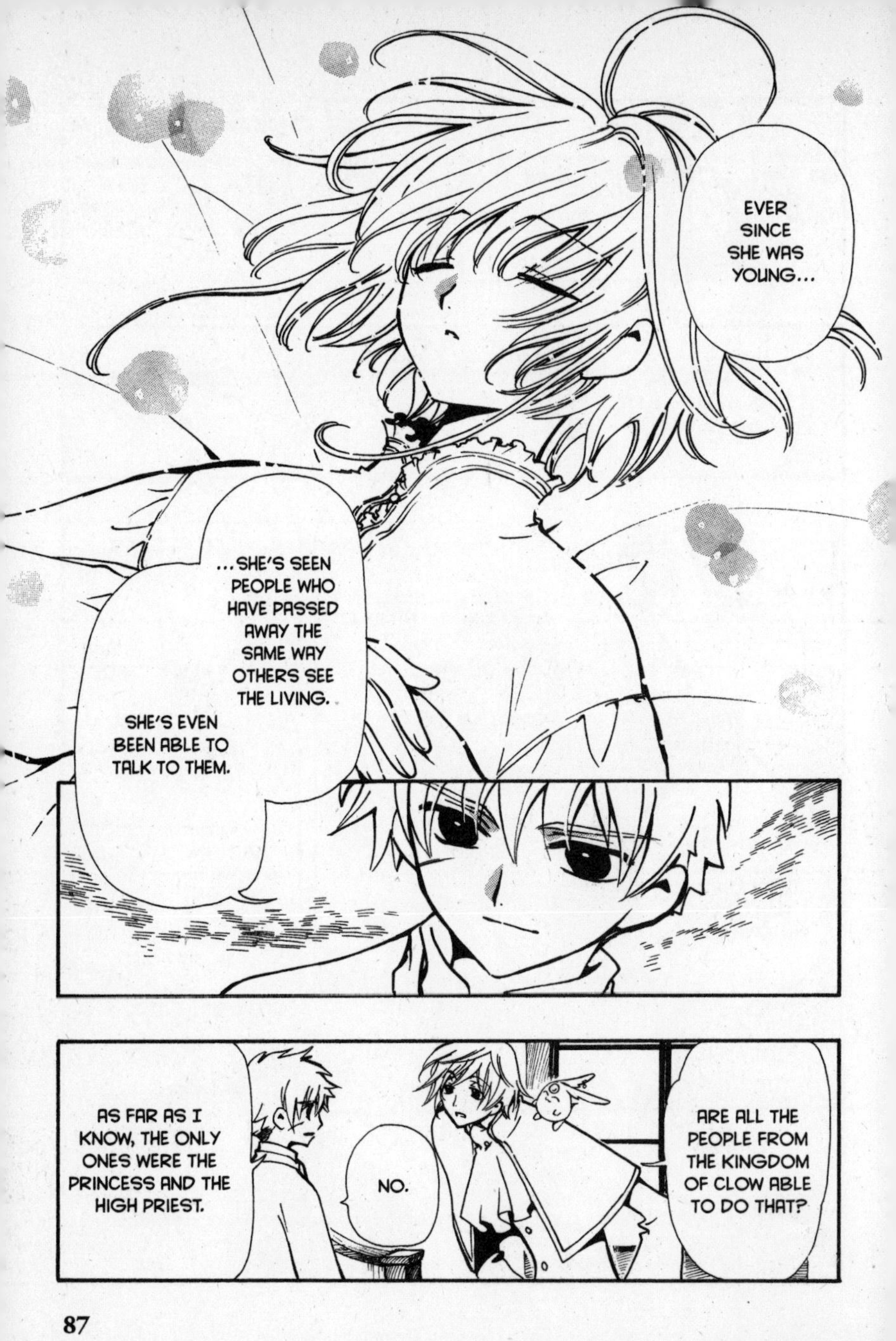
EVER SINCE SHE WAS YOUNG...
...SHE'S SEEN PEOPLE WHO HAVE PASSED AWAY THE SAME WAY OTHERS SEE THE LIVING.
SHE'S EVEN BEEN ABLE TO TALK TO THEM.
ARE ALL THE PEOPLE FROM THE KINGDOM OF CLOW ABLE TO DO THAT?
NO.
AS FAR AS I KNOW, THE ONLY ONES WERE THE PRINCESS AND THE HIGH PRIEST.

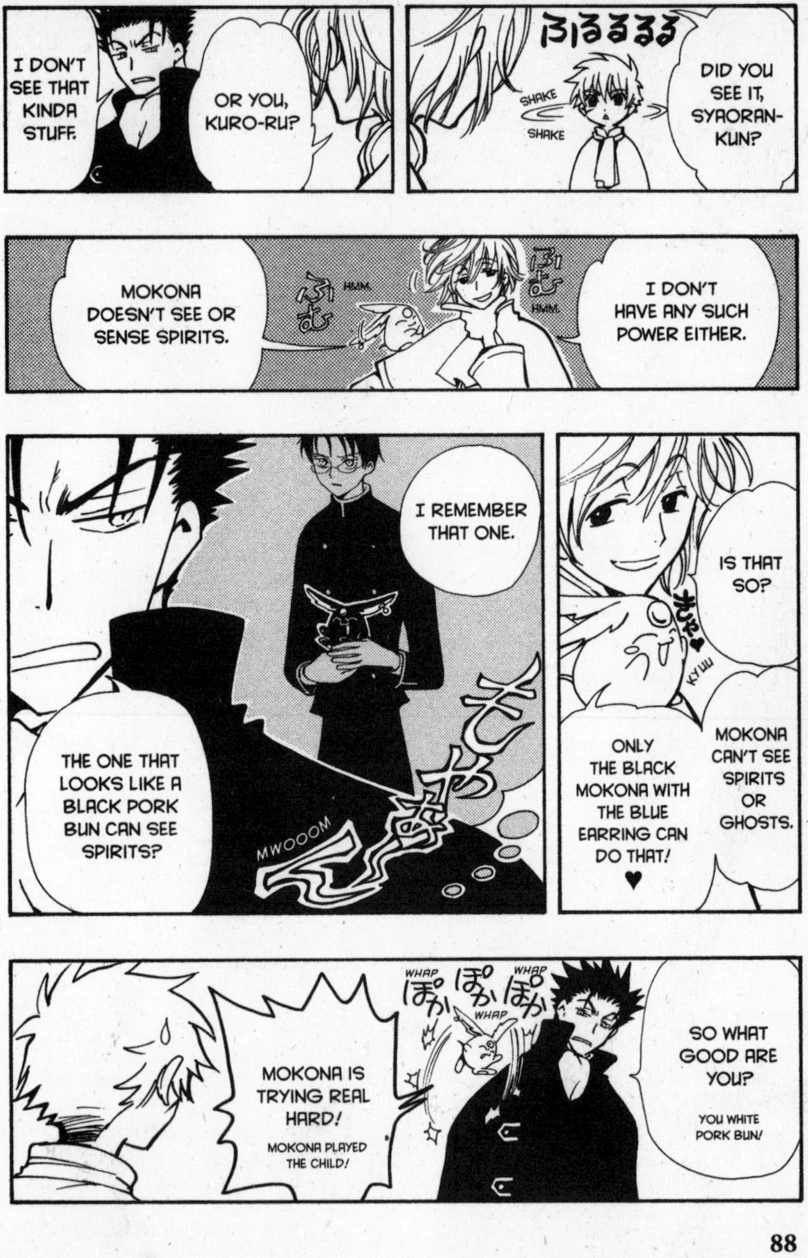

ふるるるる
DID YOU SEE IT, SYAORAN-KUN?
SHAKE
SHAKE
OR YOU, KURO-RU?
I DON'T SEE THAT KINDA STUFF.
I DON'T HAVE ANY SUCH POWER EITHER.
ふむ
HMM.
ふむ
HMM.
MOKONA DOESN'T SEE OR SENSE SPIRITS.
IS THAT SO?
きゃ♥
KYUU
MOKONA CAN'T SEE SPIRITS OR GHOSTS.
ONLY THE BLACK MOKONA WITH THE BLUE EARRING CAN DO THAT! ♥
I REMEMBER THAT ONE.
MWOOOM
THE ONE THAT LOOKS LIKE A BLACK PORK BUN CAN SEE SPIRITS?
SO WHAT GOOD ARE YOU?
YOU WHITE PORK BUN!
WHAP
ぽか
WHAP
ぽか
WHAP
ぽか
MOKONA IS TRYING REAL HARD!
MOKONA PLAYED THE CHILD!

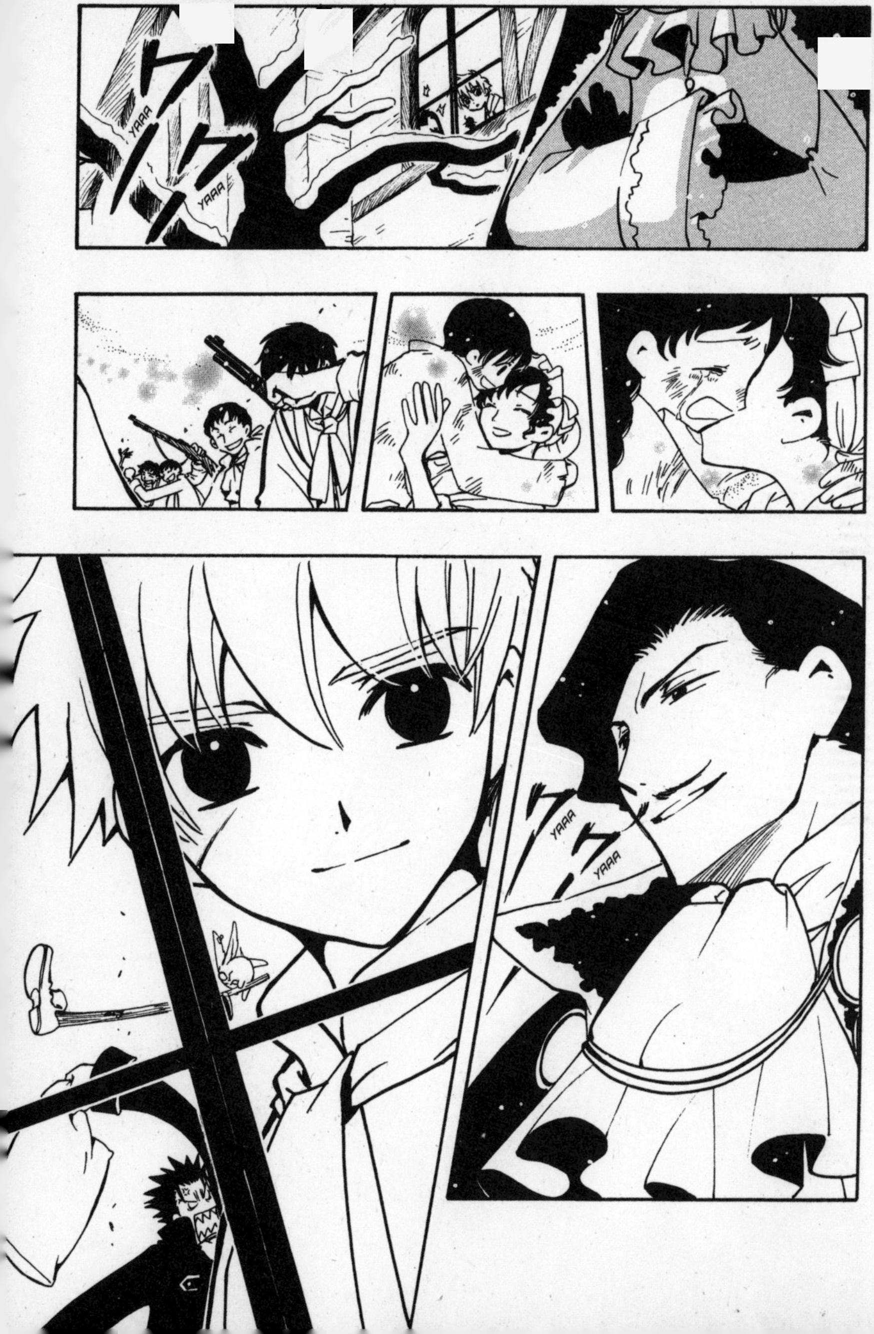
YAAA
YAAA
YAAA
YAAA

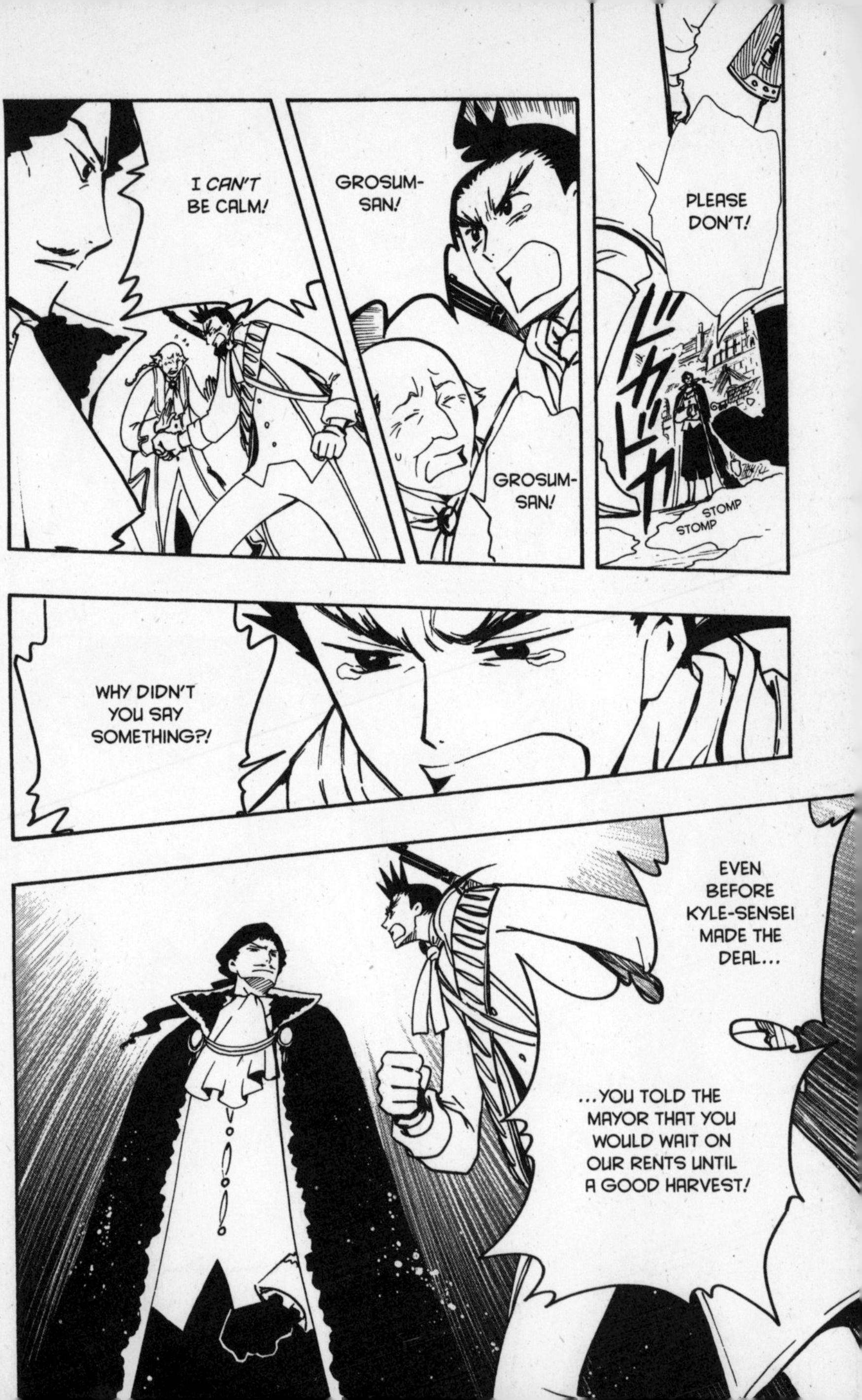
PLEASE DON'T!
ドカドカ
STOMP
STOMP
GROSUM-SAN!
GROSUM-SAN!
I CAN'T BE CALM!
WHY DIDN'T YOU SAY SOMETHING?!
EVEN BEFORE KYLE-SENSEI MADE THE DEAL...
...YOU TOLD THE MAYOR THAT YOU WOULD WAIT ON OUR RENTS UNTIL A GOOD HARVEST!

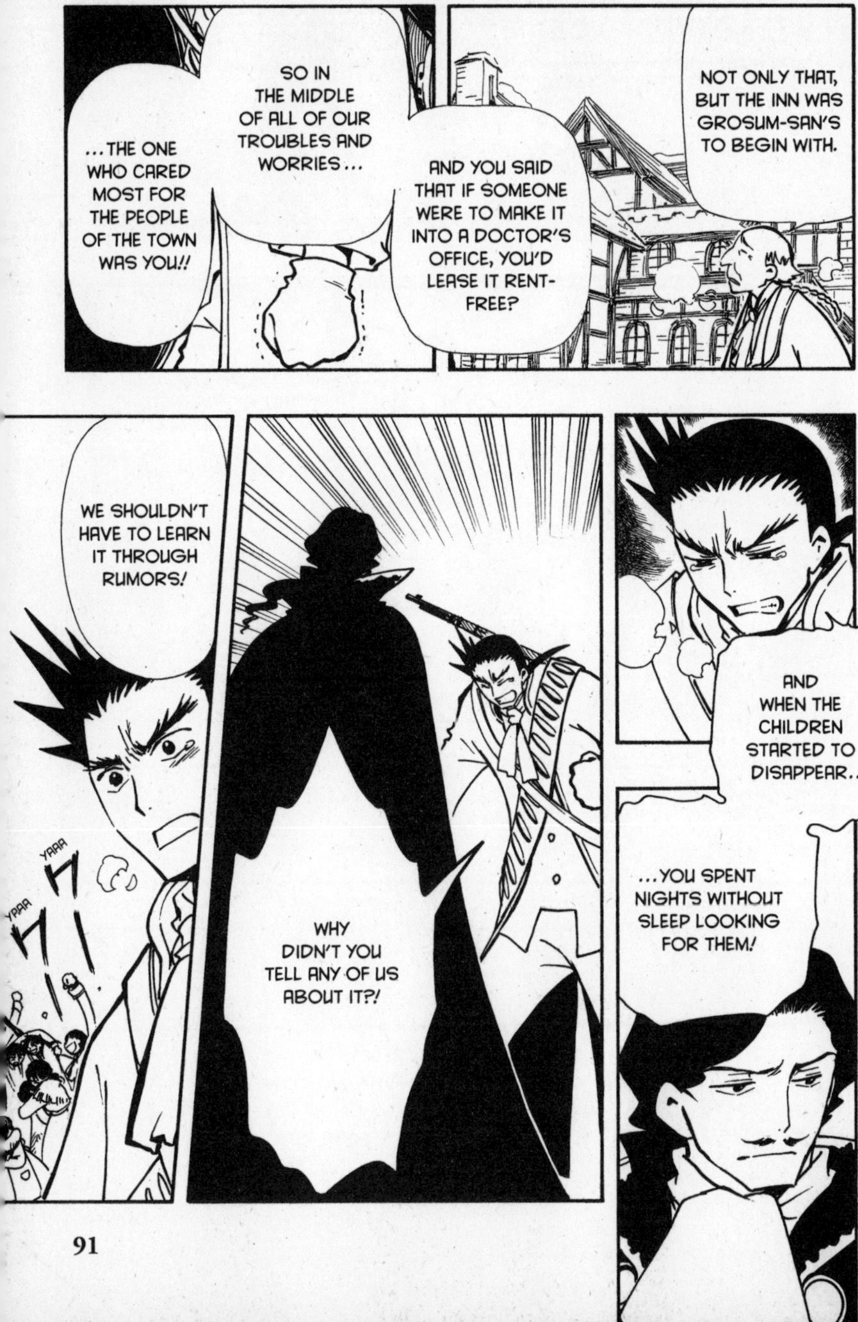
NOT ONLY THAT, BUT THE INN WAS GROSUM-SAN'S TO BEGIN WITH.
AND YOU SAID THAT IF SOMEONE WERE TO MAKE IT INTO A DOCTOR'S OFFICE, YOU'D LEASE IT RENT-FREE?
SO IN THE MIDDLE OF ALL OF OUR TROUBLES AND WORRIES...
...THE ONE WHO CARED MOST FOR THE PEOPLE OF THE TOWN WAS YOU!!
AND WHEN THE CHILDREN STARTED TO DISAPPEAR...
...YOU SPENT NIGHTS WITHOUT SLEEP LOOKING FOR THEM!
WHY DIDN'T YOU TELL ANY OF US ABOUT IT?!
WE SHOULDN'T HAVE TO LEARN IT THROUGH RUMORS!
YAAA
YAAA

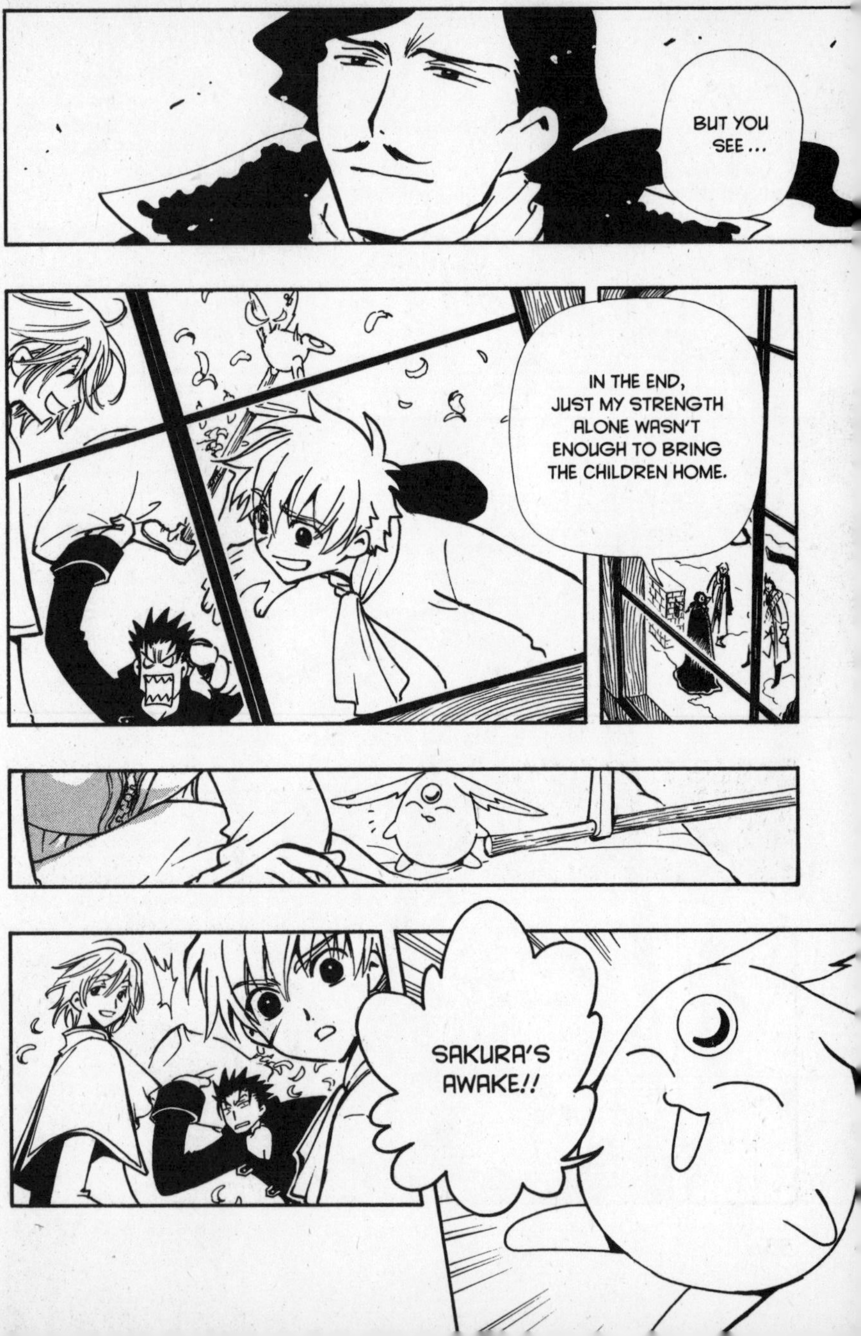
BUT YOU SEE...
IN THE END, JUST MY STRENGTH ALONE WASN'T ENOUGH TO BRING THE CHILDREN HOME.
SAKURA'S AWAKE!!

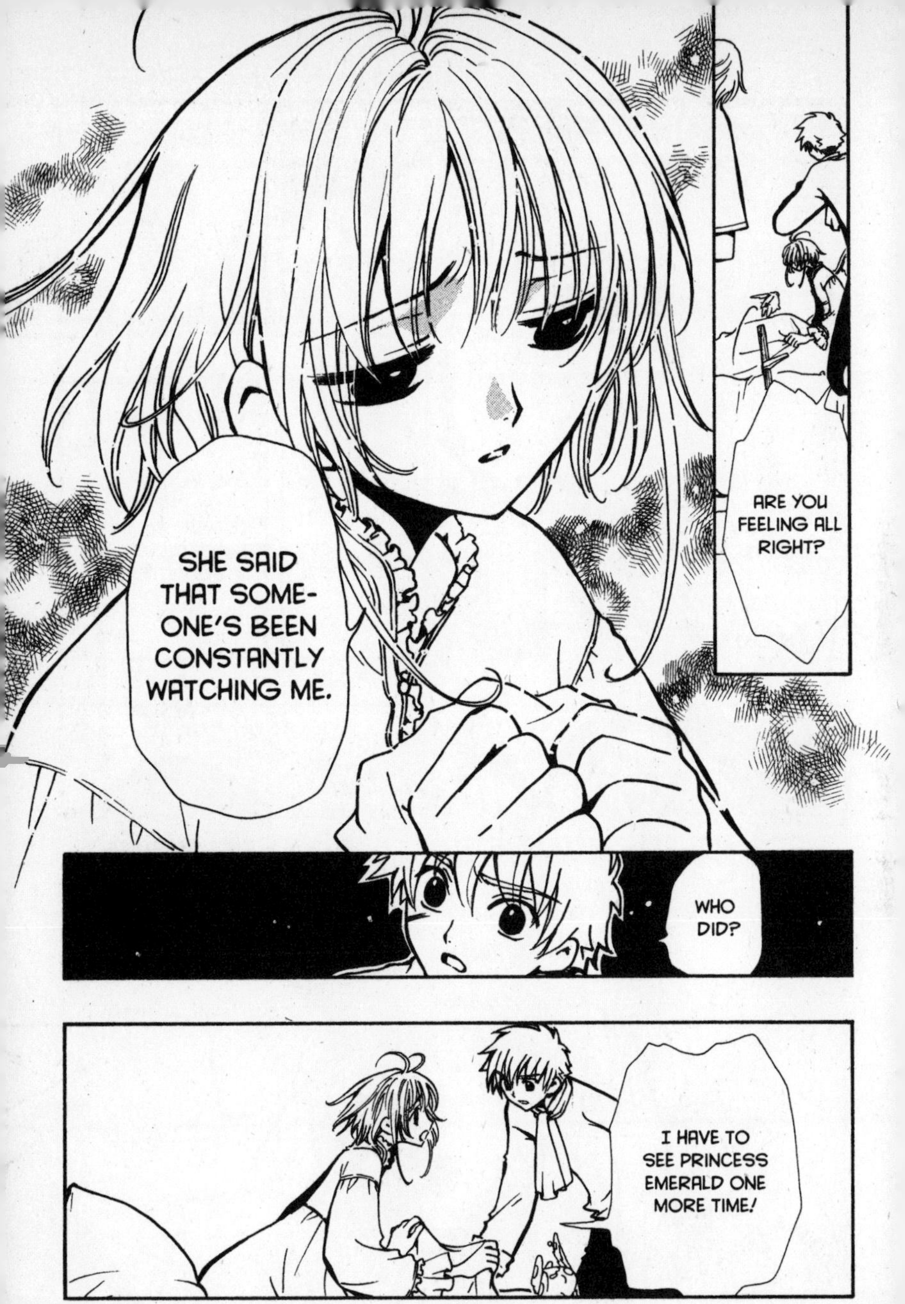
ARE YOU FEELING ALL RIGHT?
SHE SAID THAT SOME-ONE'S BEEN CONSTANTLY WATCHING ME.
WHO DID?
I HAVE TO SEE PRINCESS EMERALD ONE MORE TIME!

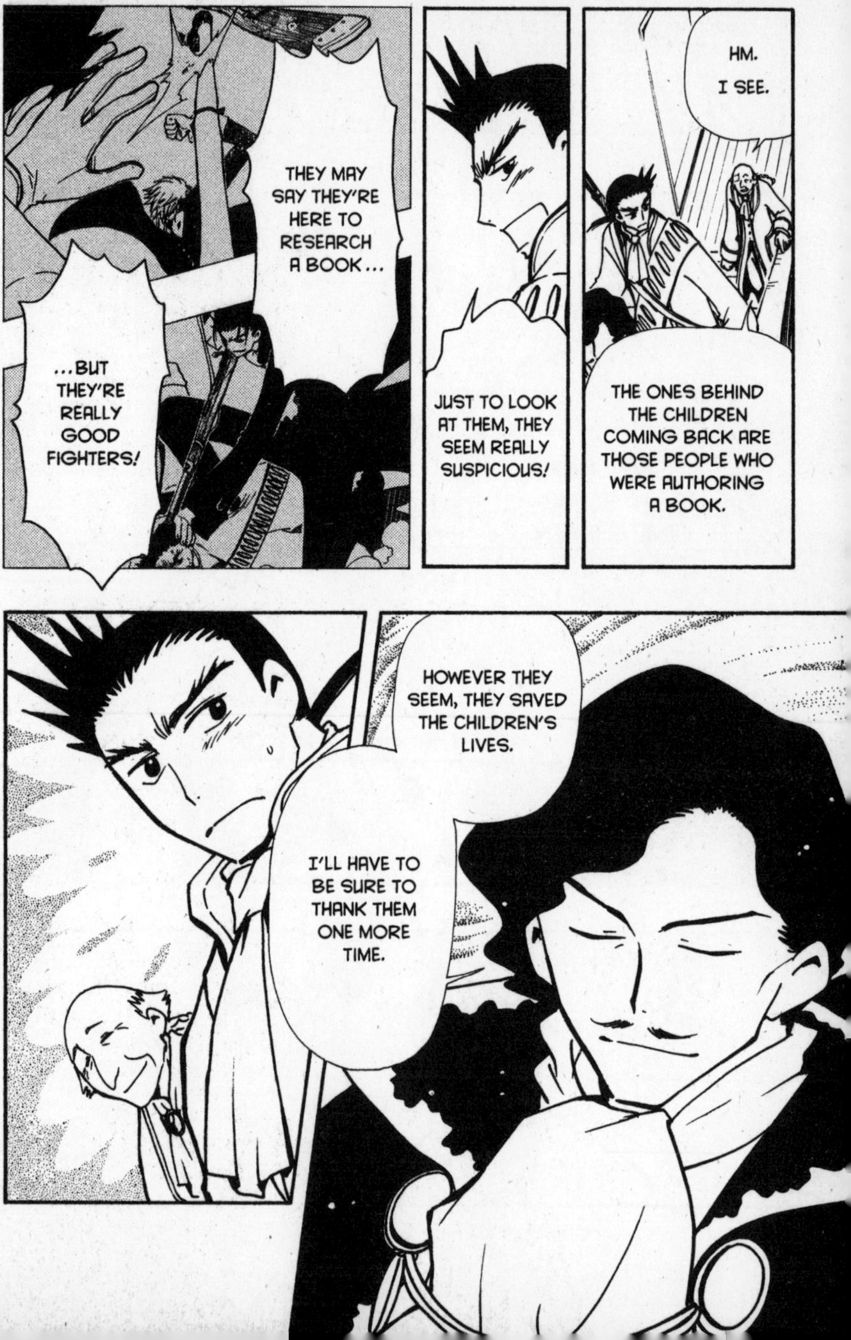
HM.
I SEE.
THE ONES BEHIND THE CHILDREN COMING BACK ARE THOSE PEOPLE WHO WERE AUTHORING A BOOK.
JUST TO LOOK AT THEM, THEY SEEM REALLY SUSPICIOUS!
THEY MAY SAY THEY'RE HERE TO RESEARCH A BOOK...
...BUT THEY'RE REALLY GOOD FIGHTERS!
HOWEVER THEY SEEM, THEY SAVED THE CHILDREN'S LIVES.
I'LL HAVE TO BE SURE TO THANK THEM ONE MORE TIME.

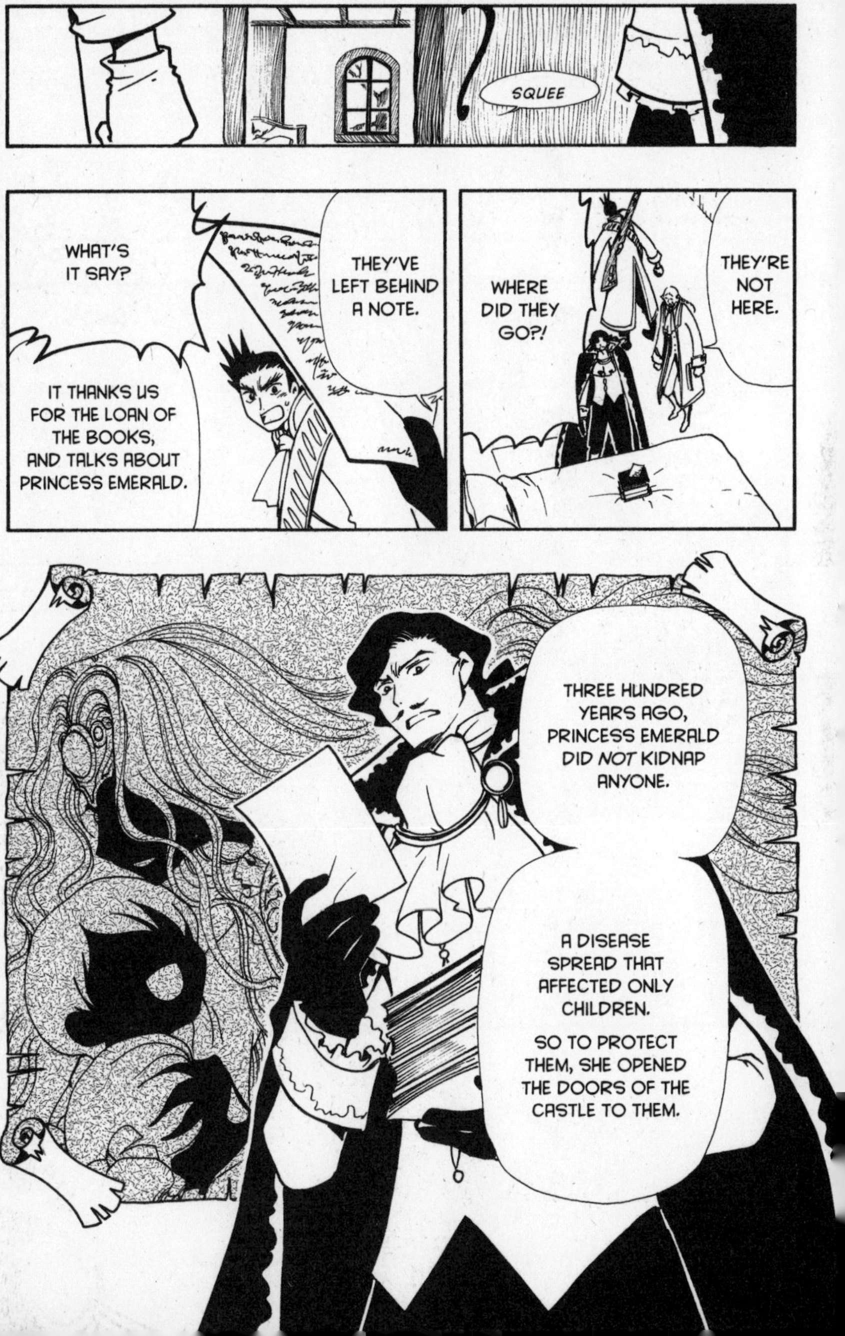
SQUEE
THEY'RE NOT HERE.
WHERE DID THEY GO?!
THEY'VE LEFT BEHIND A NOTE.
WHAT'S IT SAY?
IT THANKS US FOR THE LOAN OF THE BOOKS, AND TALKS ABOUT PRINCESS EMERALD.
THREE HUNDRED YEARS AGO, PRINCESS EMERALD DID *NOT* KIDNAP ANYONE.
A DISEASE SPREAD THAT AFFECTED ONLY CHILDREN.
SO TO PROTECT THEM, SHE OPENED THE DOORS OF THE CASTLE TO THEM.

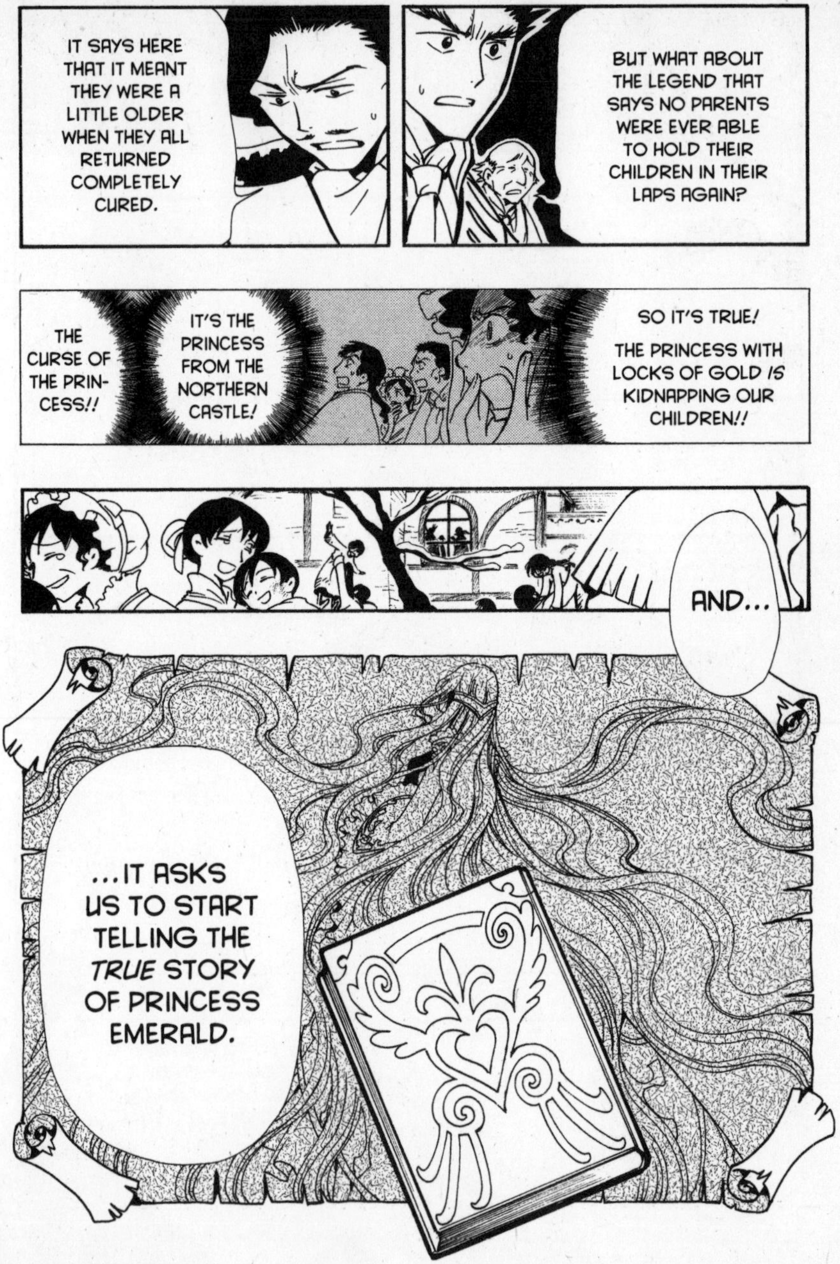
BUT WHAT ABOUT THE LEGEND THAT SAYS NO PARENTS WERE EVER ABLE TO HOLD THEIR CHILDREN IN THEIR LAPS AGAIN?
IT SAYS HERE THAT IT MEANT THEY WERE A LITTLE OLDER WHEN THEY ALL RETURNED COMPLETELY CURED.
SO IT'S TRUE!
THE PRINCESS WITH LOCKS OF GOLD *IS* KIDNAPPING OUR CHILDREN!!
IT'S THE PRINCESS FROM THE NORTHERN CASTLE!
THE CURSE OF THE PRIN-CESS!!
AND...
...IT ASKS US TO START TELLING THE *TRUE* STORY OF PRINCESS EMERALD.

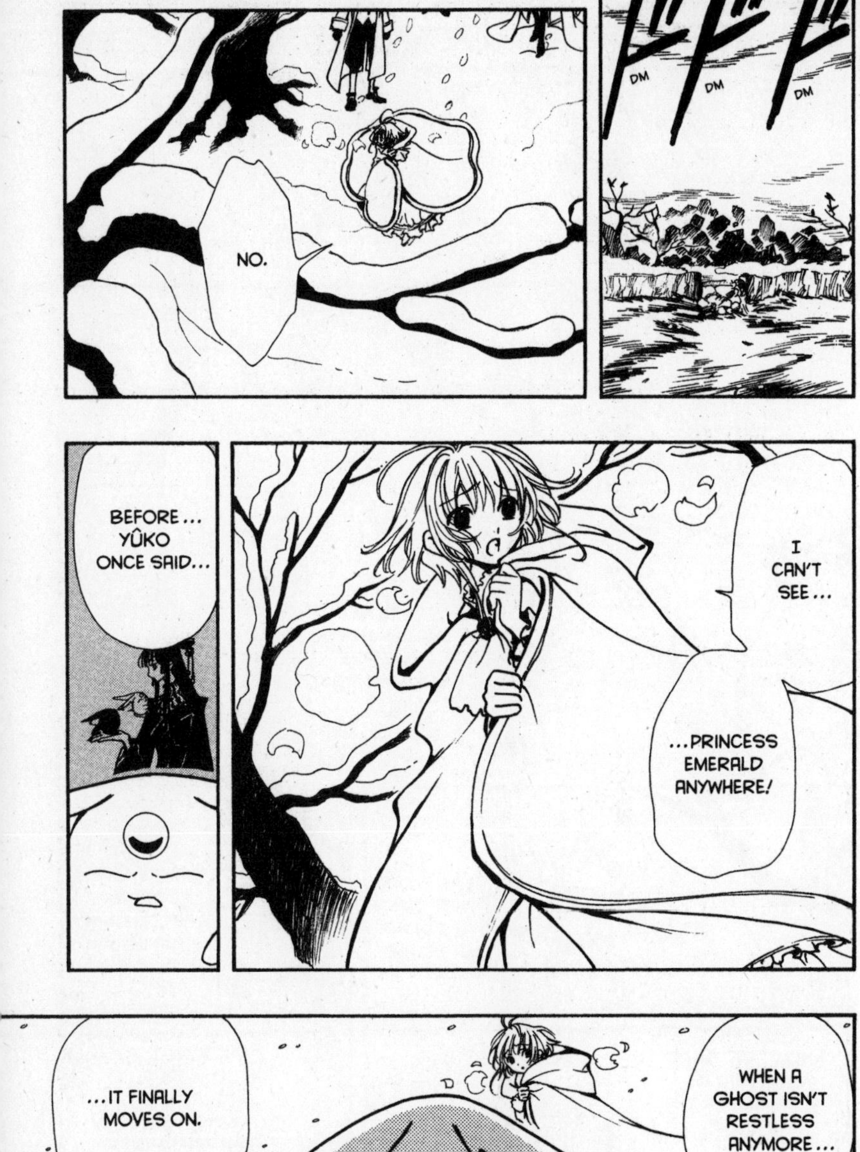
ドドド
DM
DM
DM
NO.
I CAN'T SEE...
...PRINCESS EMERALD ANYWHERE!
BEFORE... YÛKO ONCE SAID...
WHEN A GHOST ISN'T RESTLESS ANYMORE...
...IT FINALLY MOVES ON.

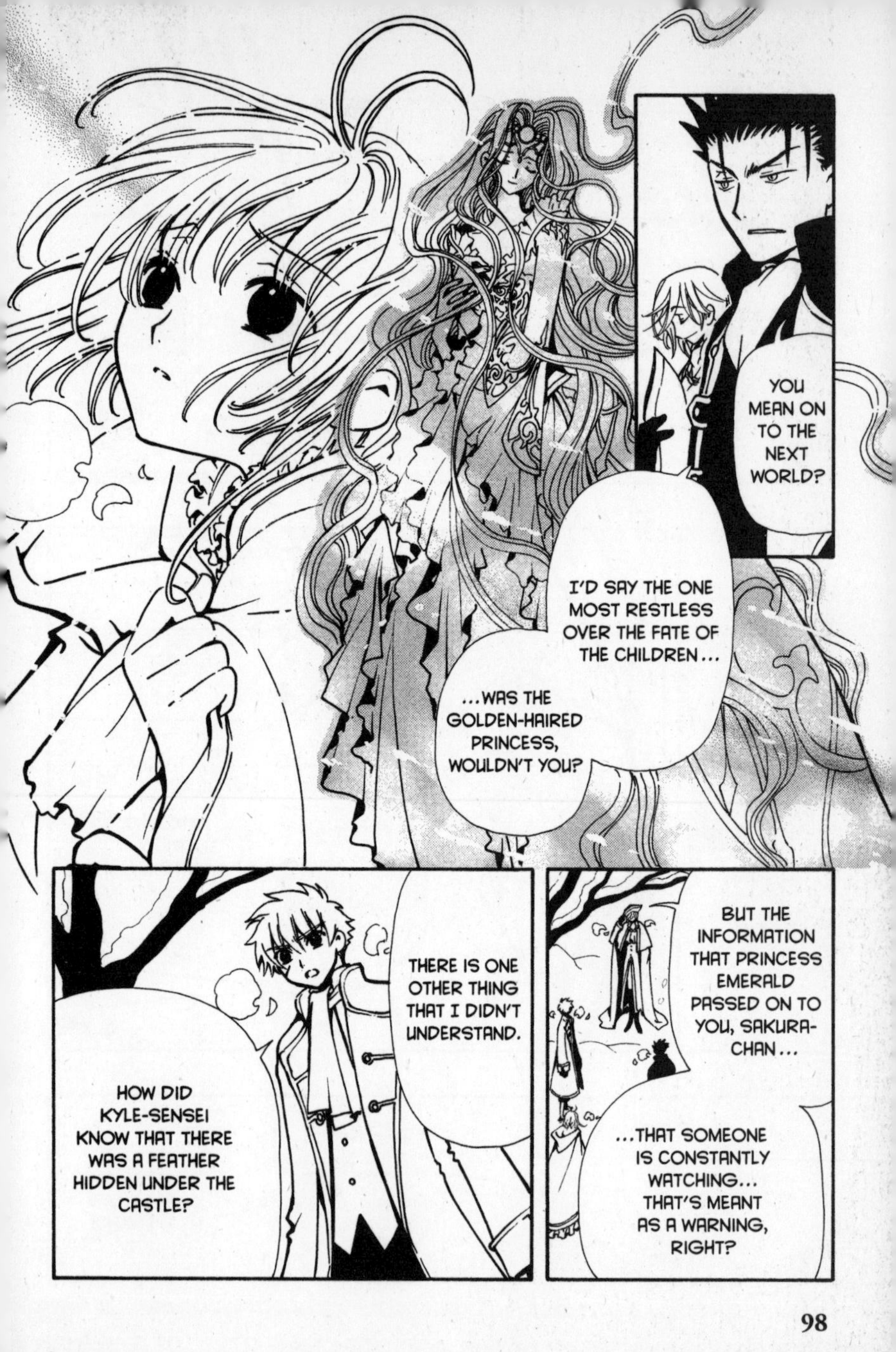
YOU MEAN ON TO THE NEXT WORLD?
I'D SAY THE ONE MOST RESTLESS OVER THE FATE OF THE CHILDREN...
...WAS THE GOLDEN-HAIRED PRINCESS, WOULDN'T YOU?
BUT THE INFORMATION THAT PRINCESS EMERALD PASSED ON TO YOU, SAKURA-CHAN...
...THAT SOMEONE IS CONSTANTLY WATCHING... THAT'S MEANT AS A WARNING, RIGHT?
THERE IS ONE OTHER THING THAT I DIDN'T UNDERSTAND.
HOW DID KYLE-SENSEI KNOW THAT THERE WAS A FEATHER HIDDEN UNDER THE CASTLE?

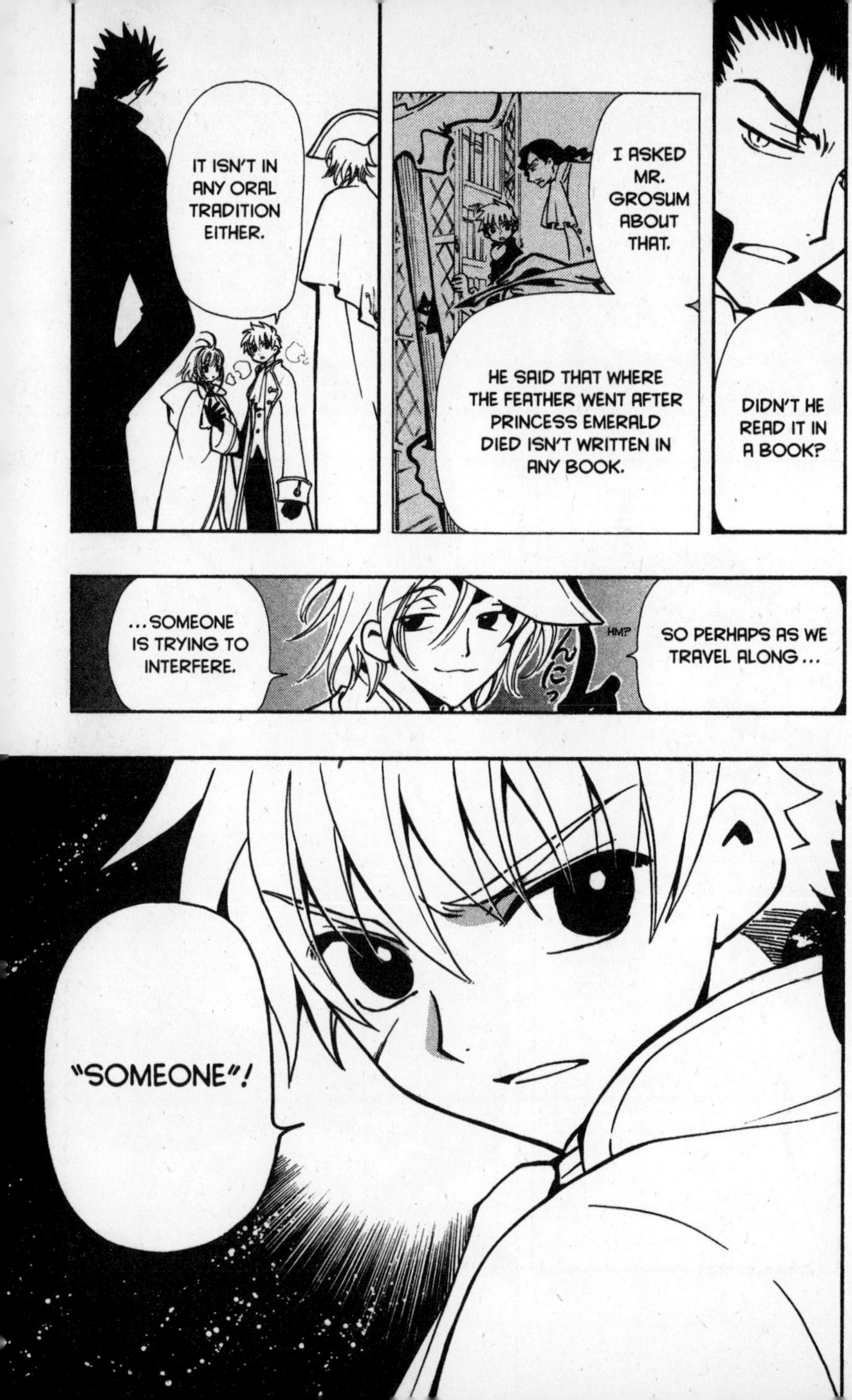
DIDN'T HE READ IT IN A BOOK?
I ASKED MR. GROSUM ABOUT THAT.
HE SAID THAT WHERE THE FEATHER WENT AFTER PRINCESS EMERALD DIED ISN'T WRITTEN IN ANY BOOK.
IT ISN'T IN ANY ORAL TRADITION EITHER.
SO PERHAPS AS WE TRAVEL ALONG...
HM?
...SOMEONE IS TRYING TO INTERFERE.
"SOMEONE"!

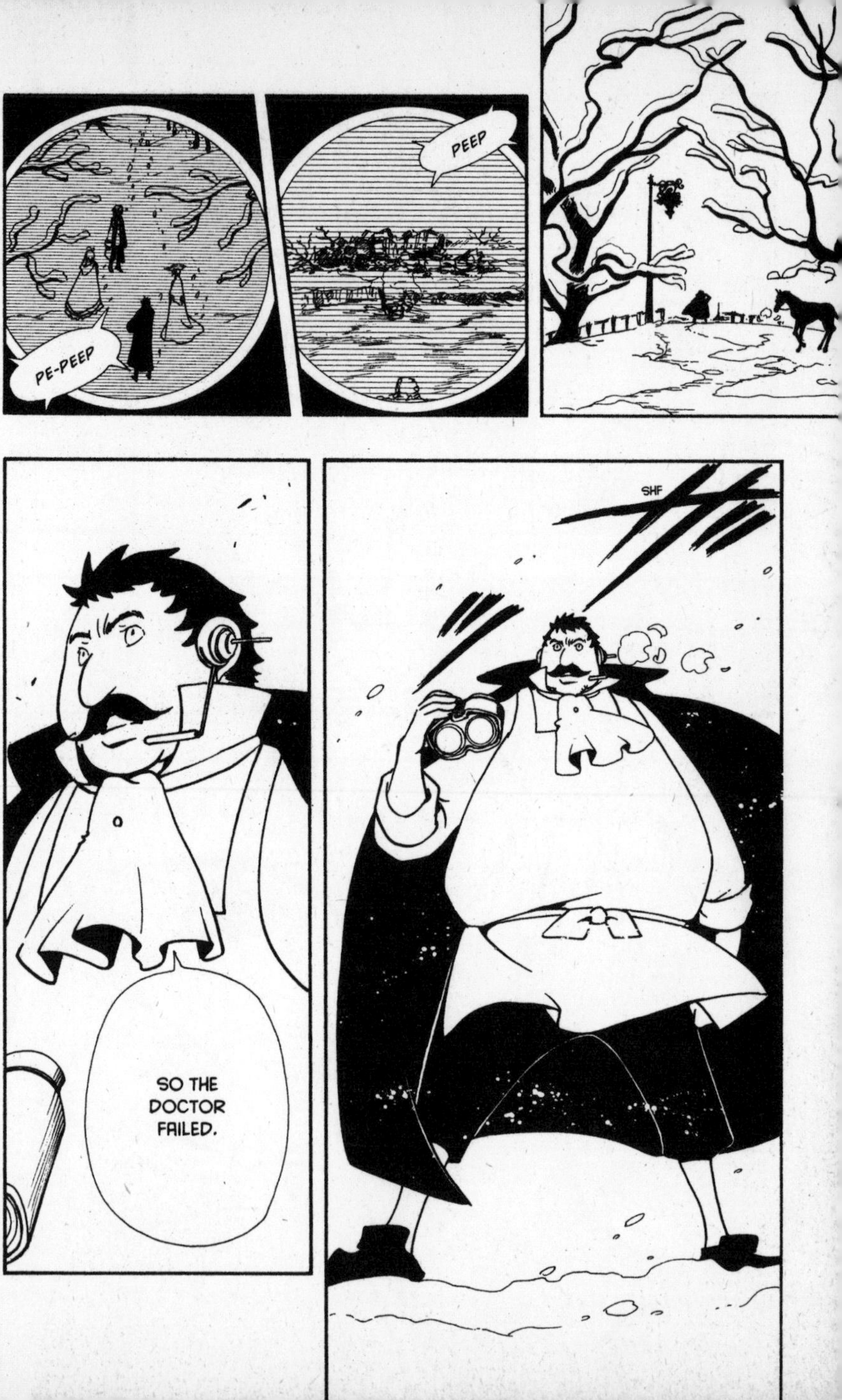
PEEP
PE-PEEP
SHF
SO THE DOCTOR FAILED.

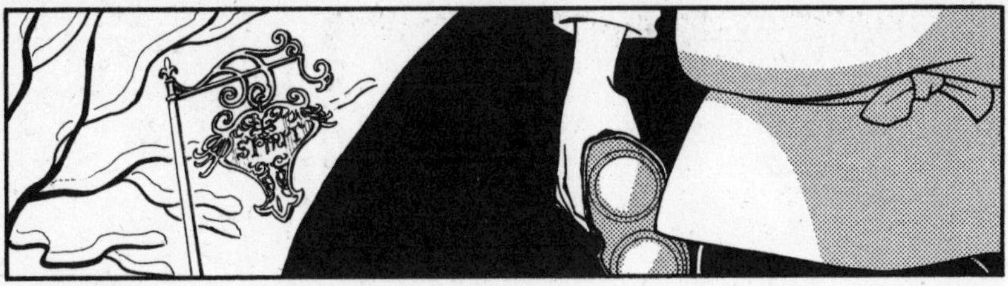

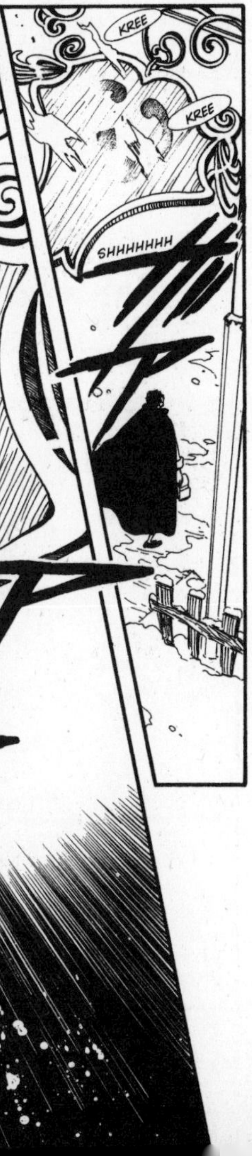
KREE
KREE
SHHHHHHH

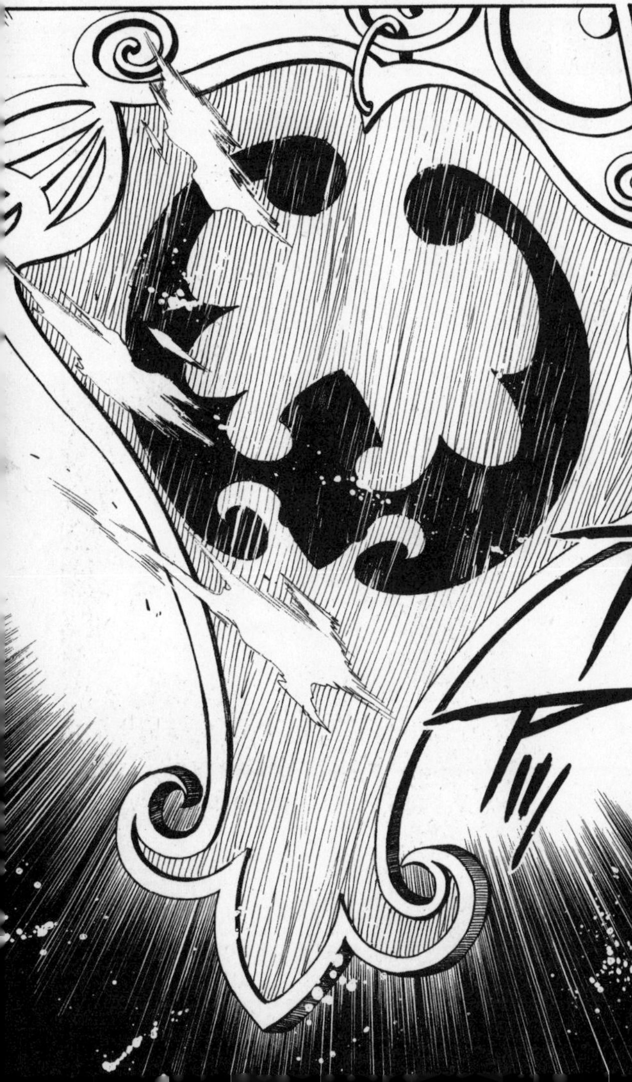

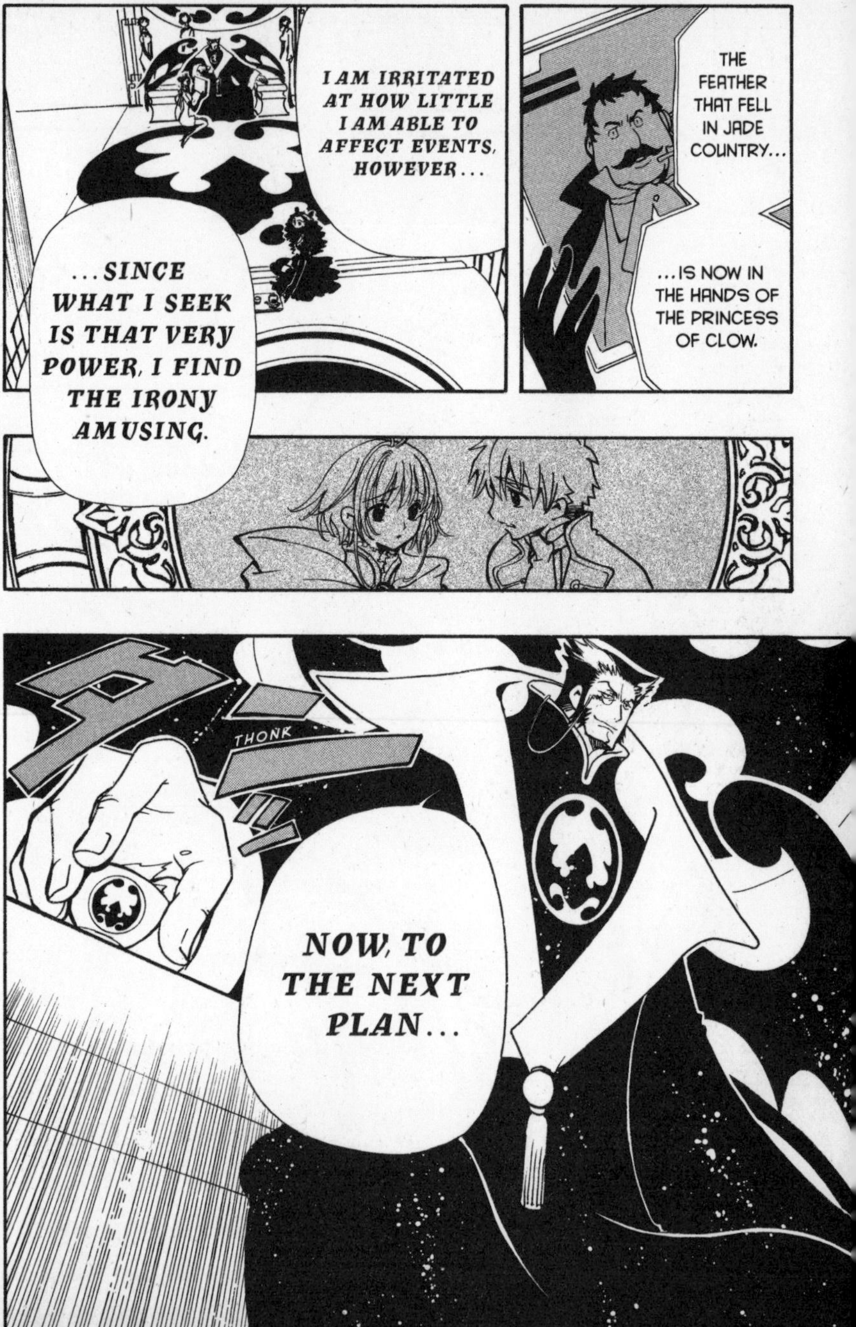
THE FEATHER THAT FELL IN JADE COUNTRY...
...IS NOW IN THE HANDS OF THE PRINCESS OF CLOW.
I AM IRRITATED AT HOW LITTLE I AM ABLE TO AFFECT EVENTS, HOWEVER...
...SINCE WHAT I SEEK IS THAT VERY POWER, I FIND THE IRONY AMUSING.
THONK
NOW, TO THE NEXT PLAN...

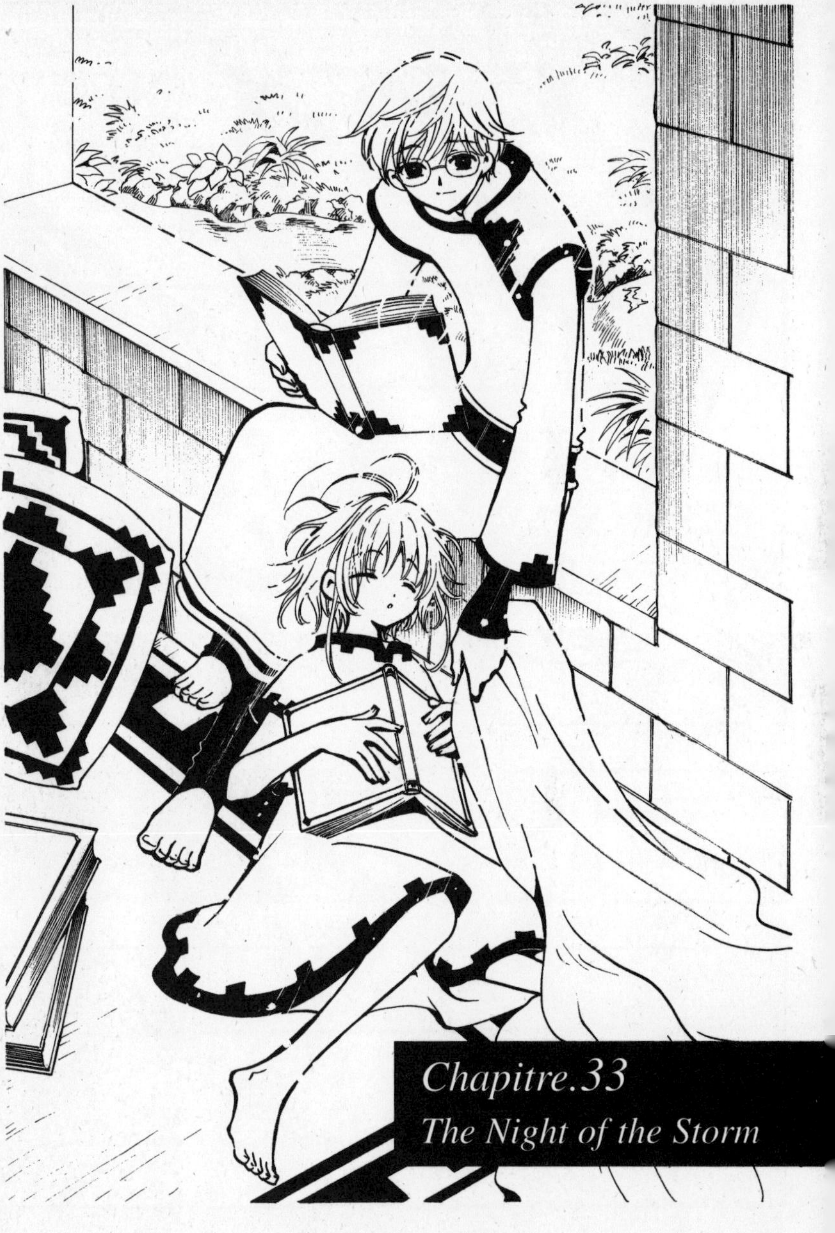

# Chapitre.33

## The Night of the Storm

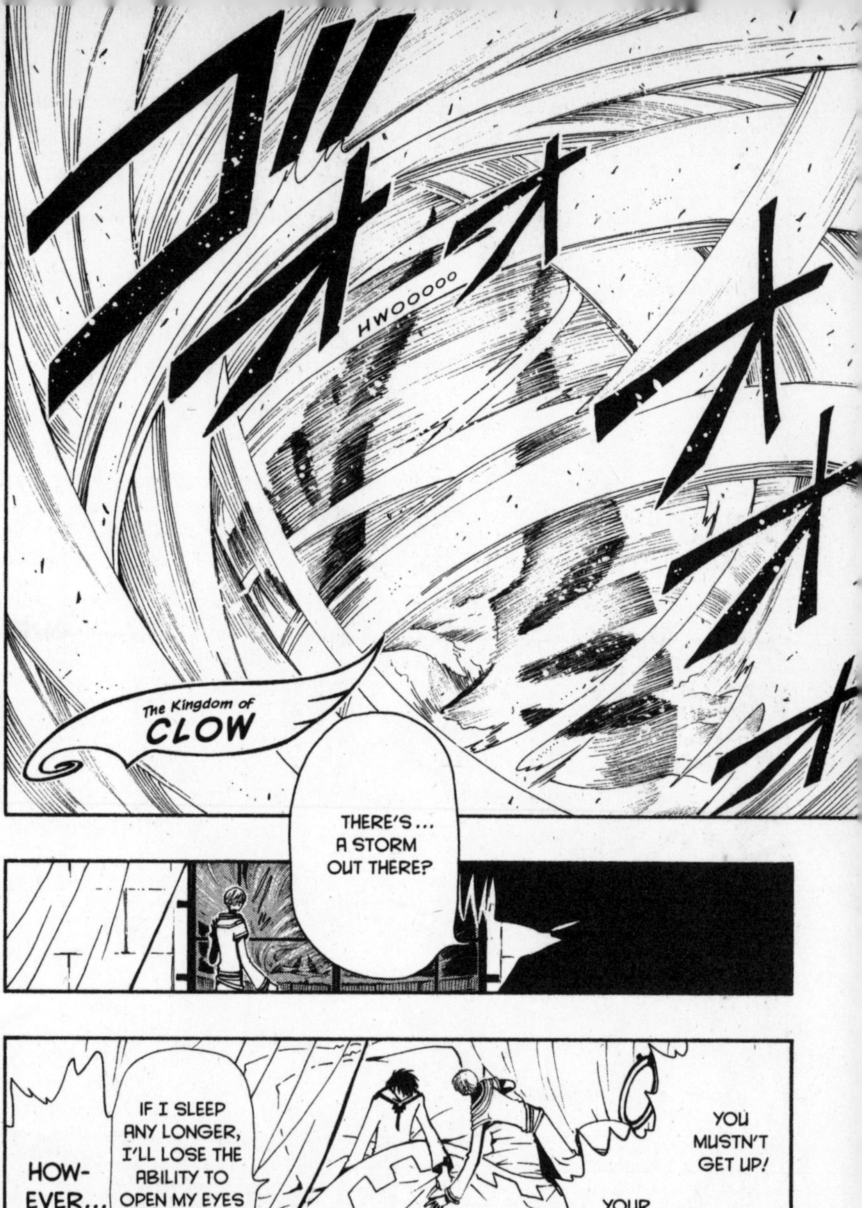
HWOOOOO
The Kingdom of CLOW
THERE'S... A STORM OUT THERE?
YOU MUSTN'T GET UP!
YOUR MAJESTY!!
IF I SLEEP ANY LONGER, I'LL LOSE THE ABILITY TO OPEN MY EYES AGAIN!
HOW-EVER...

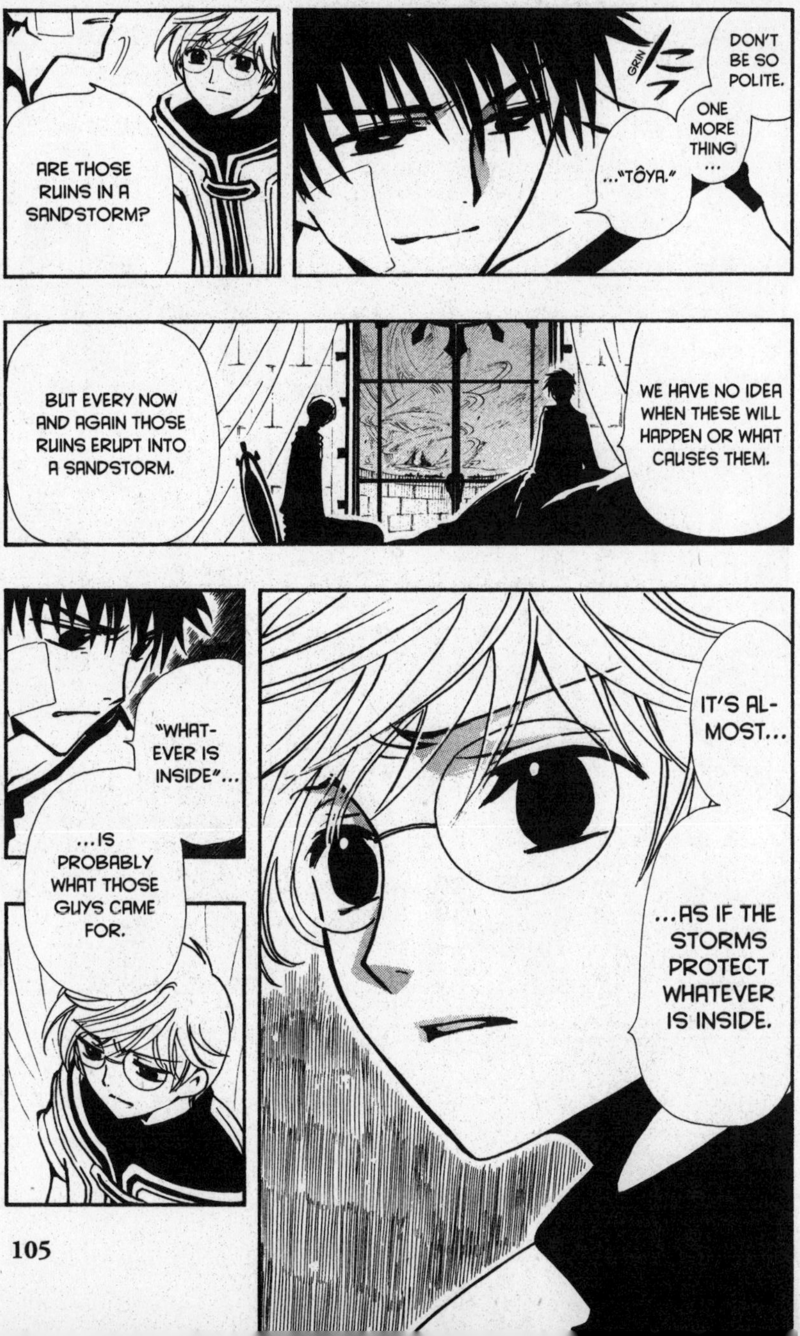
GRIN
DON'T BE SO POLITE.
ONE MORE THING ...
..."TÔYA."
ARE THOSE RUINS IN A SANDSTORM?
WE HAVE NO IDEA WHEN THESE WILL HAPPEN OR WHAT CAUSES THEM.
BUT EVERY NOW AND AGAIN THOSE RUINS ERUPT INTO A SANDSTORM.
IT'S AL-MOST...
...AS IF THE STORMS PROTECT WHATEVER IS INSIDE.
"WHAT-EVER IS INSIDE"...
...IS PROBABLY WHAT THOSE GUYS CAME FOR.

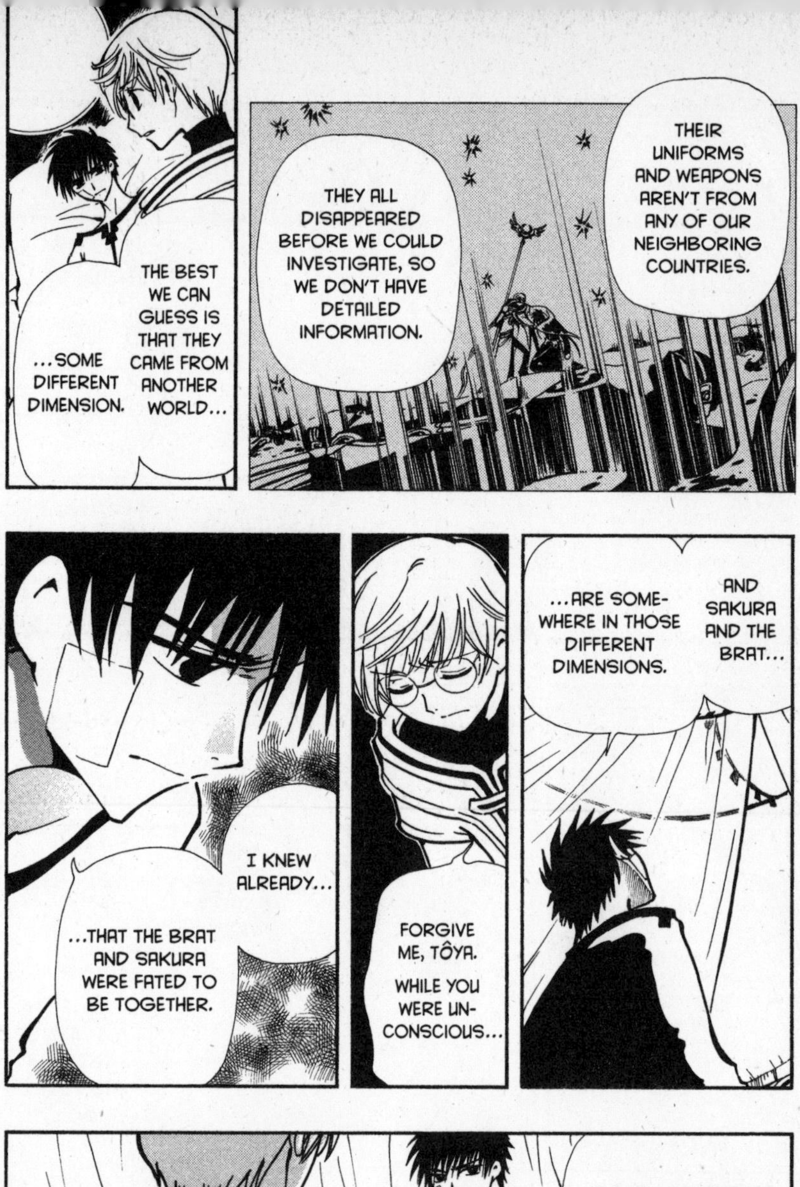
THEIR UNIFORMS AND WEAPONS AREN'T FROM ANY OF OUR NEIGHBORING COUNTRIES.
THEY ALL DISAPPEARED BEFORE WE COULD INVESTIGATE, SO WE DON'T HAVE DETAILED INFORMATION.
THE BEST WE CAN GUESS IS THAT THEY CAME FROM ANOTHER WORLD...
...SOME DIFFERENT DIMENSION.
AND SAKURA AND THE BRAT...
...ARE SOME-WHERE IN THOSE DIFFERENT DIMENSIONS.
FORGIVE ME, TÔYA.
WHILE YOU WERE UN-CONSCIOUS...
I KNEW ALREADY...
...THAT THE BRAT AND SAKURA WERE FATED TO BE TOGETHER.
DO YOU REMEMBER THE FIRST TIME WE EVER SAW HIM?

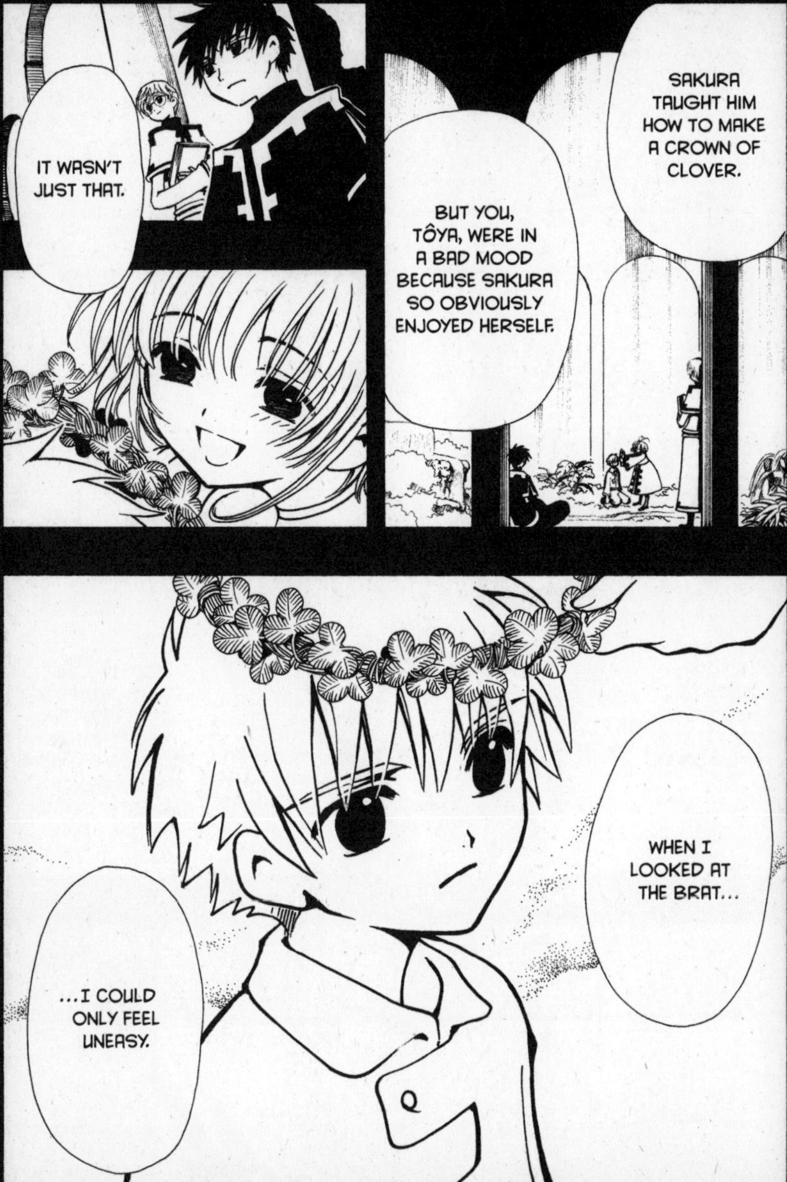
SAKURA TAUGHT HIM HOW TO MAKE A CROWN OF CLOVER.
BUT YOU, TÔYA, WERE IN A BAD MOOD BECAUSE SAKURA SO OBVIOUSLY ENJOYED HERSELF.
IT WASN'T JUST THAT.
WHEN I LOOKED AT THE BRAT...
...I COULD ONLY FEEL UNEASY.

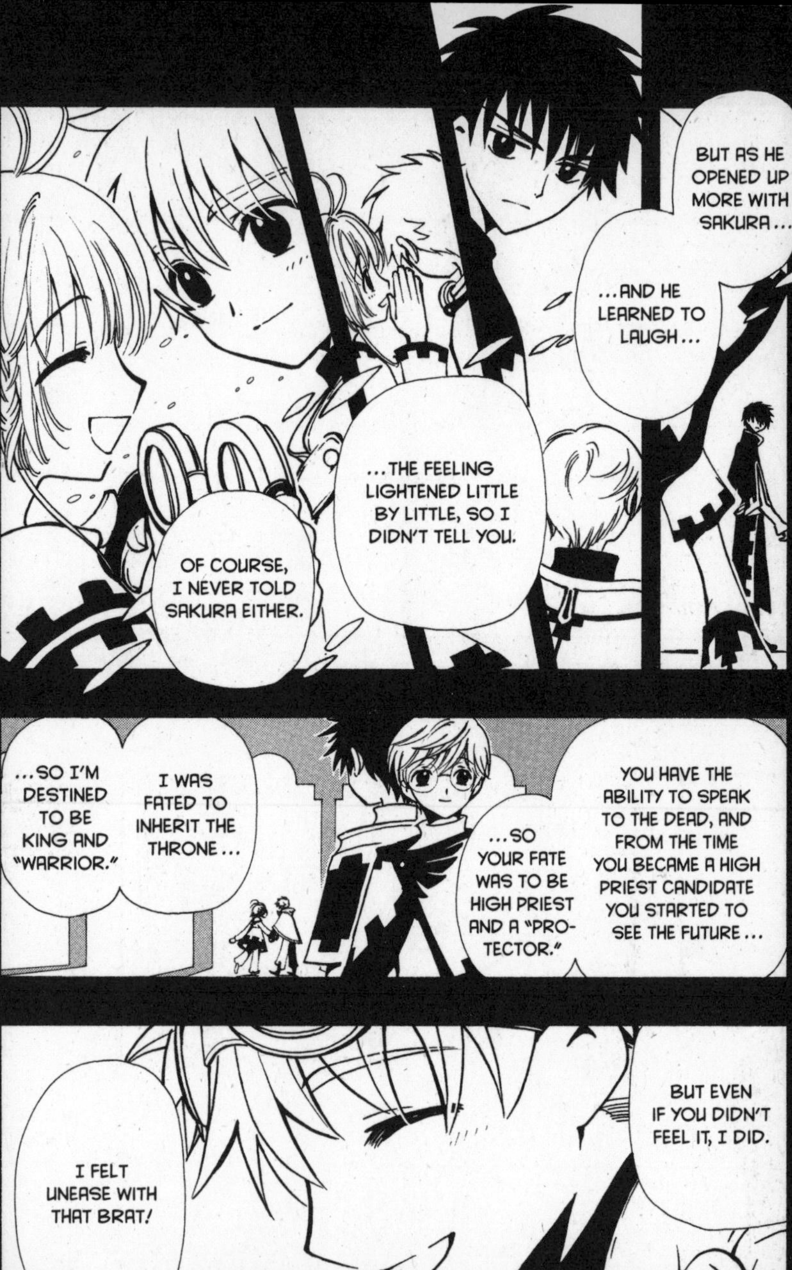
BUT AS HE OPENED UP MORE WITH SAKURA...
...AND HE LEARNED TO LAUGH...
...THE FEELING LIGHTENED LITTLE BY LITTLE, SO I DIDN'T TELL YOU.
OF COURSE, I NEVER TOLD SAKURA EITHER.
YOU HAVE THE ABILITY TO SPEAK TO THE DEAD, AND FROM THE TIME YOU BECAME A HIGH PRIEST CANDIDATE YOU STARTED TO SEE THE FUTURE...
...SO YOUR FATE WAS TO BE HIGH PRIEST AND A "PRO-TECTOR."
I WAS FATED TO INHERIT THE THRONE...
...SO I'M DESTINED TO BE KING AND "WARRIOR."
BUT EVEN IF YOU DIDN'T FEEL IT, I DID.
I FELT UNEASE WITH THAT BRAT!

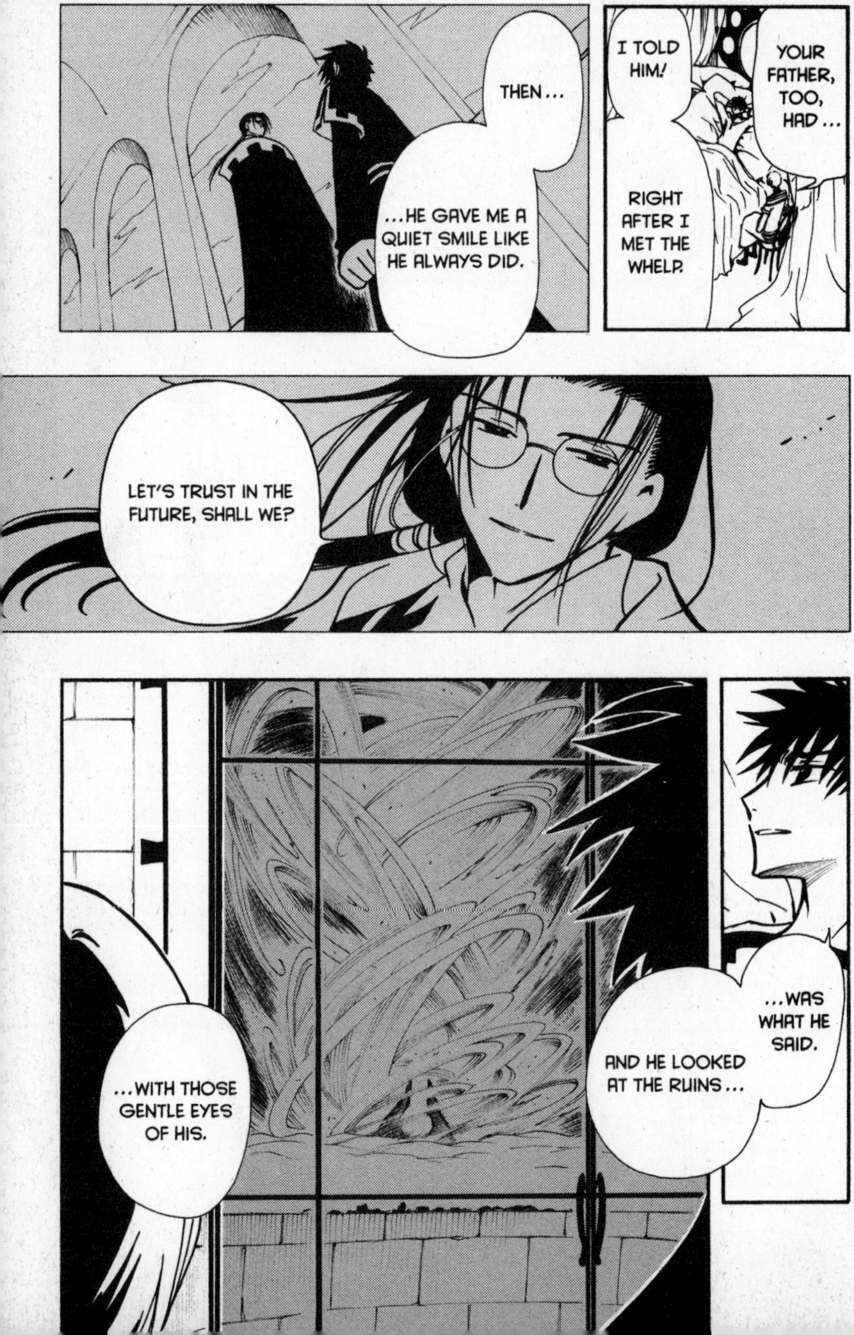
YOUR FATHER, TOO, HAD ...
I TOLD HIM!
RIGHT AFTER I MET THE WHELP.
THEN ...
... HE GAVE ME A QUIET SMILE LIKE HE ALWAYS DID.
LET'S TRUST IN THE FUTURE, SHALL WE?
... WAS WHAT HE SAID.
AND HE LOOKED AT THE RUINS ...
... WITH THOSE GENTLE EYES OF HIS.

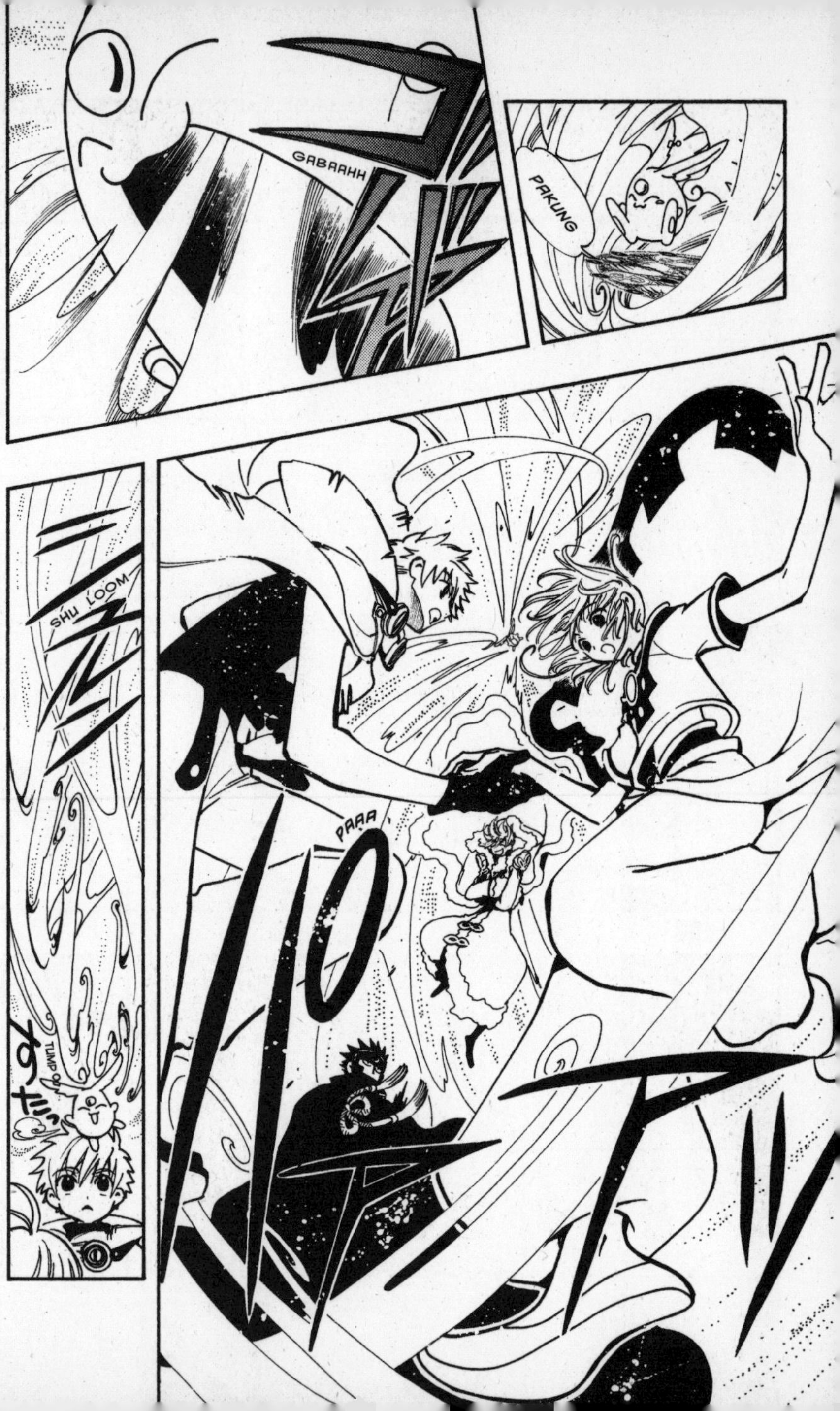
PAKUNG
GABAAHH
PAAA
SHU LOOM
TUMP
すたっ

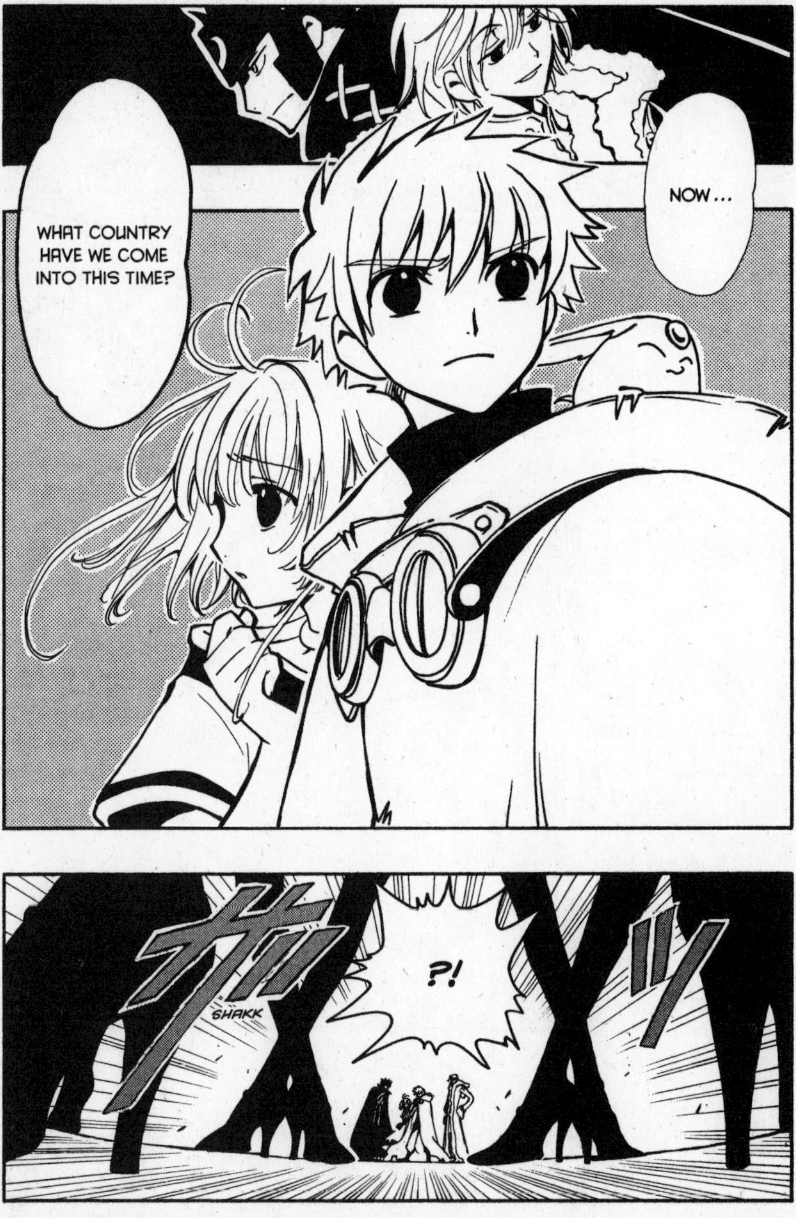
NOW...
WHAT COUNTRY HAVE WE COME INTO THIS TIME?
?!
SHAKK

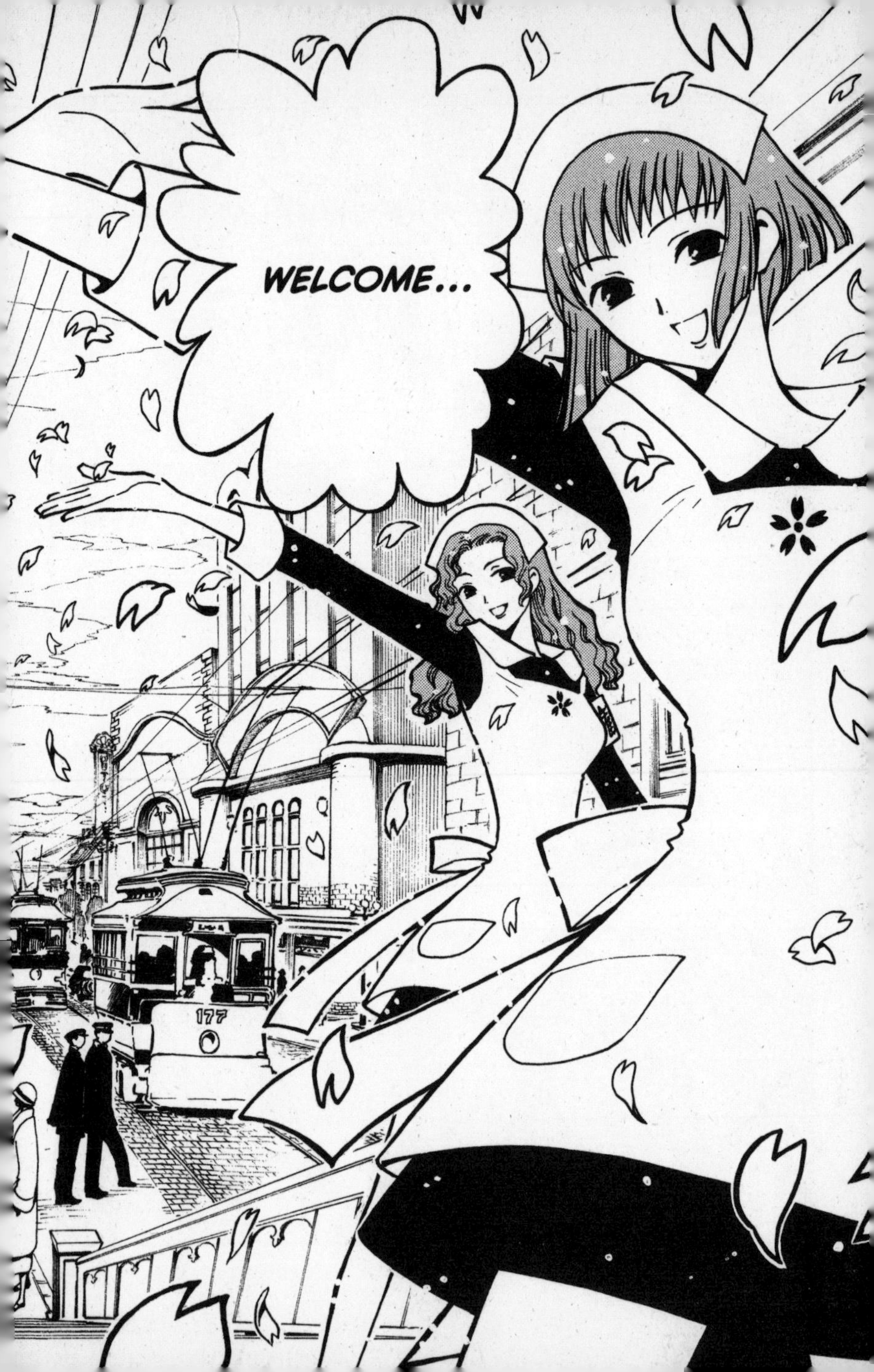
WELCOME...

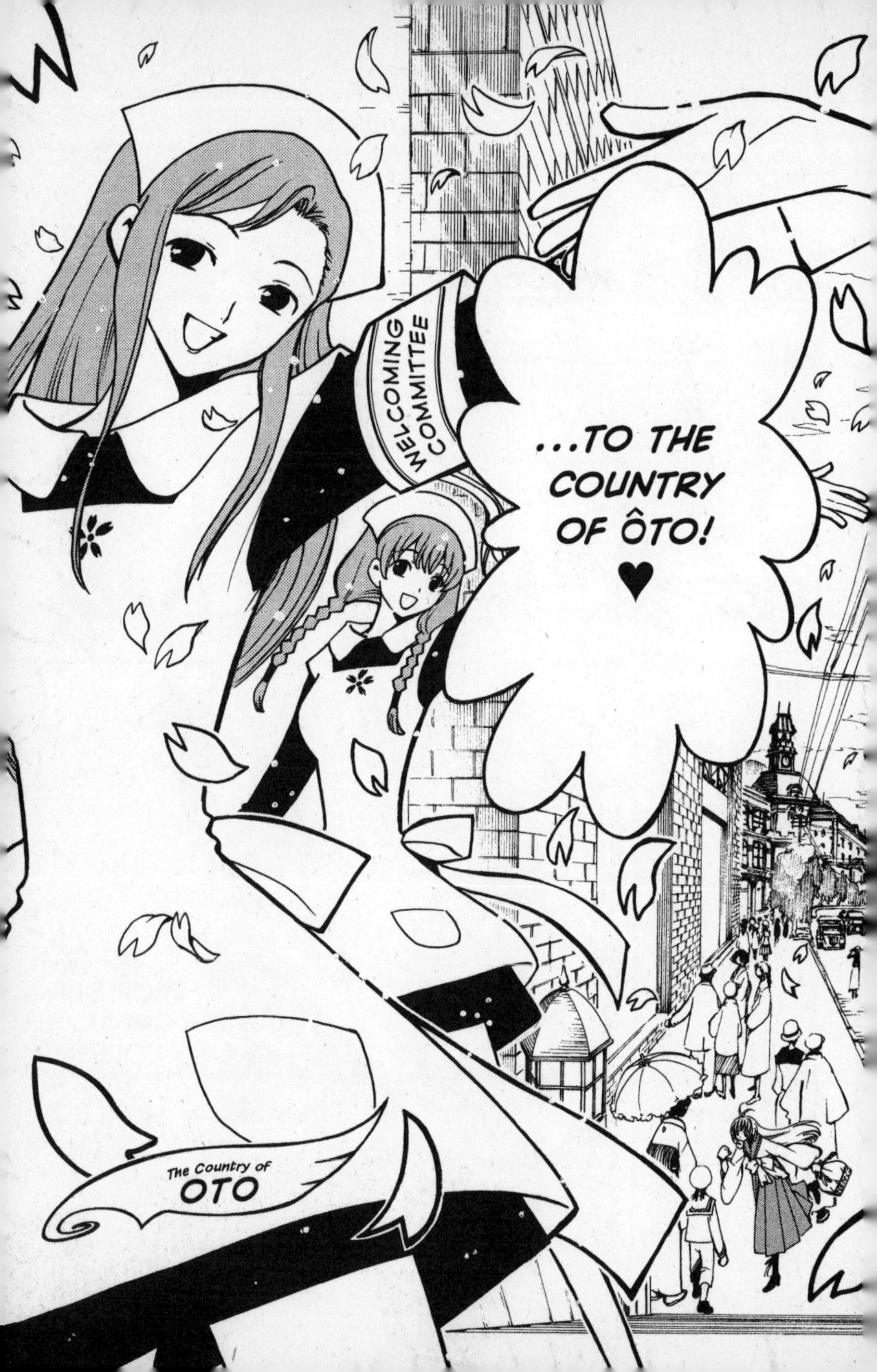
...TO THE COUNTRY OF ÔTO! ♥
WELCOMING COMMITTEE
The Country of OTO

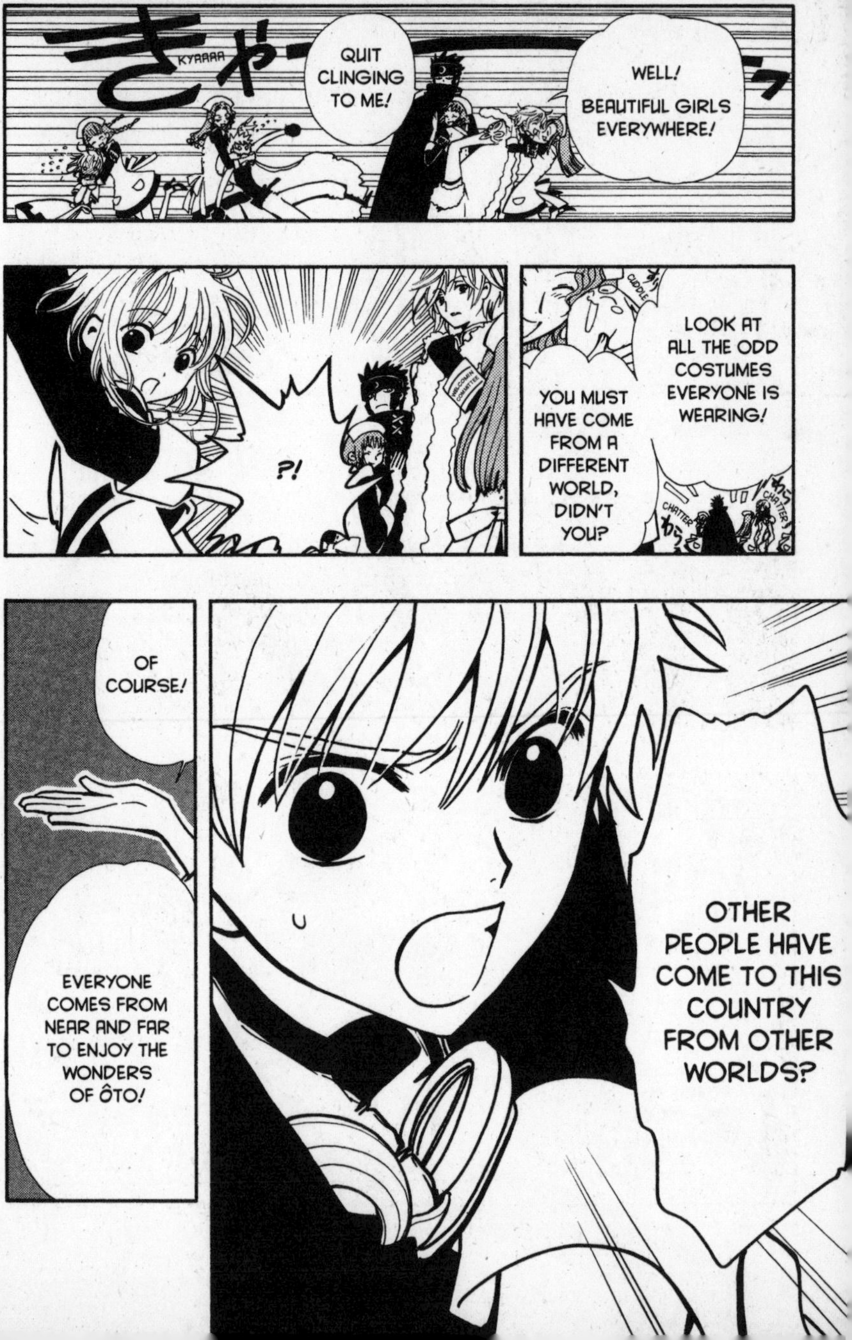
WELL! BEAUTIFUL GIRLS EVERYWHERE!
QUIT CLINGING TO ME!
KYAAAA
CUDDLE
LOOK AT ALL THE ODD COSTUMES EVERYONE IS WEARING!
YOU MUST HAVE COME FROM A DIFFERENT WORLD, DIDN'T YOU?
CHATTER
CHATTER
?!
OTHER PEOPLE HAVE COME TO THIS COUNTRY FROM OTHER WORLDS?
OF COURSE!
EVERYONE COMES FROM NEAR AND FAR TO ENJOY THE WONDERS OF ÔTO!

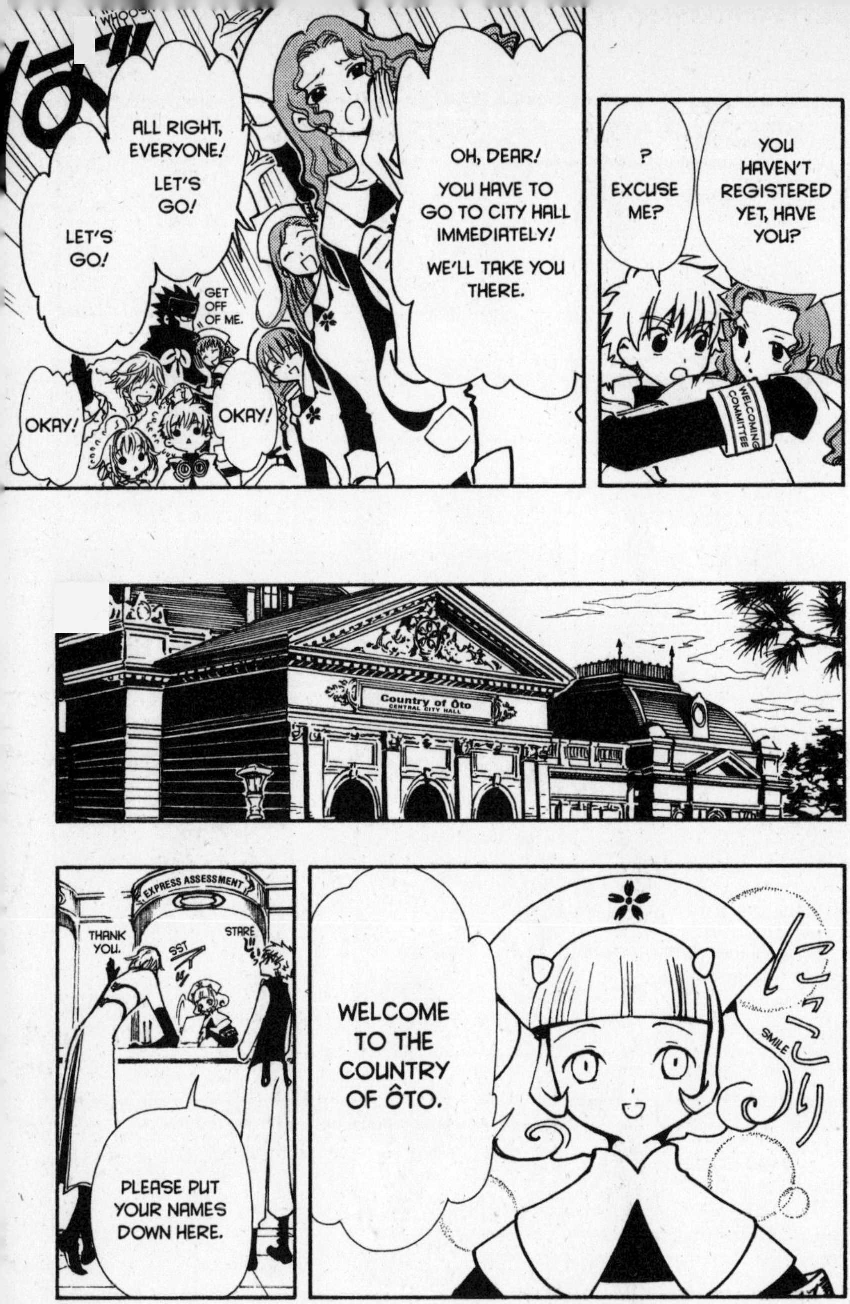
YOU HAVEN'T REGISTERED YET, HAVE YOU?
? EXCUSE ME?
WELCOMING COMMITTEE
OH, DEAR!
YOU HAVE TO GO TO CITY HALL IMMEDIATELY!
WE'LL TAKE YOU THERE.
ALL RIGHT, EVERYONE!
LET'S GO!
LET'S GO!
GET OFF OF ME.
OKAY!
OKAY!
Country of Ôto
CENTRAL CITY HALL
WELCOME TO THE COUNTRY OF ÔTO.
SMILE
EXPRESS ASSESSMENT
STARE
THANK YOU.
SST
PLEASE PUT YOUR NAMES DOWN HERE.

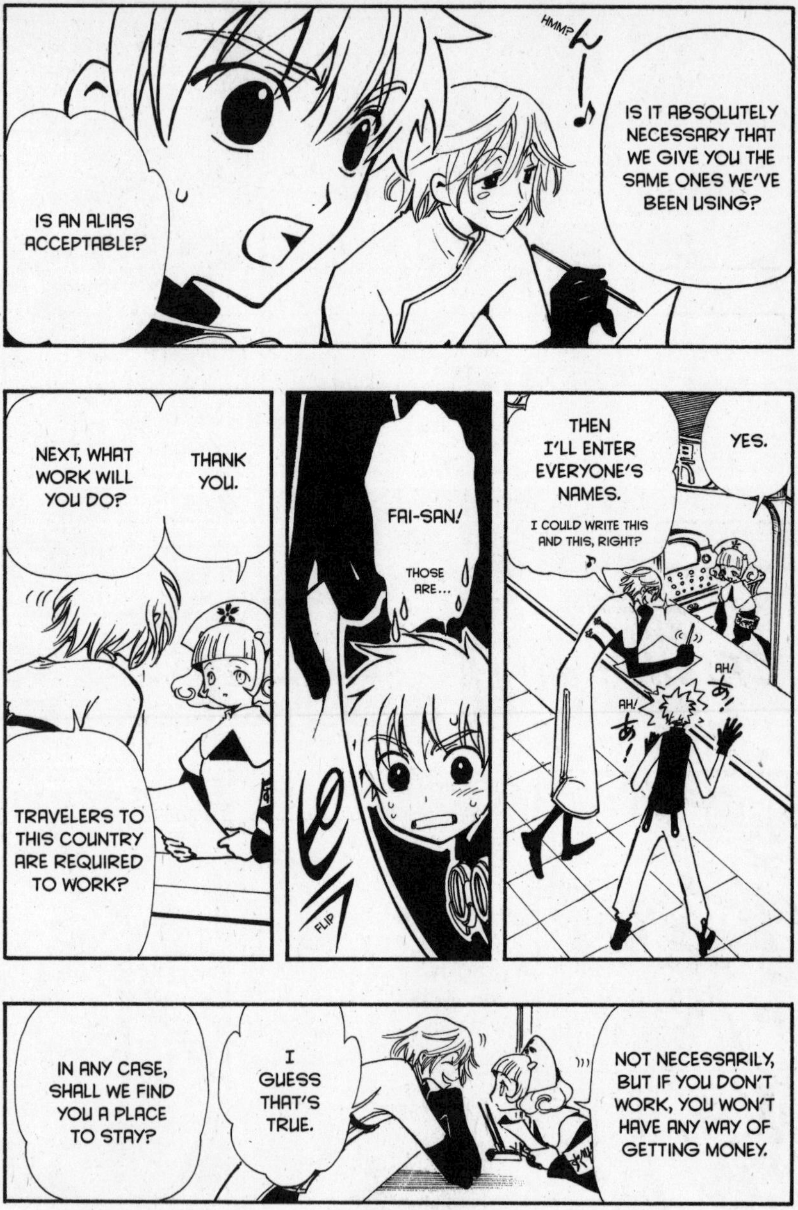
HMM?
IS IT ABSOLUTELY NECESSARY THAT WE GIVE YOU THE SAME ONES WE'VE BEEN USING?
IS AN ALIAS ACCEPTABLE?
YES.
THEN I'LL ENTER EVERYONE'S NAMES.
I COULD WRITE THIS AND THIS, RIGHT? ♪
AH! あ!
AH! あ!
FAI-SAN!
THOSE ARE...
FLIP
THANK YOU.
NEXT, WHAT WORK WILL YOU DO?
TRAVELERS TO THIS COUNTRY ARE REQUIRED TO WORK?
NOT NECESSARILY, BUT IF YOU DON'T WORK, YOU WON'T HAVE ANY WAY OF GETTING MONEY.
I GUESS THAT'S TRUE.
IN ANY CASE, SHALL WE FIND YOU A PLACE TO STAY?

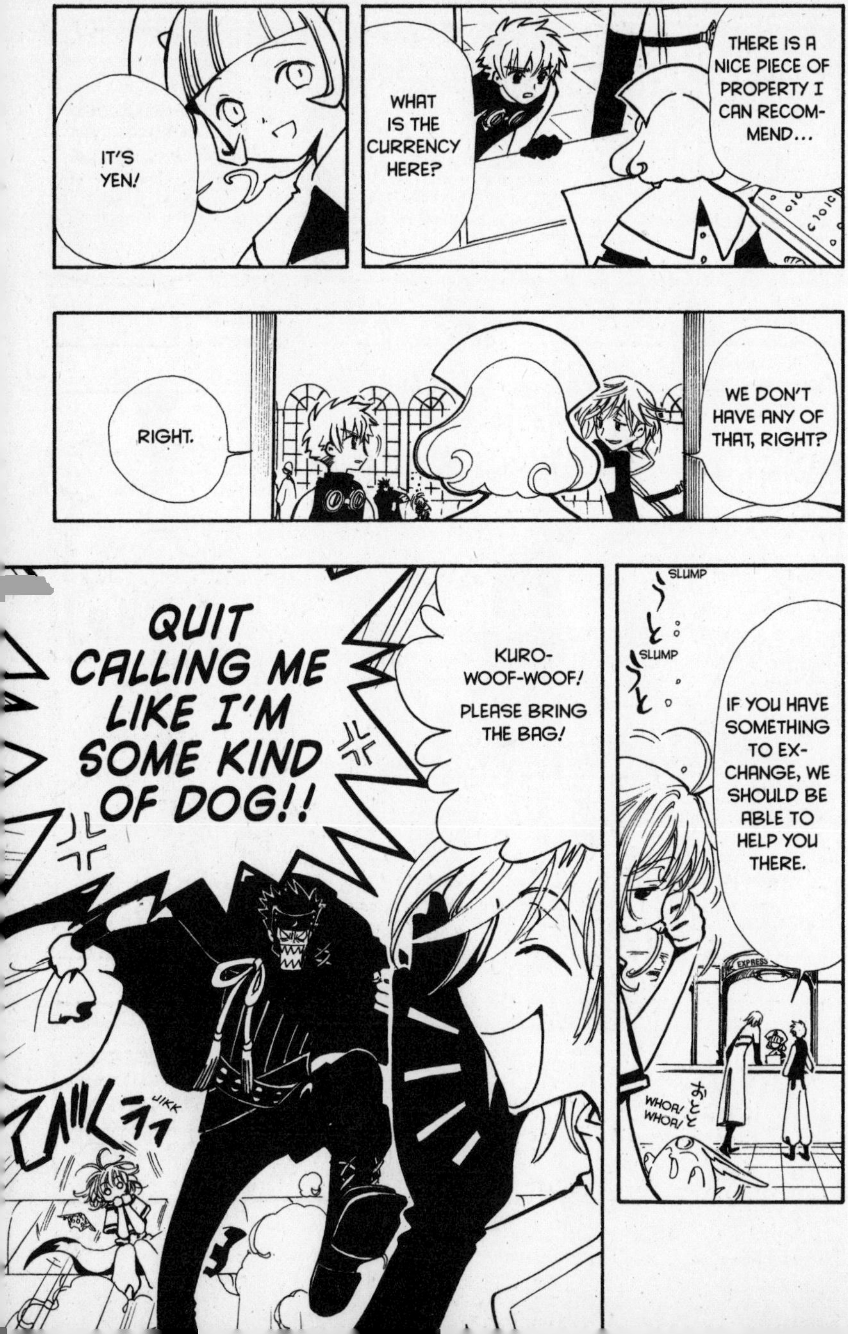
THERE IS A NICE PIECE OF PROPERTY I CAN RECOMMEND...
WHAT IS THE CURRENCY HERE?
IT'S YEN!
WE DON'T HAVE ANY OF THAT, RIGHT?
RIGHT.
SLUMP
SLUMP
IF YOU HAVE SOMETHING TO EXCHANGE, WE SHOULD BE ABLE TO HELP YOU THERE.
EXPRESS
WHOA! WHOA!
KURO-WOOF-WOOF! PLEASE BRING THE BAG!
QUIT CALLING ME LIKE I'M SOME KIND OF DOG!!
JIKK

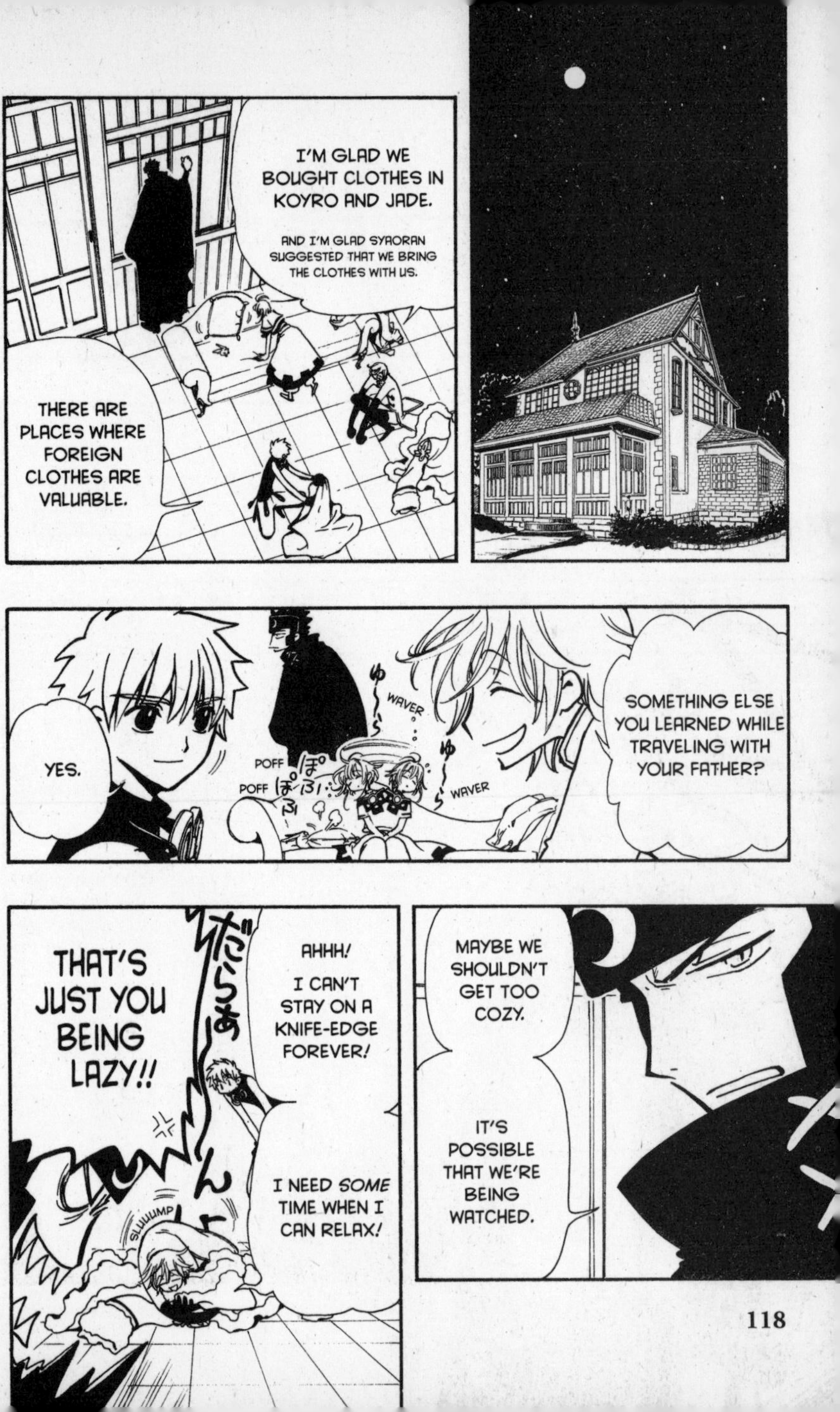
I'M GLAD WE BOUGHT CLOTHES IN KOYRO AND JADE.
AND I'M GLAD SYAORAN SUGGESTED THAT WE BRING THE CLOTHES WITH US.
THERE ARE PLACES WHERE FOREIGN CLOTHES ARE VALUABLE.
SOMETHING ELSE YOU LEARNED WHILE TRAVELING WITH YOUR FATHER?
ゆ～ら WAVER
ゆ～ら WAVER
ぽふぽふ POFF POFF
YES.
MAYBE WE SHOULDN'T GET TOO COZY.
IT'S POSSIBLE THAT WE'RE BEING WATCHED.
AHHH!
I CAN'T STAY ON A KNIFE-EDGE FOREVER!
I NEED *SOME* TIME WHEN I CAN RELAX!
だらぁ～ん SLUUUMP
THAT'S JUST YOU BEING LAZY!!

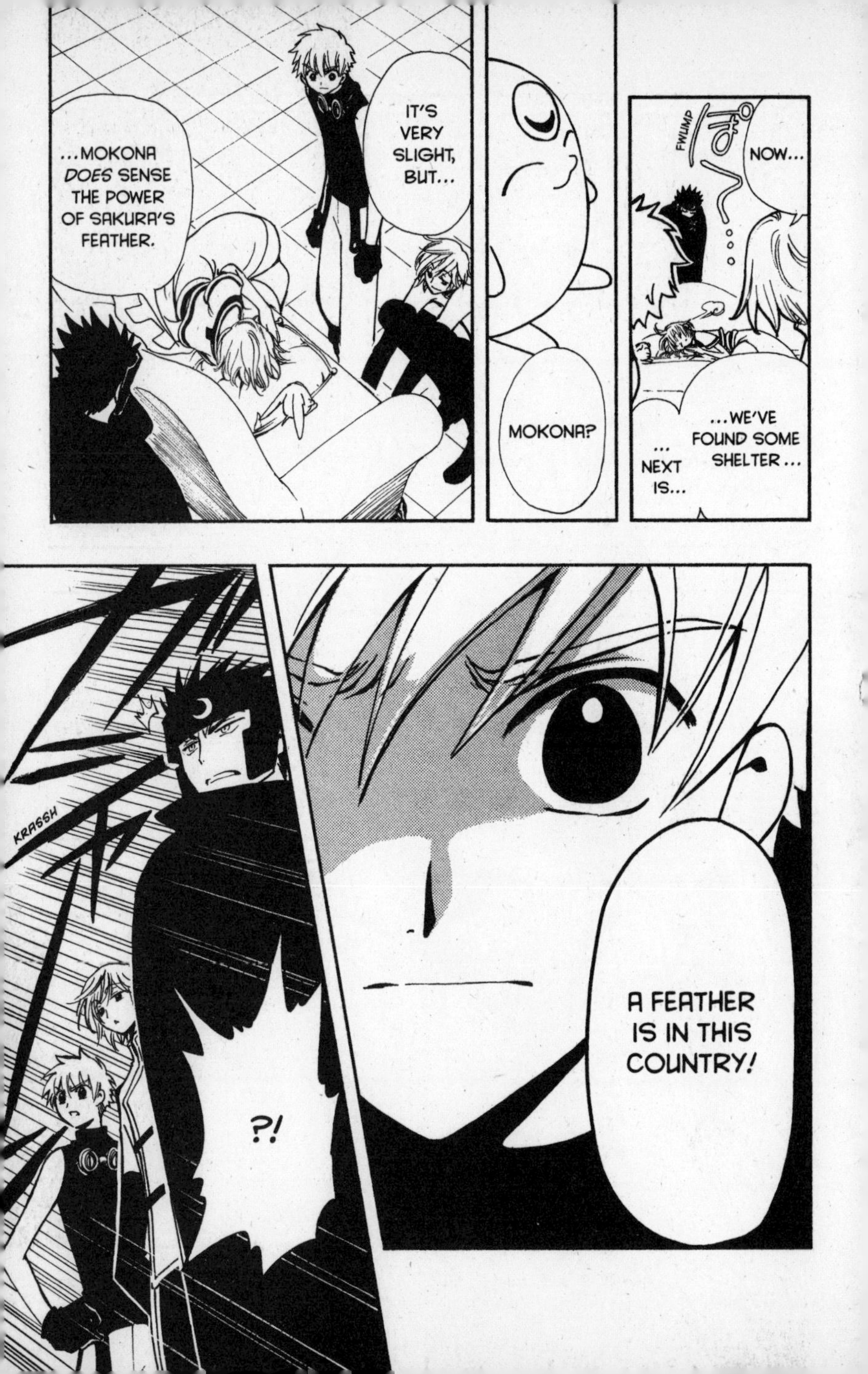
NOW...
FWUMP
...WE'VE FOUND SOME SHELTER...
... NEXT IS...
MOKONA?
IT'S VERY SLIGHT, BUT...
...MOKONA *DOES* SENSE THE POWER OF SAKURA'S FEATHER.
A FEATHER IS IN THIS COUNTRY!
KRASSH
?!

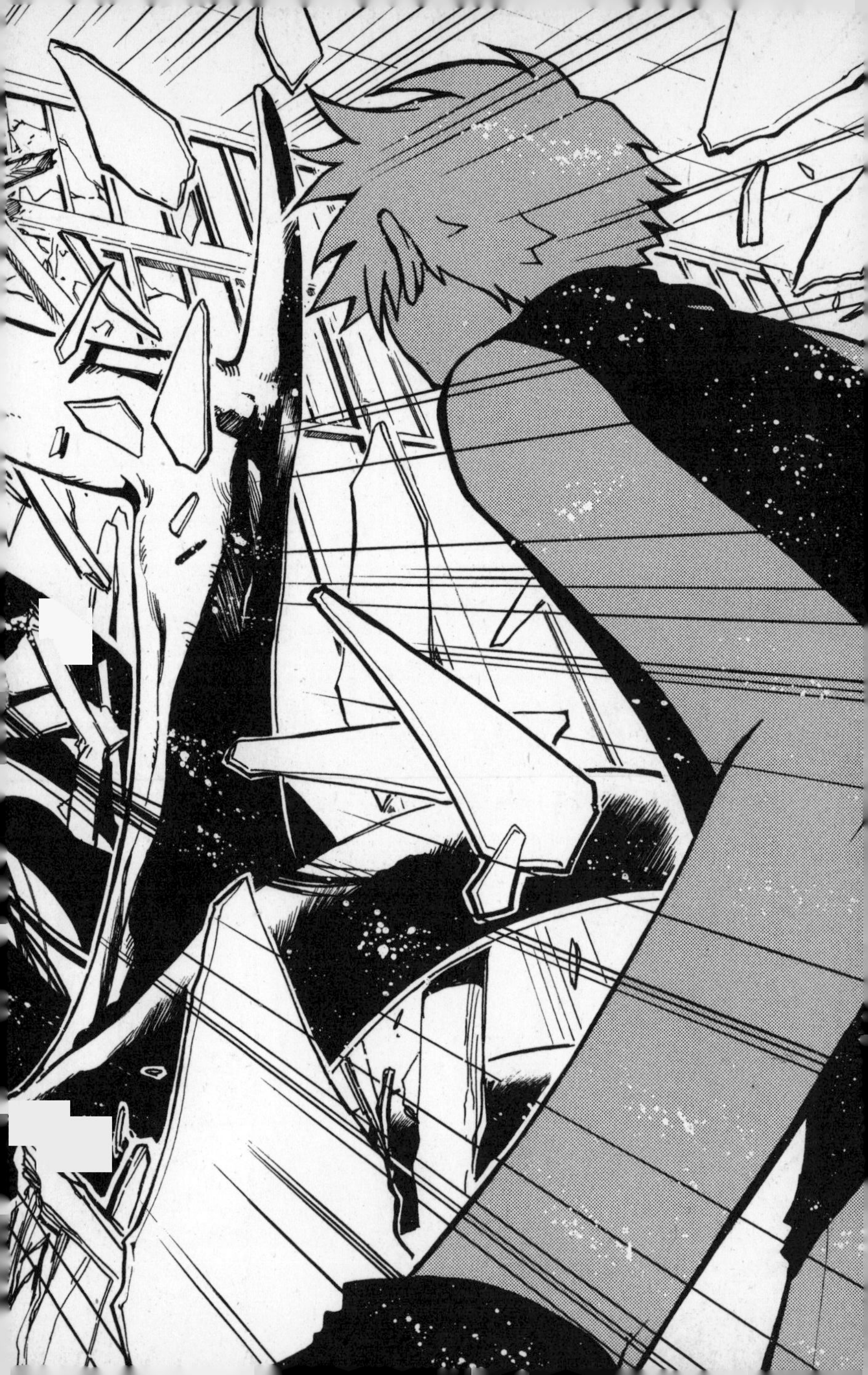

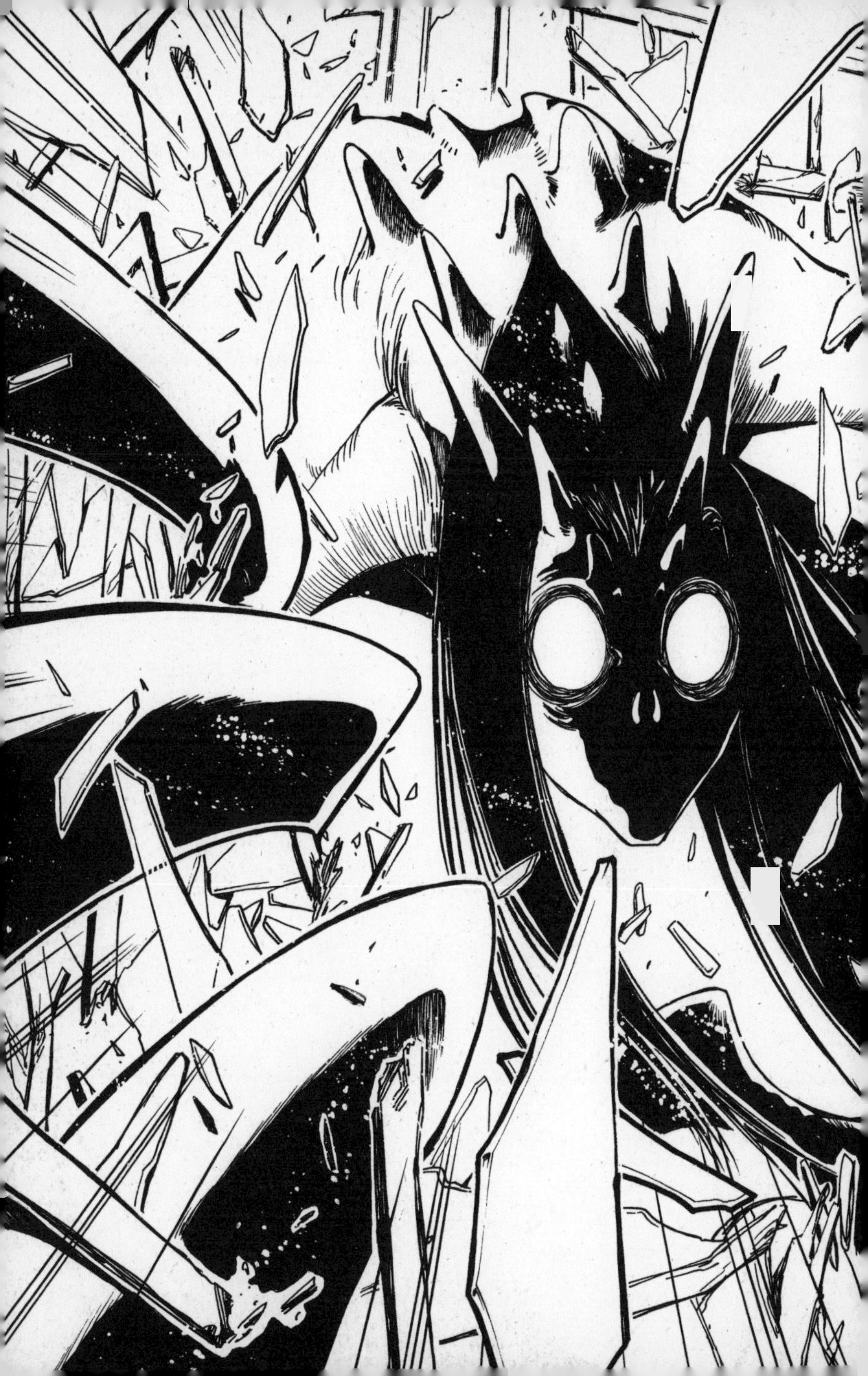

ツバサ

RESERVoir CHRoNiCLE

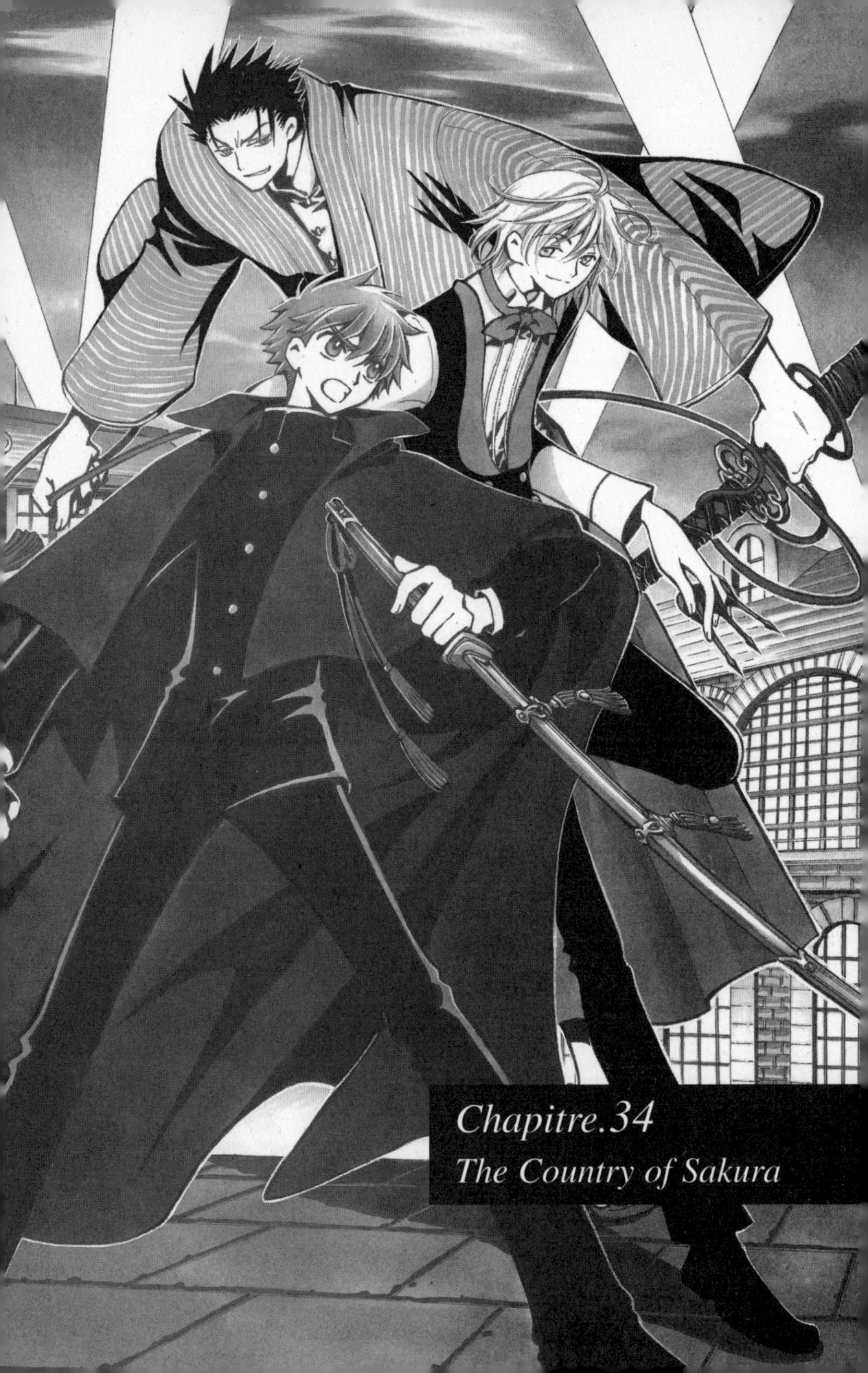
Chapitre.34
The Country of Sakura

ツバサ

RESERVoir CHRoNiCLE

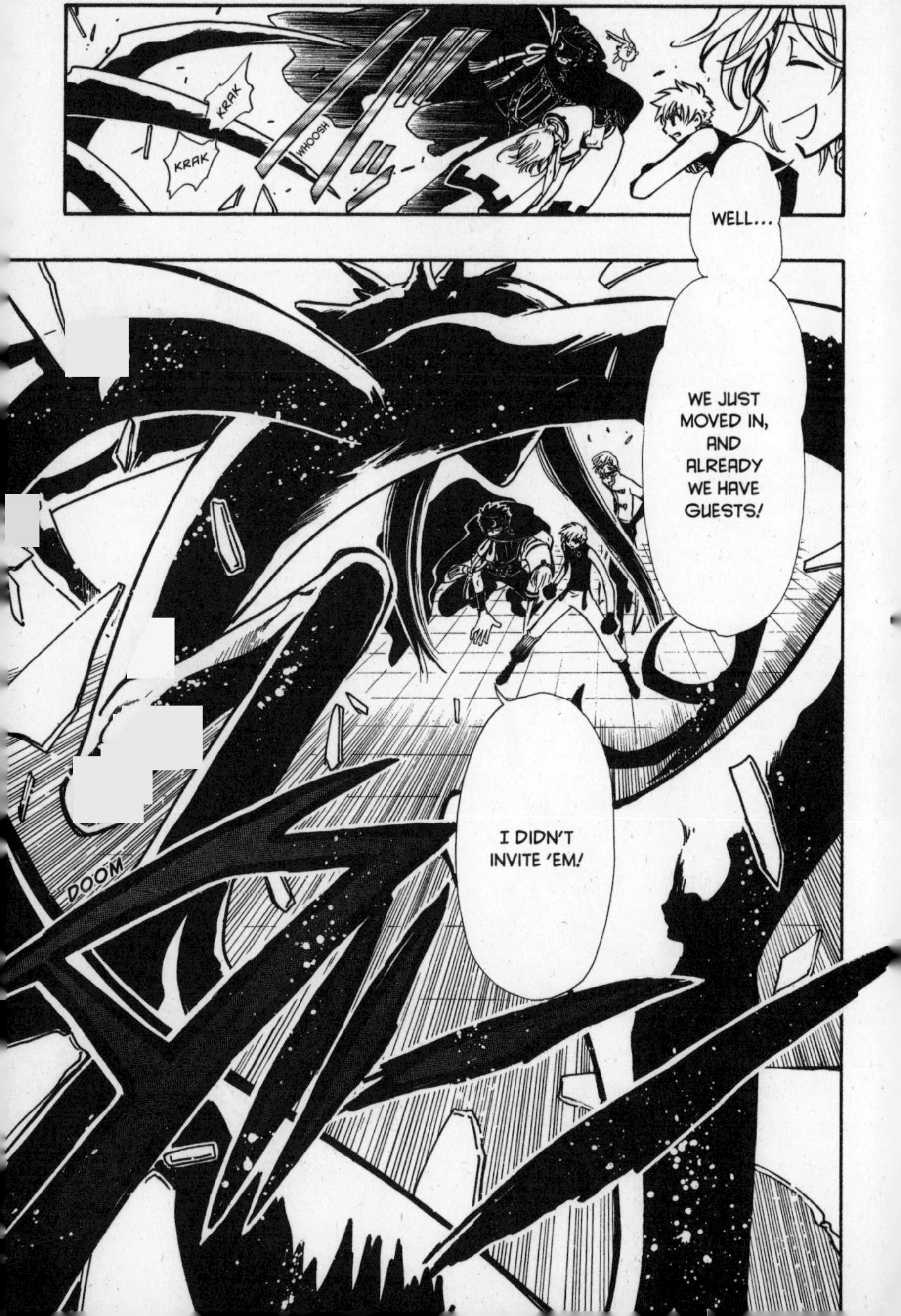
WHOOSH
KRAK
KRAK
WELL...
WE JUST MOVED IN, AND ALREADY WE HAVE GUESTS!
I DIDN'T INVITE 'EM!
DOOM

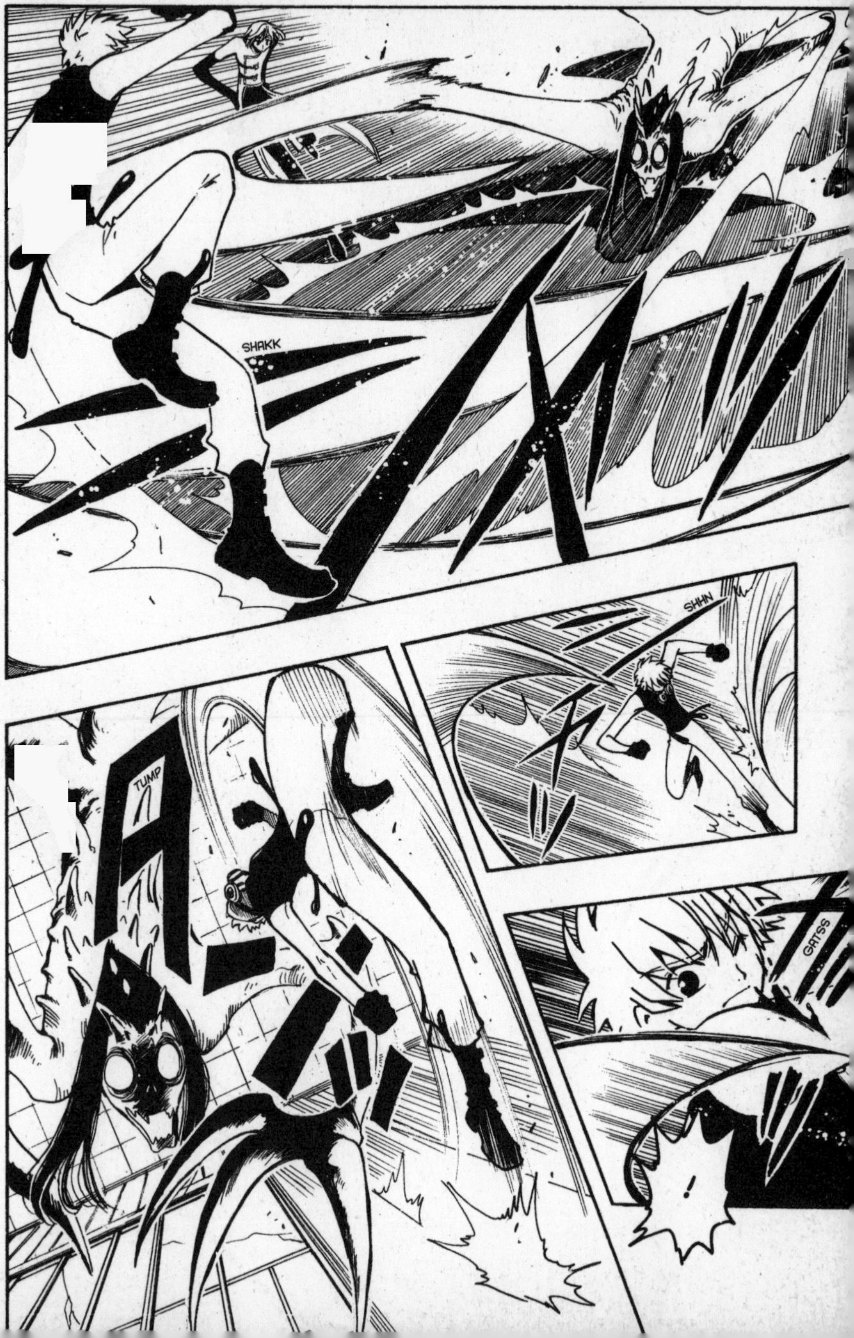
SHAKK
SHHN
GATSS
!
TUMP

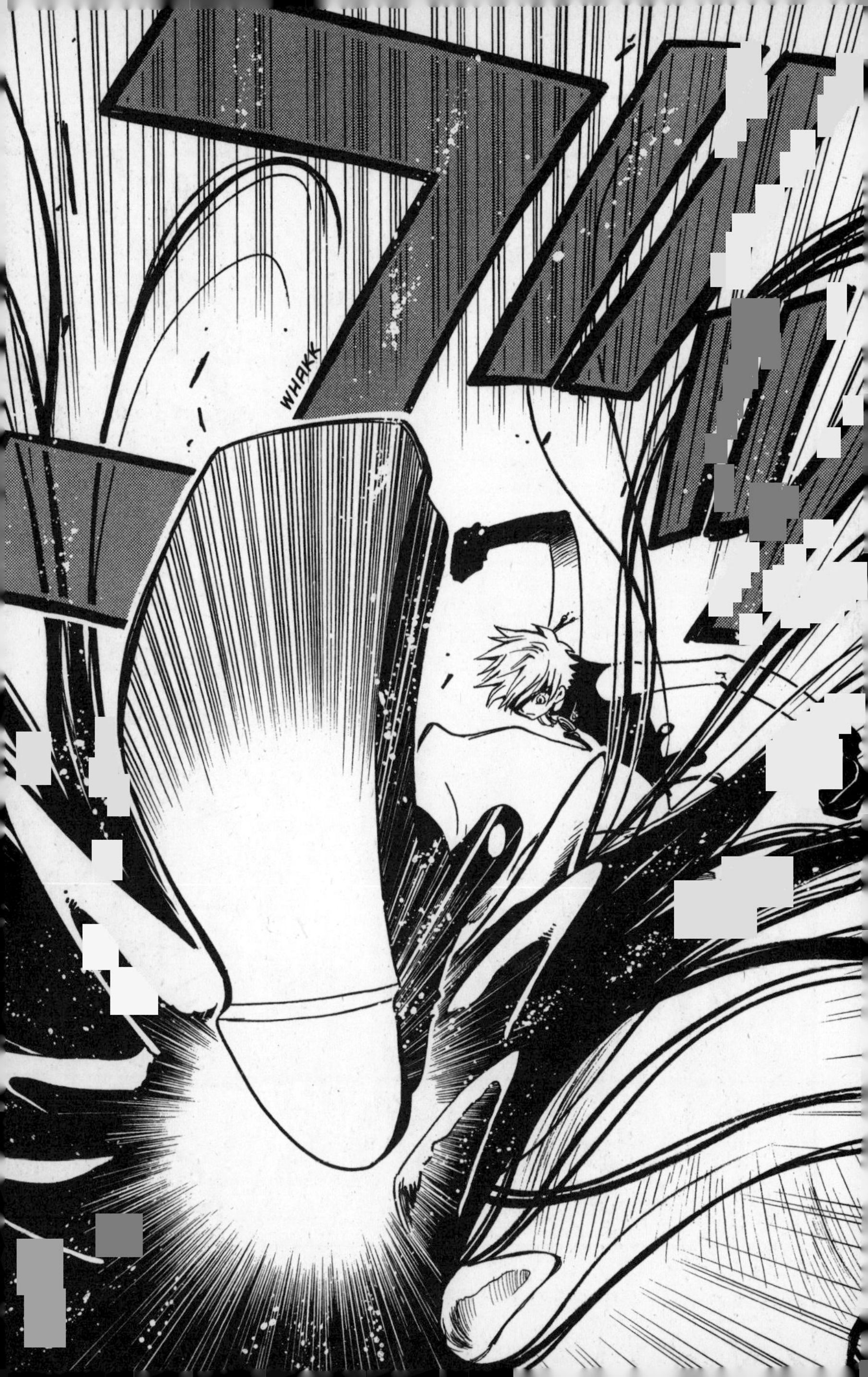
WHAKK

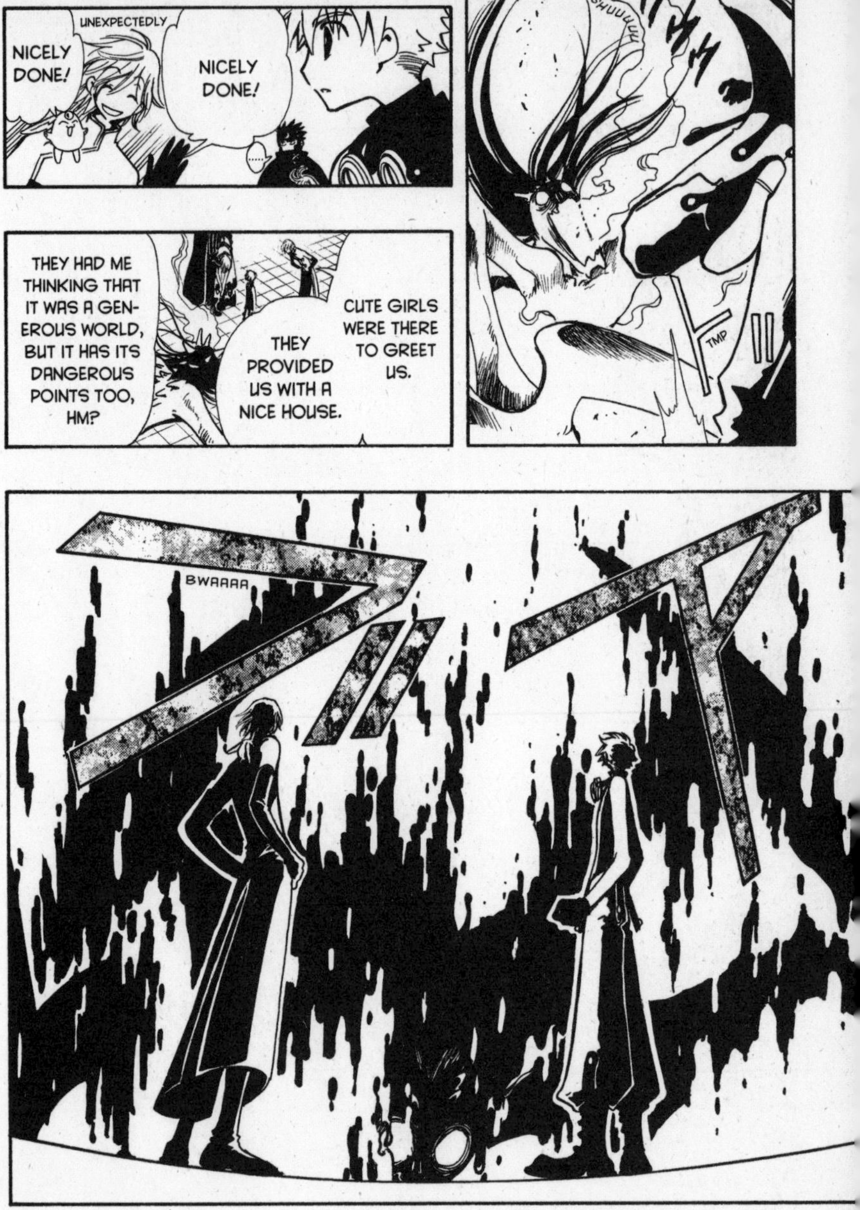
SHUUUUH
TMP
NICELY DONE!
......
UNEXPECTEDLY
NICELY DONE!
CUTE GIRLS WERE THERE TO GREET US.
THEY PROVIDED US WITH A NICE HOUSE.
THEY HAD ME THINKING THAT IT WAS A GENEROUS WORLD, BUT IT HAS ITS DANGEROUS POINTS TOO, HM?
BWAAAA

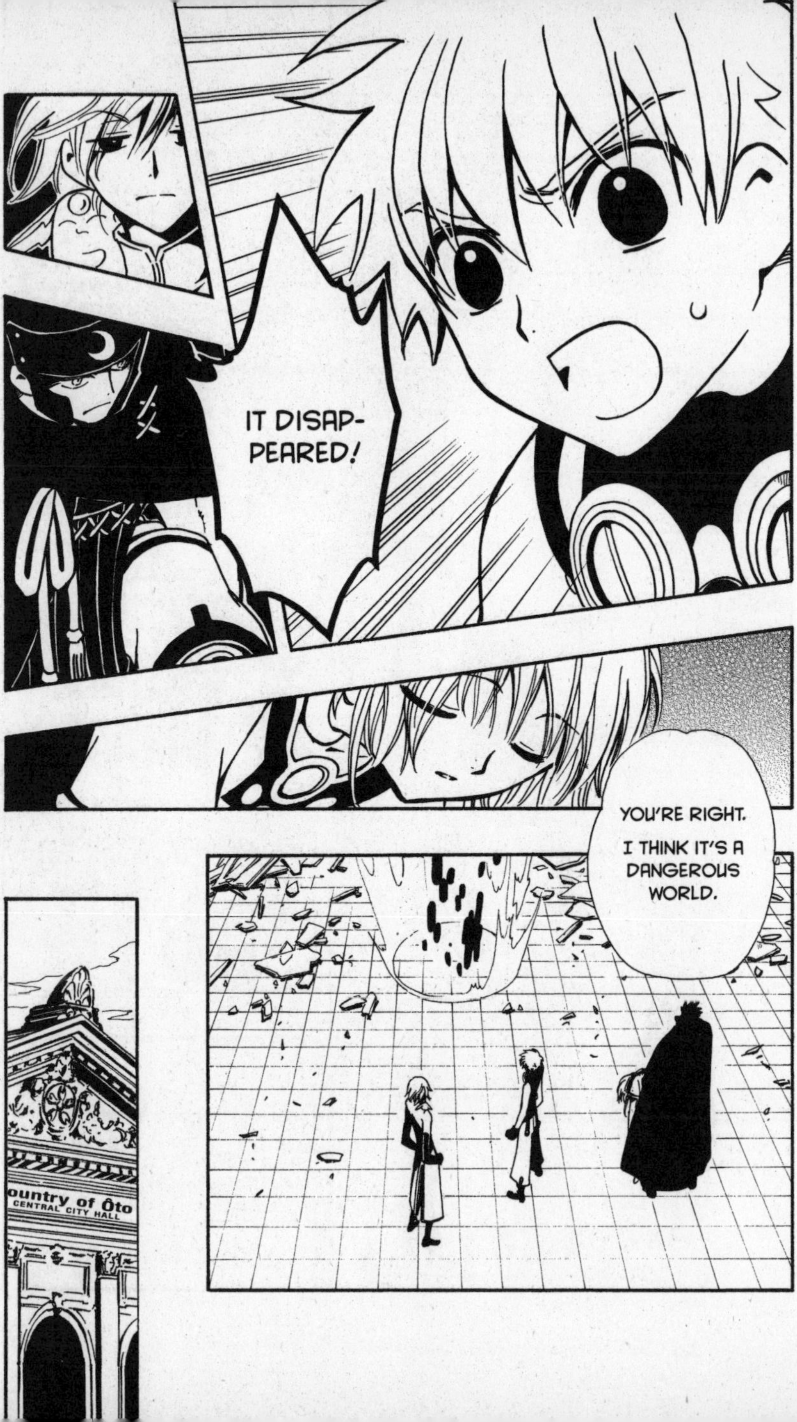
IT DISAPPEARED!
YOU'RE RIGHT. I THINK IT'S A DANGEROUS WORLD.
ountry of Ôto
CENTRAL CITY HALL

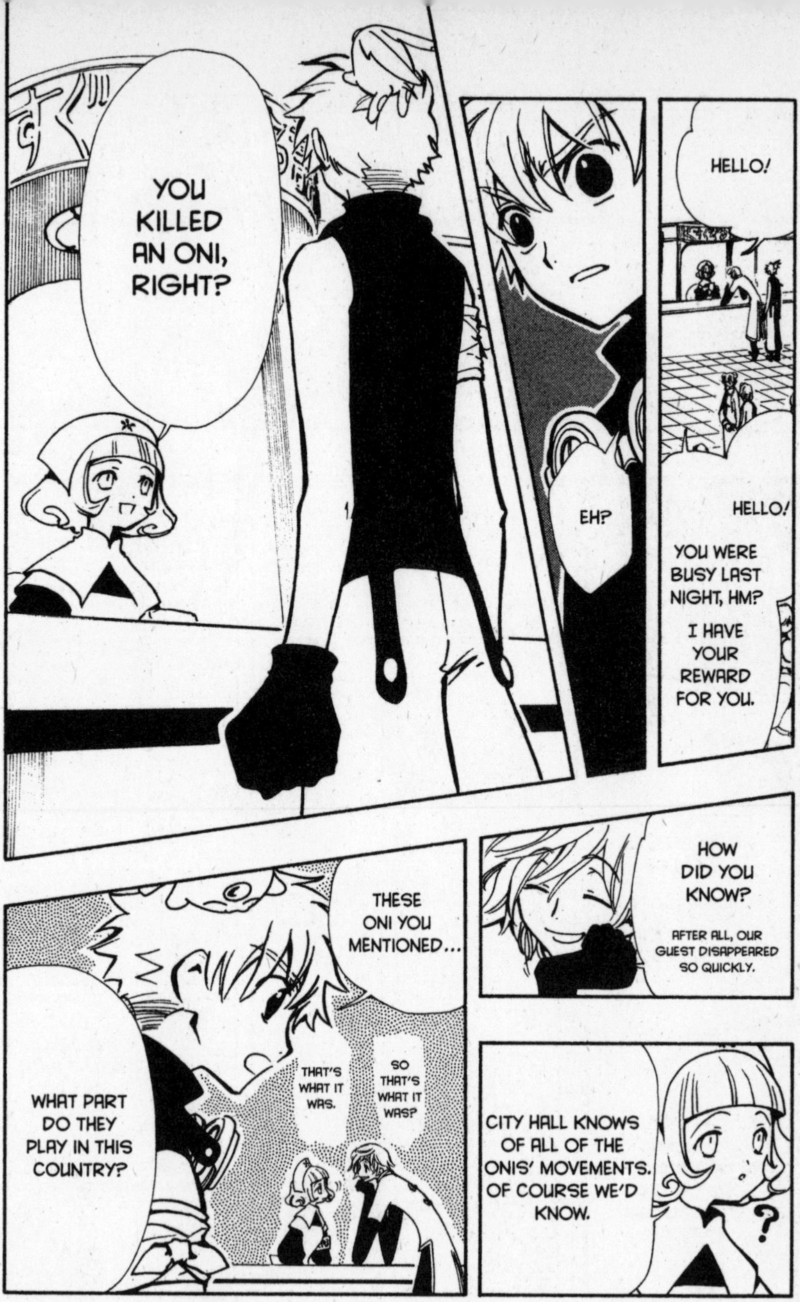
HELLO!
HELLO!
YOU WERE BUSY LAST NIGHT, HM?
I HAVE YOUR REWARD FOR YOU.
EH?
YOU KILLED AN ONI, RIGHT?
HOW DID YOU KNOW?
AFTER ALL, OUR GUEST DISAPPEARED SO QUICKLY.
CITY HALL KNOWS OF ALL OF THE ONIS' MOVEMENTS. OF COURSE WE'D KNOW.
THESE ONI YOU MENTIONED...
SO THAT'S WHAT IT WAS?
THAT'S WHAT IT WAS.
WHAT PART DO THEY PLAY IN THIS COUNTRY?

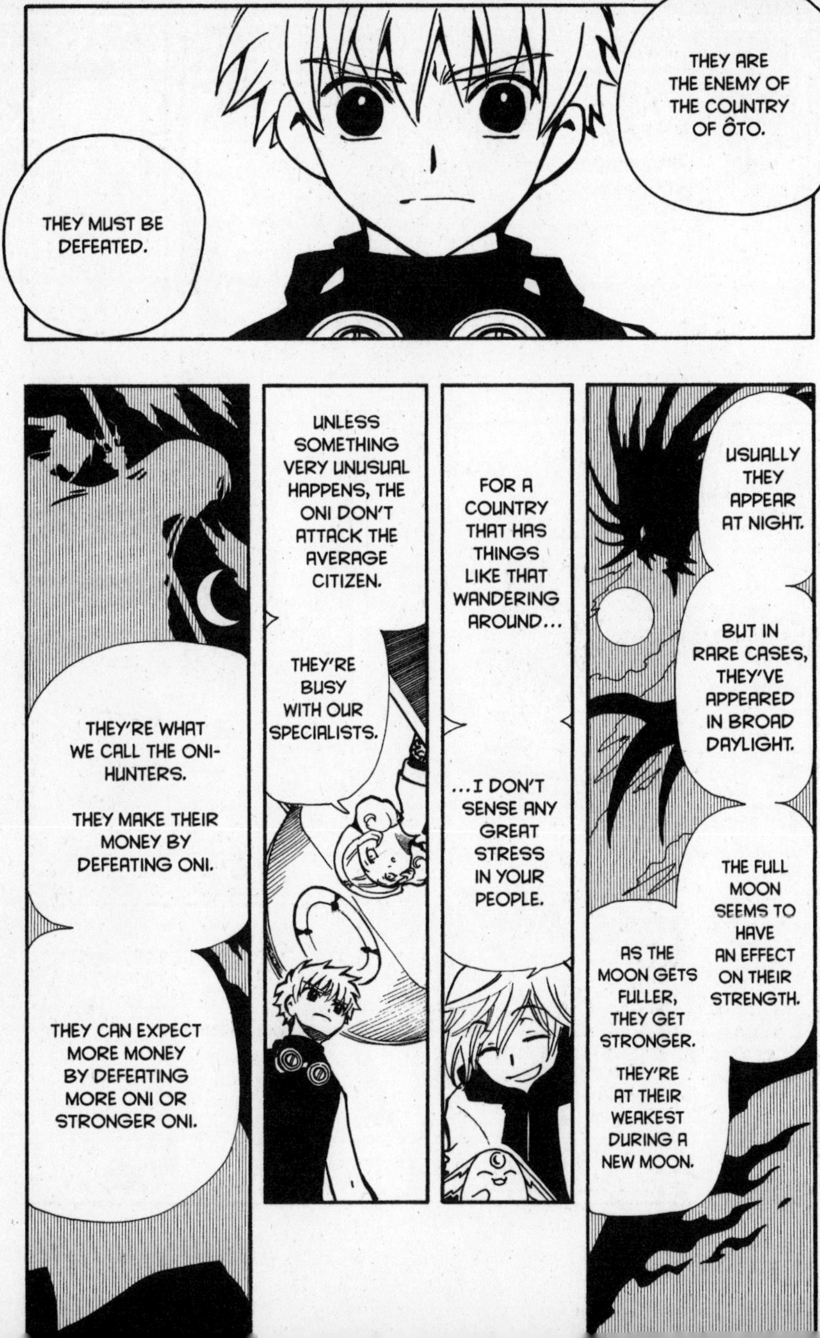
THEY ARE THE ENEMY OF THE COUNTRY OF ÔTO.
THEY MUST BE DEFEATED.
USUALLY THEY APPEAR AT NIGHT.
BUT IN RARE CASES, THEY'VE APPEARED IN BROAD DAYLIGHT.
THE FULL MOON SEEMS TO HAVE AN EFFECT ON THEIR STRENGTH.
AS THE MOON GETS FULLER, THEY GET STRONGER.
THEY'RE AT THEIR WEAKEST DURING A NEW MOON.
FOR A COUNTRY THAT HAS THINGS LIKE THAT WANDERING AROUND...
...I DON'T SENSE ANY GREAT STRESS IN YOUR PEOPLE.
UNLESS SOMETHING VERY UNUSUAL HAPPENS, THE ONI DON'T ATTACK THE AVERAGE CITIZEN.
THEY'RE BUSY WITH OUR SPECIALISTS.
THEY'RE WHAT WE CALL THE ONI-HUNTERS.
THEY MAKE THEIR MONEY BY DEFEATING ONI.
THEY CAN EXPECT MORE MONEY BY DEFEATING MORE ONI OR STRONGER ONI.

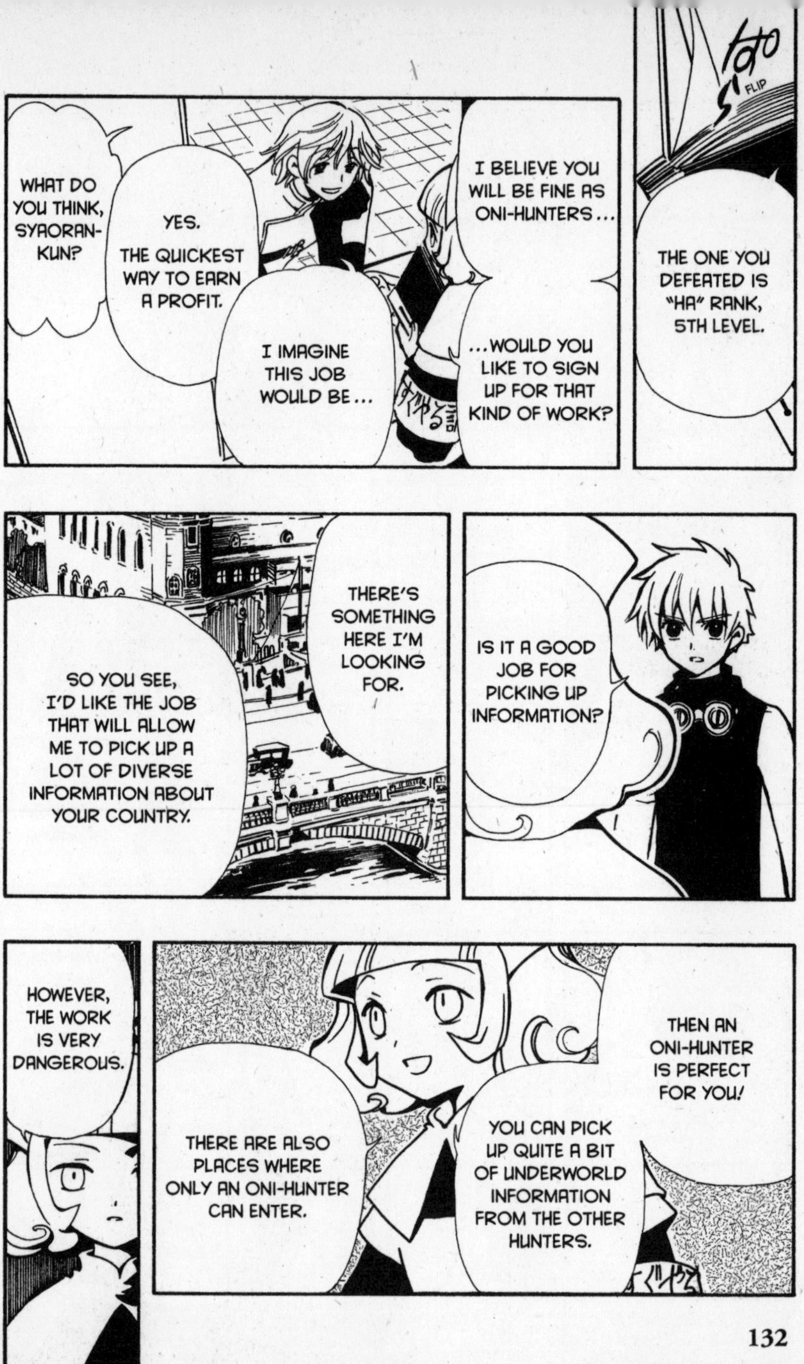
FLIP
THE ONE YOU DEFEATED IS "HA" RANK, 5TH LEVEL.
I BELIEVE YOU WILL BE FINE AS ONI-HUNTERS...
...WOULD YOU LIKE TO SIGN UP FOR THAT KIND OF WORK?
I IMAGINE THIS JOB WOULD BE...
YES. THE QUICKEST WAY TO EARN A PROFIT.
WHAT DO YOU THINK, SYAORAN-KUN?
IS IT A GOOD JOB FOR PICKING UP INFORMATION?
THERE'S SOMETHING HERE I'M LOOKING FOR.
SO YOU SEE, I'D LIKE THE JOB THAT WILL ALLOW ME TO PICK UP A LOT OF DIVERSE INFORMATION ABOUT YOUR COUNTRY.
THEN AN ONI-HUNTER IS PERFECT FOR YOU!
YOU CAN PICK UP QUITE A BIT OF UNDERWORLD INFORMATION FROM THE OTHER HUNTERS.
THERE ARE ALSO PLACES WHERE ONLY AN ONI-HUNTER CAN ENTER.
HOWEVER, THE WORK IS VERY DANGEROUS.

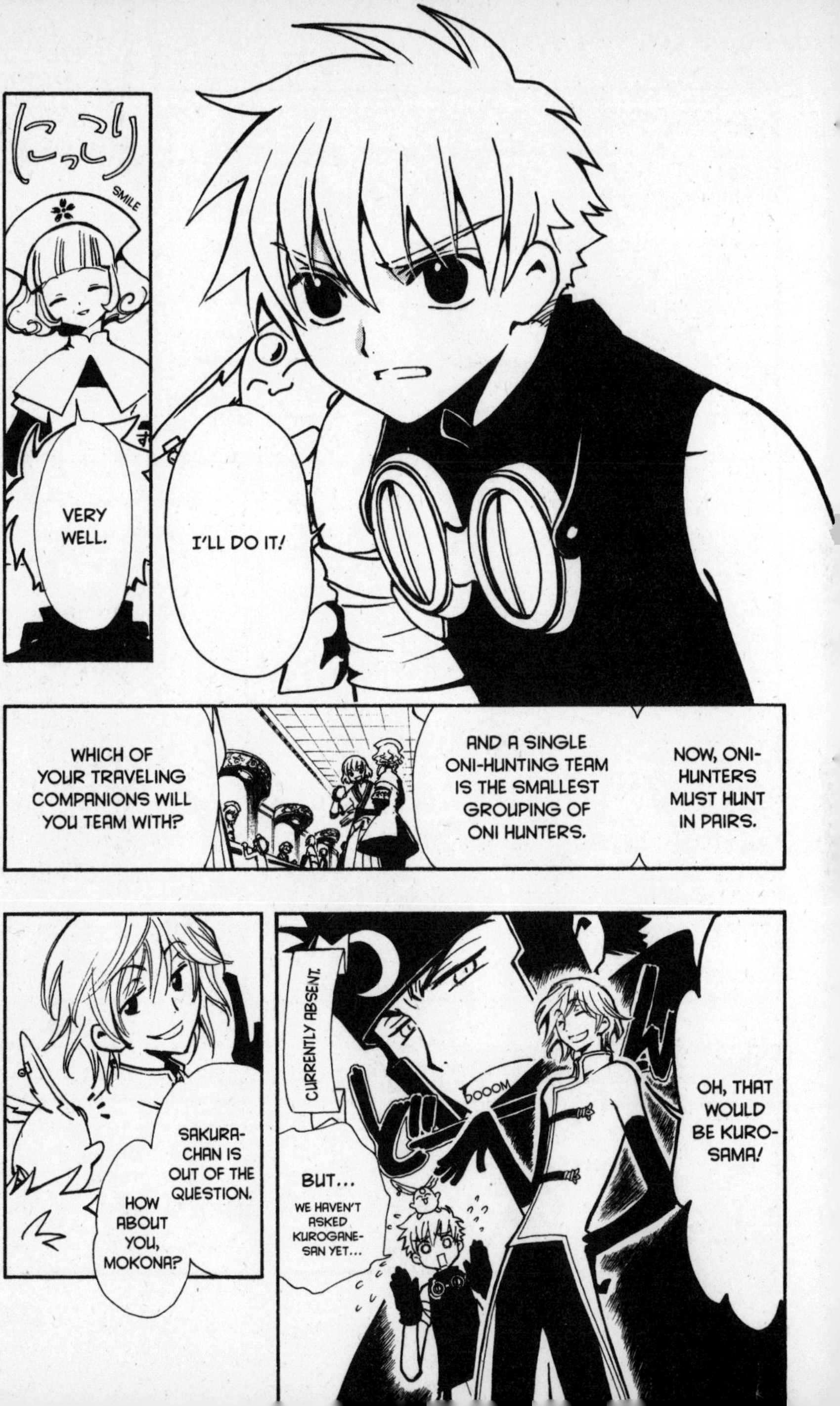
I'LL DO IT!
にっこり
SMILE
VERY WELL.
NOW, ONI-HUNTERS MUST HUNT IN PAIRS.
AND A SINGLE ONI-HUNTING TEAM IS THE SMALLEST GROUPING OF ONI HUNTERS.
WHICH OF YOUR TRAVELING COMPANIONS WILL YOU TEAM WITH?
OH, THAT WOULD BE KURO-SAMA!
BOOOM
CURRENTLY ABSENT.
BUT...
WE HAVEN'T ASKED KUROGANE-SAN YET...
SAKURA-CHAN IS OUT OF THE QUESTION.
HOW ABOUT YOU, MOKONA?

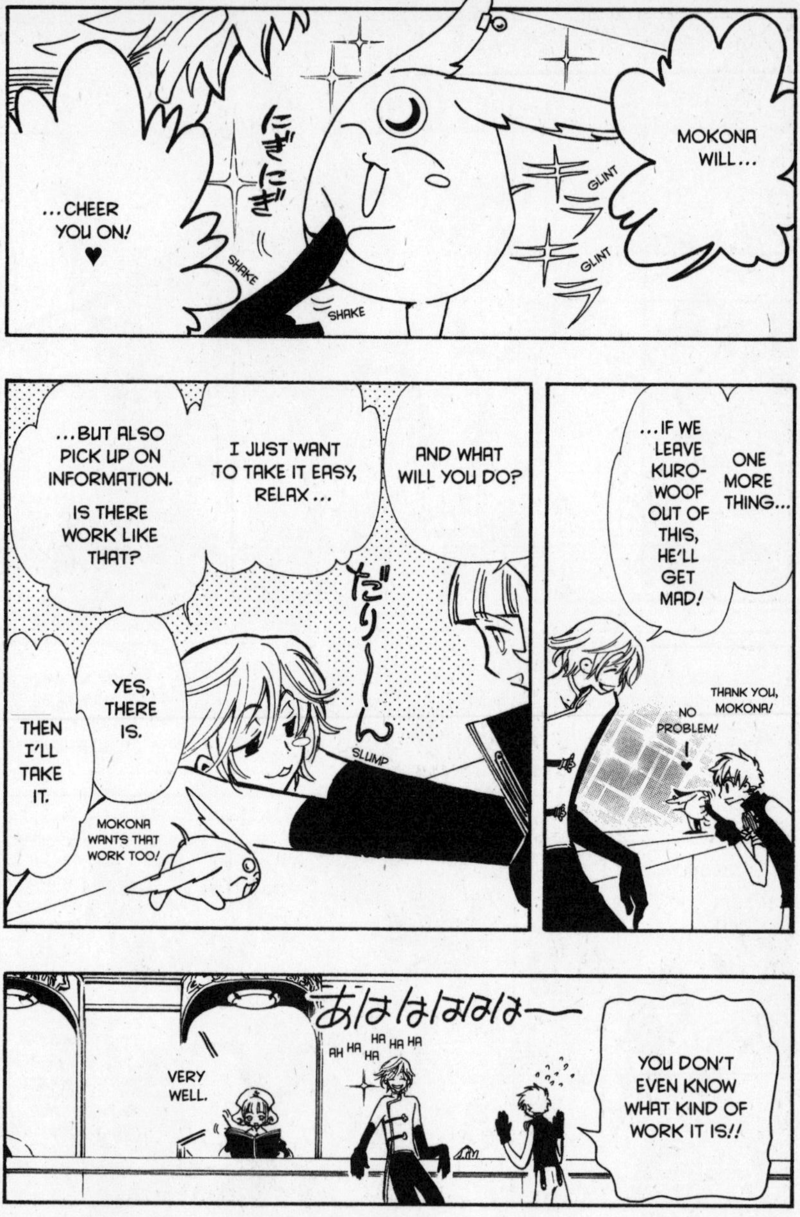
MOKONA WILL...
キラキラ
GLINT
GLINT
にぎにぎ
SHAKE
SHAKE
...CHEER YOU ON! ♥
ONE MORE THING...
...IF WE LEAVE KURO-WOOF OUT OF THIS, HE'LL GET MAD!
THANK YOU, MOKONA!
NO PROBLEM! ♥
AND WHAT WILL YOU DO?
I JUST WANT TO TAKE IT EASY, RELAX...
...BUT ALSO PICK UP ON INFORMATION.
IS THERE WORK LIKE THAT?
だりーん
SLUMP
YES, THERE IS.
THEN I'LL TAKE IT.
MOKONA WANTS THAT WORK TOO!
YOU DON'T EVEN KNOW WHAT KIND OF WORK IT IS!!
あははははは〜
AH HA HA HA HA HA
VERY WELL.

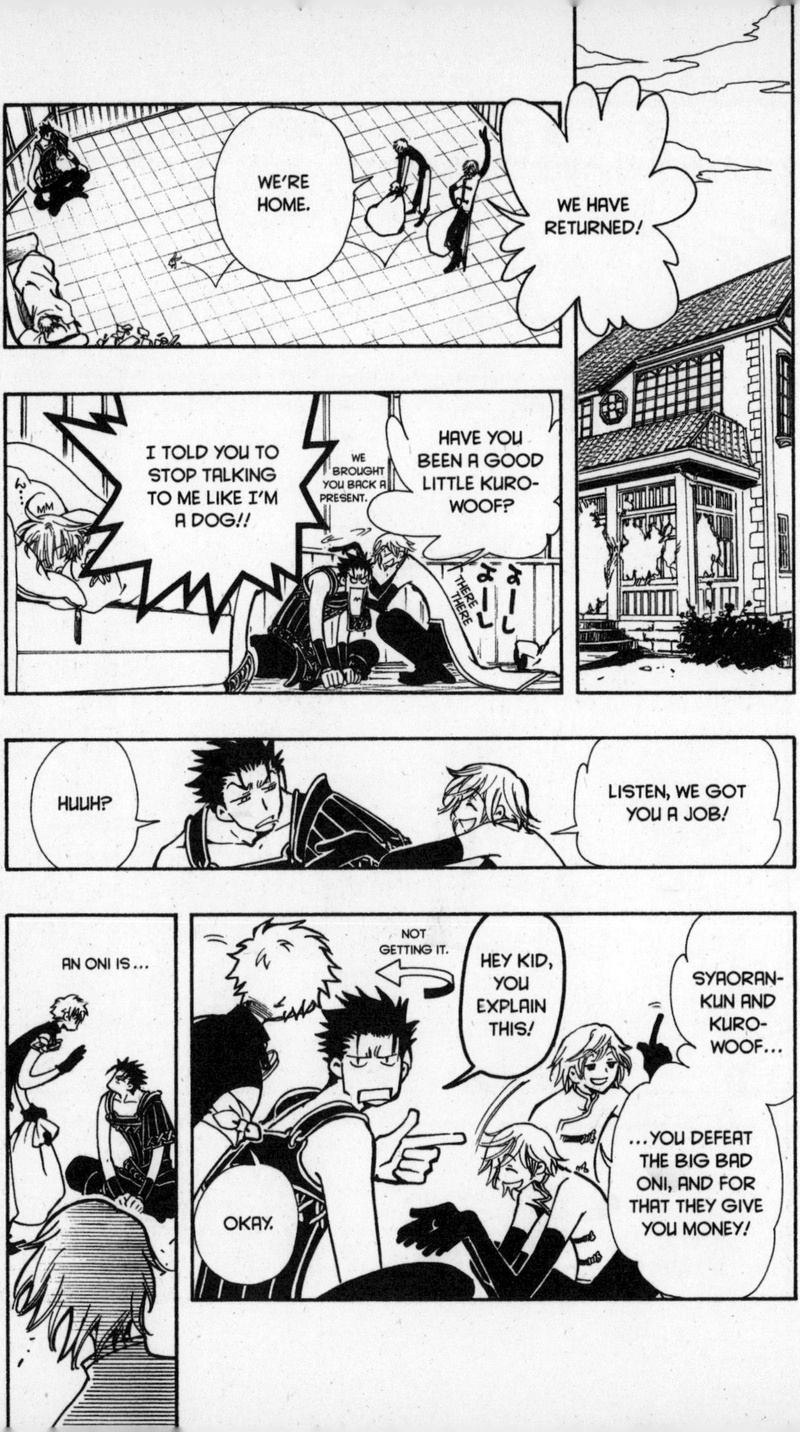
WE HAVE RETURNED!
WE'RE HOME.
HAVE YOU BEEN A GOOD LITTLE KURO-WOOF?
WE BROUGHT YOU BACK A PRESENT.
よーし よーし
THERE THERE
I TOLD YOU TO STOP TALKING TO ME LIKE I'M A DOG!!
MM
LISTEN, WE GOT YOU A JOB!
HUUH?
SYAORAN-KUN AND KURO-WOOF...
...YOU DEFEAT THE BIG BAD ONI, AND FOR THAT THEY GIVE YOU MONEY!
HEY KID, YOU EXPLAIN THIS!
NOT GETTING IT.
OKAY.
AN ONI IS...

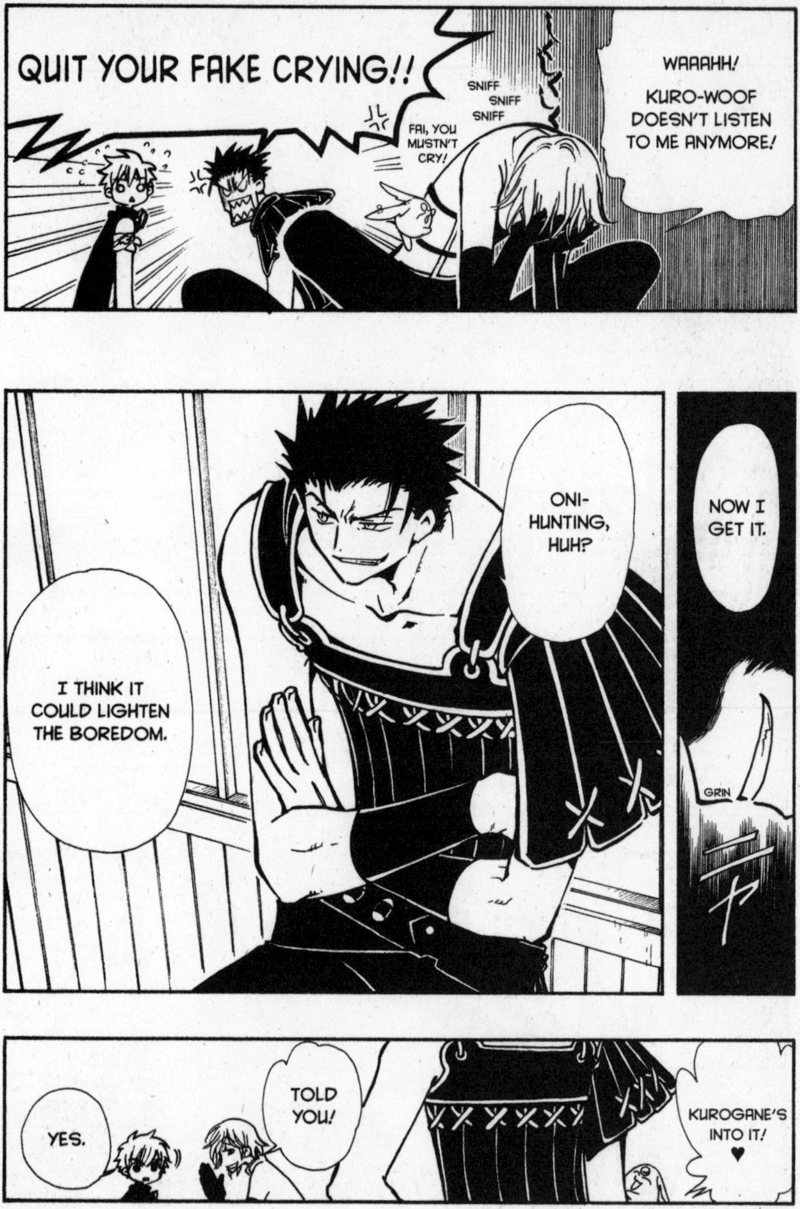
WAAAHH!
KURO-WOOF DOESN'T LISTEN TO ME ANYMORE!
SNIFF SNIFF SNIFF
FAI, YOU MUSTN'T CRY!
QUIT YOUR FAKE CRYING!!
NOW I GET IT.
GRIN
ONI-HUNTING, HUH?
I THINK IT COULD LIGHTEN THE BOREDOM.
KUROGANE'S INTO IT! ♥
TOLD YOU!
YES.

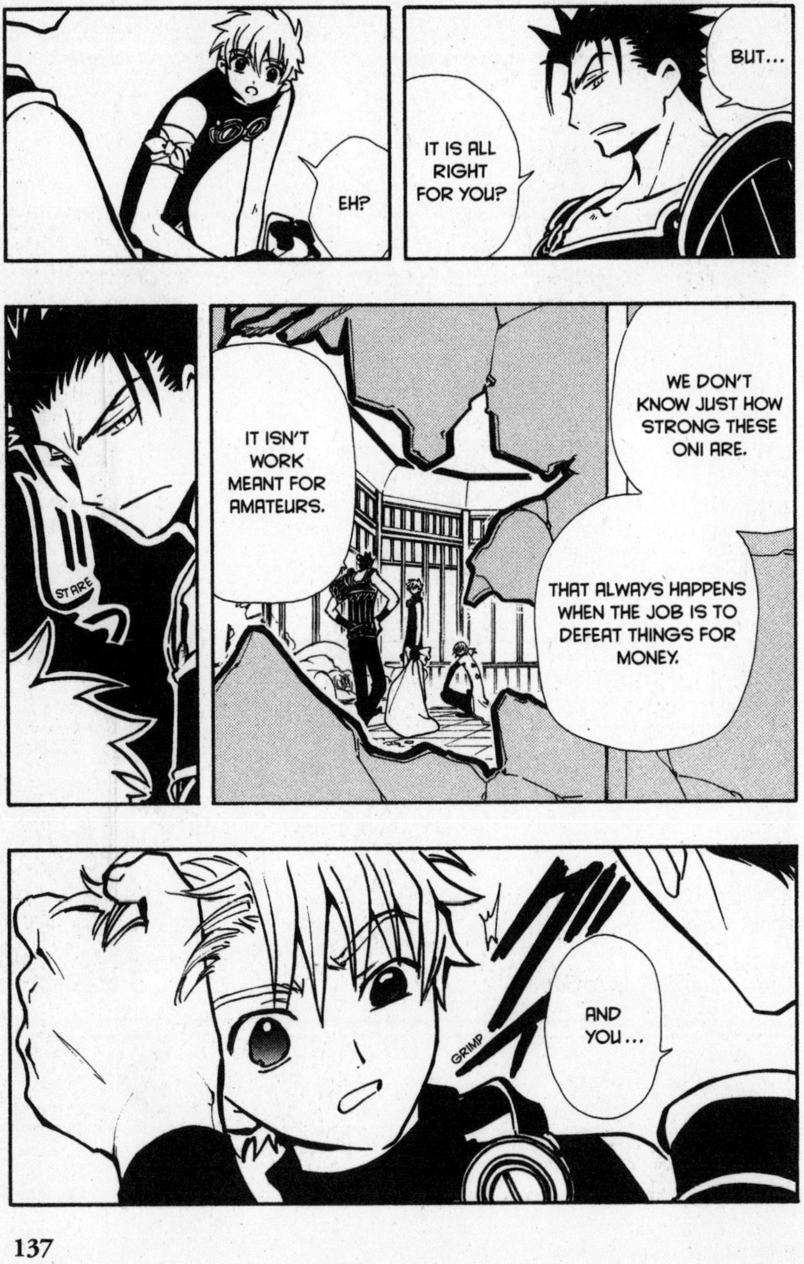
BUT...
IT IS ALL RIGHT FOR YOU?
EH?
WE DON'T KNOW JUST HOW STRONG THESE ONI ARE.
THAT ALWAYS HAPPENS WHEN THE JOB IS TO DEFEAT THINGS FOR MONEY.
IT ISN'T WORK MEANT FOR AMATEURS.
STARE
AND YOU...
GRIMP

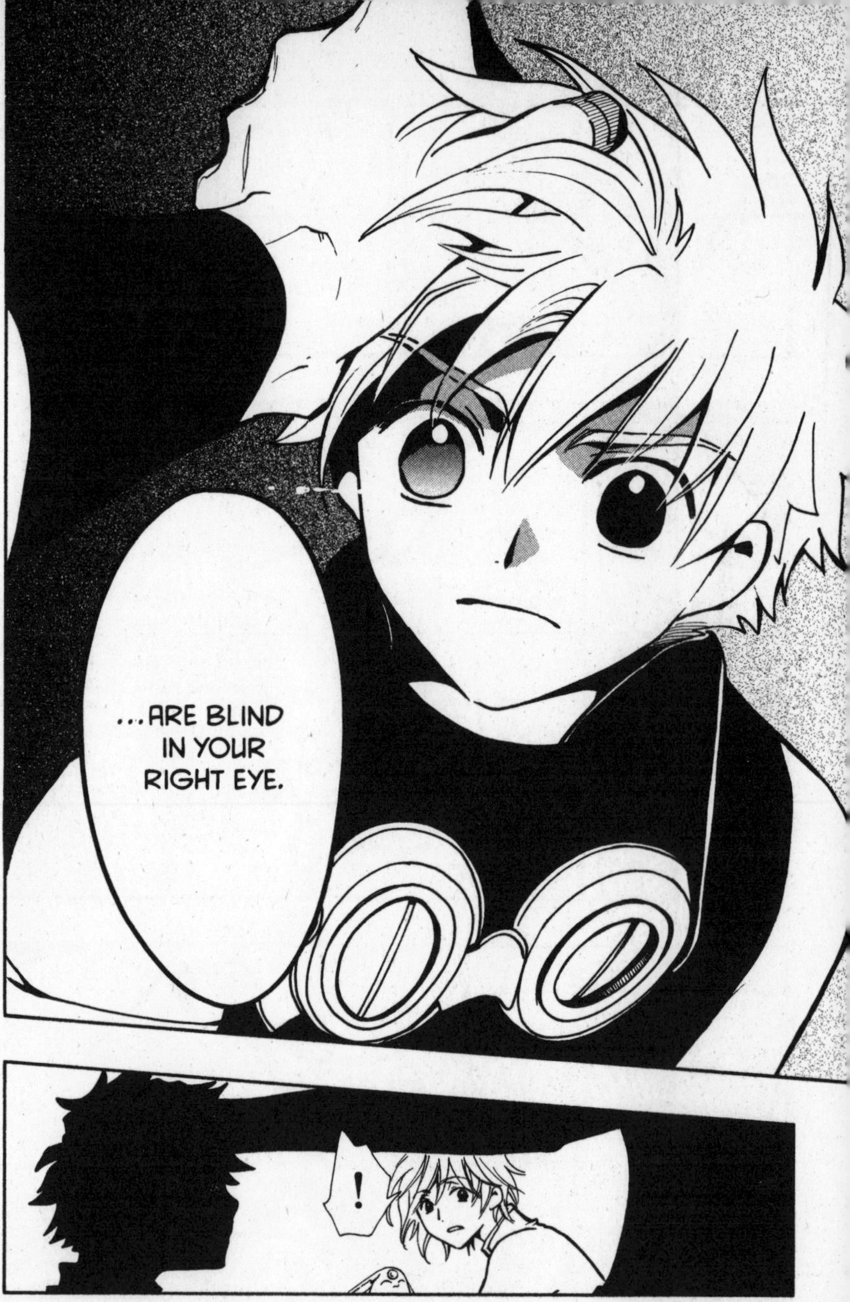
...ARE BLIND
IN YOUR
RIGHT EYE.
!

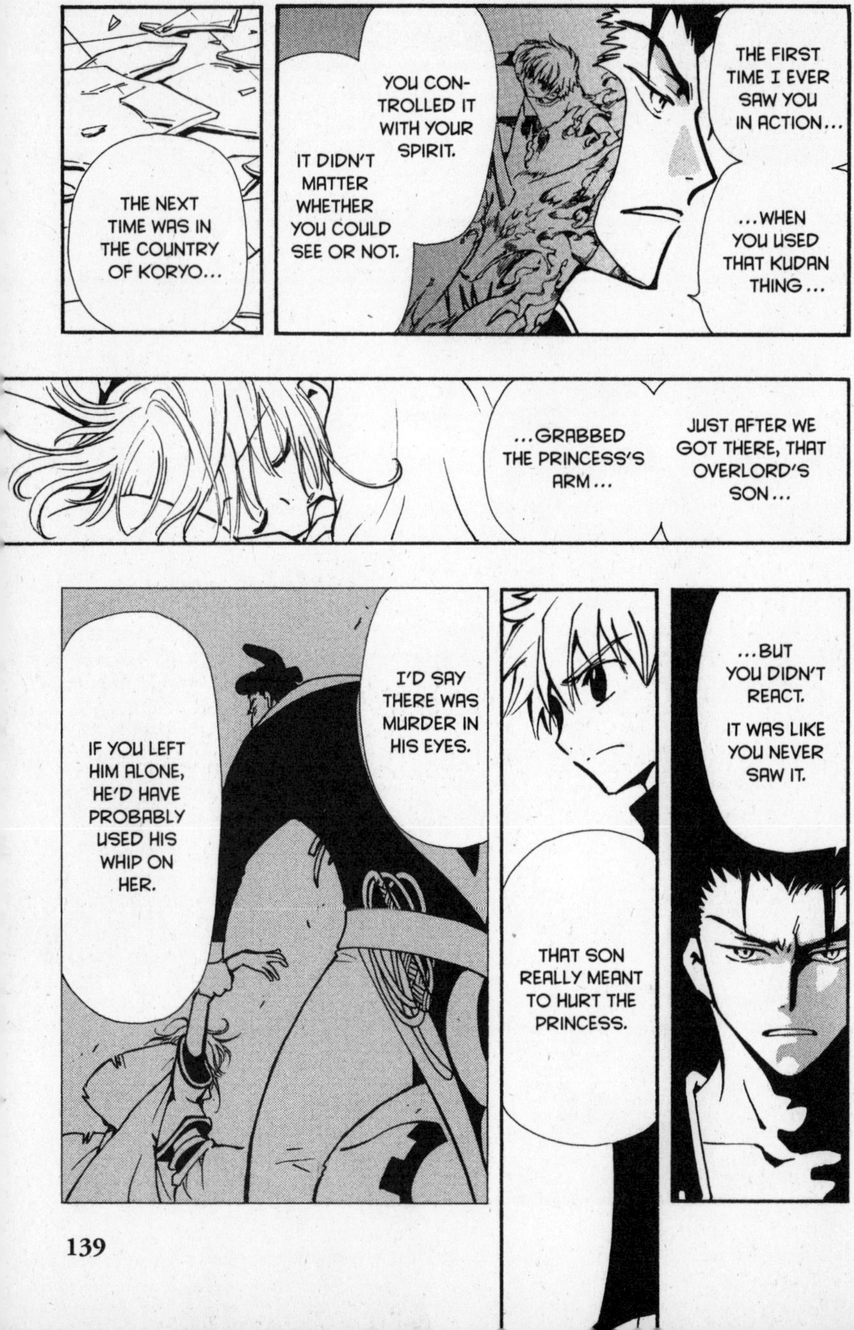
THE FIRST TIME I EVER SAW YOU IN ACTION...
...WHEN YOU USED THAT KUDAN THING...
YOU CONTROLLED IT WITH YOUR SPIRIT.
IT DIDN'T MATTER WHETHER YOU COULD SEE OR NOT.
THE NEXT TIME WAS IN THE COUNTRY OF KORYO...
JUST AFTER WE GOT THERE, THAT OVERLORD'S SON...
...GRABBED THE PRINCESS'S ARM...
...BUT YOU DIDN'T REACT.
IT WAS LIKE YOU NEVER SAW IT.
THAT SON REALLY MEANT TO HURT THE PRINCESS.
I'D SAY THERE WAS MURDER IN HIS EYES.
IF YOU LEFT HIM ALONE, HE'D HAVE PROBABLY USED HIS WHIP ON HER.

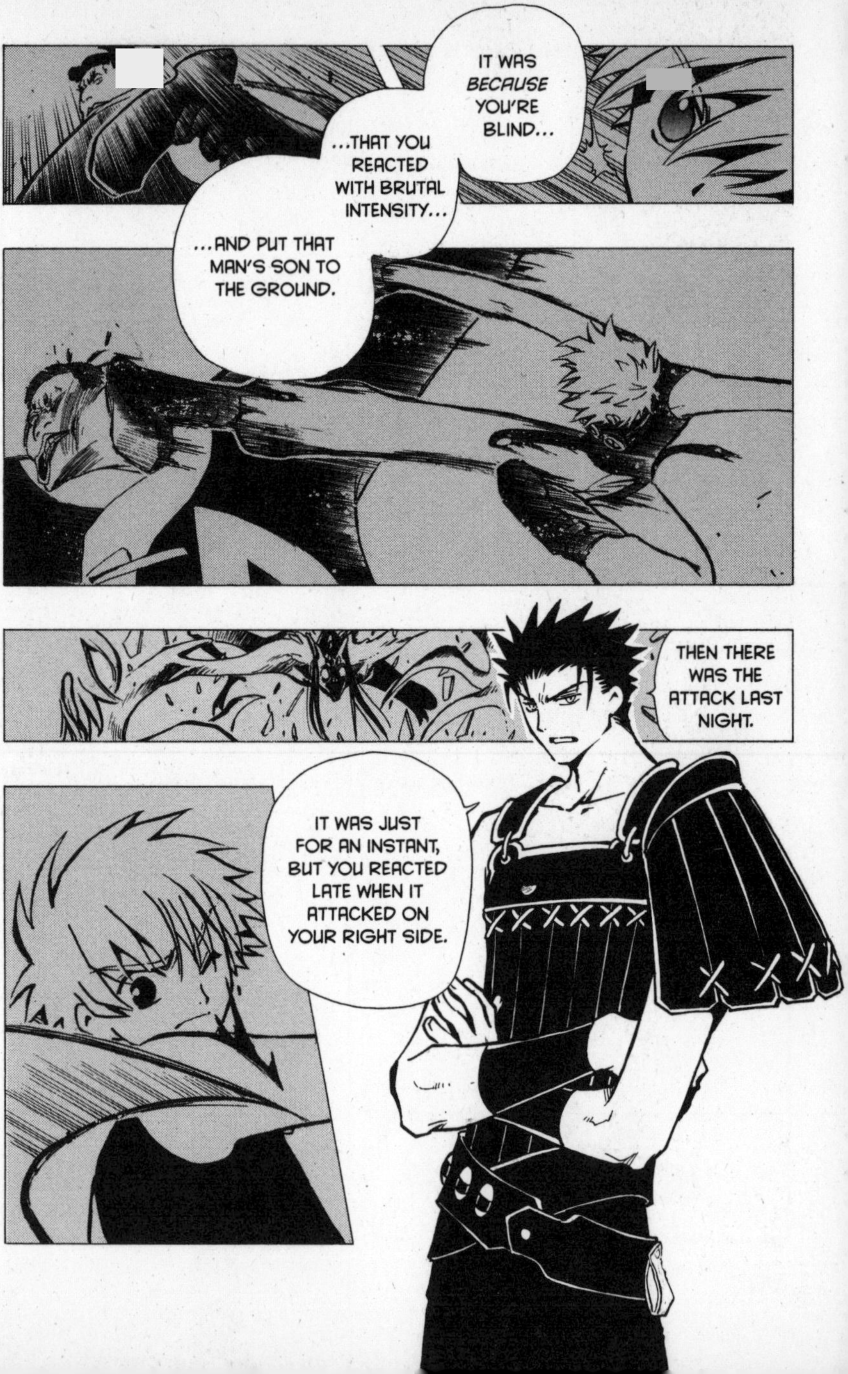
IT WAS *BECAUSE* YOU'RE BLIND...
...THAT YOU REACTED WITH BRUTAL INTENSITY...
...AND PUT THAT MAN'S SON TO THE GROUND.
THEN THERE WAS THE ATTACK LAST NIGHT.
IT WAS JUST FOR AN INSTANT, BUT YOU REACTED LATE WHEN IT ATTACKED ON YOUR RIGHT SIDE.

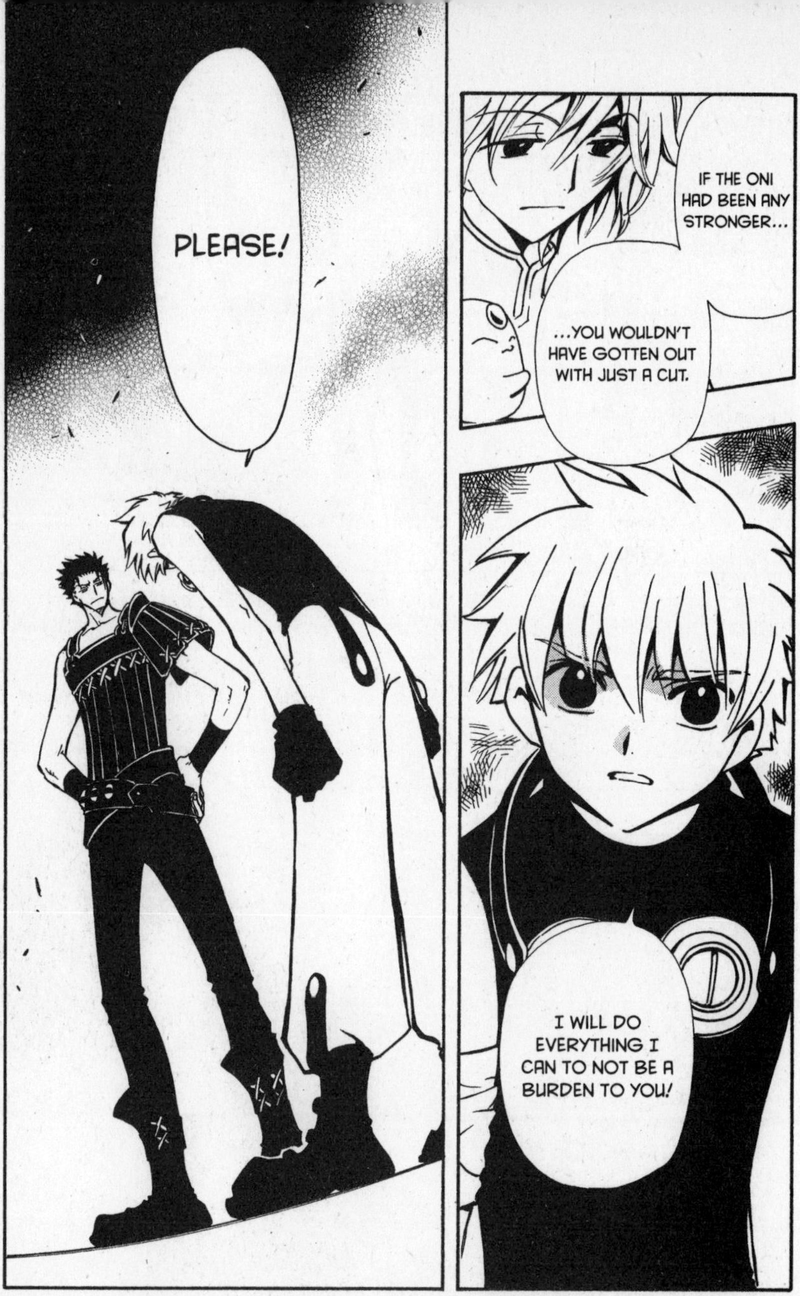
IF THE ONI HAD BEEN ANY STRONGER...
...YOU WOULDN'T HAVE GOTTEN OUT WITH JUST A CUT.
I WILL DO EVERYTHING I CAN TO NOT BE A BURDEN TO YOU!
PLEASE!

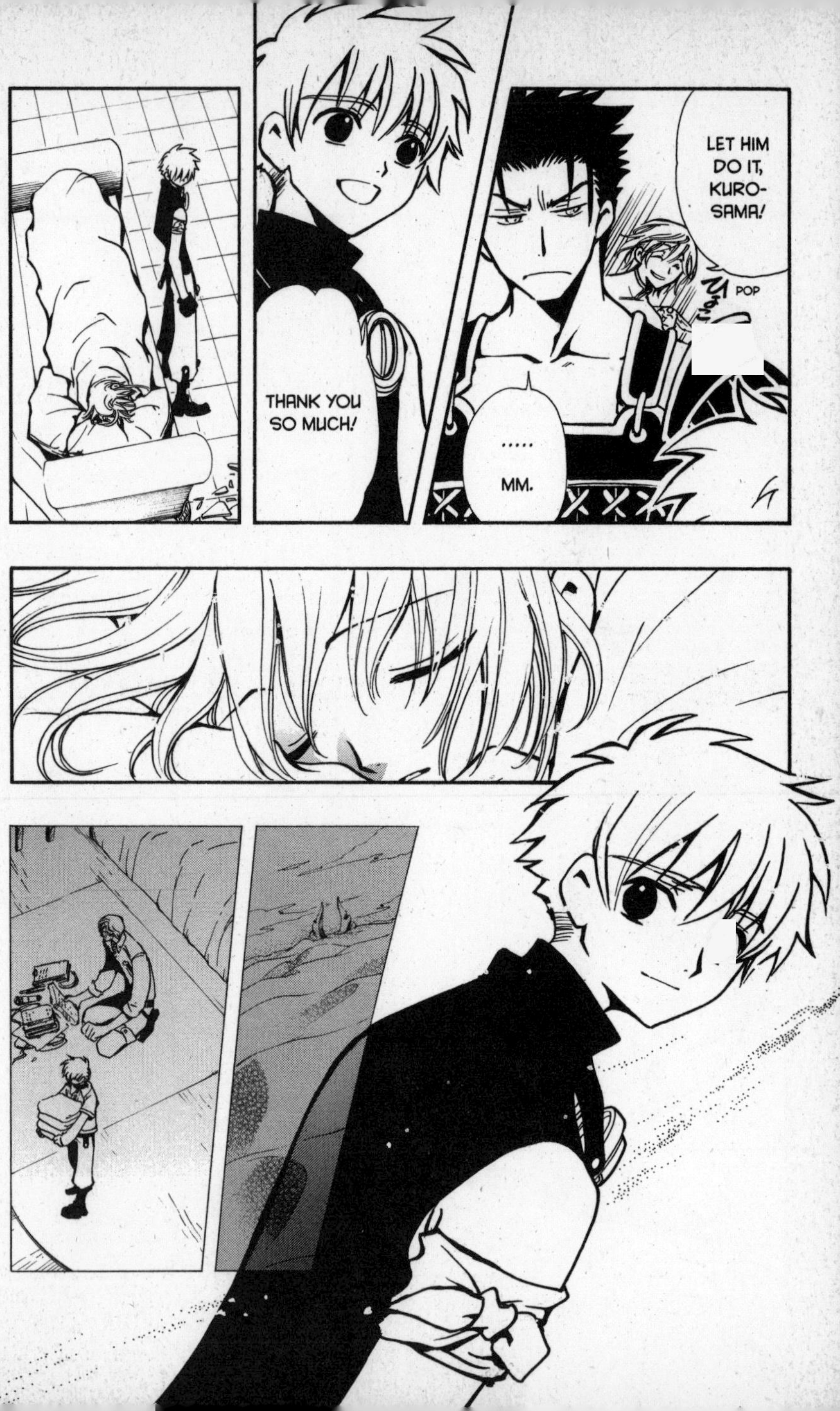
LET HIM DO IT, KURO-SAMA!
POP
..... MM.
THANK YOU SO MUCH!

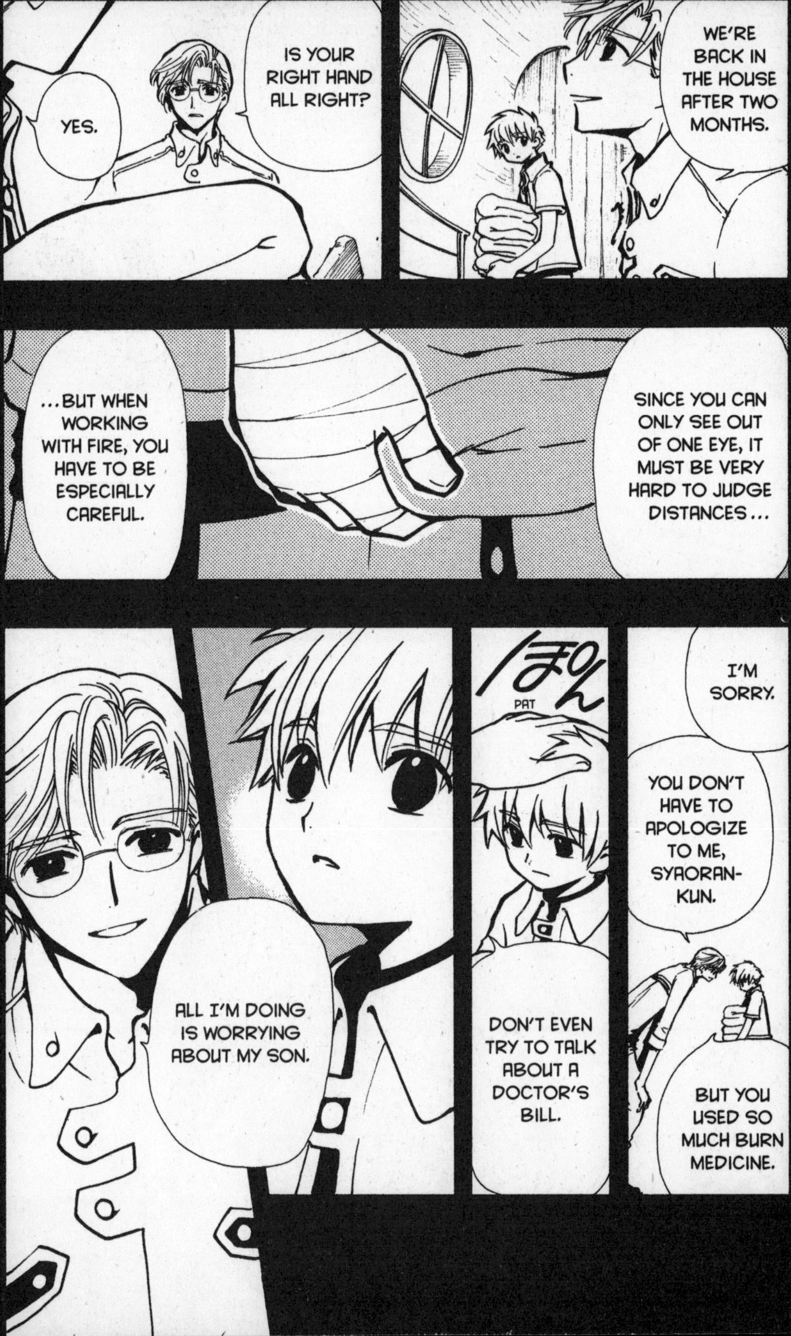
WE'RE BACK IN THE HOUSE AFTER TWO MONTHS.
IS YOUR RIGHT HAND ALL RIGHT?
YES.
SINCE YOU CAN ONLY SEE OUT OF ONE EYE, IT MUST BE VERY HARD TO JUDGE DISTANCES...
...BUT WHEN WORKING WITH FIRE, YOU HAVE TO BE ESPECIALLY CAREFUL.
I'M SORRY.
YOU DON'T HAVE TO APOLOGIZE TO ME, SYAORAN-KUN.
BUT YOU USED SO MUCH BURN MEDICINE.
ぽん
PAT
DON'T EVEN TRY TO TALK ABOUT A DOCTOR'S BILL.
ALL I'M DOING IS WORRYING ABOUT MY SON.

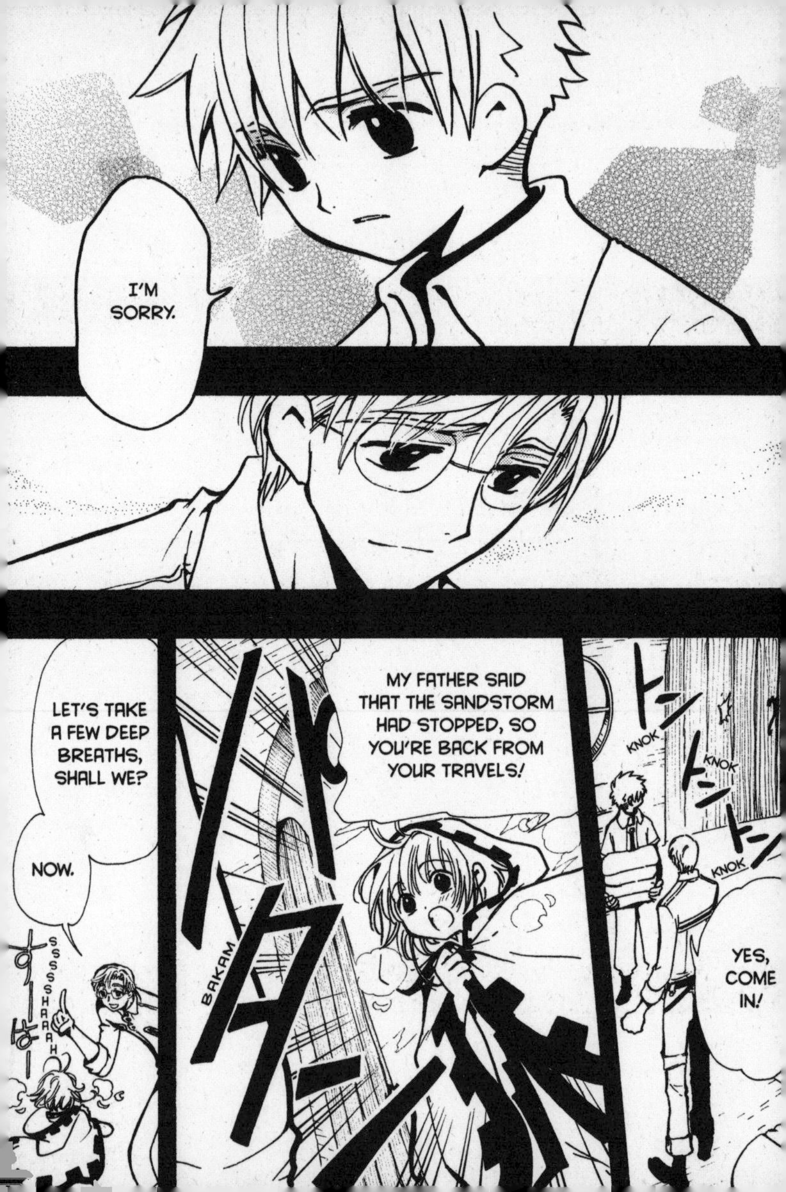
I'M SORRY.
KNOK
KNOK
KNOK
YES, COME IN!
BAKAM
MY FATHER SAID THAT THE SANDSTORM HAD STOPPED, SO YOU'RE BACK FROM YOUR TRAVELS!
LET'S TAKE A FEW DEEP BREATHS, SHALL WE?
NOW.
SSSSHAAAH

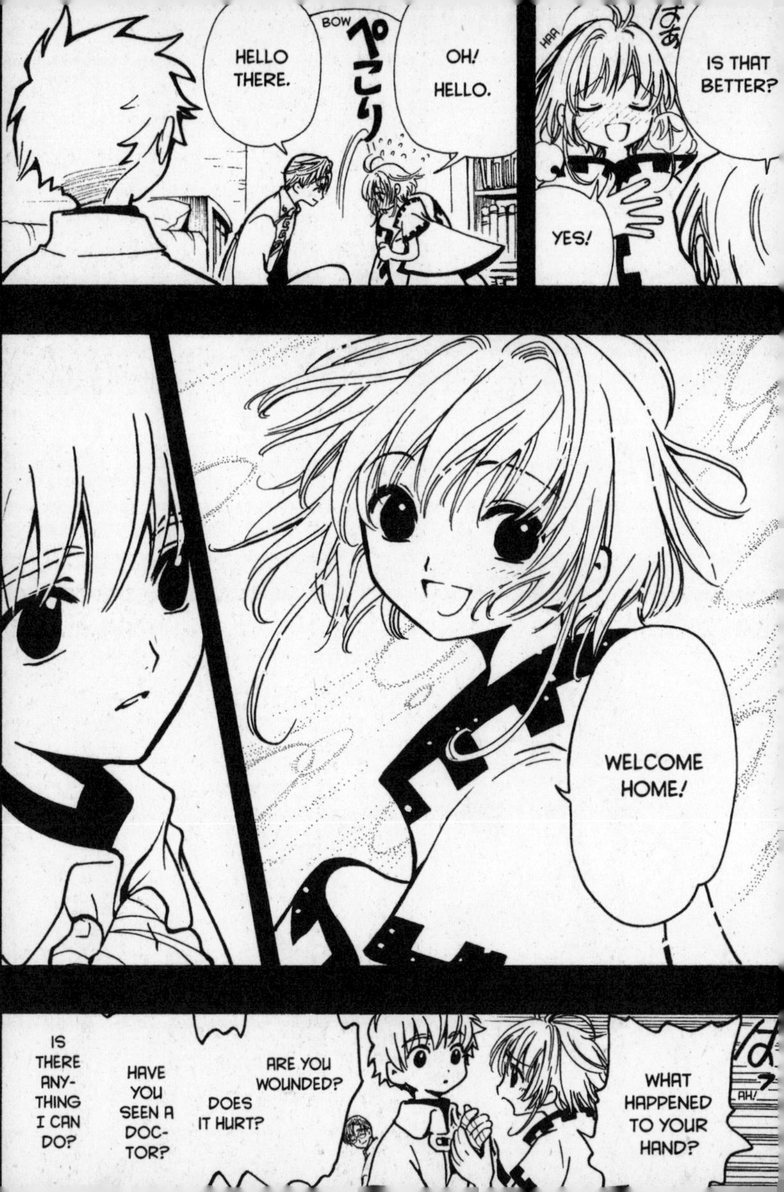
はぁ
HAA
IS THAT BETTER?
YES!
OH! HELLO.
ぺこり
BOW
HELLO THERE.
WELCOME HOME!
はっ
AH!
WHAT HAPPENED TO YOUR HAND?
ARE YOU WOUNDED?
DOES IT HURT?
HAVE YOU SEEN A DOCTOR?
IS THERE ANYTHING I CAN DO?

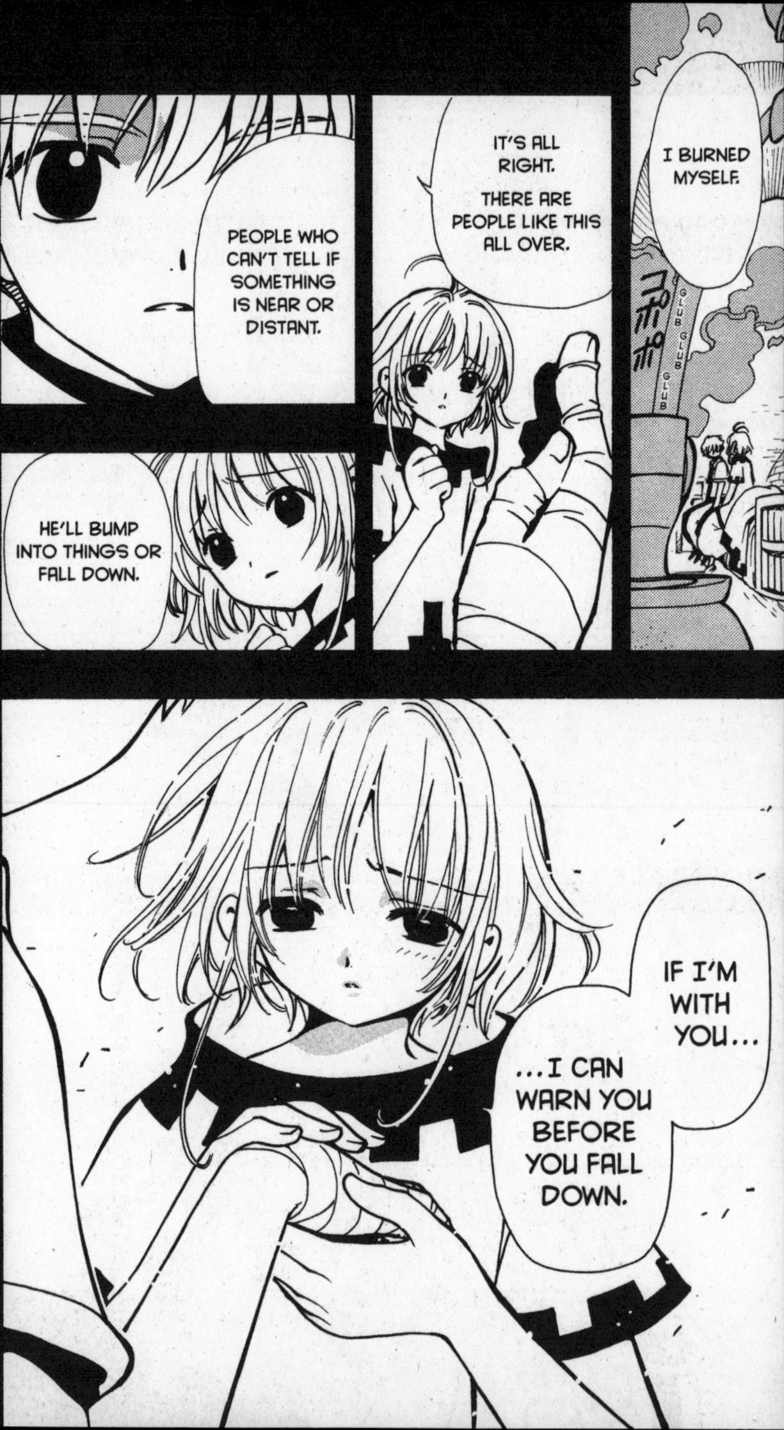
I BURNED MYSELF.
GLUB GLUB GLUB
IT'S ALL RIGHT.
THERE ARE PEOPLE LIKE THIS ALL OVER.
PEOPLE WHO CAN'T TELL IF SOMETHING IS NEAR OR DISTANT.
HE'LL BUMP INTO THINGS OR FALL DOWN.
IF I'M WITH YOU...
...I CAN WARN YOU BEFORE YOU FALL DOWN.

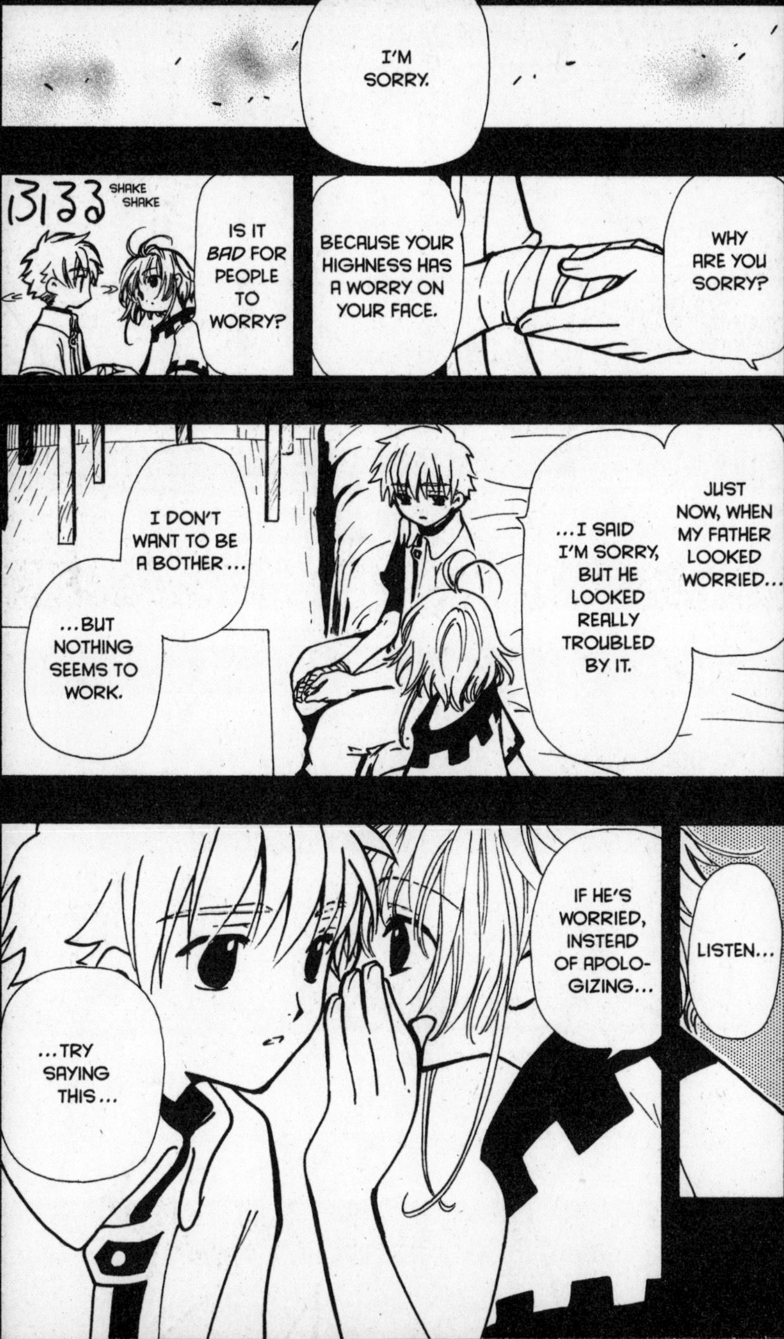
I'M SORRY.
WHY ARE YOU SORRY?
BECAUSE YOUR HIGHNESS HAS A WORRY ON YOUR FACE.
ふるふる
SHAKE SHAKE
IS IT *BAD* FOR PEOPLE TO WORRY?
JUST NOW, WHEN MY FATHER LOOKED WORRIED...
...I SAID I'M SORRY, BUT HE LOOKED REALLY TROUBLED BY IT.
I DON'T WANT TO BE A BOTHER...
...BUT NOTHING SEEMS TO WORK.
LISTEN...
IF HE'S WORRIED, INSTEAD OF APOLOGIZING...
...TRY SAYING THIS...

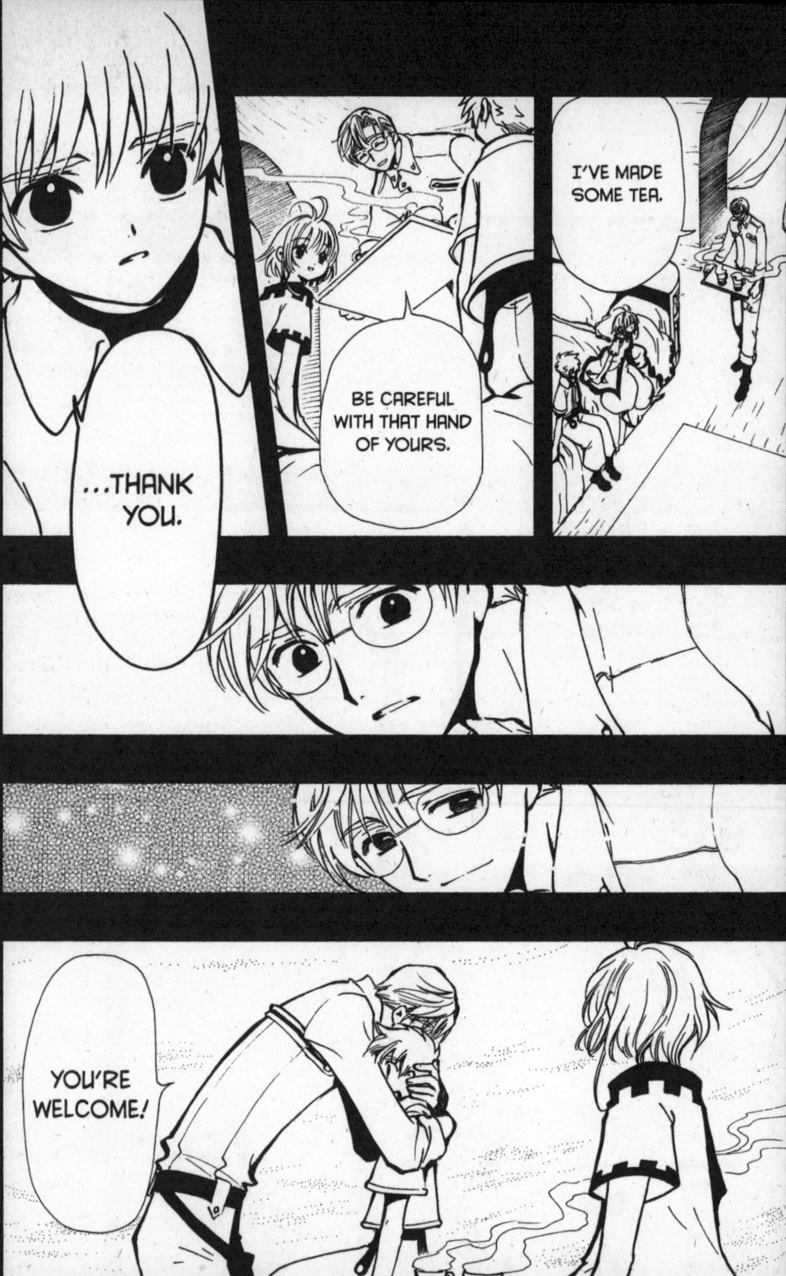
I'VE MADE SOME TEA.
BE CAREFUL WITH THAT HAND OF YOURS.
...THANK YOU.
YOU'RE WELCOME!

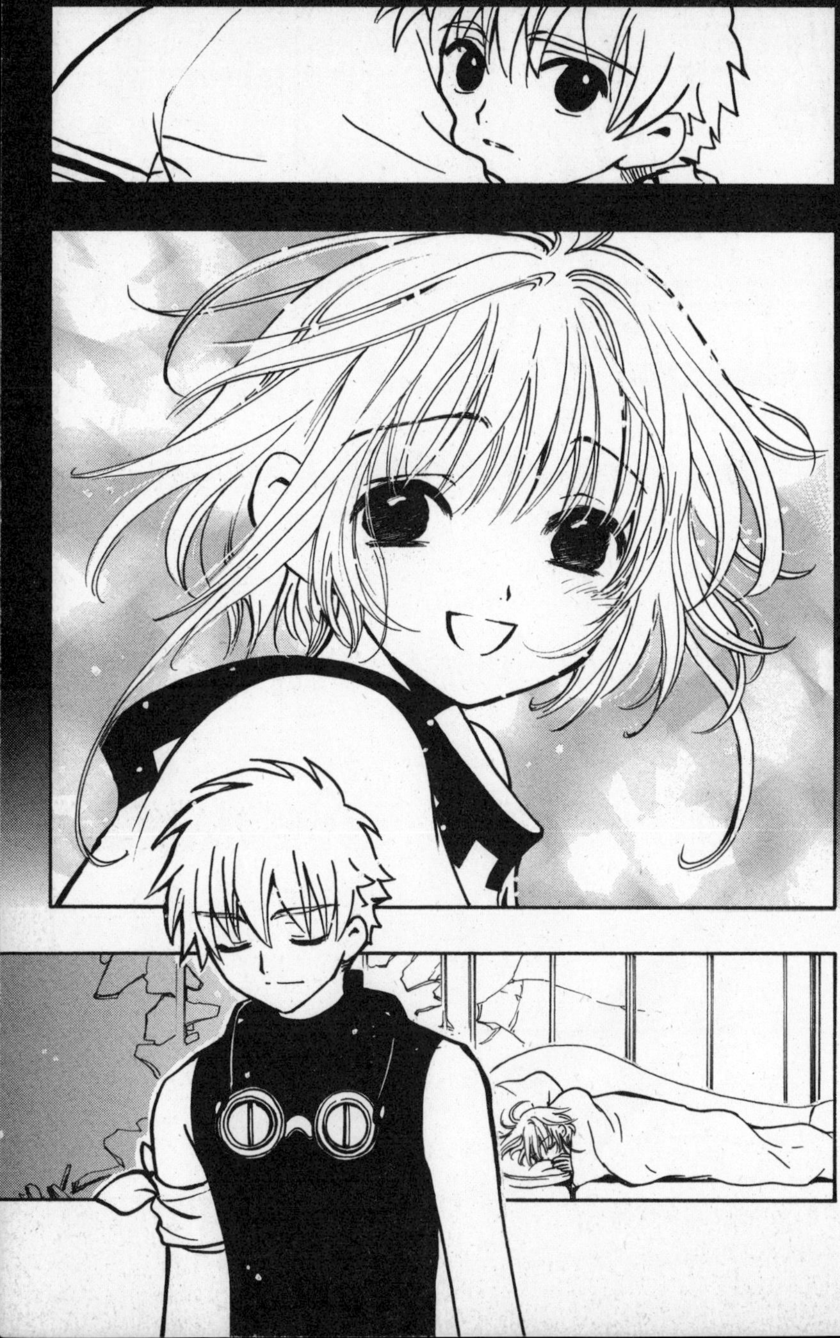

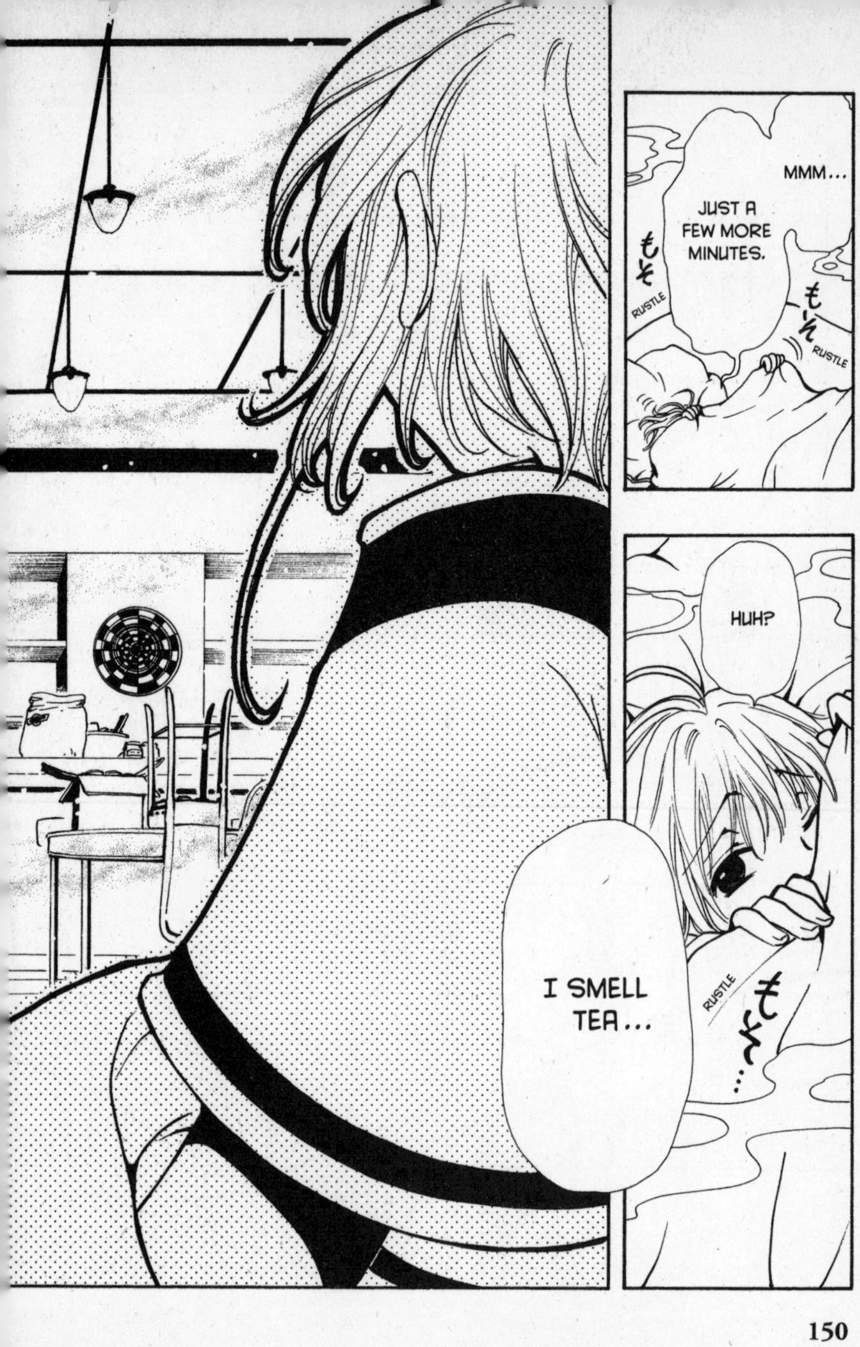
MMM...
JUST A FEW MORE MINUTES.
もそ
RUSTLE
もそ
RUSTLE
HUH?
I SMELL TEA...
もそ...
RUSTLE

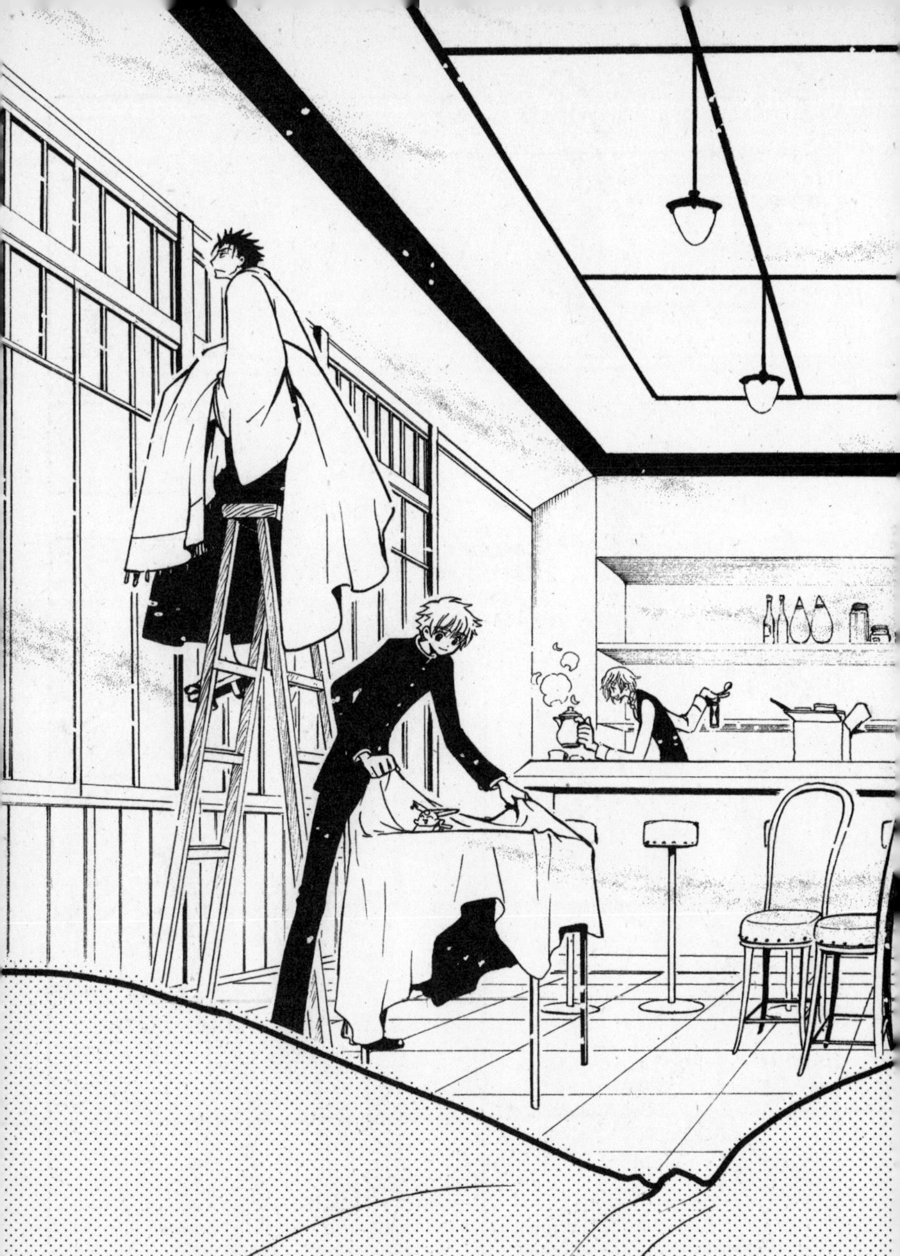

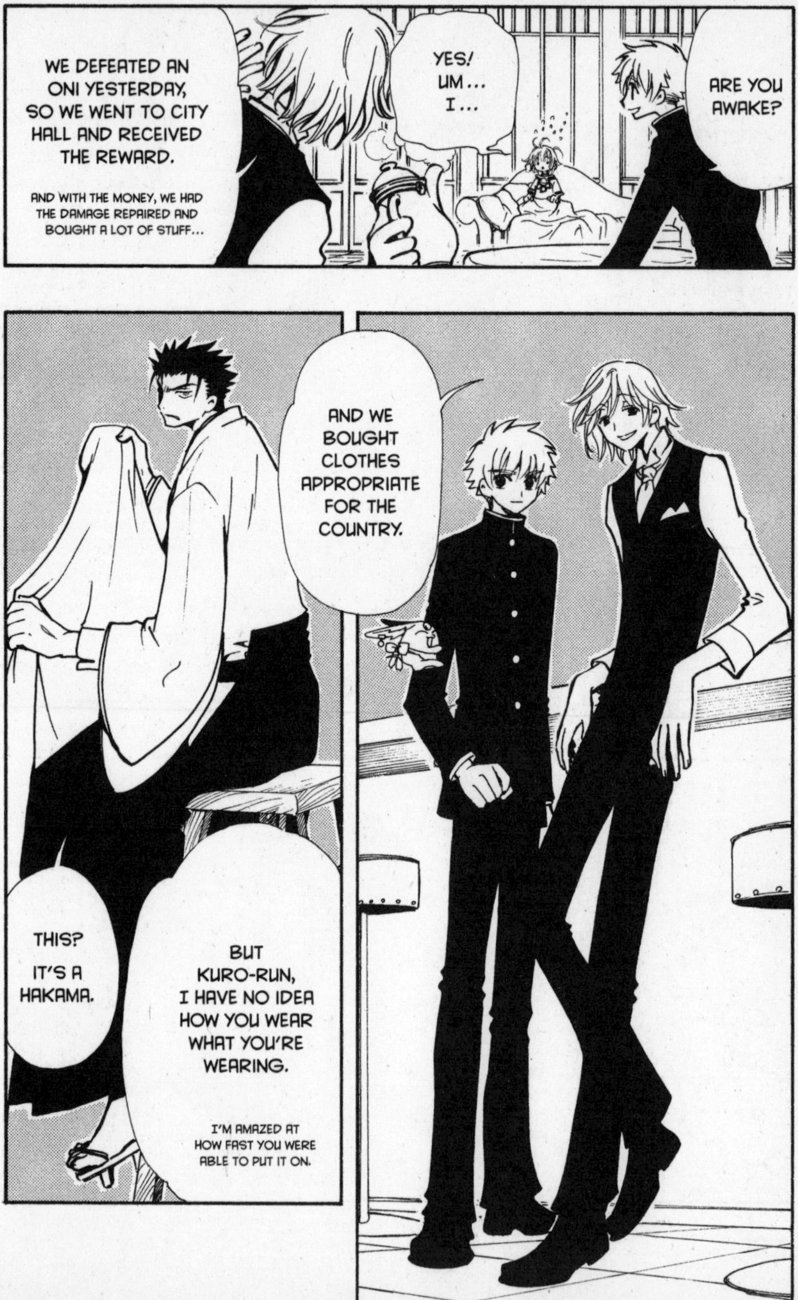
ARE YOU AWAKE?
YES! UM... I...
WE DEFEATED AN ONI YESTERDAY, SO WE WENT TO CITY HALL AND RECEIVED THE REWARD.
AND WITH THE MONEY, WE HAD THE DAMAGE REPAIRED AND BOUGHT A LOT OF STUFF...
AND WE BOUGHT CLOTHES APPROPRIATE FOR THE COUNTRY.
BUT KURO-RUN, I HAVE NO IDEA HOW YOU WEAR WHAT YOU'RE WEARING.
I'M AMAZED AT HOW FAST YOU WERE ABLE TO PUT IT ON.
THIS? IT'S A HAKAMA.

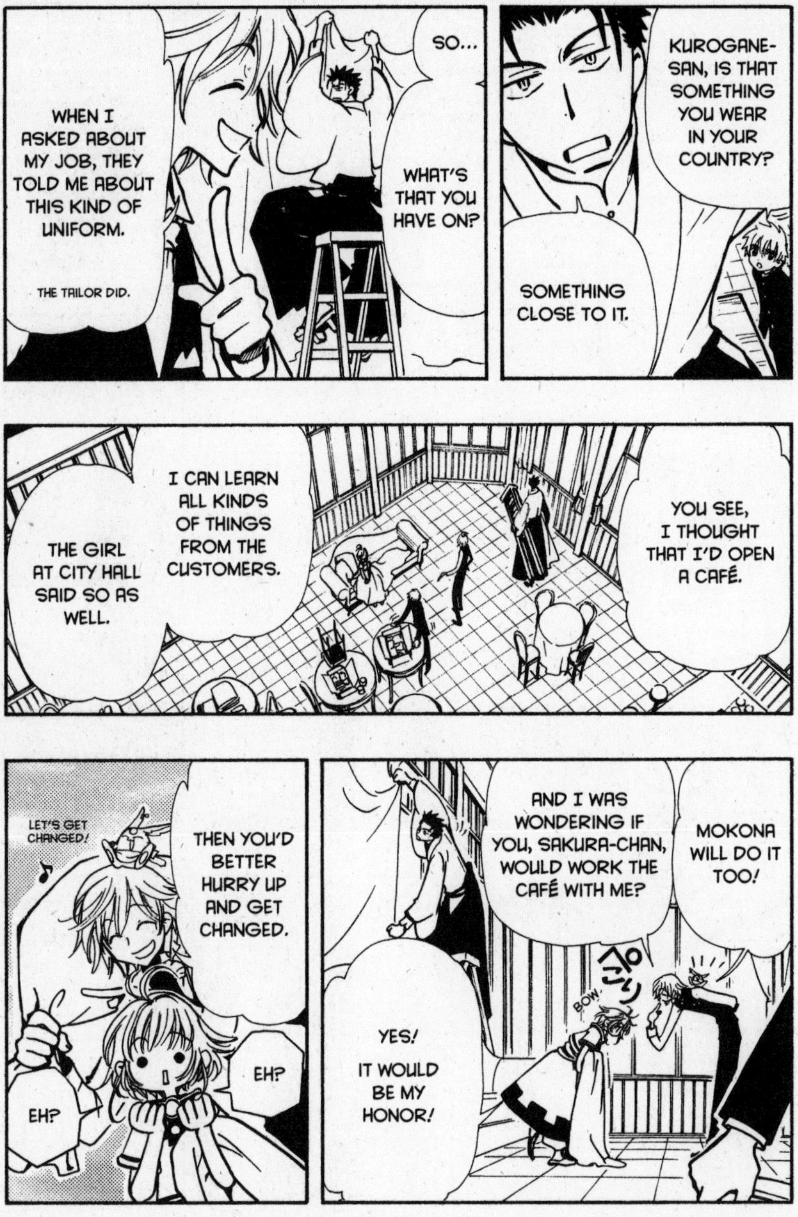
KUROGANE-SAN, IS THAT SOMETHING YOU WEAR IN YOUR COUNTRY?
SOMETHING CLOSE TO IT.
SO...
WHAT'S THAT YOU HAVE ON?
WHEN I ASKED ABOUT MY JOB, THEY TOLD ME ABOUT THIS KIND OF UNIFORM.
THE TAILOR DID.
YOU SEE, I THOUGHT THAT I'D OPEN A CAFÉ.
I CAN LEARN ALL KINDS OF THINGS FROM THE CUSTOMERS.
THE GIRL AT CITY HALL SAID SO AS WELL.
MOKONA WILL DO IT TOO!
AND I WAS WONDERING IF YOU, SAKURA-CHAN, WOULD WORK THE CAFÉ WITH ME?
BOW
YES!
IT WOULD BE MY HONOR!
THEN YOU'D BETTER HURRY UP AND GET CHANGED.
LET'S GET CHANGED!
EH?
EH?

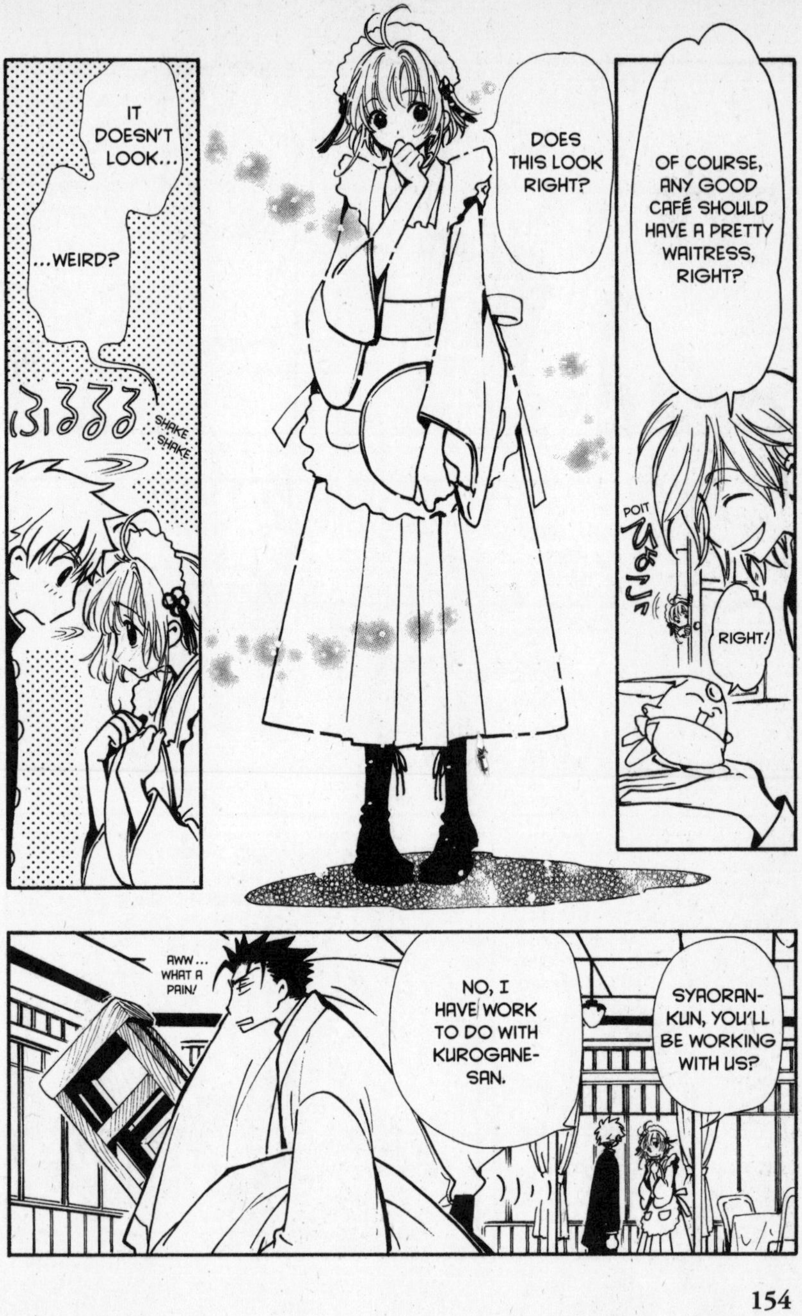
OF COURSE, ANY GOOD CAFÉ SHOULD HAVE A PRETTY WAITRESS, RIGHT?
POIT
RIGHT!
DOES THIS LOOK RIGHT?
IT DOESN'T LOOK...
...WEIRD?
SHAKE SHAKE
SYAORAN-KUN, YOU'LL BE WORKING WITH US?
NO, I HAVE WORK TO DO WITH KUROGANE-SAN.
AWW... WHAT A PAIN!

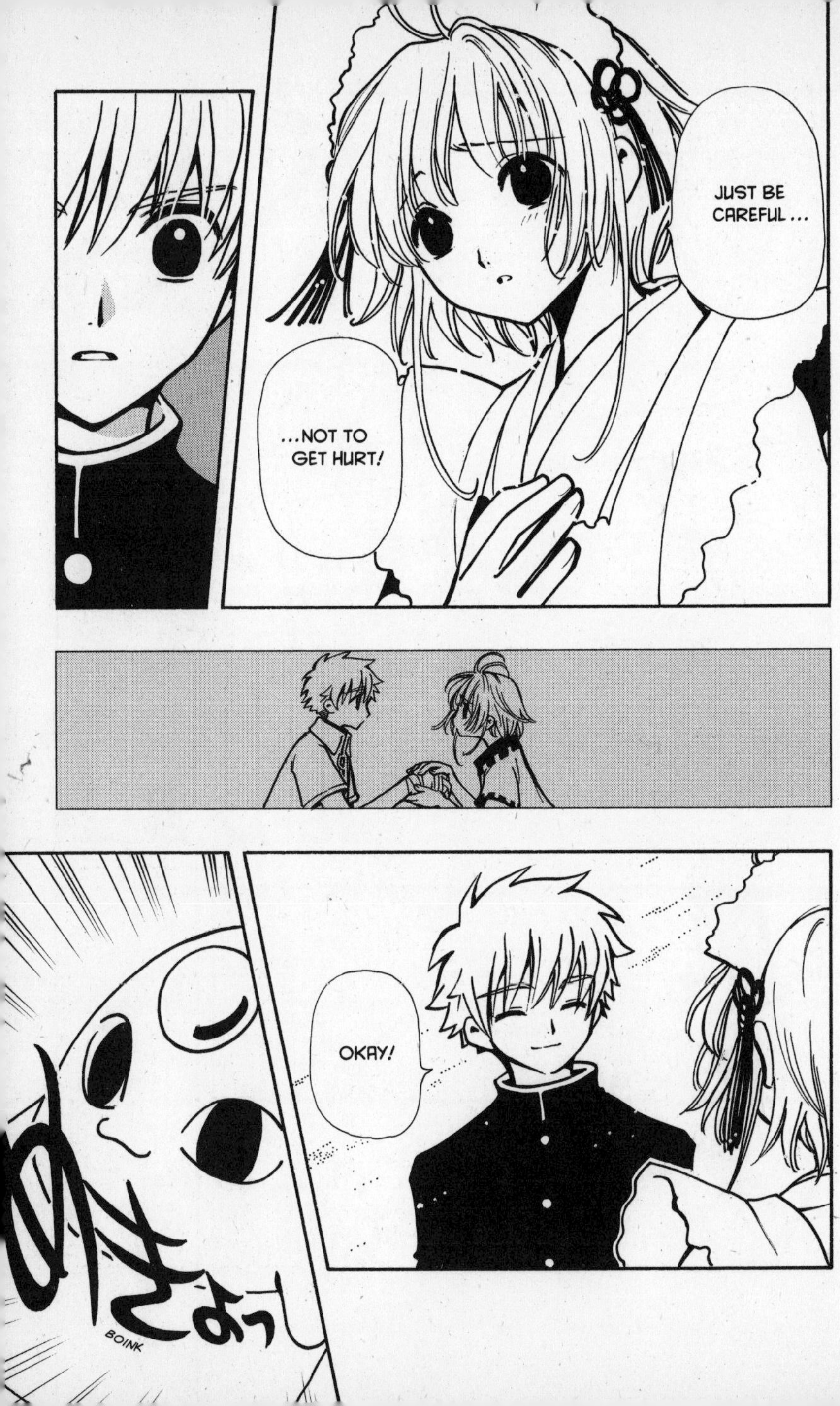
JUST BE CAREFUL...
...NOT TO GET HURT!
OKAY!
BOINK

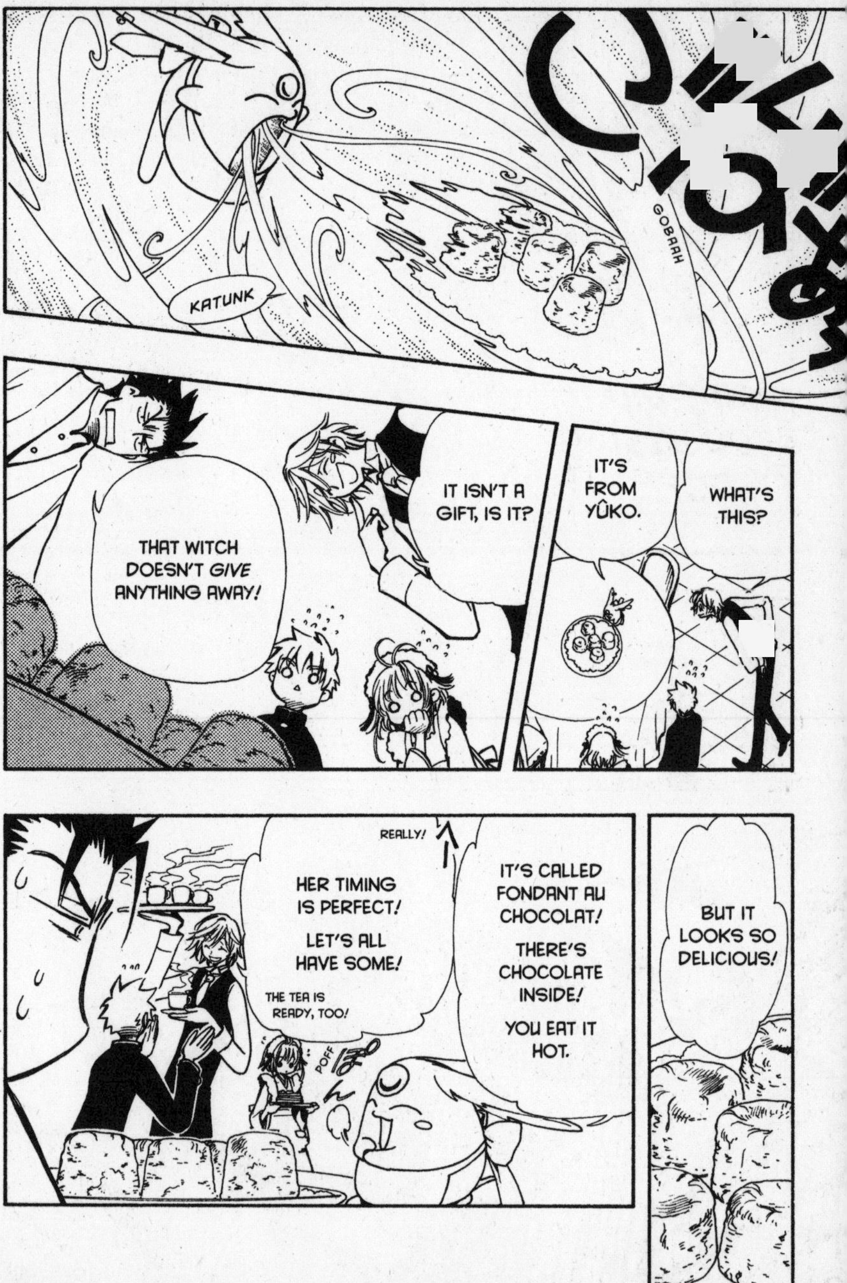
GOBAAH
KATUNK
WHAT'S THIS?
IT'S FROM YÛKO.
IT ISN'T A GIFT, IS IT?
THAT WITCH DOESN'T *GIVE* ANYTHING AWAY!
BUT IT LOOKS SO DELICIOUS!
IT'S CALLED FONDANT AU CHOCOLAT! THERE'S CHOCOLATE INSIDE! YOU EAT IT HOT.
REALLY!
HER TIMING IS PERFECT! LET'S ALL HAVE SOME!
THE TEA IS READY, TOO!
POFF

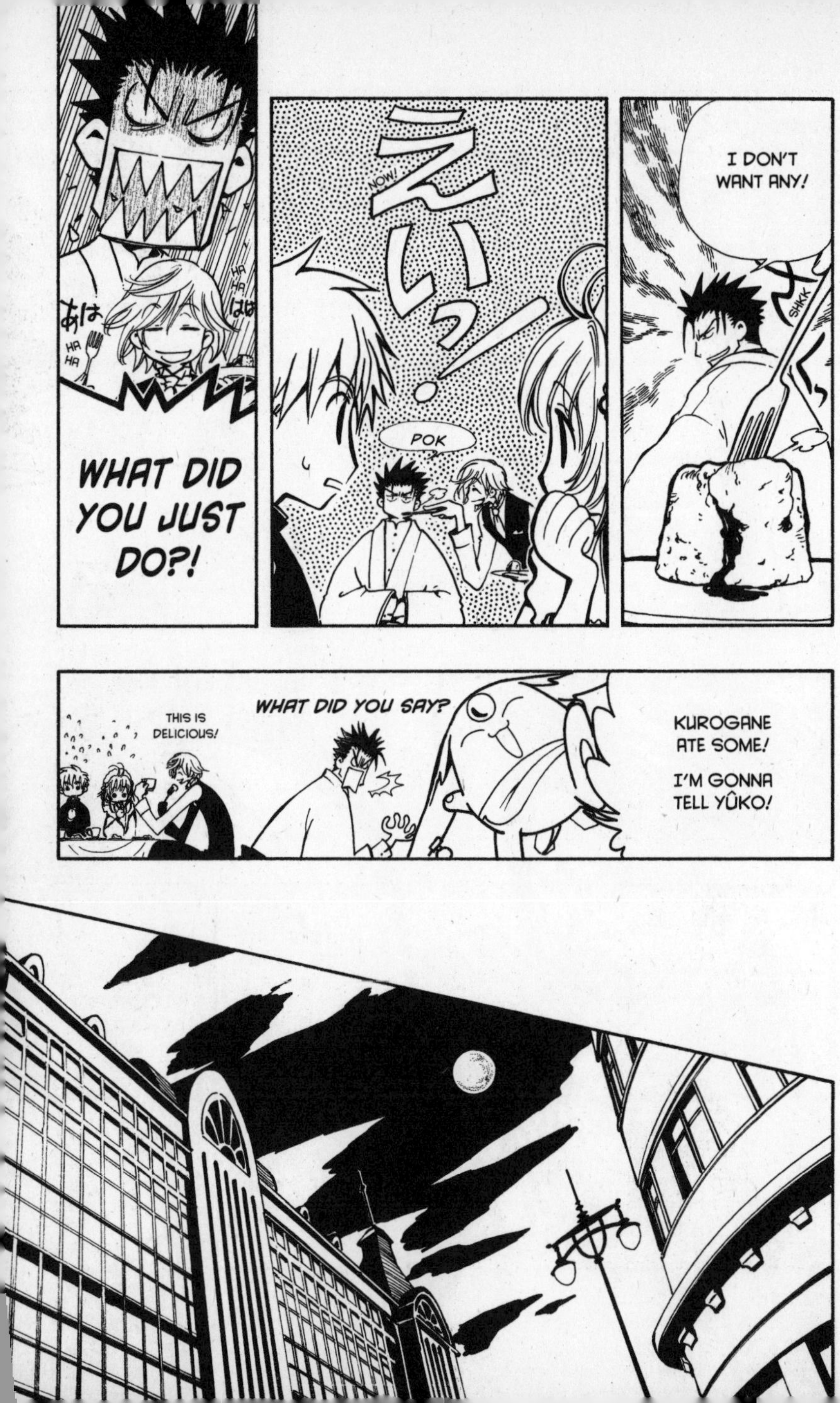
I DON'T WANT ANY!
SHKK
えいっ!
NOW!
POK
はは
HA HA
あは
HA HA
WHAT DID YOU JUST DO?!
KUROGANE ATE SOME!
I'M GONNA TELL YÛKO!
WHAT DID YOU SAY?
THIS IS DELICIOUS!

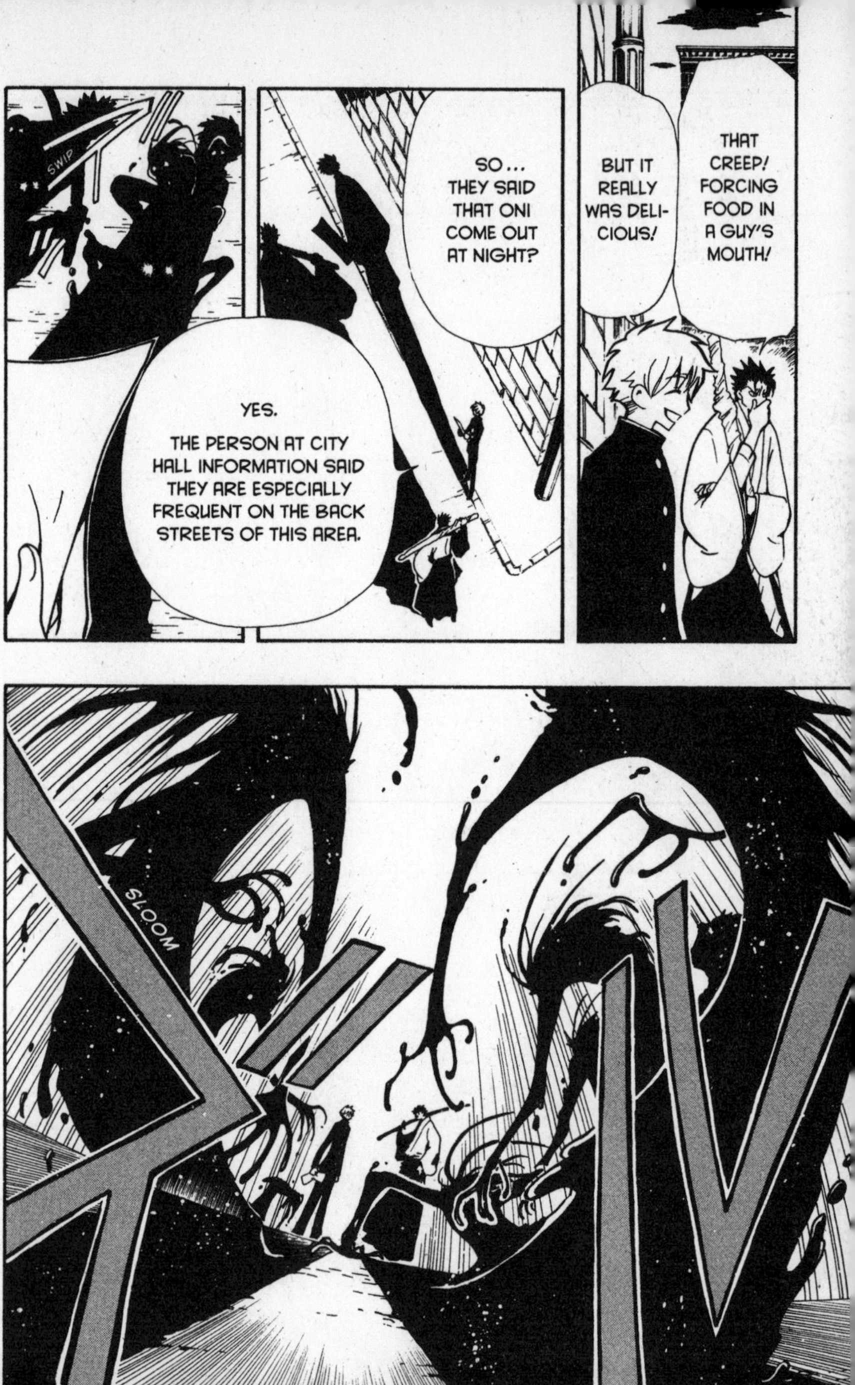
THAT CREEP! FORCING FOOD IN A GUY'S MOUTH!
BUT IT REALLY WAS DELI-CIOUS!
SO... THEY SAID THAT ONI COME OUT AT NIGHT?
YES.
THE PERSON AT CITY HALL INFORMATION SAID THEY ARE ESPECIALLY FREQUENT ON THE BACK STREETS OF THIS AREA.
SWIP
SLOOM

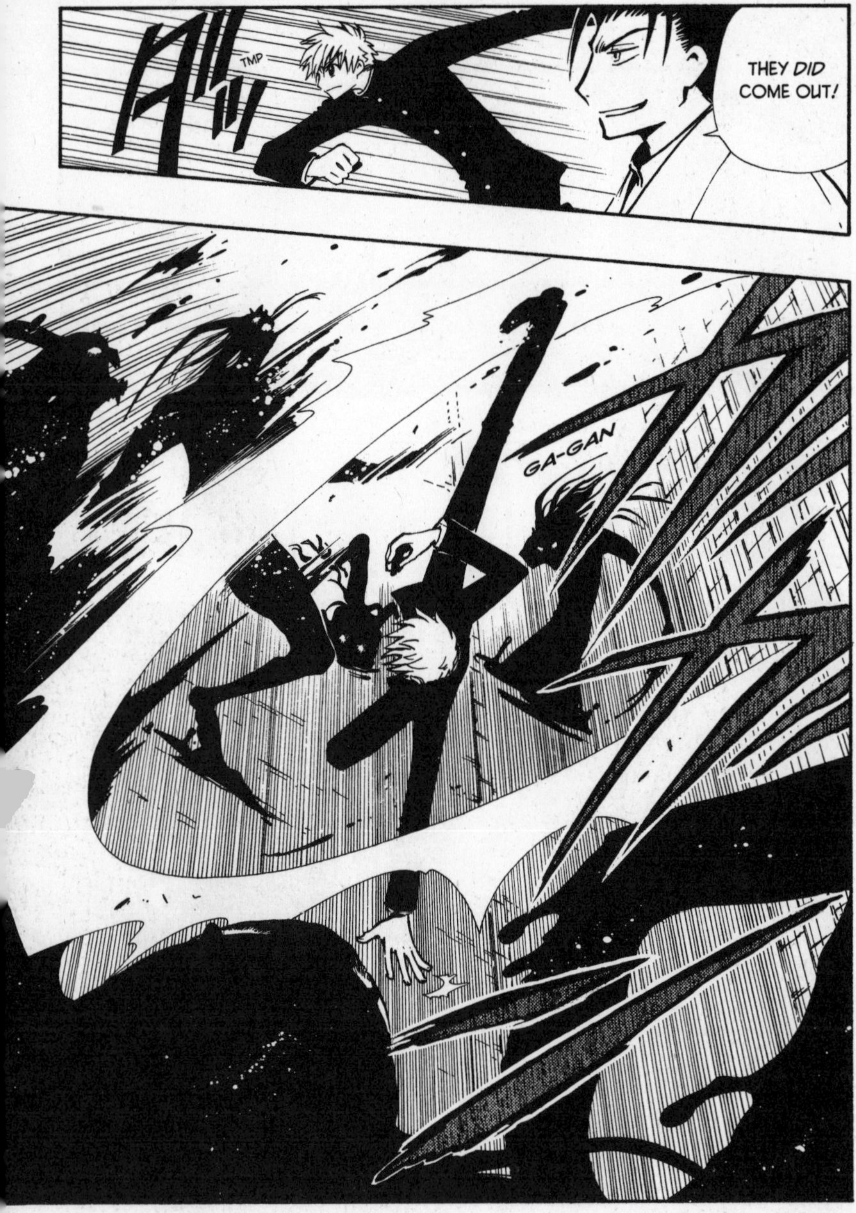
THEY *DID* COME OUT!
TMP
GA-GAN

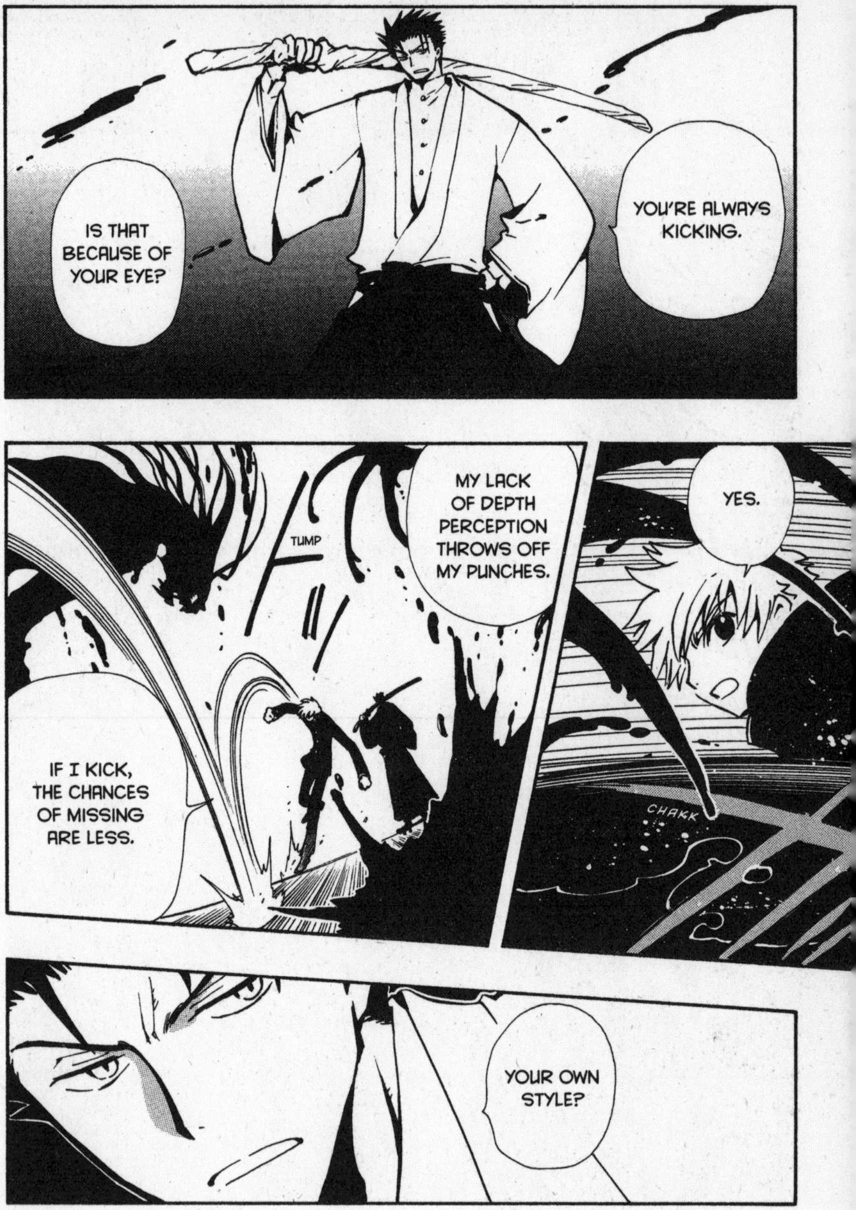
YOU'RE ALWAYS KICKING.
IS THAT BECAUSE OF YOUR EYE?
YES.
CHAKK
MY LACK OF DEPTH PERCEPTION THROWS OFF MY PUNCHES.
TUMP
IF I KICK, THE CHANCES OF MISSING ARE LESS.
YOUR OWN STYLE?

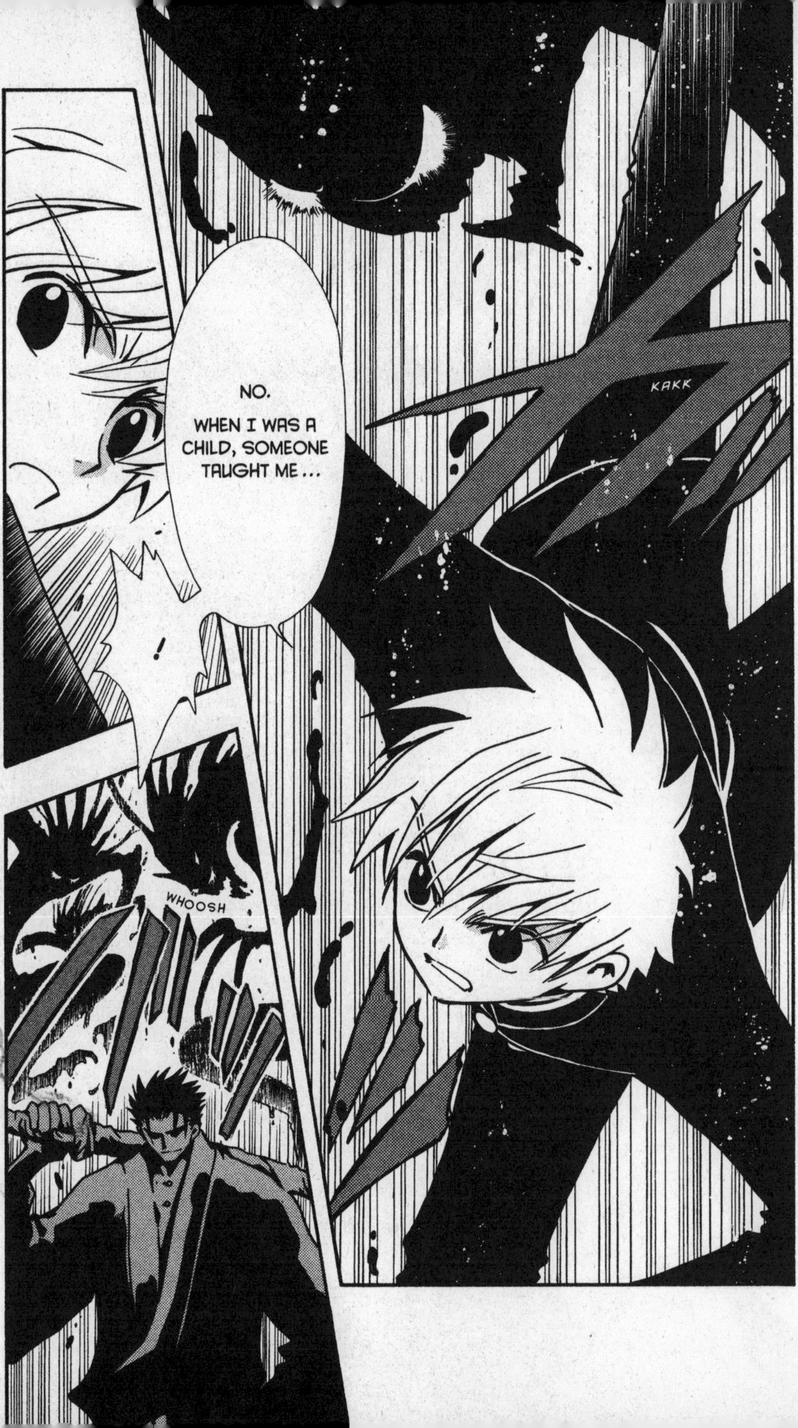
KAKK
NO.
WHEN I WAS A CHILD, SOMEONE TAUGHT ME...
!
WHOOSH

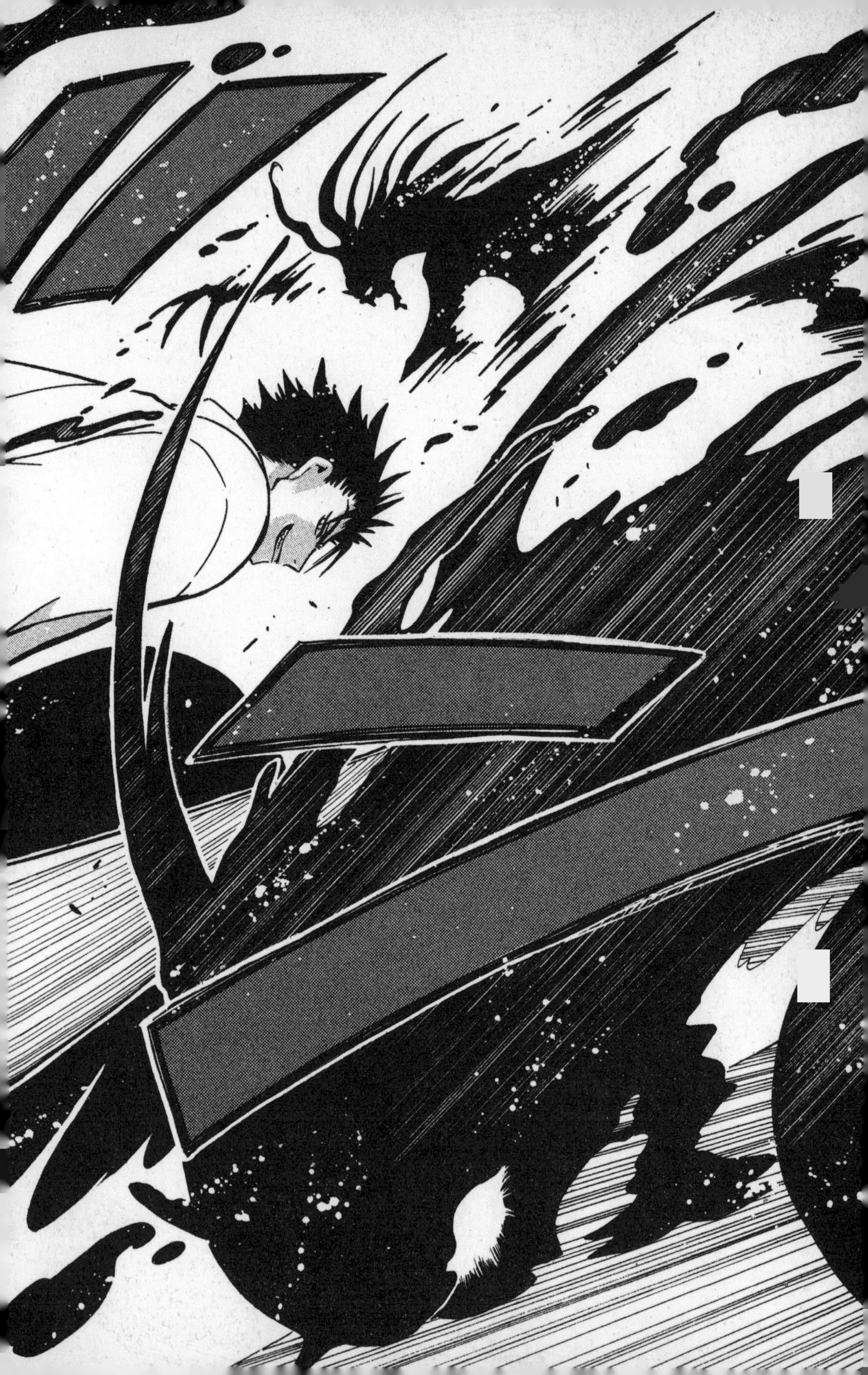

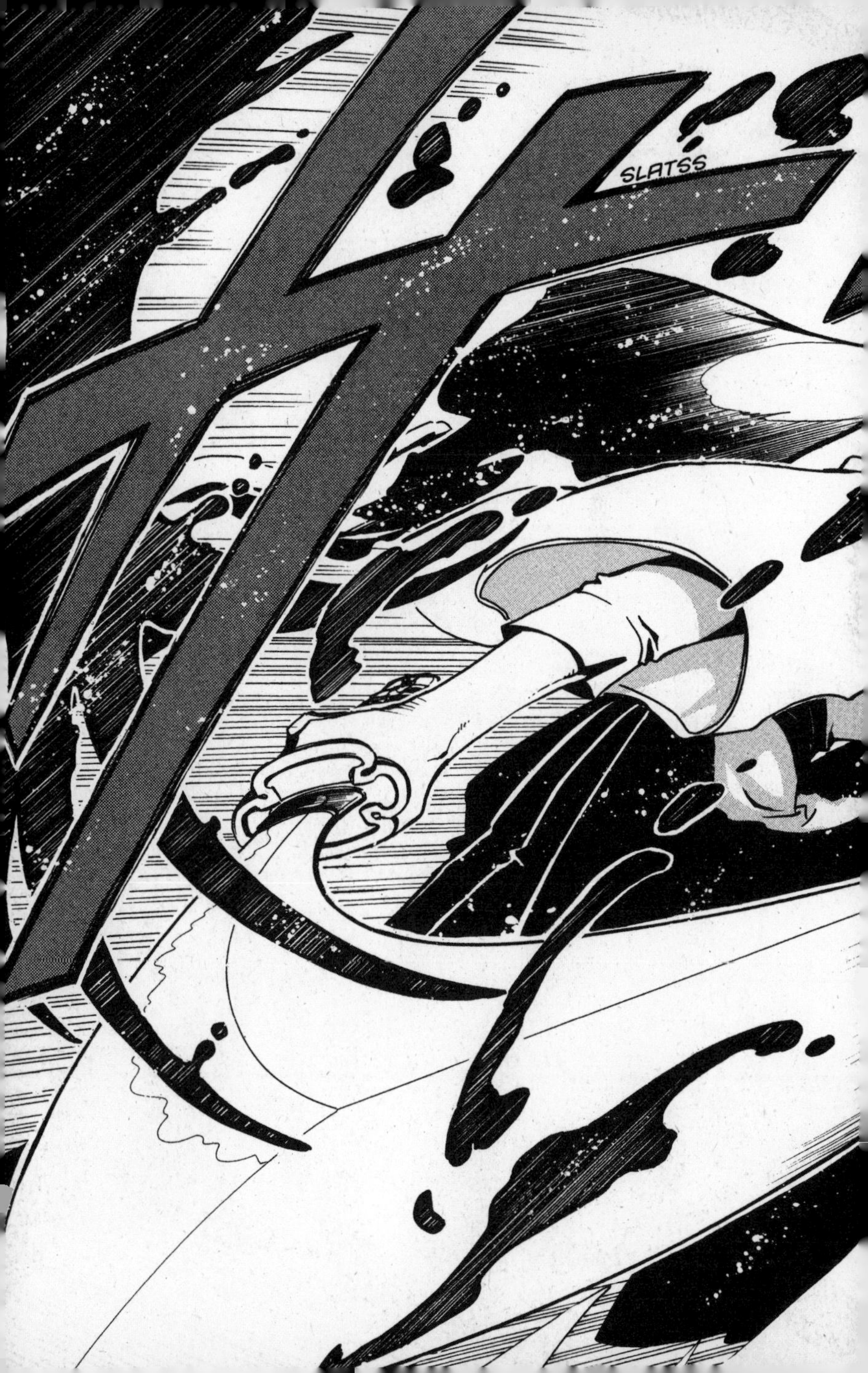
SLATSS

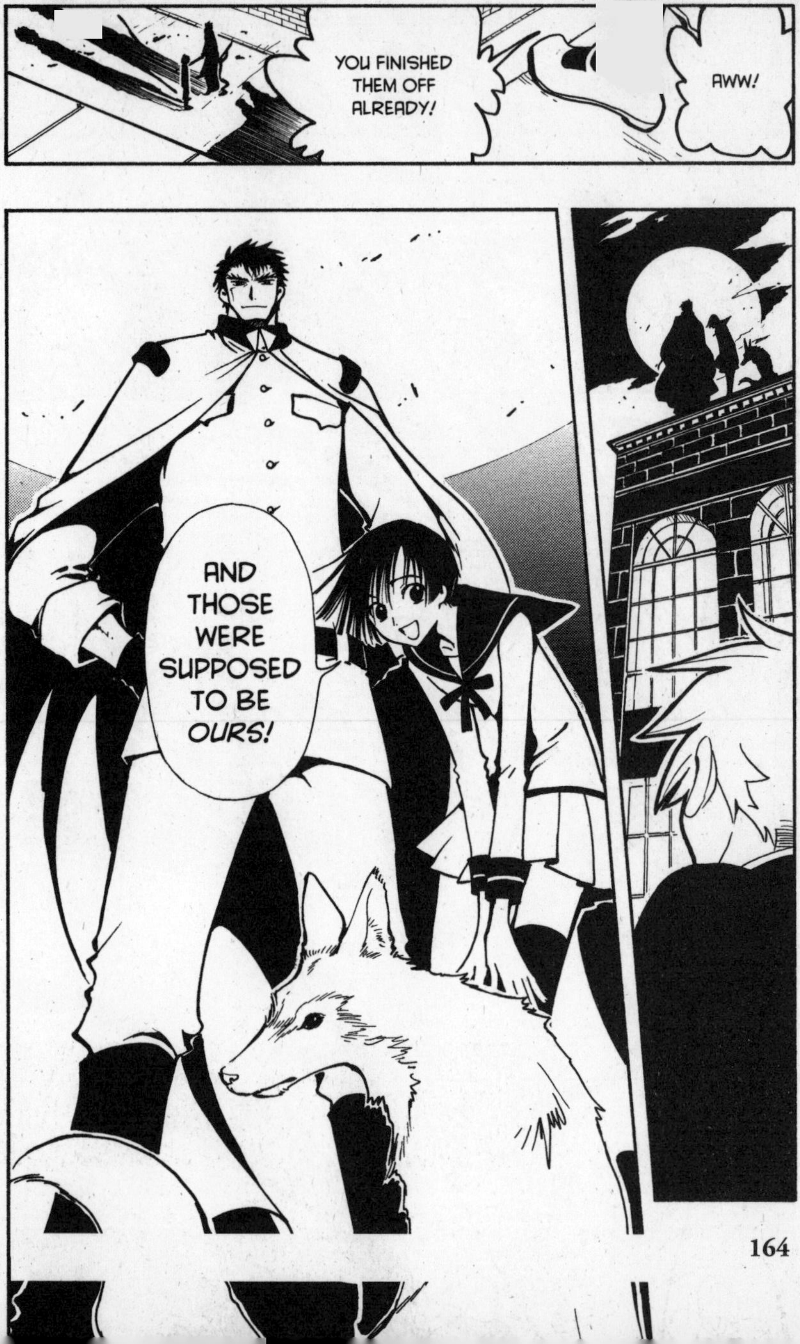
AWW!
YOU FINISHED THEM OFF ALREADY!
AND THOSE WERE SUPPOSED TO BE OURS!

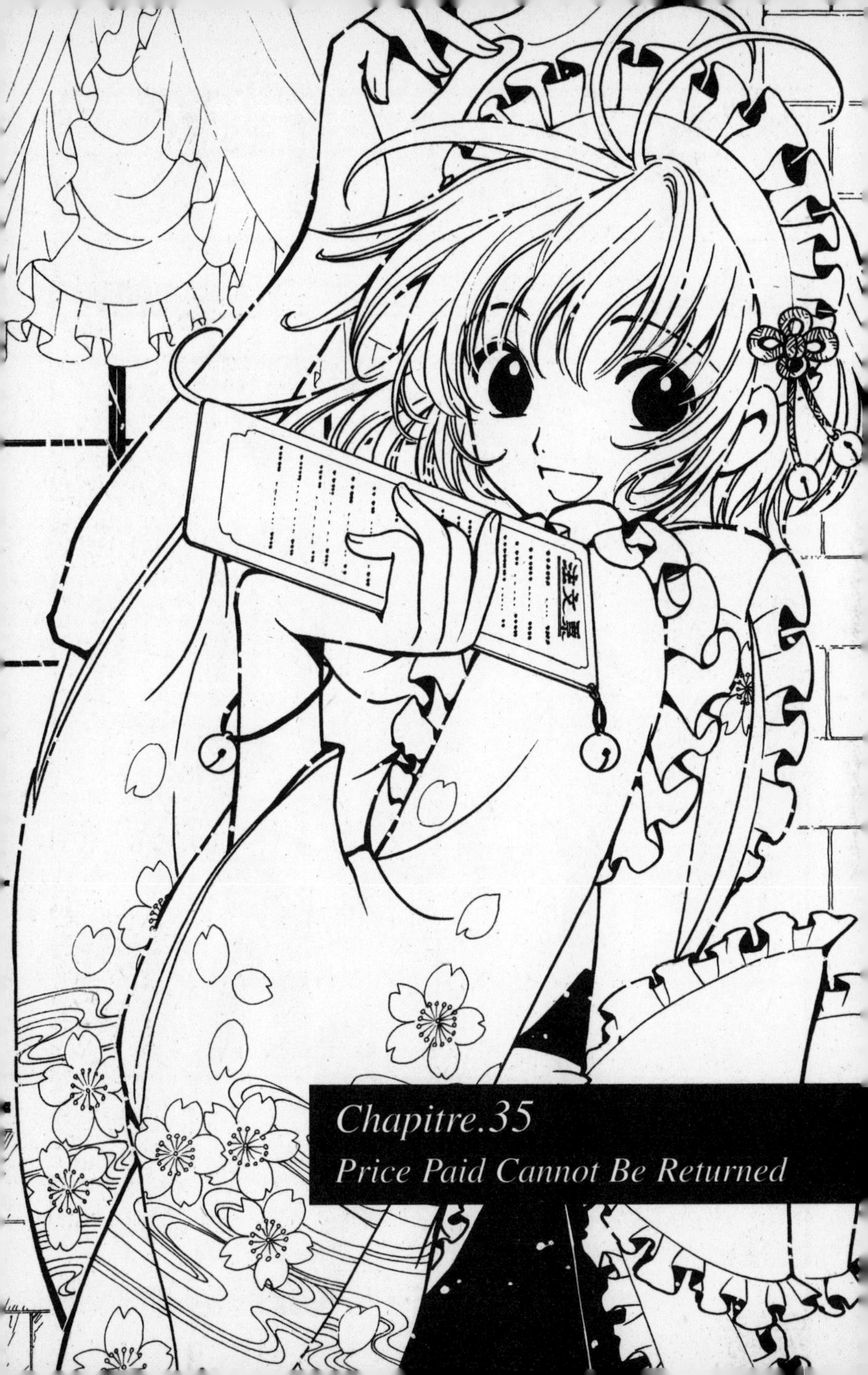

## Chapitre.35
## Price Paid Cannot Be Returned

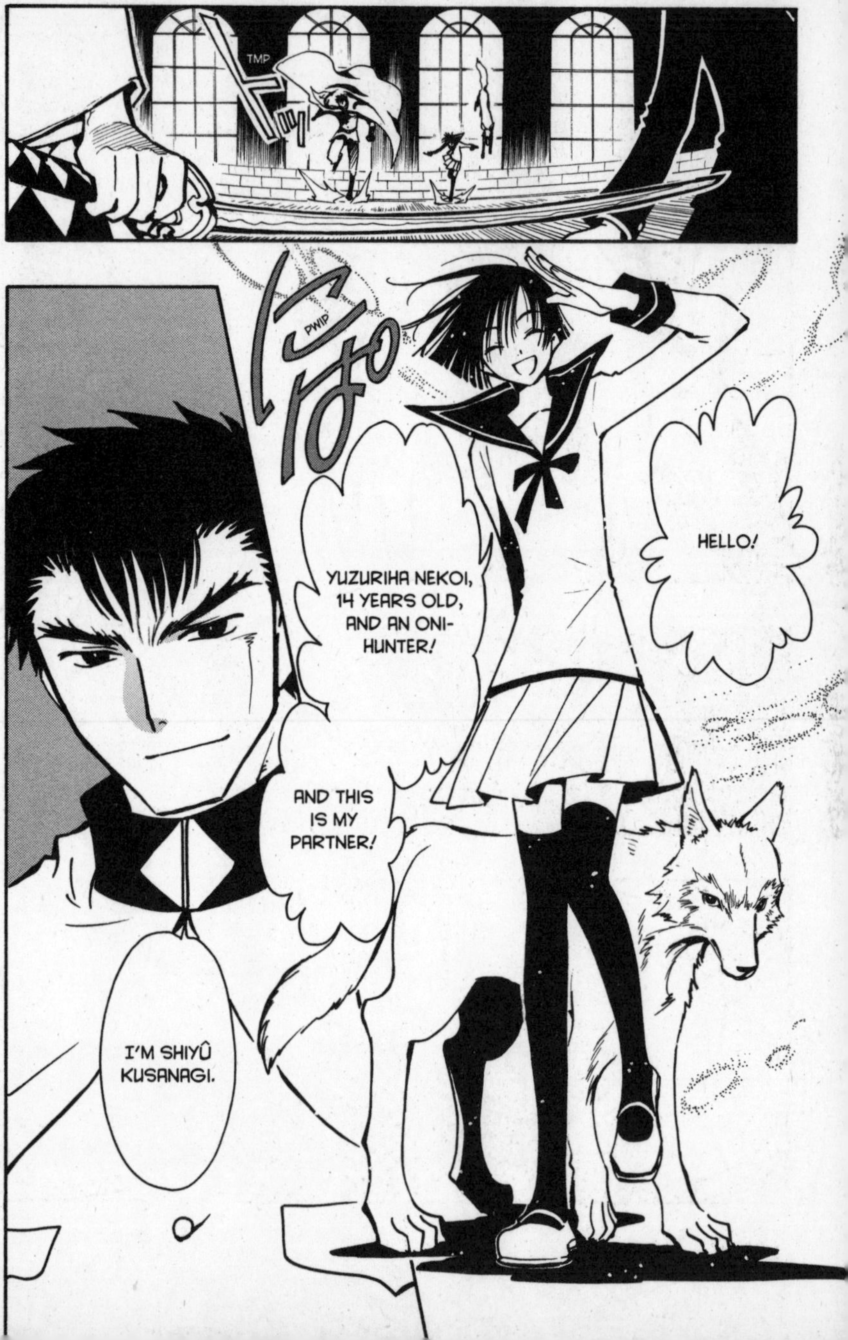
TMP
PWIP
HELLO!
YUZURIHA NEKOI, 14 YEARS OLD, AND AN ONI-HUNTER!
AND THIS IS MY PARTNER!
I'M SHIYÛ KUSANAGI.

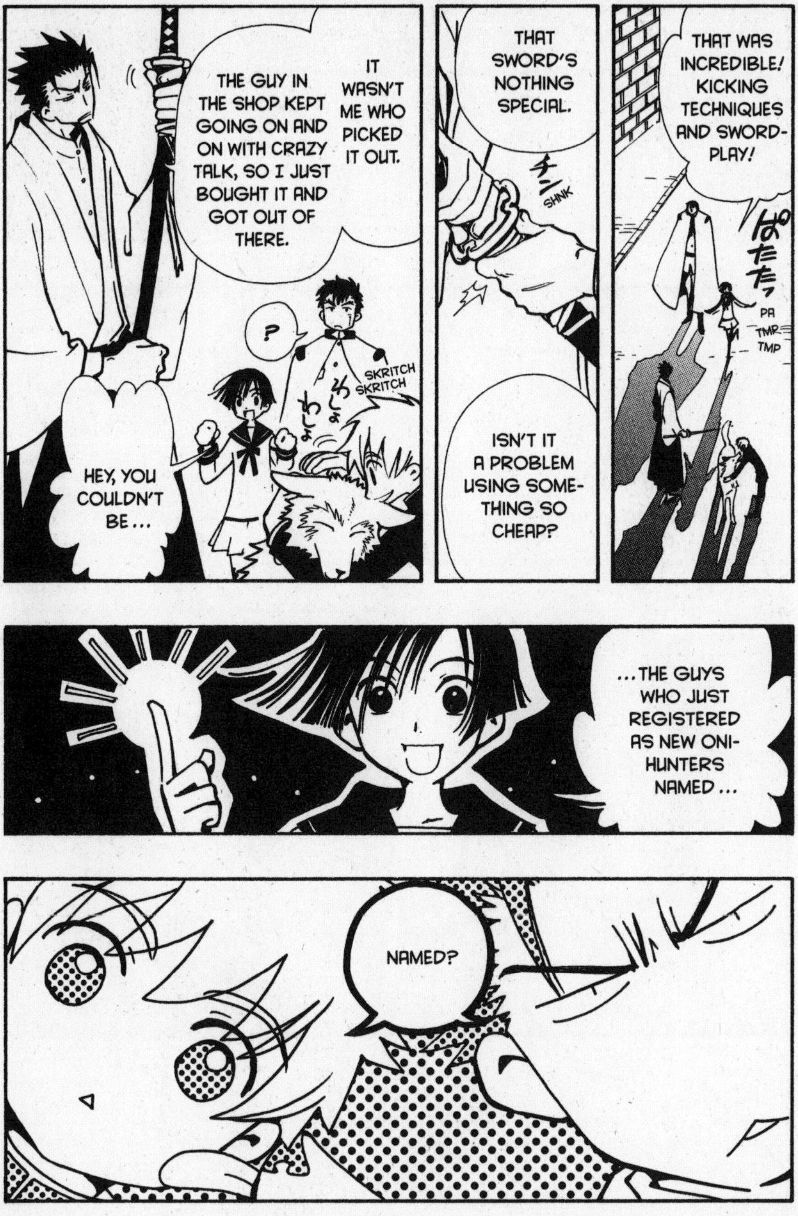
THAT WAS INCREDIBLE! KICKING TECHNIQUES AND SWORD-PLAY!
ぱたたっ
PA TMP TMP
THAT SWORD'S NOTHING SPECIAL.
チン
SHNK
ISN'T IT A PROBLEM USING SOME-THING SO CHEAP?
IT WASN'T ME WHO PICKED IT OUT.
THE GUY IN THE SHOP KEPT GOING ON AND ON WITH CRAZY TALK, SO I JUST BOUGHT IT AND GOT OUT OF THERE.
?
わしょわしょ
SKRITCH SKRITCH
HEY, YOU COULDN'T BE...
...THE GUYS WHO JUST REGISTERED AS NEW ONI-HUNTERS NAMED...
NAMED?

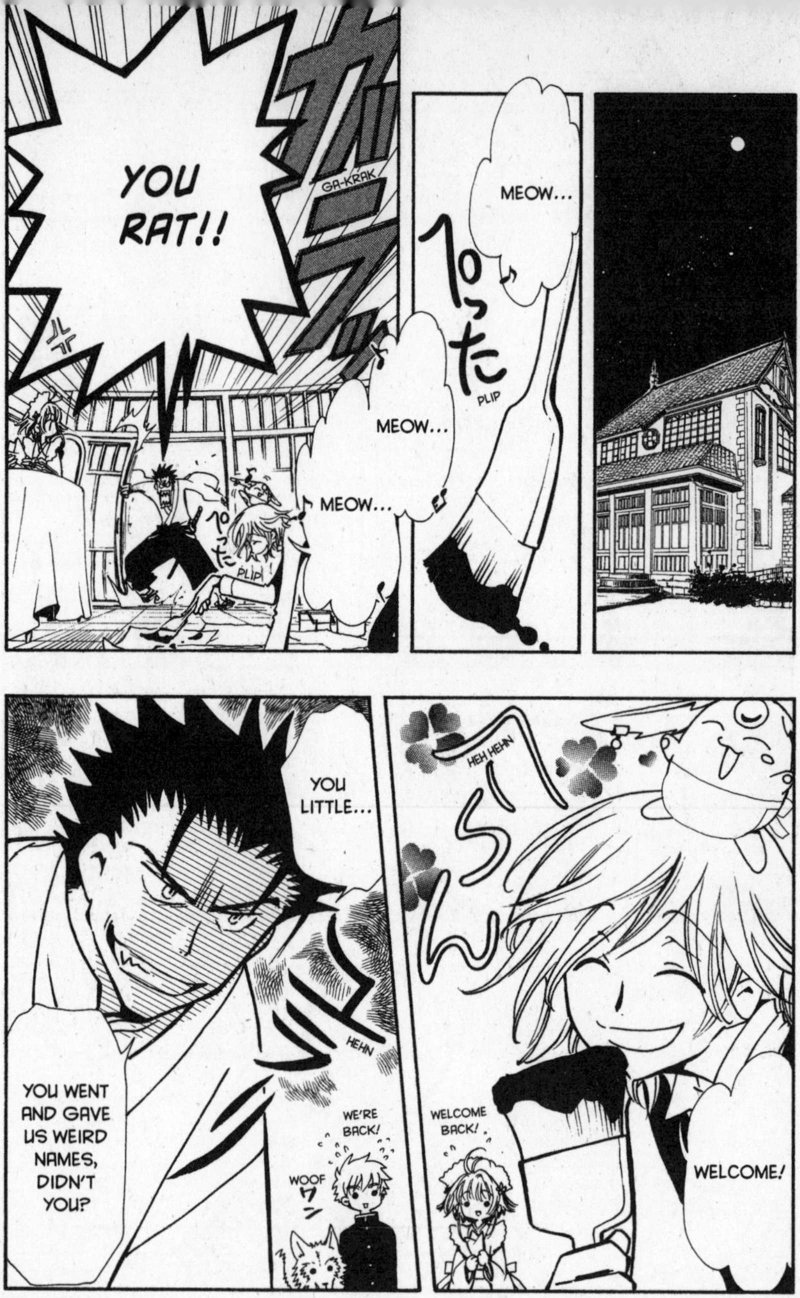
MEOW...
ぺったPLIP
GA-KRAK
YOU RAT!!
MEOW...
MEOW...
PLIP
HEH HEHN
WELCOME!
WELCOME BACK!
YOU LITTLE...
HEHN
WE'RE BACK!
WOOF
YOU WENT AND GAVE US WEIRD NAMES, DIDN'T YOU?

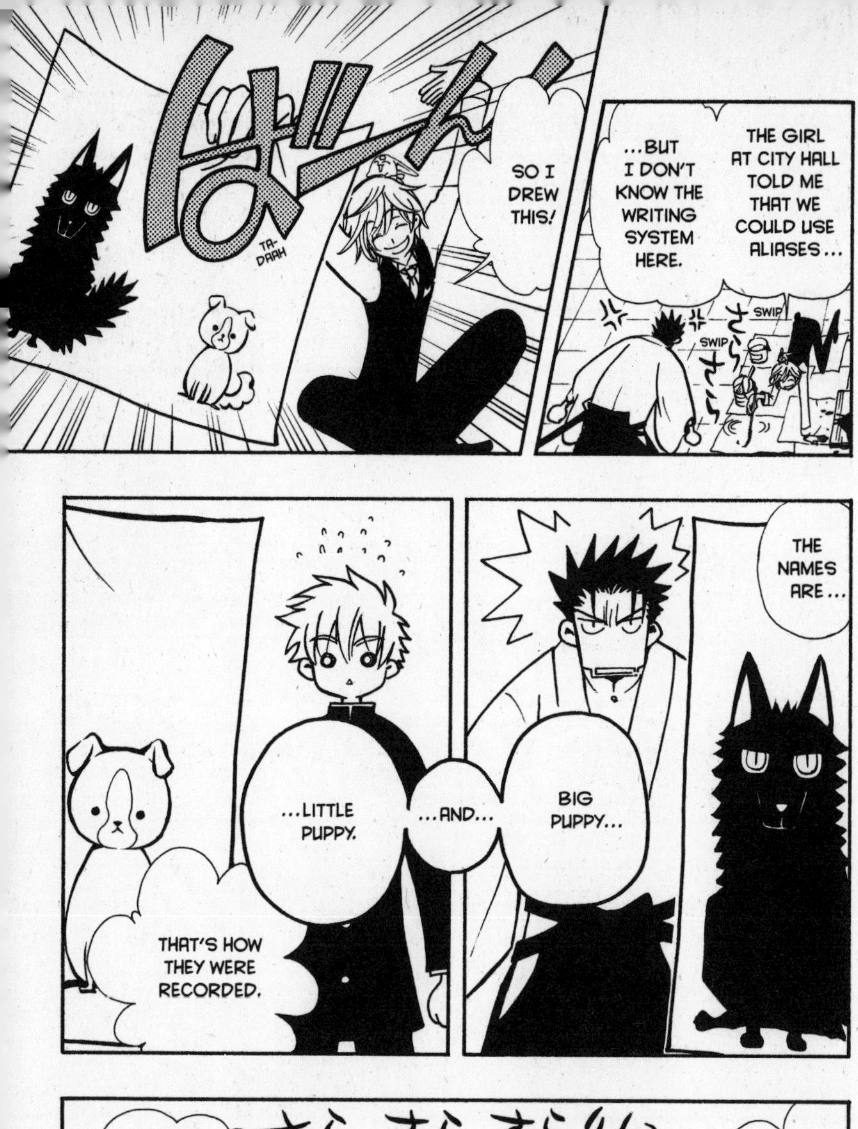
THE GIRL AT CITY HALL TOLD ME THAT WE COULD USE ALIASES...
...BUT I DON'T KNOW THE WRITING SYSTEM HERE.
SWIP
SWIP
SO I DREW THIS!
TA-DAAH
THE NAMES ARE...
BIG PUPPY...
...AND...
...LITTLE PUPPY.
THAT'S HOW THEY WERE RECORDED.
AND...
...FOR ME, I DID THIS.
SWIP
SWIP
SWIP
I DID THIS FOR SAKURA-CHAN.

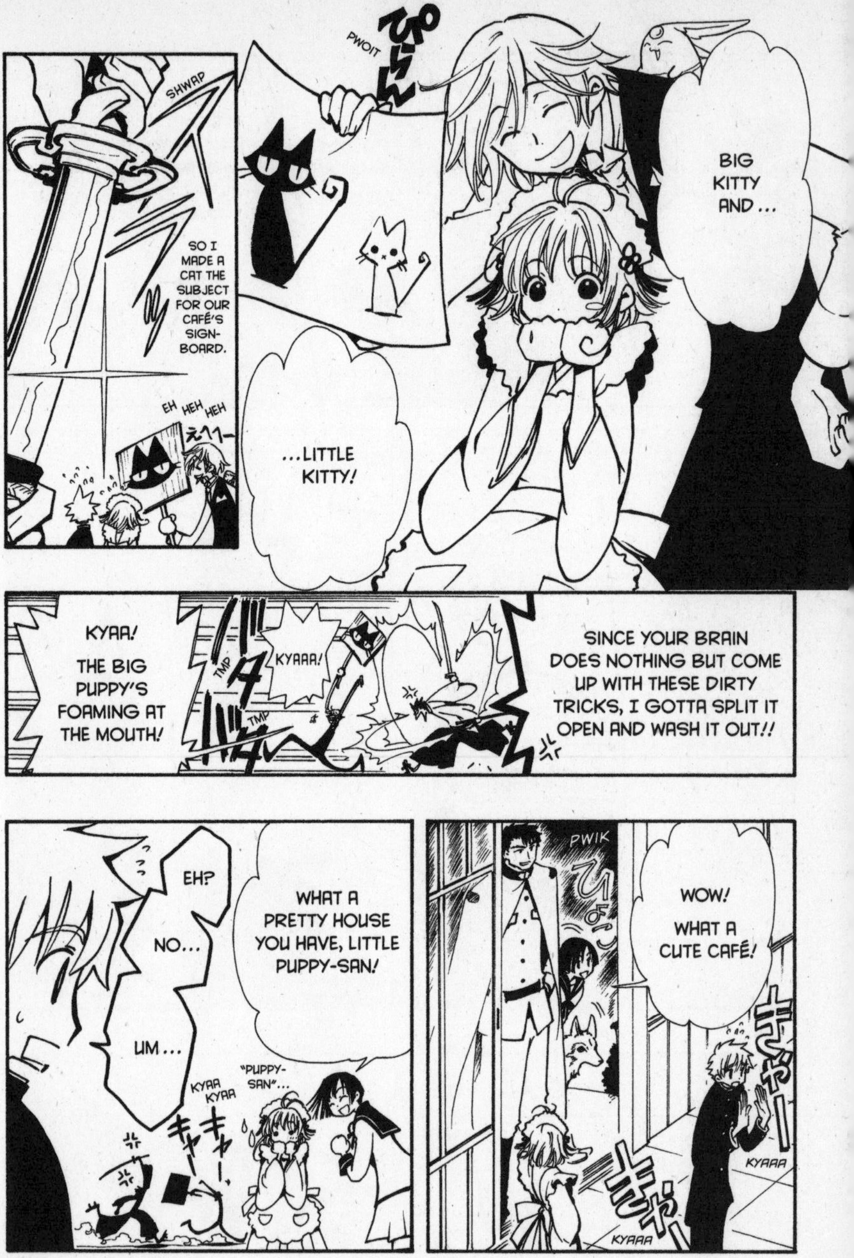
PWOIT
BIG KITTY AND...
...LITTLE KITTY!
SHWAP
SO I MADE A CAT THE SUBJECT FOR OUR CAFÉ'S SIGN-BOARD.
EH HEH HEH
SINCE YOUR BRAIN DOES NOTHING BUT COME UP WITH THESE DIRTY TRICKS, I GOTTA SPLIT IT OPEN AND WASH IT OUT!!
KYAAA!
TMP
TMP
KYAA!
THE BIG PUPPY'S FOAMING AT THE MOUTH!
PWIK
WOW!
WHAT A CUTE CAFÉ!
KYAAA
KYAAA
WHAT A PRETTY HOUSE YOU HAVE, LITTLE PUPPY-SAN!
EH?
NO...
UM...
"PUPPY-SAN"...
KYAA KYAA

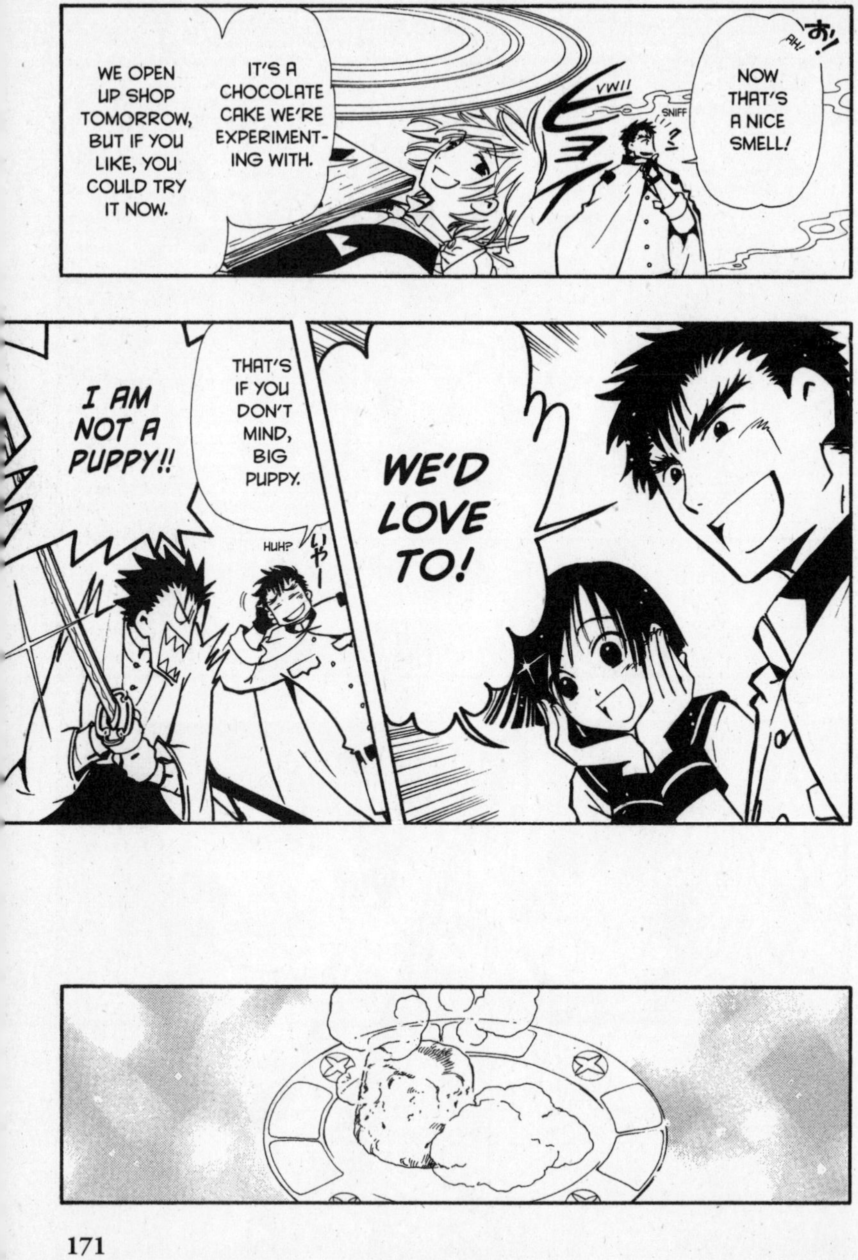
AH! お!
NOW THAT'S A NICE SMELL!
SNIFF
VWII
IT'S A CHOCOLATE CAKE WE'RE EXPERIMENT-ING WITH.
WE OPEN UP SHOP TOMORROW, BUT IF YOU LIKE, YOU COULD TRY IT NOW.
WE'D LOVE TO!
THAT'S IF YOU DON'T MIND, BIG PUPPY.
HUH?
I AM NOT A PUPPY!!

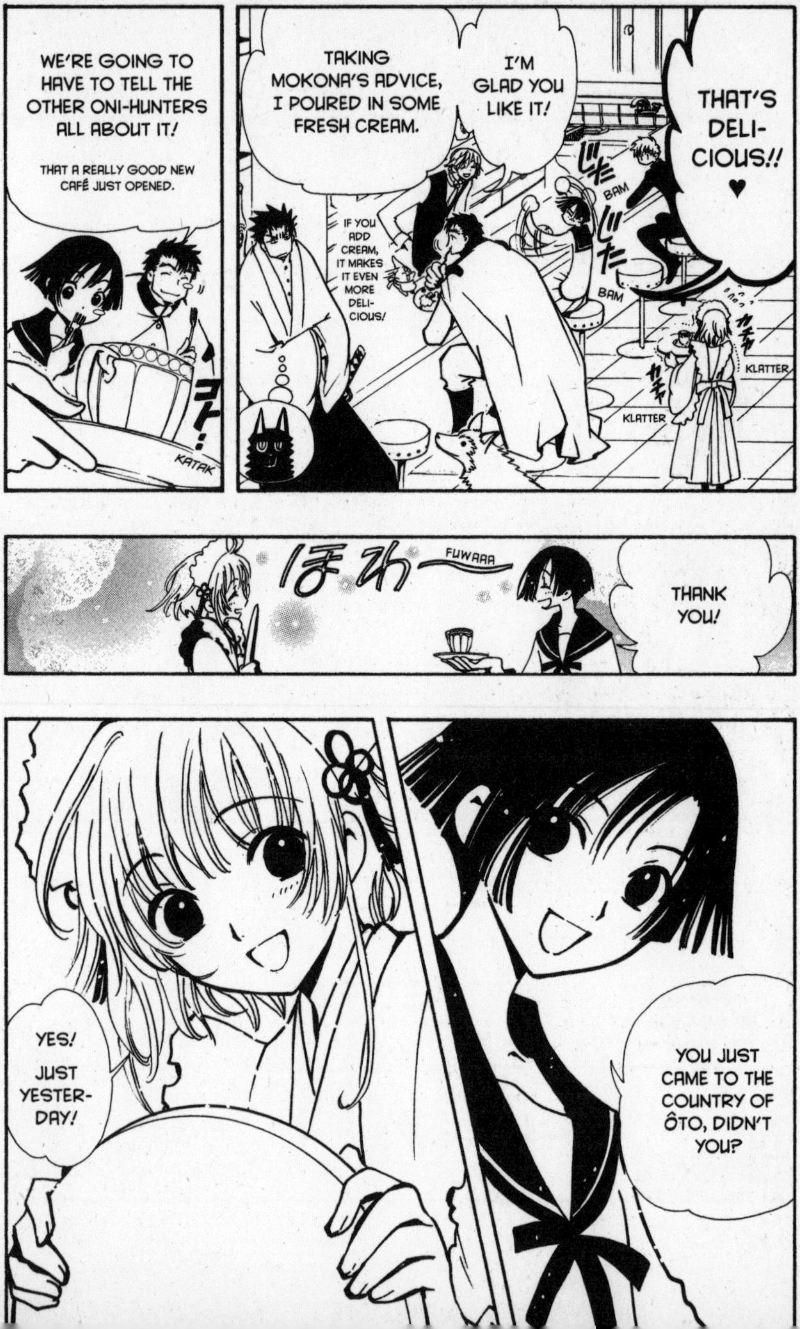
THAT'S DELICIOUS!! ♥
BAM
BAM
I'M GLAD YOU LIKE IT!
TAKING MOKONA'S ADVICE, I POURED IN SOME FRESH CREAM.
IF YOU ADD CREAM, IT MAKES IT EVEN MORE DELICIOUS!
KLATTER
KLATTER
WE'RE GOING TO HAVE TO TELL THE OTHER ONI-HUNTERS ALL ABOUT IT!
THAT A REALLY GOOD NEW CAFÉ JUST OPENED.
KATAK
THANK YOU!
FUWAAA
YOU JUST CAME TO THE COUNTRY OF ÔTO, DIDN'T YOU?
YES! JUST YESTERDAY!

BUT MAYBE YOU COULD HELP.

THE GIRL AT CITY HALL MENTIONED RANKS AND LEVELS OF ONI.

WHAT ARE THEY?

ON THE VERY NIGHT WE ARRIVED, AN ONI ATTACKED OUR HOUSE.

IT WAS TOUCH-AND-GO FOR A BIT.

CHART OF ONI RANKS AND LEVELS

ÔTO OFFICIAL CHARTS

RANKS AND LEVELS

| | |
|---|---|
| I | 1 2 3 4 5 |
| RO | 1 2 3 4 5 |
| HA | 1 2 3 4 5 |
| NI | 1 2 3 4 5 |
| HO | 1 2 3 4 5 |
| HE | 1 2 3 4 5 |
| TO | 1 2 3 4 5 |

STRONGEST

WEAKEST

AND THERE ARE FIVE LEVELS FOR EACH RANK.

ONI COME IN DIFFERENT RANKS WITH "I" BEING THE STRONGEST.

THEN, IN DESCENDING STRENGTHS ARE "RO," "HA," "NI," "HO," "HE," AND "TO."

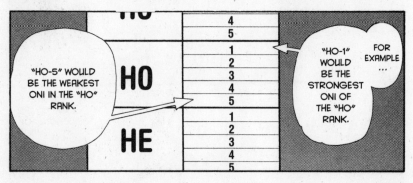

"HO-5" WOULD BE THE WEAKEST ONI IN THE "HO" RANK.

"HO-1" WOULD BE THE STRONGEST ONI OF THE "HO" RANK.

FOR EXAMPLE...

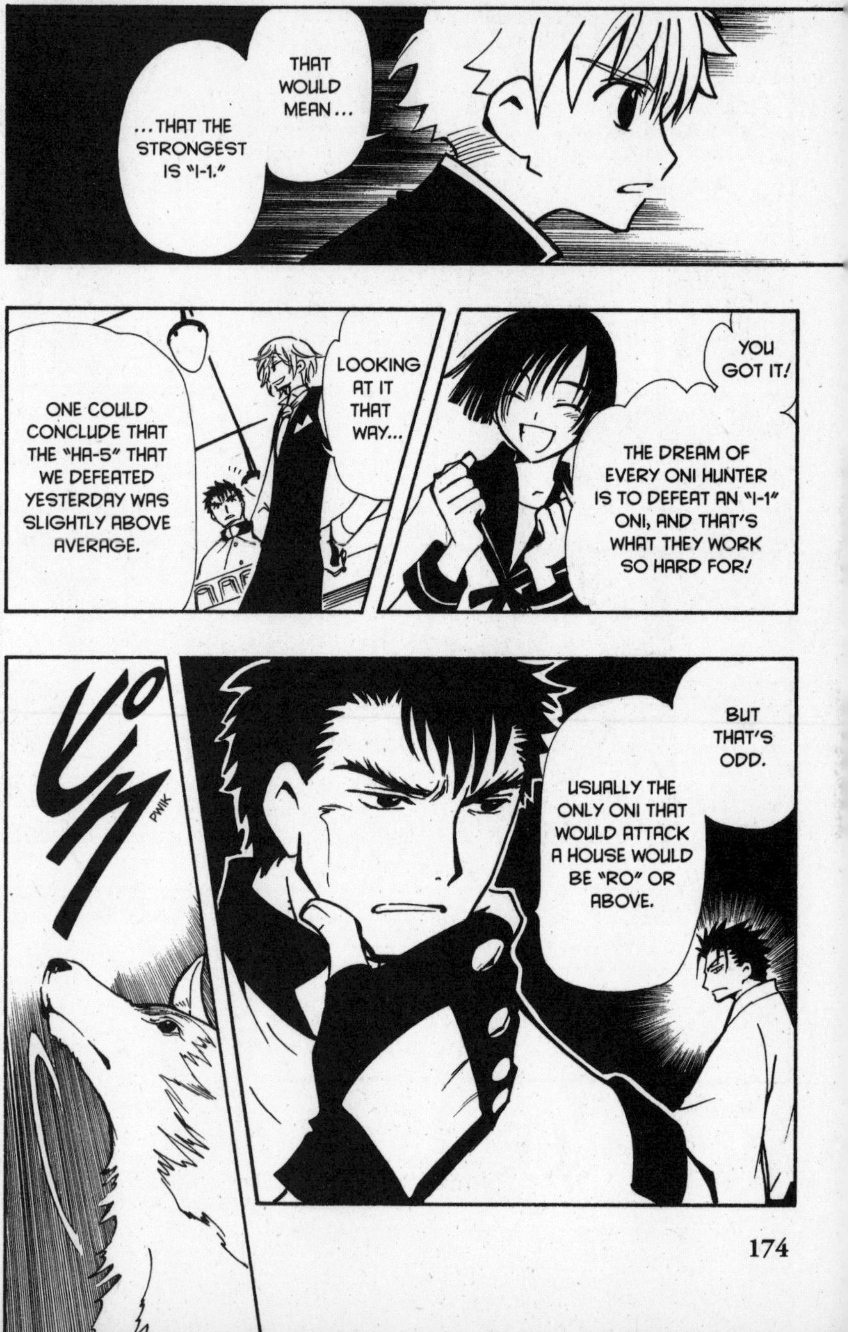
THAT WOULD MEAN...
...THAT THE STRONGEST IS "I-1."
YOU GOT IT!
THE DREAM OF EVERY ONI HUNTER IS TO DEFEAT AN "I-1" ONI, AND THAT'S WHAT THEY WORK SO HARD FOR!
LOOKING AT IT THAT WAY...
ONE COULD CONCLUDE THAT THE "HA-5" THAT WE DEFEATED YESTERDAY WAS SLIGHTLY ABOVE AVERAGE.
BUT THAT'S ODD.
USUALLY THE ONLY ONI THAT WOULD ATTACK A HOUSE WOULD BE "RO" OR ABOVE.
PWIK

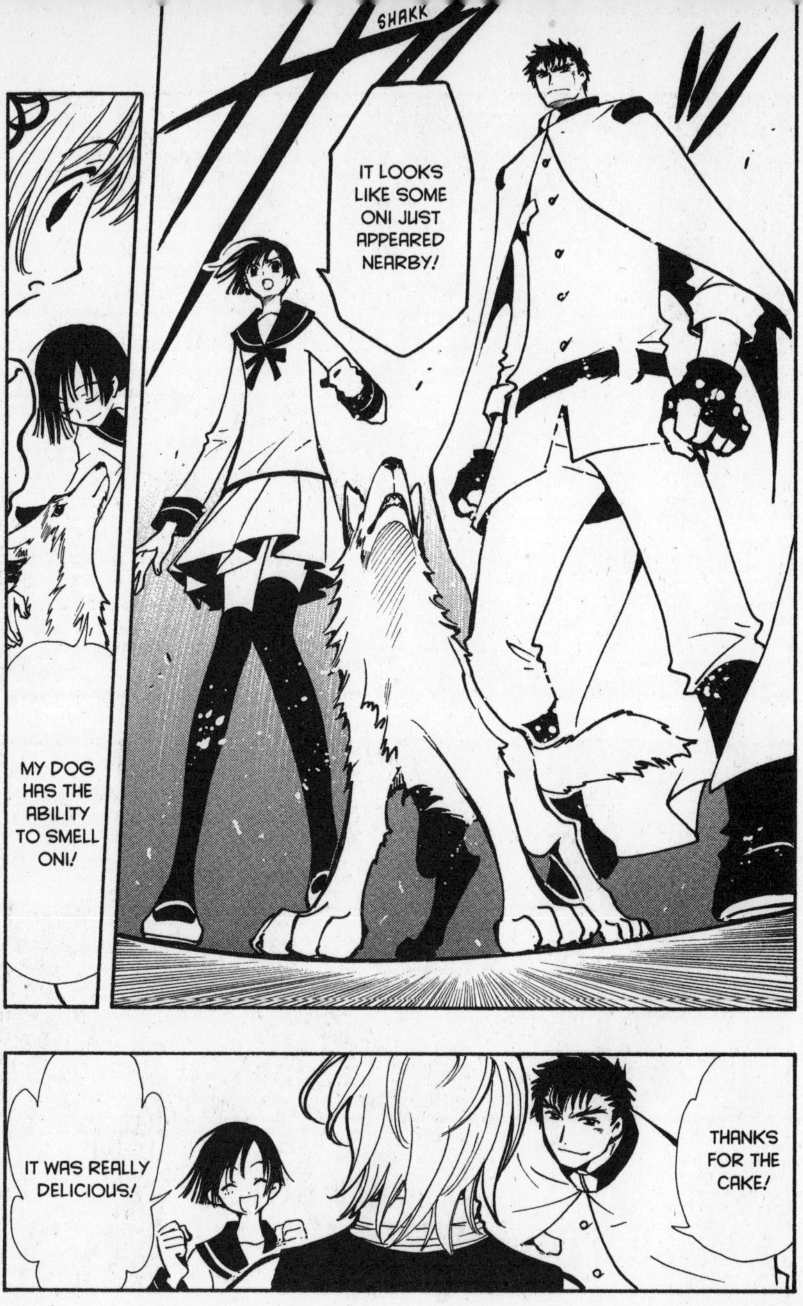
SHAKK
IT LOOKS LIKE SOME ONI JUST APPEARED NEARBY!
MY DOG HAS THE ABILITY TO SMELL ONI!
THANKS FOR THE CAKE!
IT WAS REALLY DELICIOUS!

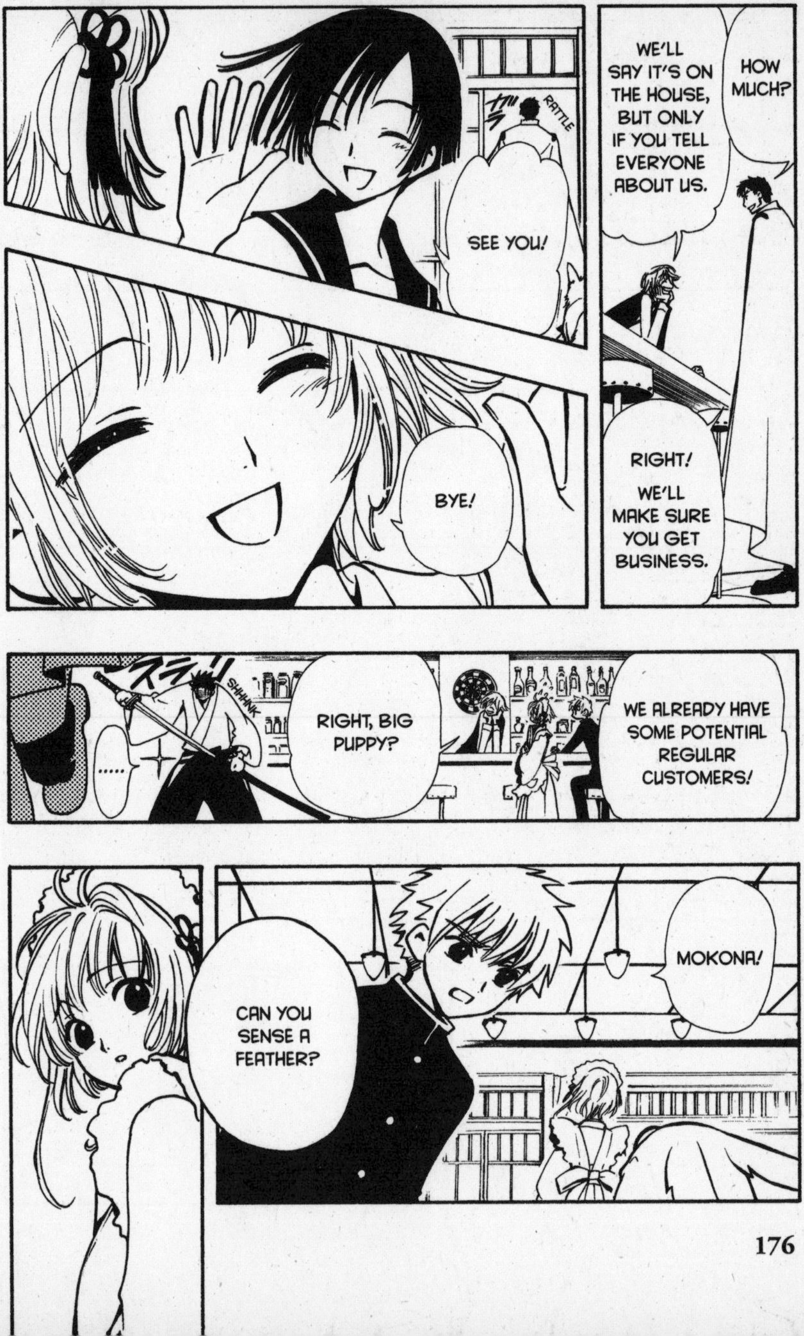
HOW MUCH?
WE'LL SAY IT'S ON THE HOUSE, BUT ONLY IF YOU TELL EVERYONE ABOUT US.
RIGHT! WE'LL MAKE SURE YOU GET BUSINESS.
RATTLE
SEE YOU!
BYE!
WE ALREADY HAVE SOME POTENTIAL REGULAR CUSTOMERS!
RIGHT, BIG PUPPY?
SHHHNK
......
MOKONA!
CAN YOU SENSE A FEATHER?

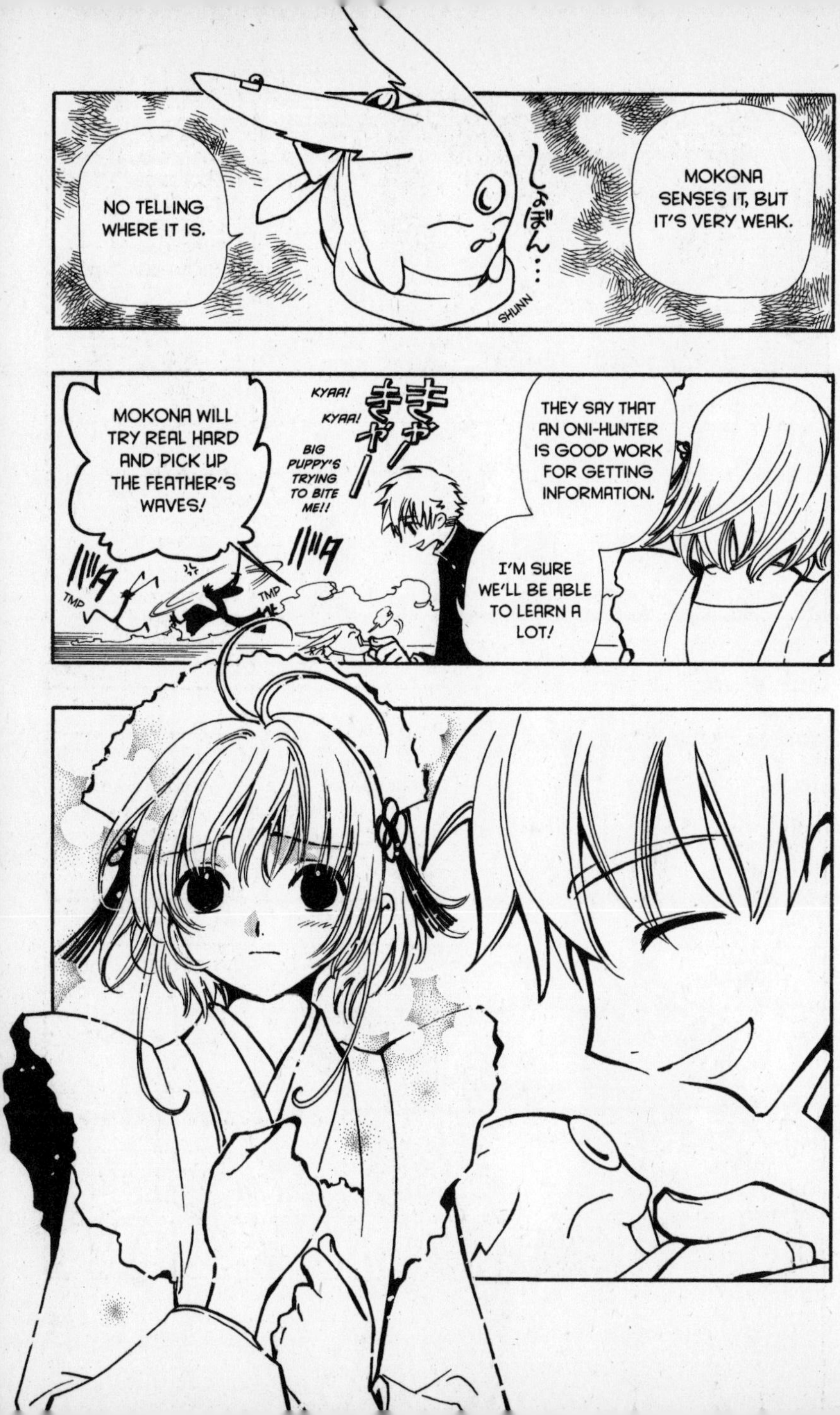
MOKONA SENSES IT, BUT IT'S VERY WEAK.
しょぼん…
SHUNN
NO TELLING WHERE IT IS.
THEY SAY THAT AN ONI-HUNTER IS GOOD WORK FOR GETTING INFORMATION.
I'M SURE WE'LL BE ABLE TO LEARN A LOT!
きゃーきゃー
KYAA!
KYAA!
BIG PUPPY'S TRYING TO BITE ME!!
MOKONA WILL TRY REAL HARD AND PICK UP THE FEATHER'S WAVES!
パタ
TMP
パタ
TMP

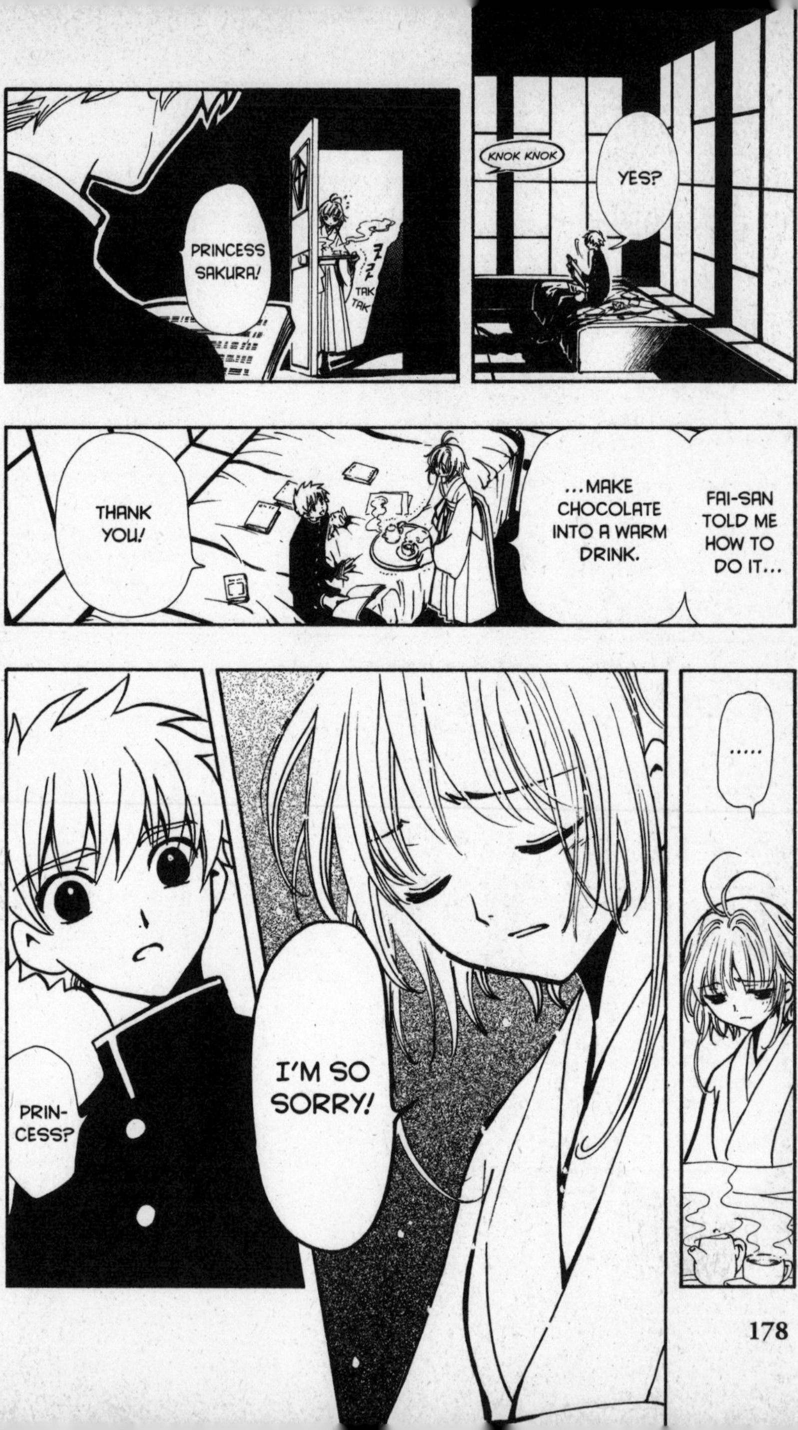
KNOK KNOK
YES?
PRINCESS SAKURA!
TAK TAK
FAI-SAN TOLD ME HOW TO DO IT...
...MAKE CHOCOLATE INTO A WARM DRINK.
THANK YOU!
.....
I'M SO SORRY!
PRIN-CESS?

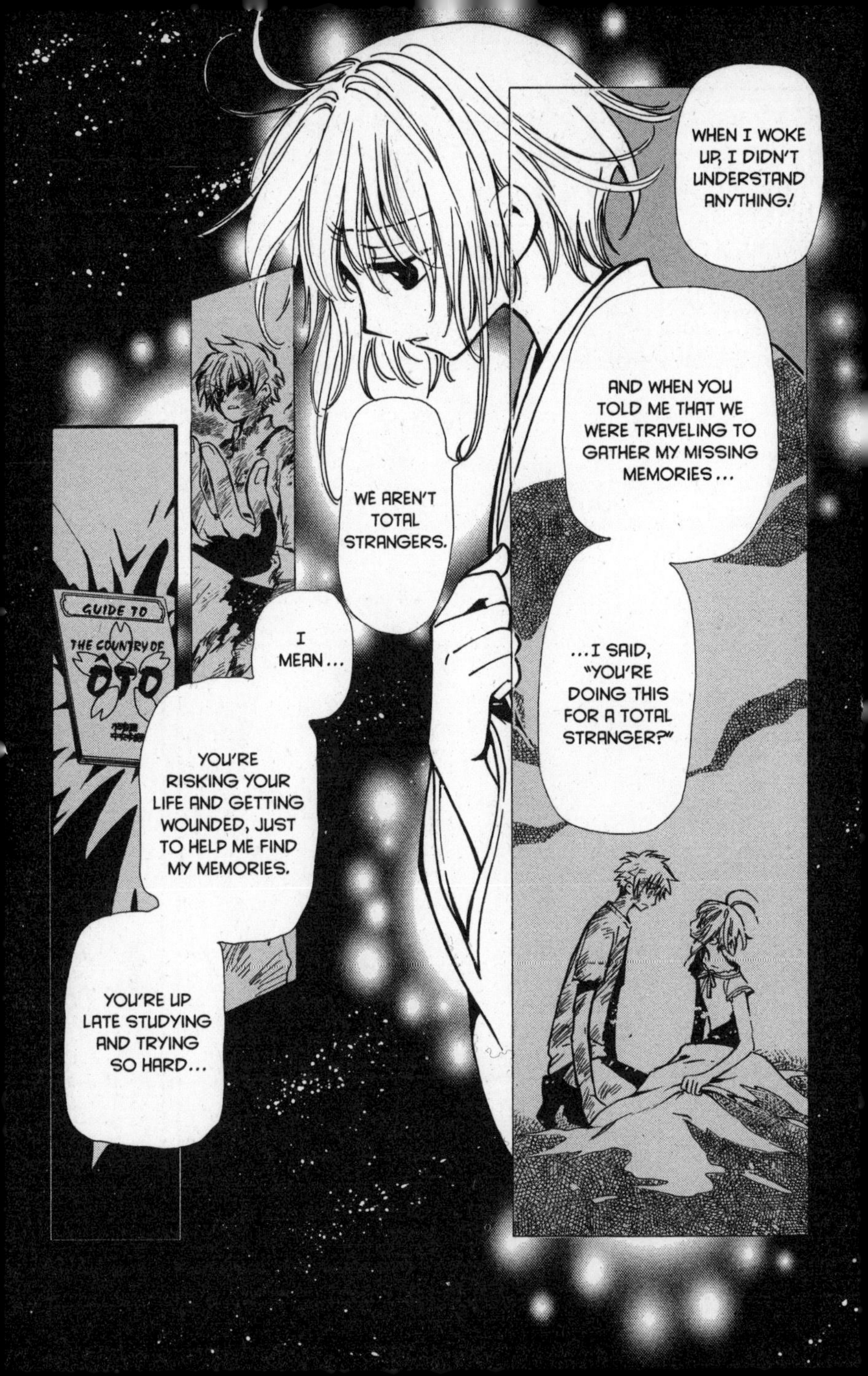
WHEN I WOKE UP, I DIDN'T UNDERSTAND ANYTHING!
AND WHEN YOU TOLD ME THAT WE WERE TRAVELING TO GATHER MY MISSING MEMORIES...
...I SAID, "YOU'RE DOING THIS FOR A TOTAL STRANGER?"
WE AREN'T TOTAL STRANGERS.
I MEAN...
YOU'RE RISKING YOUR LIFE AND GETTING WOUNDED, JUST TO HELP ME FIND MY MEMORIES.
YOU'RE UP LATE STUDYING AND TRYING SO HARD...
GUIDE TO
THE COUNTRY OF
OTO

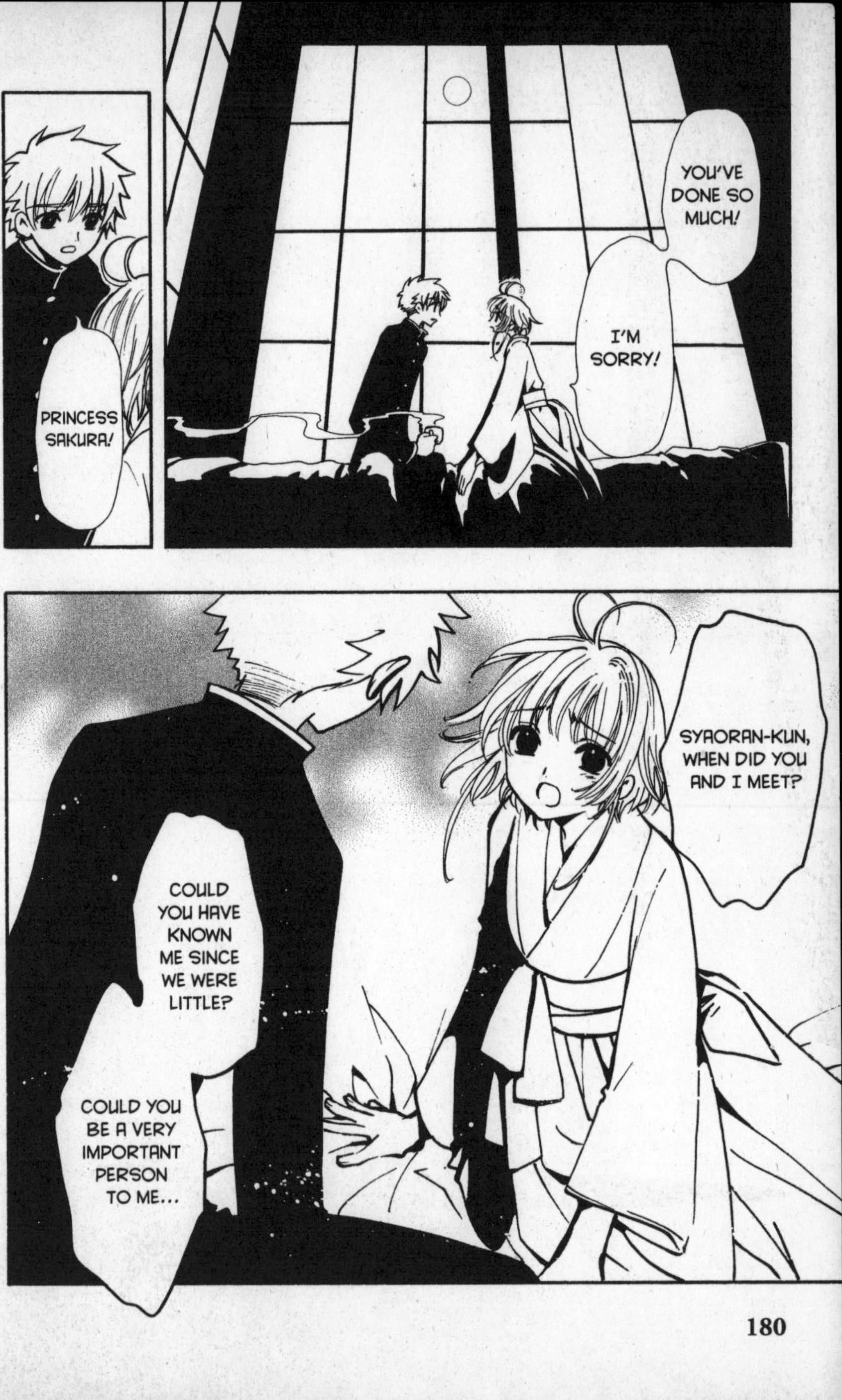
YOU'VE DONE SO MUCH!
I'M SORRY!
PRINCESS SAKURA!
SYAORAN-KUN, WHEN DID YOU AND I MEET?
COULD YOU HAVE KNOWN ME SINCE WE WERE LITTLE?
COULD YOU BE A VERY IMPORTANT PERSON TO ME...

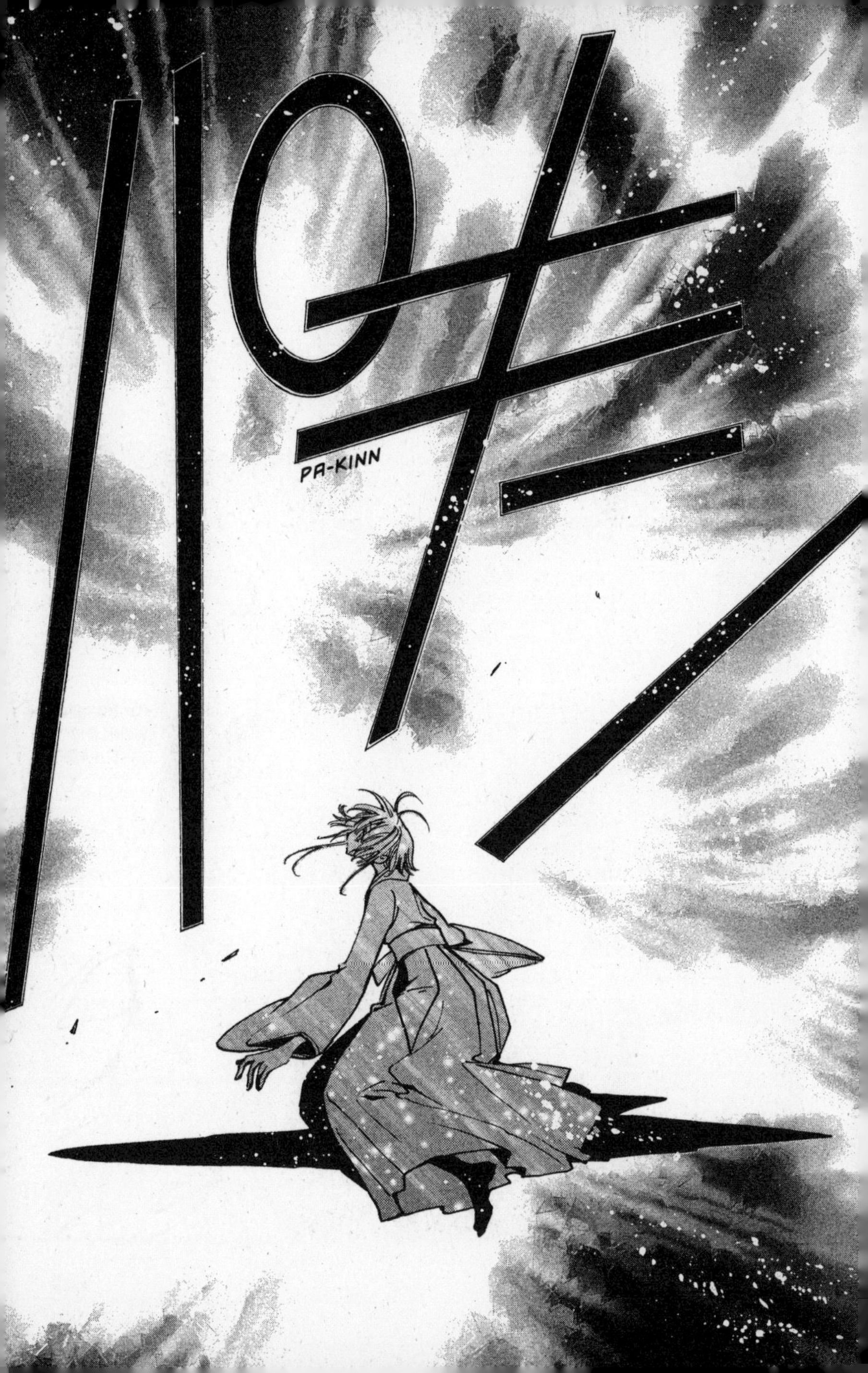
PA-KINN

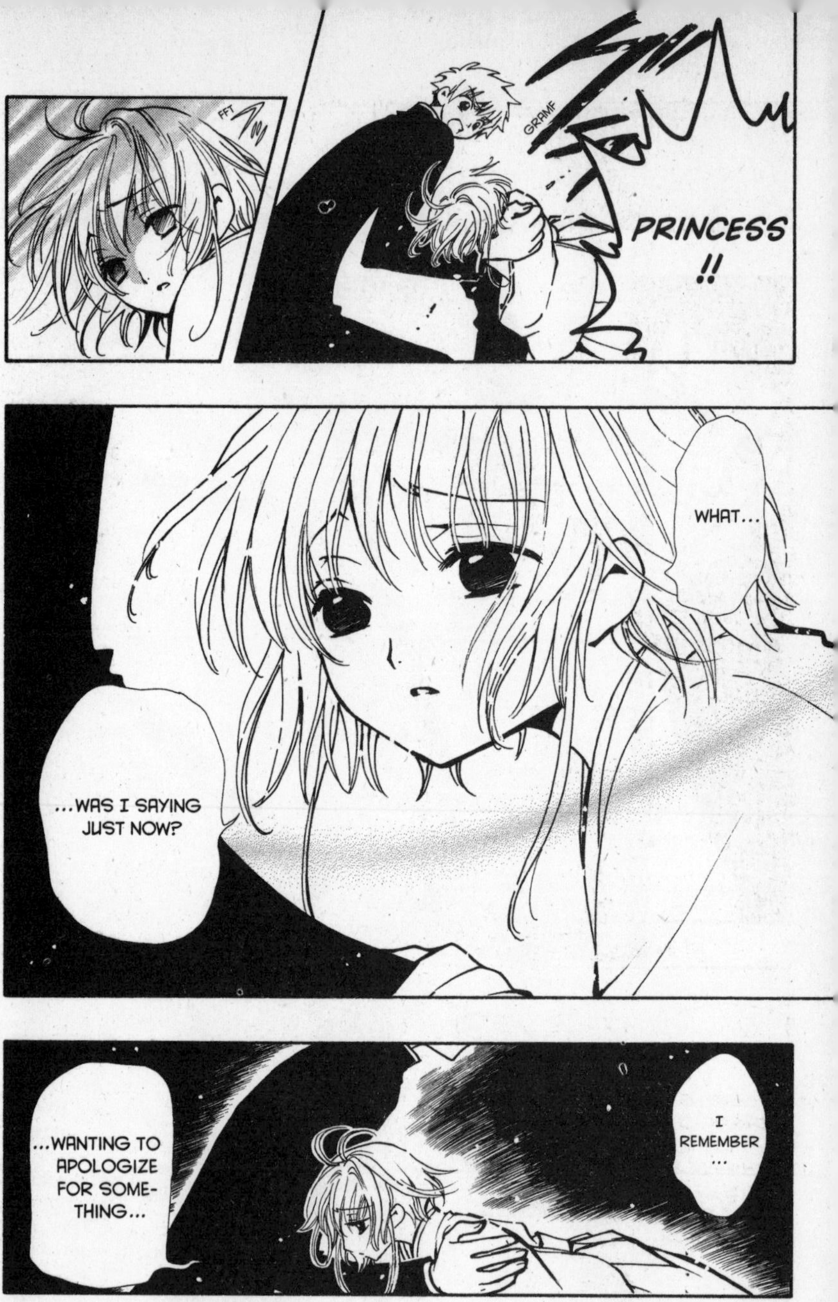
GRAMF
PRINCESS !!
FFT
WHAT...
...WAS I SAYING JUST NOW?
I REMEMBER ...
...WANTING TO APOLOGIZE FOR SOME-THING...

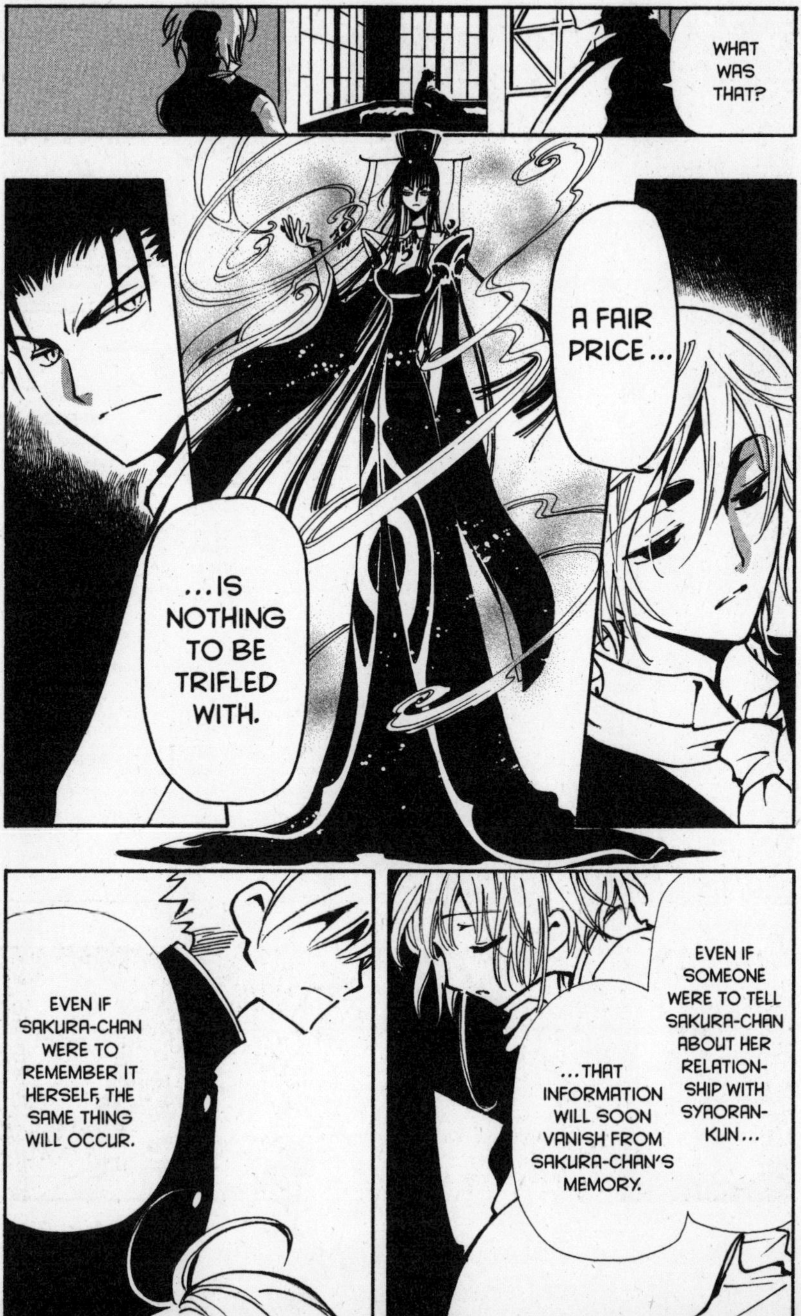
WHAT WAS THAT?
A FAIR PRICE...
...IS NOTHING TO BE TRIFLED WITH.
EVEN IF SOMEONE WERE TO TELL SAKURA-CHAN ABOUT HER RELATION-SHIP WITH SYAORAN-KUN...
...THAT INFORMATION WILL SOON VANISH FROM SAKURA-CHAN'S MEMORY.
EVEN IF SAKURA-CHAN WERE TO REMEMBER IT HERSELF, THE SAME THING WILL OCCUR.

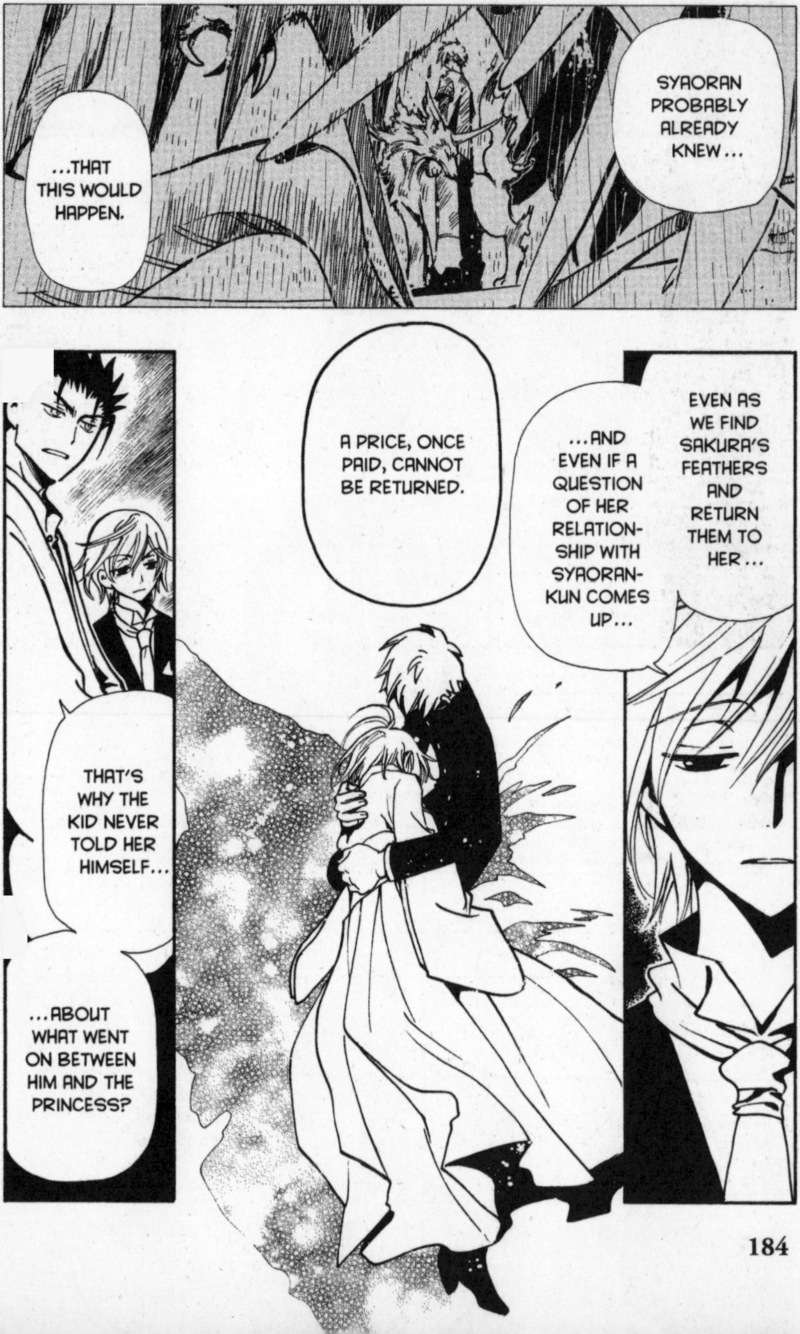
SYAORAN PROBABLY ALREADY KNEW...
...THAT THIS WOULD HAPPEN.
EVEN AS WE FIND SAKURA'S FEATHERS AND RETURN THEM TO HER...
...AND EVEN IF A QUESTION OF HER RELATIONSHIP WITH SYAORAN-KUN COMES UP...
A PRICE, ONCE PAID, CANNOT BE RETURNED.
THAT'S WHY THE KID NEVER TOLD HER HIMSELF...
...ABOUT WHAT WENT ON BETWEEN HIM AND THE PRINCESS?

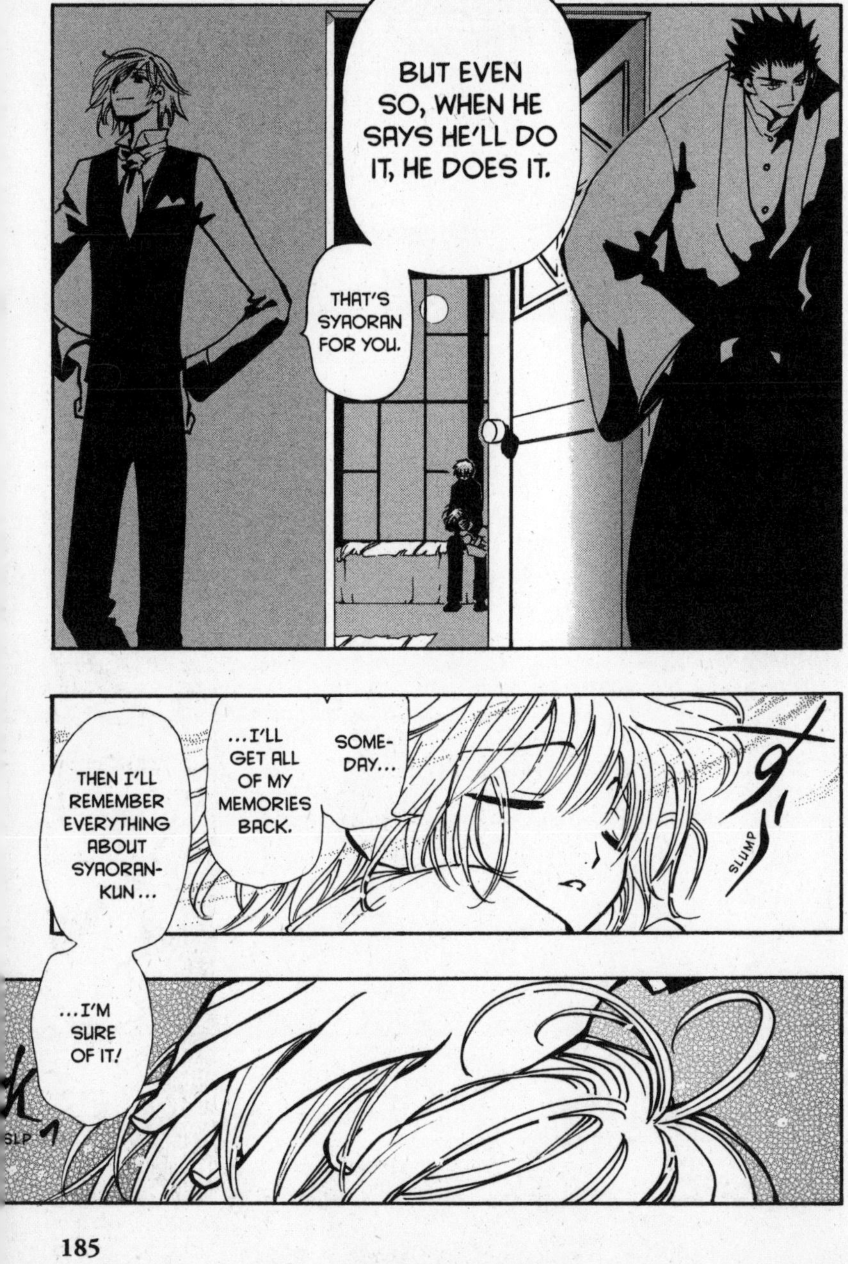
BUT EVEN SO, WHEN HE SAYS HE'LL DO IT, HE DOES IT.
THAT'S SYAORAN FOR YOU.
SLUMP
SOME-DAY...
...I'LL GET ALL OF MY MEMORIES BACK.
THEN I'LL REMEMBER EVERYTHING ABOUT SYAORAN-KUN...
...I'M SURE OF IT!
SLP

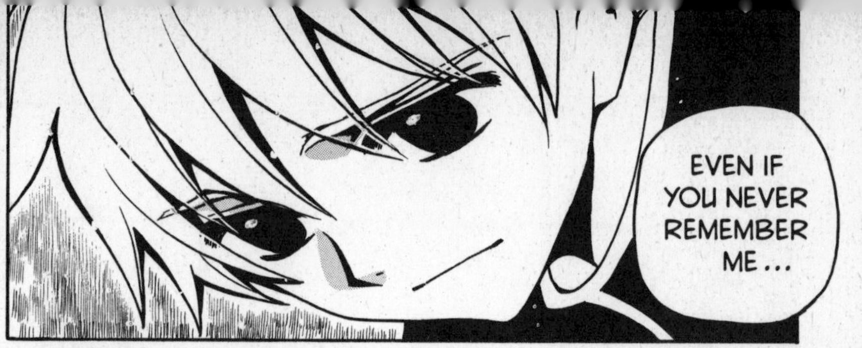
EVEN IF YOU NEVER REMEMBER ME...
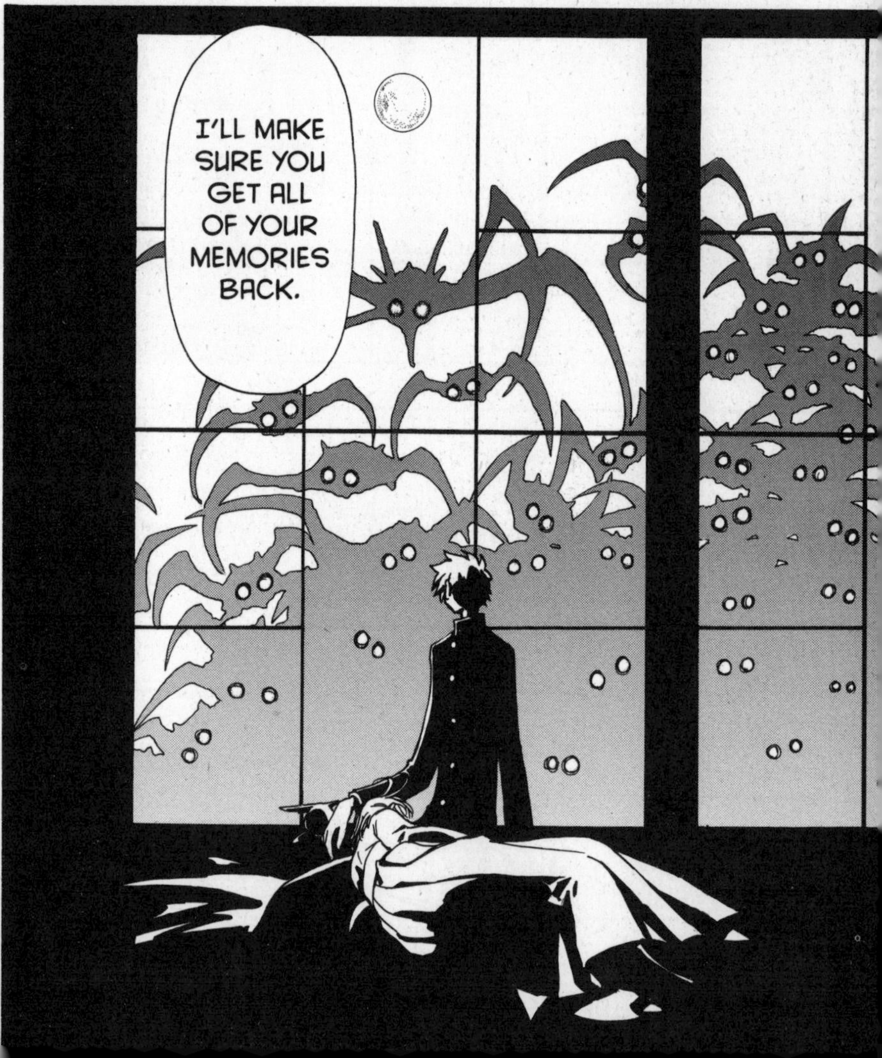
I'LL MAKE SURE YOU GET ALL OF YOUR MEMORIES BACK.

*To Be Continued*

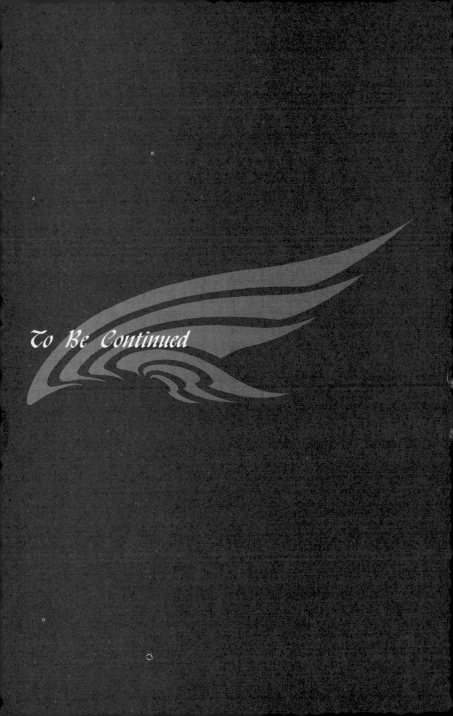

# About the Creators

CLAMP is a group of four women who have become the most popular manga artists in America—Satsuki Igarashi, Tsubaki Nekoi, Mokona, and Ageha Ohkawa. They started out as doujinshi (fan comics) creators, but their skill and craft brought them to the attention of publishers very quickly. Their first work from a major publisher was *RG Veda*, but their first mass success was with *Magic Knight Rayearth*. From there, they went on to write many series, including *Cardcaptor Sakura* and *Chobits*, two of the most popular manga in the United States. Like many Japanese manga artists, they prefer to avoid the spotlight, and little is known about them personally.

CLAMP is currently publishing three series in Japan: *Tsubasa* and *xxxHOLiC* with Kodansha and *Gohou Drug* with Kadokawa.

# Translation Notes

Japanese is a tricky language for most Westerners, and translation is often more art than science. For your edification and reading pleasure, here are notes on some of the places where we could have gone in a different direction in our translation of the work, or where a Japanese cultural reference is used.

## The country of Ôto

Many anime and manga fans have heard of the Meiji era—between 1867 and 1912. It was a time when Japan moved at lightning speed from the technology of a medieval feudal society to the modern age. America is also familiar with the Shôwa era (maybe not by that name) from 1926 through 1989, when the Shôwa emperor (Hirohito) was emperor of Japan. That era covered the pre-war militaristic movement, the war, and the post-war rebuilding of Japan. But the Taishô era, 1912 through 1926, is largely ignored in the West. On the other hand, Taishô is a romantic time for Japanese novelists because it is an era where traditional Japanese customs lived alongside the westernized elements of more modern Japan. Wooden trolleys, Edwardian houses, brick-paved streets filled with rickshaws, and kimono-clad women carrying their parasols are all standard images of the time. The country of Ôto is based on the Taishô era.

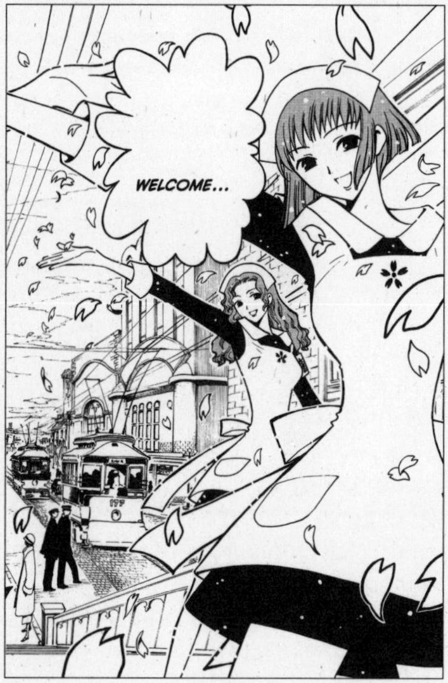
WELCOME...

## Country of Sakura

Chapitre.34
The Country of Sakura

The kanji that makes up the spelling for "Ôto" is cherry blossom ("sakura") and capital. Cherry blossoms are a symbol of Japan since they are one of the first colorful flowers to bloom in spring—and they represent the color and joy of spring and rebirth.

USUALLY THEY APPEAR AT NIGHT.
BUT IN RARE CASES, THEY'VE APPEARED IN BROAD DAYLIGHT.
THE FULL MOON SEEMS TO HAVE AN EFFECT ON THEIR STRENGTH.
AS THE MOON GETS FULLER, THEY GET STRONGER.
THEY'RE AT THEIR WEAKEST DURING A NEW MOON.

## Oni

In Japanese legends and fairy tales, oni play the role we usually reserve for ogres and goblins in Western stories—the bad guy. They are usually portrayed as big, brutish men with a single stubby horn on the top of their heads, bearing studded or spiked clubs, wearing animal hide (tiger skin is popular), and looking for ways to be troublesome. The oni of Ôto are somewhat different from the traditional idea of oni.

## Cafés

Nearly as prevalent as convenience stores, cafés—also called *kissaten* ("tea shops") or coffee shops—are everywhere in Japan, and they've taken on a unique cultural significance. Coffee shops are where you arrange to meet with friends, business contacts, or dates. They are where one can wait for a show to start or a train to come; they are the place to get off the street for a quiet conversation. And sometimes people even go to cafés when they're thirsty or want a snack. The price of a cup of coffee (the cheapest is usually called "American") is less than 500 yen, and it is a small price to pay for the enormous convenience of cafés.

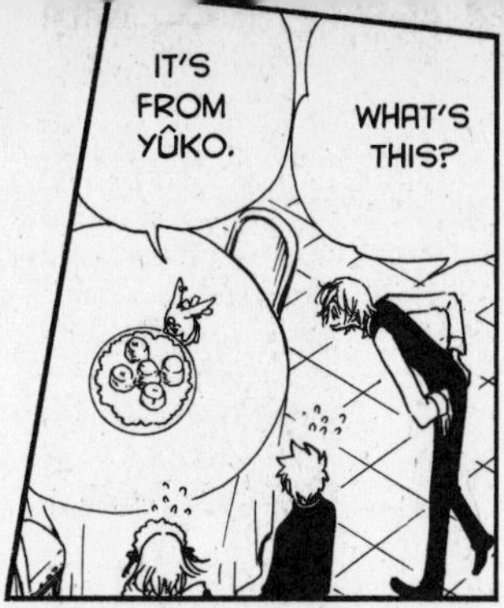
WHAT'S THIS?
IT'S FROM YÛKO.

### Fondant au Chocolat

If you want to see where the Fondant au Chocolat came from and what nefarious plan Yûko had in sending it, see *xxxHOLiC*, Volume 4.

### Yuzuriha Nekoi and Shiyû Kusanagi

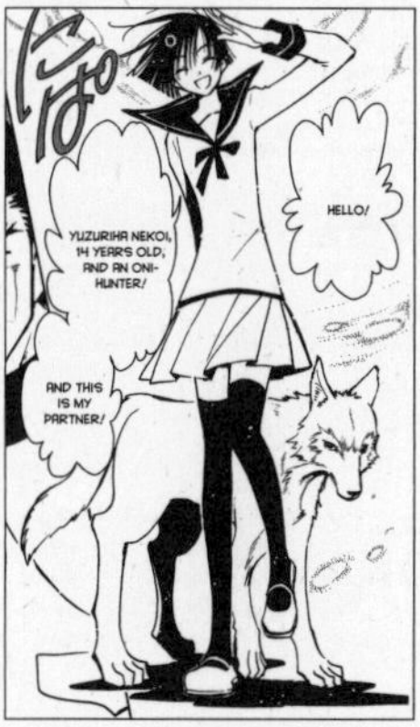
HELLO!
YUZURIHA NEKOI, 14 YEARS OLD, AND AN ONI-HUNTER!
AND THIS IS MY PARTNER!

Fans who follow *X* (*X/1999*) will recognize the extremely enthusiastic Yuzuriha Nekoi and her spirit dog (real dog in this universe), Inuki. As she grew up, everyone called her a liar since she was the only one who could see Inuki. But just before meeting and joining the Dragons of Heaven, she met the muscular and brave Shiyû Kusanagi, the first person other than herself who saw the dog. The two shared a connection that was almost romance. However, neither one knew that they were on opposite sides of a battle that could be the end of the earth. Happily, in this world they are on the same side.

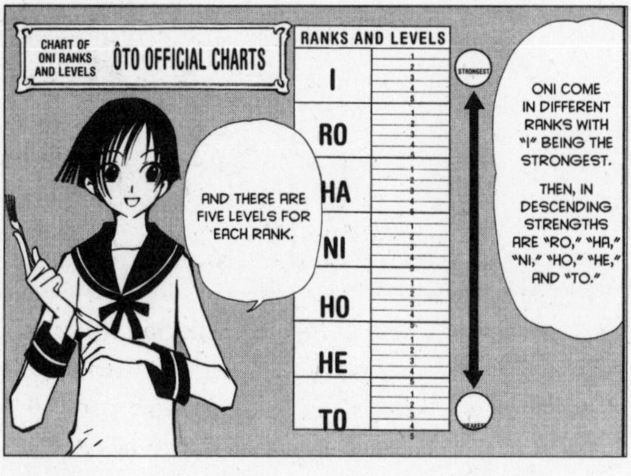
ONI COME IN DIFFERENT RANKS WITH "I" BEING THE STRONGEST.
THEN, IN DESCENDING STRENGTHS ARE "RO," "HA," "NI," "HO," "HE," AND "TO."
STRONGEST
RANKS AND LEVELS
I
RO
HA
NI
HO
HE
TO
CHART OF ONI RANKS AND LEVELS
ÔTO OFFICIAL CHARTS
AND THERE ARE FIVE LEVELS FOR EACH RANK.

### Iroha

Before modern reforms of the written Japanese language and *kana* (written symbols of the Japanese-language syllables) were put in the present order, children would recite a poem that used all the *kana* only once and made sense as a poem. It's sort of like a combination of the alphabet song and "the quick brown fox jumps over the lazy dog" in English. And just like we use the alphabet to number things, so too do the Japanese use the Iroha poem as a substitute for a numbering system.

HOW MUCH?
WE'LL SAY IT'S ON THE HOUSE, BUT ONLY IF YOU TELL EVERYONE ABOUT US.
RIGHT! WE'LL MAKE SURE YOU GET BUSINESS.

### On the House (Service)

The first time a person goes to a Japanese retail shop or restaurant, the customer may receive some small free gift to encourage them to come again later and to encourage the customer's friends to patronize the business as well. (Don't expect it. It doesn't happen everywhere.) The word the Japanese use for this gift is the English word "service." Fans of anime may recognize "fan service" as a word that has grown out of the "service" custom.

# Preview of Volume 6

Here is an excerpt from Volume 6, on sale in English now.

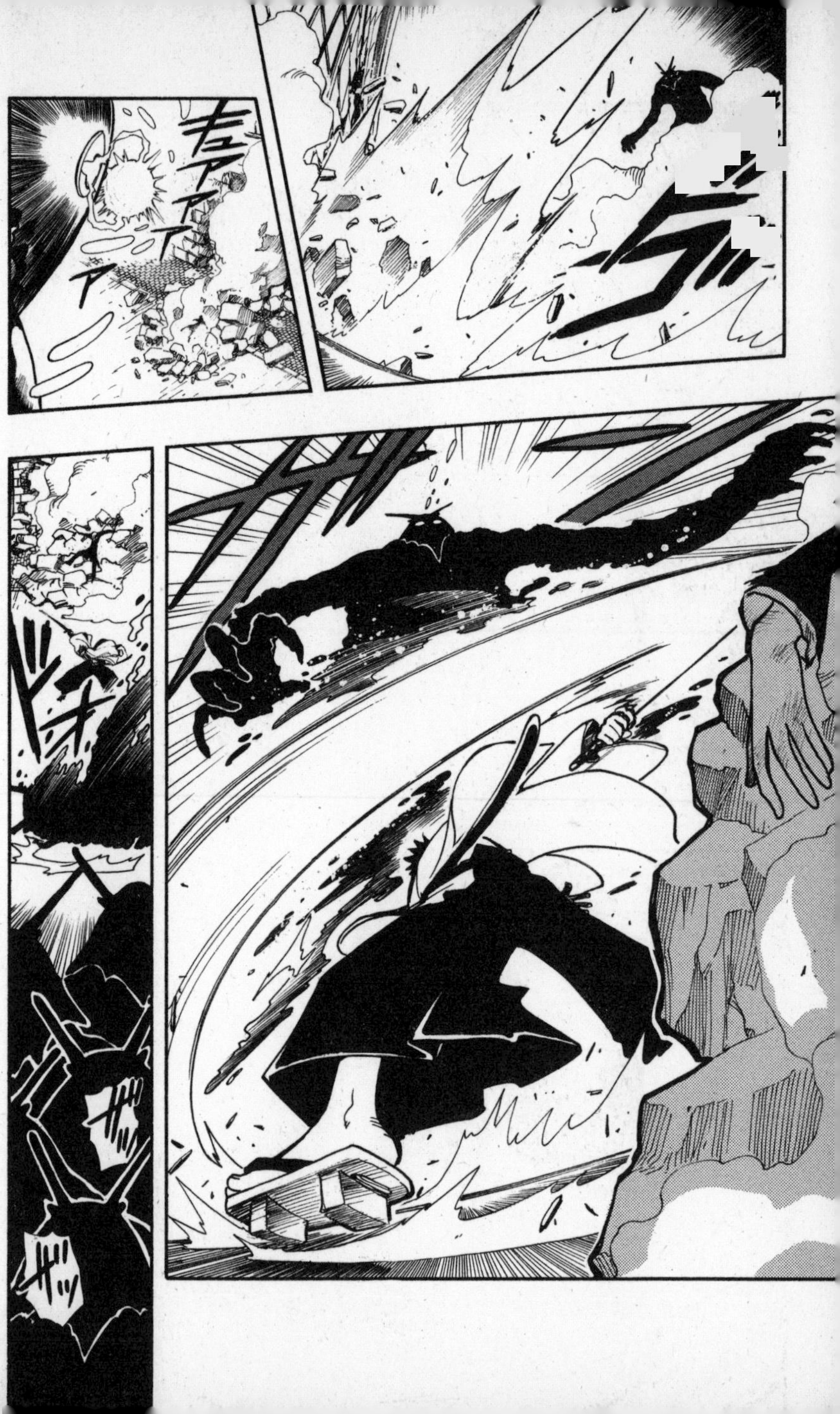
キュアアアァ
ドォ
ザッ
ザッ

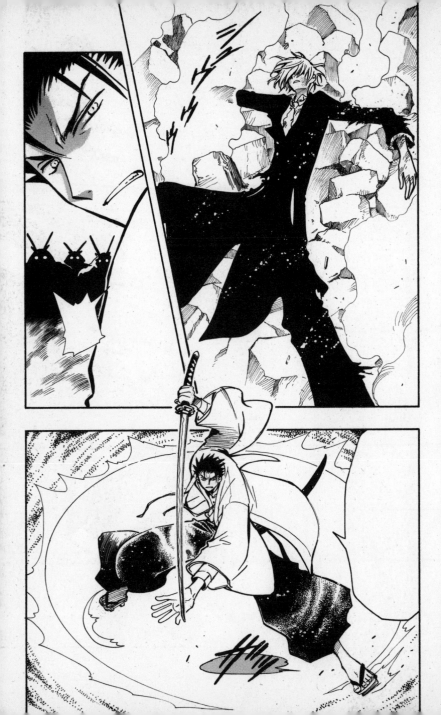

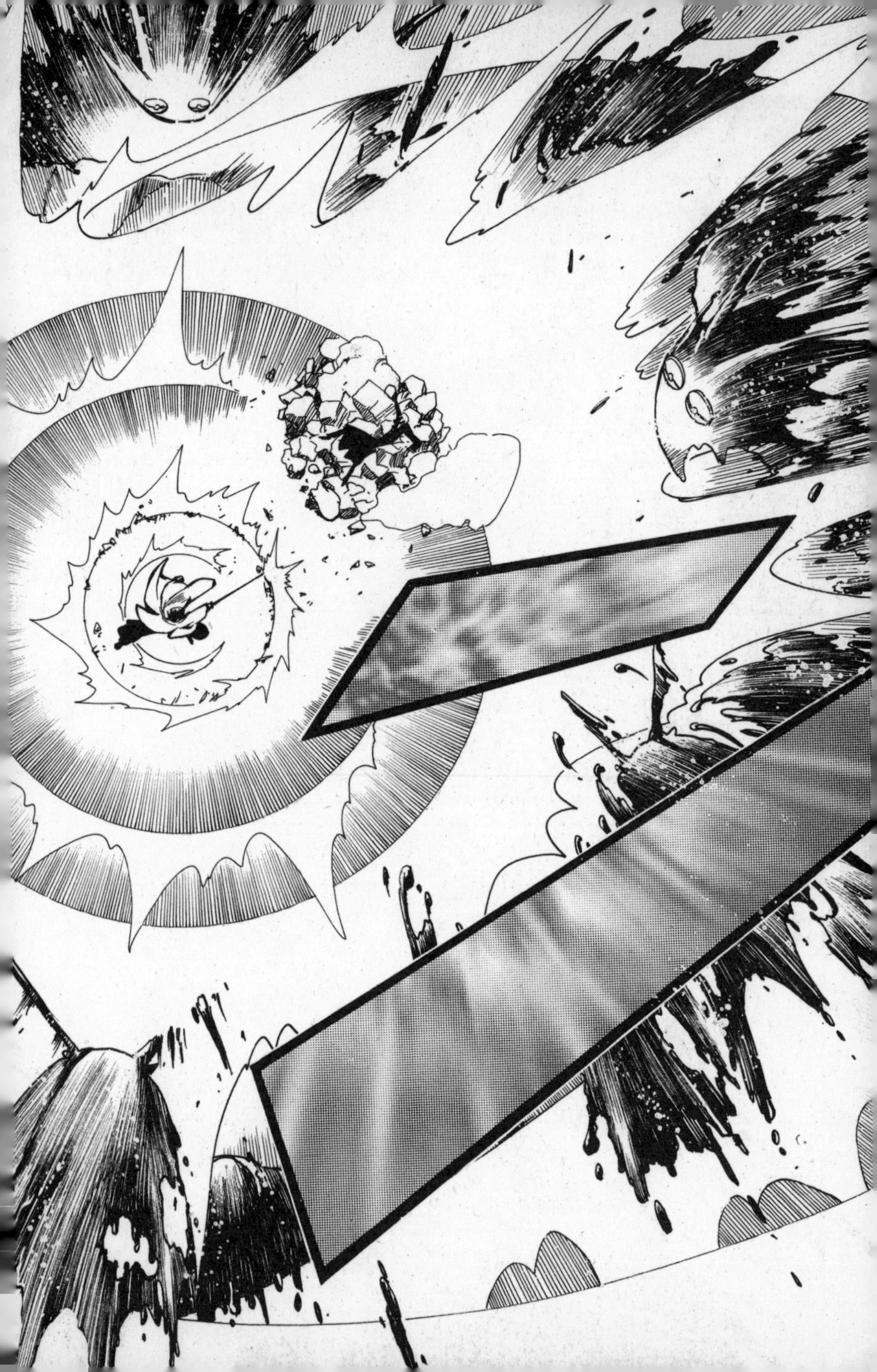

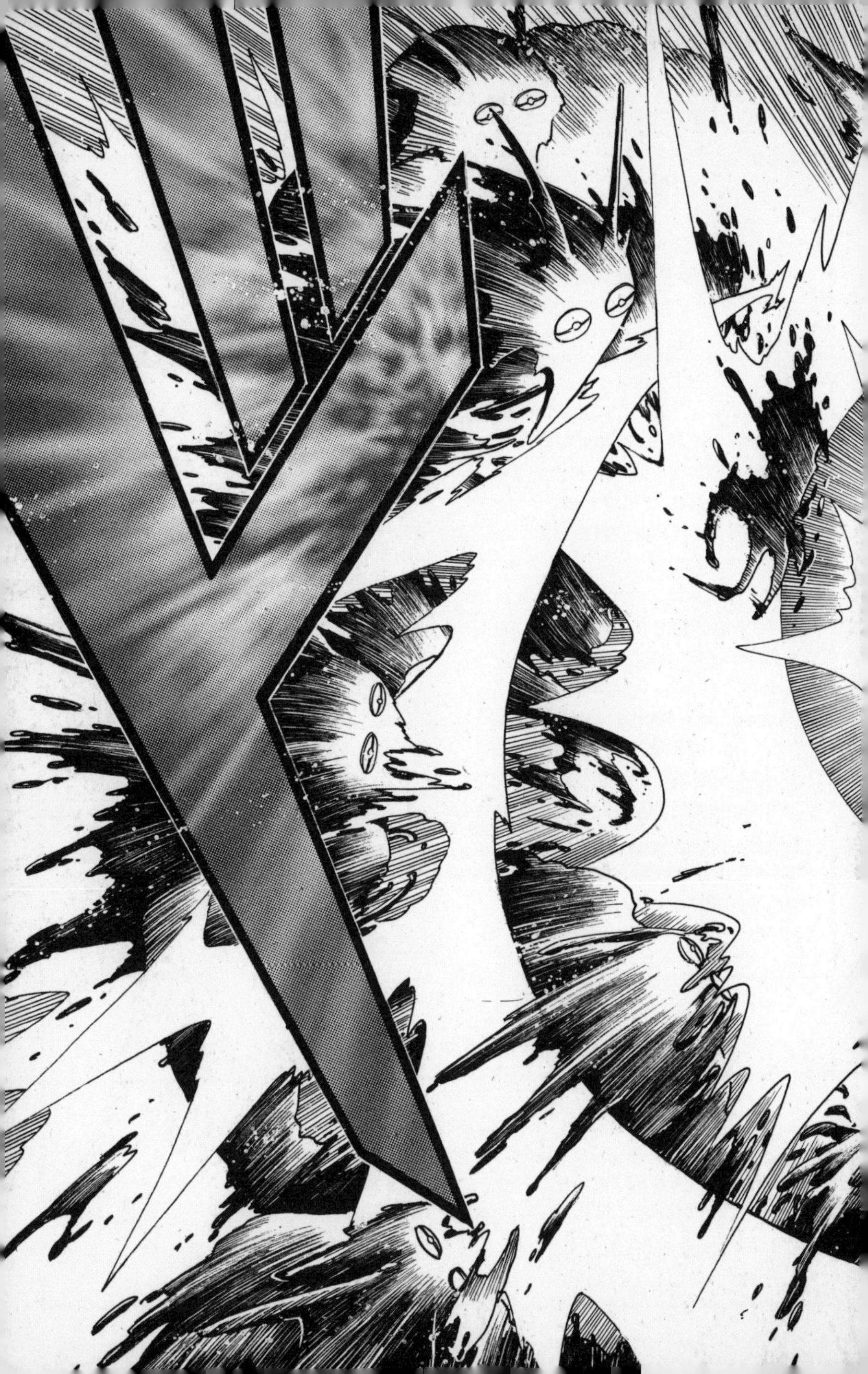

# THE Wallflower

## YAMATONADESHIKO SHICHIHENGE

**BY TOMOKO HAYAKAWA**

It's a beautiful, expansive mansion, and four handsome, fifteen-year-old friends are allowed to live in it for free! But there is one condition—within three years the young men must take the owner's niece and transform her into a proper lady befitting the palace in which they all live! How hard can it be?

Enter Sunako Nakahara, the horror-movie-loving, pock-faced, frizzy-haired, fashion-illiterate hermit who has a tendency to break into explosive nosebleeds whenever she sees anyone attractive. This project is going to take far more than our four heroes ever expected; it needs a miracle!

1
THE Wallflower
YAMATONADESHIKO SHICHIHENGE
TOMOKO HAYAKAWA

**Ages: 16+**

***Special extras in each volume! Read them all!***

DEL REY

**VISIT WWW.DELREYMANGA.COM TO:**

- View release date calendars for upcoming volumes
- Sign up for Del Rey's free manga e-newsletter
- Find out the latest about new Del Rey Manga series

## BY CLAMP

**W**atanuki Kimihiro is haunted by visions. When he finds himself irresistibly drawn into a shop owned by Yûko, a mysterious witch, he is offered the chance to rid himself of the spirits that plague him. He accepts, but soon realizes that he's just been tricked into working for the shop to pay off the cost of Yûko's services! But this isn't any ordinary kind of shop . . . In this shop, Yûko grants wishes to those in need. But they must have the strength of will not only to truly understand their need, but to give up something incredibly precious in return.

Ages: 13+

*Special extras in each volume! Read them all!*

# NEGIMA!™

## BY KEN AKAMATSU

**N**egi Springfield is a ten-year-old wizard teaching English at an all-girls Japanese school. He dreams of becoming a master wizard like his legendary father, the Thousand Master. At first his biggest concern was concealing his magic powers, because if he's ever caught using them publicly, he thinks he'll be turned into an ermine! But in a world that gets stranger every day, it turns out that the strangest people of all are Negi's students! From a librarian with a magic book to a centuries-old vampire, from a robot to a ninja, Negi will risk his own life to protect the girls in his care!

Ages: 16+

### Special extras in each volume! Read them all!

# Othello

## BY SATOMI IKEZAWA

satomi ikezawa

**Y**aya Higuchi has a rough life. Constantly teased and tormented by her classmates, she takes her solace in dressing up as a member of her favorite rock band, Juliet, on the weekends. Things begin to look up for Yaya when a cute classmate befriends her. Her devotion to Juliet, however, eventually just brings her more of the teasing and harassment she gets at school. Unable to cope, Yaya . . . changes. Suddenly, Yaya is gone—and in the blink of an eye, a new personality emerges. She is now Nana and she is tough, confident, and in charge. Nana can do things that Yaya could never do—like beating up the boys and taking care of all of Yaya's problems. How will Yaya live with this new, super-confident alternate personality? Who will be the dominant one, and who is the REAL Yaya?

**Ages: 16+**

*Special extras in each volume! Read them all!*

# TOMARE!

## [STOP!]

You're going the wrong way!

Manga is a completely different type of reading experience.

To start at the *beginning,* go to the *end!*

That's right! Authentic manga is read the traditional Japanese way—from right to left. Exactly the *opposite* of how American books are read. It's easy to follow: Just go to the other end of the book, and read each page—and each panel—from right side to left side, starting at the top right. Now you're experiencing manga as it was meant to be.